Advanced
C Primer ++

D0117401

Advanced
C Primer ++

Stephen Prata

HOWARD W. SAMS & COMPANY

A Division of Macmillan, Inc.
4300 West 62nd Street
Indianapolis, Indiana 46268 USA

© 1986 by The Waite Group, Inc.

FIRST EDITION
FOURTH PRINTING—1987

All rights reserved. No part of this book shall be reproduced, stored in a retrieval system, or transmitted by any means, electronic, mechanical, photocopying, recording, or otherwise, without written permission from the publisher. No patent liability is assumed with respect to the use of the information contained herein. While every precaution has been taken in the preparation of this book, the publisher and author assume no responsibility for errors or omissions. Neither is any liability assumed for damages resulting from the use of the information contained herein.

International Standard Book Number: 0-672-22486-0
Library of Congress Catalog Card Number: 86-61876

Acquisitions Editor: *James S. Hill*
Development and Production Editors: *Brown Editorial Service*
Designer: *T. R. Emrick*
Illustrator: *Don Clemons*
Cover Artist: *Ned Shaw*
Compositor: *Shepard Poorman Communications, Indianapolis*

Printed in the United States of America

Trademark Acknowledgments

All terms mentioned in this book that are known to be trademarks or service marks are listed below. In addition, terms suspected of being trademarks or service marks have been appropriately capitalized. Howard W. Sams & Co. cannot attest to the accuracy of this information. Use of a term in this book should not be regarded as affecting the validity of any trademark or service mark.

IBM, IBM C Compiler, IBM PC, IBM PC AT, and IBM PC XT are registered trademarks and PC-DOS is a trademark of International Business Machines Corporation.

Intel is a registered trademark of Intel Corporation.

Lifeboat is a trademark and Lattice C Compiler is a registered trademark of Lifeboat Associates.

Microsoft, Microsoft C Compiler, Microsoft MASM assembler, MS-DOS, and XENIX are registered trademarks of Microsoft Corporation.

Motorola® a registered trademark of Motorola, Inc.

UNIX is a trademark of AT&T Bell Laboratories, Inc.

WordStar is a registered trademark of Micropro International Corporation.

To my friends and to what they have added to my life.

Contents

Preface

We have two goals for this book. The first is to help you learn more about the C language. The second is to help you learn more about the IBM PC and similar computers. These two goals are related, for one of the most interesting things about C is how it can be used to exploit all the capabilities of a computer. That is not the only interesting thing about C, however, and most of the first half of the book concerns advanced C topics that are not tied to any one computer system.

This book looks, for example, at

- [ ] I/O problems and solutions
- [ ] pointer usage
- [ ] bit operations
- [ ] memory operations
- [ ] standard library functions

The second half of the book develops the IBM connection and covers

- [ ] the interface between C and DOS
- [ ] the interface between C and BIOS
- [ ] the segmented memory scheme used by the IBM PC's Intel 8088 processor
- [ ] how to access the whole memory in C

Advanced C Primer + + also introduces assembly language and shows how to create assembly language modules that can be used in C programs. In short, the books covers a host of interesting and useful topics.

To help you along, this book provides many examples, as well as questions and answers. We have kept the examples fairly short to encourage you to type and experiment with them, for that is one of the most effective ways to learn programming techniques and concepts. We hope that you enjoy this guide to the exciting world of advanced C.

Stephen Prata

Acknowledgments

Thanks to Michael Lindbeck for discussions on C and on the IBM environment, and thanks to Robert Lafore and Mitchell Waite for editorial suggestions and guidance.

1
Introduction

■ Setting up
■ Our approach
■ About computers and compilers

Introduction

After you have learned the basics of C, what comes next? What topics and techniques should you study? In this book, we bring together a number of key subjects that are possible answers to these questions. Mastering them will move you from the basics into the world of advanced programming.

In the first part of the book, we cover advanced topics such as pointer use, function design, input/output for text and for binary files, and bit operations, plus writing programs that don't "sulk" when they encounter unexpected input. We show how to make full use of the C library and how to make effective use of memory.

These initial topics deal with standard C, that is, the implementation of C shared among various computer systems. However, many advanced topics in C involve exploiting the resources of a specific computer. Therefore, in the second part of the book, we get down to the nitty gritty (or, sometimes, just the nitty) of computer hardware and show you how C works in the world of the IBM family of computers (the PC, XT, AT, and clones). Here you will learn how to access the routines built into the ROM (read-only memory) of the IBM, how to use the system calls found in DOS (the disk operating system), how to use input/output ports, how to control the video screen, how to access *all* of the PC's memory, and how to write simple assembly language routines and integrate them into a C program. The details are specific to the IBM, but the principles apply to any computer system.

Finding out how a language works and what you can do with it is interesting and exciting. But after you have learned the basics, you become aware of what you don't yet know how to do. Perhaps you aren't all that comfortable with certain language features, such as pointers or bitwise operators. Or maybe you want to know more about some of the library functions, such as low-level I/O functions or memory allocation functions. Or you run up against programming problems, such as making interactive I/O respond smoothly in the face uncooperative users. Maybe you want to take more direct control over what the screen displays, or you want to know more about the interface between C and a particular operating system or between C and assembly language.

In brief, you want to advance your knowledge of C. The purpose of this book is to help you do that.

Topic Selection

Many of the points we mention in this book are general in nature. The required knowledge is much the same for whatever computer system you work with. Other language features, however, depend on the particular system. The interface between C and UNIX, for instance, is not the same as the interface between C and DOS. If we limit ourselves to the first group of topics, we miss out on some fascinating and useful matters. Investigating the second group of topics, however, means limiting ourselves to one particular system (or family of systems) if the book is to be a reasonable size.

We have chosen a compromise route. Most of the first half of the book is devoted to general topics, whereas the second half concentrates on the adaptation of C to the IBM PC/XT/AT environment, where we get into all the specialized topics we mention in the first half of the book. (For more information on the C-UNIX interface see the second half of *Advanced UNIX—A Programmer's Guide* by Stephen Prata, published by Sams in 1985.)

The choice of topics does provide two different views of C. Much of the first half of the book deals with generic C, that is, with C programs that run with little or no modification in a variety of environments. Here we uphold the ideal of portability, generally recognized as one of C's great virtues. Most of the second half of the book deals with IBM-specific C, that is, with programs that explicitly exploit the unique capabilities and idiosyncrasies of the IBM PC. Here we uphold the ideals of power and flexibility, two more of C's great virtues. Both aspects—portability and specificity—raise interesting problems and are important to understanding C.

Exploring the ways C can be used on an IBM PC involves looking closely at how the PC works; this naturally leads the book to IBM-specific topics such as the use of ports, the system of segmented memory, how the processor uses registers, and other hardware matters that general introductions to a language ignore. So this is a book about the IBM PC design as well as about C.

What You Should Know

By calling this a book on advanced C, we don't mean that it is for advanced C programmers. Instead, we intend it to help you *become* a advanced C programmer. Naturally, we assume you have studied C already, that you know how to put together a program, call a function, declare variables, use

C operators such as the increment operator, use types and arrays, and the like. We assume that you are familiar with, or at least exposed to, the basic C concepts presented in *C Primer Plus* (Waite, Prata, and Martin, Indianapolis: Sams, 1984) or its equivalent.

We will take the time to review some of the more troublesome topics, such as pointers, functions, storage classes, arrays, and structures. And we will try to remind you of important points as we go along.

When additional information is needed, such as knowledge of IBM PC memory segmentation or of the basics of assembly language, the book provides it rather than assuming you've learned it elsewhere. After all, this book is here to help you!

Approach of This Book

There are many ways to present advanced topics. One is to concentrate on a few major programs for which a variety of skills and knowledge is needed. This has the advantages of illustrating the organization of large programs and of presenting realistic problems. One disadvantage of that approach is that several concepts may get intertangled, complicating the problem of understanding what is happening. Second, this approach reduces the variety of examples.

The approach here is more tutorial. To illustrate a concept, we use a short example that concentrates on the concept. This makes it easier to see how the concept works, and it helps you to try out the example on a computer. This approach enables us to include many examples, exposing you to more ideas and to more ways of looking at the same idea. Keeping the examples simple sometimes (but not always!) results in programs that are more illustrative than useful, but that doesn't hinder the learning process. After all, musicians improve their skills by playing scales as well as sonatas. Also, it is easier for you to type in a short example than a long one.

One aspect of keeping examples short is keeping error-checking at a minimum, except, of course, for examples illustrating error-checking concepts. Error-checking is a vital part of serious programming, but including it in our examples would only muddle the particular points you are trying to study. You can, if you like, regard this lack as an advantage, for it gives you the opportunity to exercise your skills by adding error-checking to examples you find useful.

In line with this tutorial approach, we often will raise questions for you to answer; you'll find the answers at the end of each chapter. Questions look like this:

☐ *Question 1-1*   Where will you find the answer to this question?

Most of the chapters also will have exercises (but no answers) at the chapter's end.

We suggest that you answer the questions and do the exercises as you go along. They will help you check your level of understanding and perhaps develop your comprehension a bit further. Probably one of the most instructive activities you can do is to reproduce examples, then modify them to see what happens and to test your own understanding. Most people find learning programming by *doing* is much more effective than learning solely by *reading*.

Hardware and Software You Will Need

You should have access to a computer system with a C compiler. Roughly half the book is general enough that its examples will run with little or no change on most systems, including UNIX-based computers. The other half contains examples specifically intended for the IBM PC. For these, you need a PC-compatible system and a suitable compiler.

Which Computer?

Just which computers can you use? The machine-dependent programs in this book were written and tested on an IBM PC. They also run, however, on the IBM XT and IBM AT. Some of the programs use routines stored in the ROM. They should run on any machine using the IBM ROM or one of the IBM-compatible ROMs. Other programs use routines from DOS. IBM products come with PC-DOS, while many competitors come with MS-DOS. Both were developed by Microsoft, and programs using the DOS routines should run with either form of DOS. Some programs, however, do require the DOS (PC or MS) to be Version 2 or later. Some programs use specific port addresses and video memory locations. They require machines that are compatible with the PC on those points. IBM's dominance of the industry is such that many machines are compatible in all these areas.

For simplicity, we will refer to the IBM PC when we talk about a specific computer, but we really will mean the IBM PC, XT, AT, and compatibles.

Which Compiler?

We have used the IBM and Microsoft C compilers for our examples (the two are nearly identical). Many of these examples can be duplicated with other PC compilers with few or no changes, but some examples use library functions or definitions that are unique to IBM and Microsoft. That doesn't mean such examples cannot be done with other compilers, however, because they may have other functions or facilities to perform the same task in a somewhat different manner. The main point is to understand how a given example works. Once you do that, you should be able to reproduce the essential features with other compilers, providing that they have the necessary capabilities.

The IBM and Microsoft C Compilers—Let's look at the background and features of the compilers we'll be using to understand which features make them different from other compilers.

Microsoft originally marketed a version of Lifeboat's Lattice C compiler. With Version 3.0, however, Microsoft introduced its own product, one which IBM has adopted, with small modifications, as the official IBM C compiler, which it terms Version 1.0. Microsoft, of course, also developed the operating system PC-DOS that is most used on IBM PCs. Similar MS-DOS operating systems are standard for a host of IBM clones, look-alikes, and somewhat-resembles. We often will use the term DOS to represent MS-DOS and PC-DOS. Microsoft also developed the MASM assembler, which has been adopted as the standard IBM PC assembler. We'll use it in the last two chapters.

The import of all this is that the IBM and Microsoft C compilers have a lot of clout behind them, being backed by two industry giants that would like to see these compilers become industry standard. Fortunately, they are good compilers, ones that produce fast and compact code. They are full-featured compilers, providing several memory models and the ability to generate code for the 80186 and 80286 processors as well as for the PC's 8088 processor. There are other good compilers, and we don't intend to debate which is best. Suffice it to say we chose to work with IBM and Microsoft C because of their industry position and because they are very capable compilers.

Compiler Differences—In principle, all compilers should implement the same basic C language, and in practice they nearly do. It is in the libraries and in the adaptations to the IBM PC environment, not in the language implementations, that the most important differences come. Some of the differences are in the extent of the library; one compiler may offer more string-handling functions than another. Other differences are in the names and designs of those functions intended to handle the interface between C and the IBM. For instance, more limited compilers may not give full access to all the built-in BIOS and DOS routines. Those that do may use different names and argument formats for the interface functions.

The 8088 processor in the IBM PC uses a segmented memory system. Most compilers, by default, use one 64K-segment of memory for code and a second 64K-segment for data, even though the PC can use up to 640K of memory. The IBM and Microsoft C compilers offer several ways to overcome this limitation and to access the whole memory. Several other compilers offer similar facilities, but the details differ.

We'll look at how assembly language routines can be incorporated into IBM and Microsoft C programs. Again, many other compilers offer similar facilities, but with differing details.

How do these differences affect you if you are using another compiler? We feel that the most important aspect is understanding the basic principles, understanding what a particular function call accomplishes.

That understanding, combined with the documentation for your particular compiler, should help you to make the transition from one compiler to another.

IBM and Microsoft C System Requirements

As you might expect of IBM and Microsoft products, these C versions are not petite. They require a minimum of 256 kilobytes of memory, two double-sided disk drives, and DOS Version 2.0 (Microsoft C) or DOS Version 2.1 (IBM C) or later. They can be run on a PC, XT, AT, or clone.

These are the minimum requirements, but more memory and a hard disk makes using the compiler much faster and more convenient.

The IBM and Microsoft compilers come with excellent, two-volume manuals. We have, however, summarized some of the compilation basics in Appendix C. Some minor differences between the IBM and the Microsoft versions are discussed there, but the two are essentially the same. For brevity, we will use the term IBM C to mean either.

Closing Words

Programming is a fascinating, sometimes addictive, subject. We hope this book helps satisfy some of your cravings. And don't forget to do the examples!

Answer to Question in the Chapter

■   *1-1.*   Here.

2

Advanced C Warmup

- Pointer constants and pointer variables
- The address operator (&) and the indirect value operator (*)
- Pointer arithmetic
- Pointers and arrays
- Pointers and strings
- Pointers and structures
- Functions as program building blocks
- Separate compilation
- Function arguments: actual and formal
- Function return values and function types
- Pointer arguments
- Functions and arrays
- Storage classes: automatic, external, static, external static, register
- Pointers and functions

Advanced C Warmup

There is no sharp demarcation between beginning C and advanced C, but most programmers consider pointers and the effective use of functions to be advanced concepts. Certainly, much of this book features pointers and functions, so a good way to begin is with a summary of the basic properties of pointers and of functions. In passing, we'll touch on arrays, strings, and structures. This chapter offers you the opportunity to review, consolidate, and perhaps extend your knowledge of these topics.

Basic Pointers

One of the most important tools of a C programmer is the pointer. It is used mainly in:

> constructing functions capable of modifying variables in the calling program
>
> handling dynamically allocated memory in array-processing functions
>
> constructing certain data representations, such as linked lists.

To review what a pointer is and how it works, however, we will study it in a simpler context.

First, what is a pointer? It is a variable or an expression representing the address of a memory location. You can think of the address as identifying or pointing to whatever value is stored at the memory location—hence the name *pointer*.

Pointer Constants and the Address Operator (&)

C has two fundamental ways of representing a pointer. The first is to apply the *address operator,* &, to a variable. The resulting expression is the address of the variable. Thus, if x is a variable, &x is the variable's address. Suppose, for example, that we have the following program fragment:

```
int fowls = 5;

printf("The value %d is stored at location %u\n", fowls, &fowls);
```

Addresses are stored as unsigned integers, so we use the %u format to print them. The output of this fragment would look like this:

```
The value 5 is stored at location 3620
```

Here, &fowls is a *pointer constant*. We can change the value of fowls to 4 or 10 or some other number, but the new value still will be stored at the same address, 3620. We can think of fowls as being the identifier for the value 5, while &fowls is the identifier for the address 3620.

The exact significance of the numerical value of the address depends on the computer system we are using. When the usual small-memory model is used with the IBM PC, the pointer value is an *offset* measured from the beginning of the *data segment*. Thus, the value 3620 is not an absolute address but an address relative to the beginning of a block of memory used for holding data. We'll return to these concepts in Chapter 6. Anyway, the numerical value usually is of interest just to the computer and not to the programmer. We use the symbolic representation of the address to make our programming points.

Pointer Variables and the Indirect Value Operator (∗)

The second way to represent a pointer is to declare a *pointer variable*. This kind of variable can be assigned to an address as its value. For instance, if pt were the proper kind of pointer variable, we could assign fowls's address to it:

```
pt = &fowls; /* assign an address to a pointer variable */
```

The conceptual difference between pt and &fowls is that the value of &fowls is fixed for the duration of the program, but pt can be assigned other addresses; &fowls is a constant, pt is a variable.

☐ *Question 2-1* What would the numerical value of pt be after the indicated assignment?

The C *indirect value* operator (∗) is used to represent the value a pointer points to. Thus, in our fowl example, pt is the address of fowls, and ∗pt is the value stored at that address (5, when last seen). We'll return to this operator soon.

Before we examine how to declare a pointer variable, let's look more closely at what is meant by the address of a variable. Suppose we have the following declarations:

```
char letter;
int boxcars;
float taxes;
```

The variable `letter`, being type `char`, occupies just one byte, while each of the other two variables occupies more than one byte. How is that reflected in the address? Not at all. In all cases, the address is the address of the *first* byte of the data object. Thus, all addresses look alike; there is no way to tell a `char` from a `float` just by the value of the address.

Nonetheless, a program needs to know the data type a given pointer points to. For instance, if the indirect value operator (`*`) gives the value of what the pointer points to, then we must tell the program how many bytes to use and how to interpret them. For this reason, a pointer declaration must not only identify the variable as a pointer, it also must identify the data type it points to. The technique C uses to declare pointers is demonstrated in the following declarations:

```
char *pc;  /* pc is a pointer to type char */
int *pi;   /* pi is a pointer to type int */
float *pf; /* pf is a pointer to type float */
```

These declarations create variables intended to hold addresses of data of the indicated types. Since the `*` operator is applied to pointers, these declarations indicate that `pc`, `pi`, and `pf` are pointers. (Otherwise, it would make no sense to apply the `*` operator to them.) Each of these variables is allocated enough memory space to store an address. The rest of each declaration indicates the data type to be found at the stored address. It is important to realize that `pc` and not `*pc` is the pointer. The program would use `pc` where an address is called for, and it would use `*pc` where the value stored is called for.

□ *Question 2-2*   How does the storage space allocated for `pf` compare to the storage space allocated for `pc` in the last example?

Figure 2-1 illustrates how a value is assigned to a pointer.

□ *Question 2-3*   In Figure 2-1, what would &pt be?

Let's look at another example. Suppose we have these statements:

```
float net;
float gross = 650.00;
float taxes = 100.00;
float *pf;

pf = &taxes;
```

Figure 2–1
Assigning a Value to a Pointer-to-Int

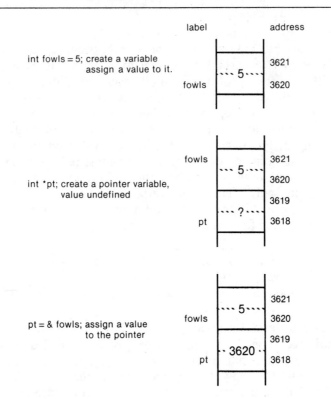

Then *pf can be used exactly as taxes would be:

```
net = gross — *pf; /* same as net = gross — taxes; */
printf("Taxes are %.2f\n", *pf);
*pf = 112.0;    /* same as taxes = 112.0 */
```

The final statement, for example, can be paraphrased this way: Find the address stored in the variable pf. Go to that address and place the number 112.0 there.

Similarly, pf could be used in place of &taxes:

```
scanf("%f", pf); /* same as scanf("%f", &taxes); */
```

In short, pf and &taxes are equivalent ways of specifying the address, and *pf and taxes are equivalent ways of specifying the value found there. Figure 2–2 illustrates using a pointer to change the value of a variable.

Figure 2–2
Changing Values Indirectly

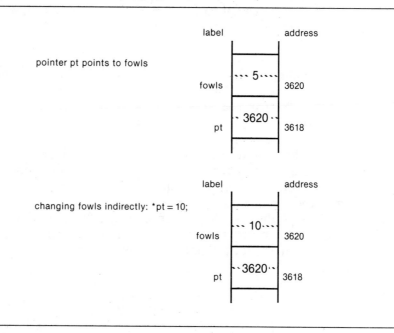

Pointers Should Come with Good References

A pointer should refer to a specific address before the ∗ operator is applied to it. The following code, for instance, is trouble:

```
int *pi;
*pi = 1492;    /* uh-uh */
```

This says to place the number 1492 at the memory address indicated by pi. But we haven't yet set pi to an address, so the program will interpret whatever garbage value happens to be sitting in pi to be an address. This will place or attempt to place the 1492 in some highly unsuitable location. So make sure a pointer is assigned an address value *before* you attempt to use the ∗ operator.

Pointer Arithmetic

You've seen how to create pointer constants and pointer variables. Once you have a pointer, you can add or subtract from it. Let's see by example what that does:

```
#include <stdio.h>
main()
{
```

```
char ch;
float fl;
printf("&ch is %u and &ch + 1 is %u\n", &ch, &ch + 1);
printf("&fl is %u and &fl + 1 is %u\n", &fl, &fl + 1);
}
```

Running this little program produces results like the following:

```
&ch is 4048 and &ch + 1 is 4049
&fl is 4050 and &ch + 1 is 4054
```

Adding 1 to a `char` address increases the address by 1, and adding 1 to a `float` address increases the address by 4. (This is on a system that uses a 4-byte `float`.) In general, adding 1 to a pointer increases it by 1 unit of the data type it points to. This provides a convenient way to handle arrays. Set a pointer to the first element of an array, then, as shown in Figure 2–3, use pointer addition to get pointers to the other elements of the array. We'll present examples of this approach later.

Figure 2–3
Pointer Addition

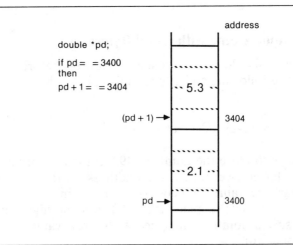

Pointer subtraction also is possible. Subtracting one from a pointer produces a pointer to a location one data-type unit before the original location.

Finally, pointer arithmetic can determine the difference between two pointers. In this case, both pointers must point to the same data type, and the difference is expressed in units of that data type. For example, if p1 and p2 are both pointers to four-byte `int`s, then p2 − p1 would be the actual numerical difference divided by four. For example, p1 could point to the beginning of an array and p2 to some value found in the array. The difference would give the number of array elements from the first element to the other one.

Pointers, Array Names, and Function Names

In C, the name of an array is a pointer to the first element of the array. Suppose we have this array declaration:

```
int cards[52];
```

In this case, `cards` is a pointer to `cards[0]`, the first element of the array. That is, it is the same as `&cards[0]`. Note that the array name points to the first element, not to the whole array. This means that the type for `cards` is pointer-to-`int`, not pointer-to-array-of-52-ints. This means, for example, that `cards + 1` points to the next `int`, which is `cards[1]`, and not to the next block of 52 `int`s. See Figure 2–4.

Figure 2–4
Array Name Is a Pointer to the First Element in an Array

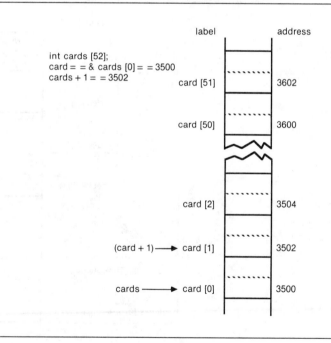

Suppose we have a two-dimensional array:

```
int decks[10][52];
```

Think of it as an array of arrays. Then `decks` is an array of 10 elements, with each element being an array of 52 `ints`. Since an array name points to its first element, `decks` points to the first array of 52 `ints`. So, in this case, `decks` *is* a pointer-to-52-`ints`. That means that `decks + 1` points to the next array of 52 `ints`.

Furthermore, because `decks` is an array of arrays, its first element, `decks[0]` is itself an array. That makes `decks[0]` the name of an array of 52 `ints`, so `decks[0]` is a pointer to its first element, `decks[0][0]`. Thus, `decks[0]`, like `cards` earlier, is a pointer of type pointer-to-`int`. This means, for example, that `decks[0] + 1` points to the `int` following `decks[0][0]`, namely, `decks[0][1]`. This concept is illustrated in Figure 2–5.

Figure 2–5
An Array of Arrays

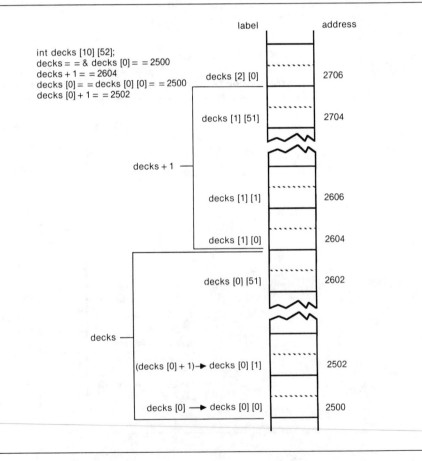

Because array names are pointers, pointer notation can be used to represent array members. For instance, the fifth member of the `cards` array is cards[4]. But `cards + 4` points to that element, so we also can use the membership operator to represent the same element: `*(cards + 4)`. Figure 2–6 shows how this is done.

Figure 2–6
Pointer Notation and Array Notation

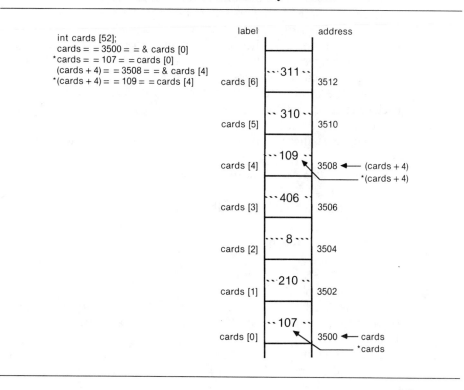

Array names are pointer *constants*. When we discuss functions later, we'll see that pointer *variables* can be used as if they were array names.

Much as the name of an array serves as a pointer to the first element of an array, the name of a function serves as a pointer to where the function code is stored. This fact is used in designing functions that take other functions as arguments. We'll return to this topic later in the book.

Pointers and Strings

In C a string is a series of characters terminated by the *null character*. This is the character whose ASCII code is 0; often it is represented by the notation `'\0'`. A string can be stored in a named array, or it can be represented by a string constant. Here are two ways to initialize a named array to a string:

```
static char guy[6] = {'C', 'h', 'u', 'c', 'k', '\0' };
static char gal[6] = "Ellie";
```

Only static and external storage class arrays (as discussed later in this chapter) can be initialized. The first form is the standard one for any form of array: a comma-separated list of elements enclosed in braces. The second form is a shortcut usable only with strings. The part in quotes is a string constant; it implicitly includes the null character.

In C, a string constant is treated as a pointer. That is, if you say printf(''beans''), the actual argument provided to the printf() function is the address of the first character (b) in the string "beans". Thus, the expression "beans" acts much like an array name. One difference is that if you use the string "beans" twice, you actually use two separate strings, each with its own address. (Not all C compilers follow this rule, but it is the current C standard.)

To verify these facts, try running the following statement:

```
printf("%s %u %u %c\n", "beans", "beans", "beans", * "beans");
```

The output should be of this form:

```
beans 131 125 b
```

Here, 131 is the address of one "beans" string, while 125 is the address of the other.

Note the final argument. If "beans" is a pointer to the first element of a string, then *"beans" should be the value of the first element, and it is.

The fact that a quoted string is really an address makes the following common idiom possible:

```
char *ps = "Karen";
```

Superficially, this resembles

```
static char sis[6] = "Karen";
```

but the forms are quite different. The second form establishes an array called sis and fills it with the letters in "Karen," plus a null character, thus using six bytes of memory. The first form establishes a single *pointer,* ps (just two bytes), and assigns it the address of the beginning of a "Karen" string. The string itself is stored in the data section of memory, where it occupies six bytes. Because ps is a pointer, not an array, it doesn't need to be of static or external storage class to be initialized.

Typically, programs use char pointers, like ps, to represent strings built into a program and char arrays to receive strings that are read in during run time. The relevant difference is that creating an array allocates space to hold a new string, while creating a pointer only allocates space to hold an address.

In short, we have three common ways to represent a string: a quoted string constant, a named `char` array, and a pointer-to-`char` variable. The unifying concept for these three forms is that all can be treated as pointers so that string-handling functions can use them equivalently. Thus, with the declarations we have shown, we can make the following statement:

```
printf("%s %s %s\n", gal, " saw ", ps);
```

Here `gal` is the name of an array, and hence a pointer; `" saw "` is a string constant, and hence a pointer; and `ps` is a declared pointer.

Pointers and Structures

Like arrays, structures are *aggregate* data objects, meaning they can hold several data items. A given array is limited to one data type, but a structure can hold a variety of data types. A general structure definition consists of the keyword `struct` followed by a "tag" that can be used to identify other structures of the same format. Then comes a *template* that details the construction of the structure. The template is followed by a list of identifiers that label specific structure variables using this particular template. Here is a sample set of structure declarations:

```
struct player {
            char fname[12];        /* first name */
            char lname[14];        /* last name */
            float ba;              /* batting average */
            int rbi;               /* runs batted in */
          } ruth, cobb, prata, giants[25];

struct player alstars[25], nlstars[25], *pps;
```

Here, `player` is the structure tag. The template holds a small sample of baseball statistics. The identifier `ruth` names one particular variable using the indicated format. The identifier `giants` is the name of an array of `player` structures. The tag `player` is used again, along with the keyword `struct`, to declare more variables using this particular template. Here `pps` is a pointer to a `player` structure.

Names and Pointers—Now let's look at some pointer matters. First, unlike the case for arrays, the name of a structure is *not* a pointer to a structure. If, for instance, a function uses a pointer to a structure for an argument, you would use the expression `&ruth`, not `ruth`, as the actual argument.

Second, the name of an array of structures—like any array name—*is* a pointer to its first element. Thus, in our example, `giants` is a pointer to a player structure. But `giants[2]`, being an element of the array, *is* a player structure.

Structure Membership—The membership operator, which is a period, is used to identify particular members of a named structure. First comes the structure name, then the operator, then the particular member type. Thus, Cobb's batting average would be represented by `cobb.ba`. The type of the expression is the type of the right-hand identifier, so `cobb.ba` is a `float`.

For arrays, the same principle holds. Because `giants[10]` is a particular structure, then `giants[10].rbi` is an `int` representing a particular player's RBIs.

Now for pointers. Suppose, for example, we assign the address of a particular structure to a pointer:

```
pps = &ruth;
```

There are two notations for accessing members of a structure by using a pointer to a structure. The first is to note that if `pps` is the address of `ruth`, then `*pps` represents `ruth` itself. So we can say `(*pps).rbi` instead of `ruth.rbi`. The parentheses are used because the membership operator has higher precedence than the indirect value operator here.

The second method is to use the indirect membership operator, which looks like this: `->`. It's created by typing a hyphen, then a greater than symbol. It works like the period, but it is used with pointers-to-structures instead of with structure names. In this notation `pps->rbi` represents the RBI value. Again, the type is of the right-hand identifier; `pps` may be a pointer, but `pps->rbi` is an `int`. Note that since an array name is a pointer, we can use `(giants + 10)->rbi` instead of `giant[10].rbi`.

Pointer Uses

The first examples of pointers in this chapter, although valid, often were not typical of the uses of pointers. There is little point in assigning `&taxes` to `pf` and then using `*pf` when we more easily could have used `taxes` all along. There are places, however, in which pointers are essential. One, as we've seen, is in handling strings. Another is as formal function arguments for functions designed to alter values in the calling program. Array-processing functions in particular use pointers. We'll see examples of these uses soon. A third use is in programs that use explicit dynamic memory allocation. These programs request additional memory as they run, and pointers are used to keep track of the new memory. A fourth use is in linked data structures, in which each structure contains one or more pointers to other structures. Chapter 6 takes up the preceding two topics. Fifth, C's standard I/O package uses pointers to indicate files. We'll take that up in Chapter 3.

Book Mark

HOWARD W. SAMS & COMPANY
Excellence In Publishing

fff

DEAR VALUED CUSTOMER:

Howard W. Sams & Company is dedicated to bringing you timely and authoritative books for your personal and professional library. Our goal is to provide you with excellent technical books written by the most qualified authors. You can assist us in this endeavor by checking the box next to your particular areas of interest.

We appreciate your comments and will use the information to provide you with a more comprehensive selection of titles.

Thank you,

Vice President, Book Publishing
Howard W. Sams & Company

SUBJECT AREAS:

Computer Titles:
- ☐ Apple/Macintosh
- ☐ Commodore
- ☐ IBM & Compatibles
- ☐ Business Applications
- ☐ Communications
- ☐ Operating Systems
- ☐ Programming Languages

Electronics Titles:
- ☐ Amateur Radio
- ☐ Audio
- ☐ Basic Electronics
- ☐ Electronic Design
- ☐ Electronic Projects
- ☐ Satellites
- ☐ Troubleshooting & Repair

Other interests or comments:

_____

_____

Name_____
Title_____
Company_____
Address_____
City_____
State/Zip_____
Daytime Telephone No. _____

fff

HOWARD W. SAMS & COMPANY

A Division of Macmillan, Inc.
4300 West 62nd Street
Indianapolis, Indiana 46268 USA

22486

Book Mark

BUSINESS REPLY CARD

FIRST CLASS   PERMIT NO. 1076   INDIANAPOLIS, IND.

POSTAGE WILL BE PAID BY ADDRESSEE

HOWARD W. SAMS & CO.
ATTN: Public Relations Department
P.O. BOX 7092
Indianapolis, IN 46206

NO POSTAGE
NECESSARY
IF MAILED
IN THE
UNITED STATES

HOWARD W. SAMS
& COMPANY

Function Basics

C encourages a modular programming style, with functions used as the modular building blocks. A C program is a collection of functions. Part of programming is deciding how to break down a design into separate functions; we'll look into that throughout this book. Right now, however, we'll look at the more technical aspects: how to define functions, how to join functions together to make a program, and how to arrange for individual functions to communicate with one another.

Programs and Functions

A C program consists of one or more functions. One of the functions must be called `main()`, for execution of a C program begins with the function of that name. Aside from that distinction, all C functions are on equal footing. That means each is defined by itself, outside of any other function. Unlike Pascal, C doesn't allow a function definition to be nested inside another function definition.

Function definitions in C look much like the definitions of `main()` you've seen; since `main()` is just another function, this should be no surprise. Here, for example, is a simple function definition:

```
printpluses()            /* function name--no semicolon */
{                        /* opening brace */
    int n;               /* declare variables */

    for ( n = 0; n < 25; n++)
        putchar('+');
    putchar('\n');       /* function code */
}                        /* closing brace */
```

The `printpluses()` function can be called (or *invoked*) by other functions by using its name:

```
#include <stdio.h>
main()
{

    printf("\n\n\n\n");              /* skip 4 lines */
    printpluses();                   /* a function call */
    printf("\nMetamorphic Rock, Inc.\n");
    printf("324 Sizzle Place\n");
    printf("Hipville, CA 90010\n\n");
    printf("We transform music!\n\n");
    printpluses();
}
```

This code tells `main()` to use `printpluses()`. But how do we let `main()` know where to find the `printpluses()` function? The simplest way is to place both functions in the same file:

```
#include <stdio.h>
main()
{

    printf("\n\n\n\n");                    /* skip 4 lines */
    printpluses();                         /* a function call */
    printf("\nMetamorphic Rock, Inc.\n");
    printf("324 Sizzle Place\n");
    printf("Hipville, CA 90010\n\n");
    printf("We transform music!\n\n");
    printpluses();
}

printpluses()              /* function name--no semicolon */
{                          /* opening brace */
    int n;                 /* declare variables */

    for ( n = 0; n < 25; n++)
       putchar('+');
    putchar('\n');         /* function code */
}                          /* closing brace */
```

Here, `main()` is listed first, then `printpluses()`, but the order just as easily could have reversed. (Remember, C uses the name `main()` to tell where to start execution.) In either case, compiling and running the program would produce these results:

```
+++++++++++++++++++++++++

Metamorphic Rock, Inc.
324 Sizzle Place
Hipville, CA 90010

We transform music!

+++++++++++++++++++++++++
```

Usually, especially for larger programs, you'll want to place distinct functions (or groups of functions) into separate files and use C's separate compilation feature.

Separate Compilation—Suppose we place `main()` in a file called *letter-head.c* and `printpluses()` in a file called *printpluses.c*. The contents of these files are termed the *source code* for the two functions. In C, the two files can be compiled separately, then linked to form the final program. With IBM C, we can compile and link the program with this sequence of commands:

```
cc letterhead
cc printpluses
clink letterhead printpluses
```

This produces a file of executable code called *letterhead.exe* that we can run to produce the same results we saw earlier. It also creates two new files called *letterhead.obj* and *printpluses.obj*. These contain the *object code* for the two functions. Object code is the machine-language translation of the original source code. To produce the executable code, the object code files are combined (*linked*) with one another and with object code for the library functions (such as `printf()`) used.

Suppose, now, that we want to change the *letterhead.c* file. To produce a new executable program, we need to recompile *letterhead.c* after changing it, but we don't have to recompile *printpluses.c*, because *printpluses.obj* already has the compiled version. Instead, we can give this sequence of commands:

```
cc letterhead
clink letterhead printpluses
```

These commands compile *letterhead.c,* producing a new *letterhead.obj* file. This file then is linked with the existing *printpluses.obj* file and any required library files to produce the executable file *letterhead.exe*. Appendix C provides more information about the compilation process.

This approach has three big advantages compared to recompiling the whole program. First, compiling is much slower than linking, so using precompiled modules saves much time. The more function files you have for a program, the more important the savings become. Second, particularly useful modules can be incorporated with ease into other programs; just include the object code file in the list of files following the `clink` command. Third, for debugging purposes, you can use `cc` to compile an individual file even if it is not a complete program. Then you can see the errors, if any, turned up by the compiler. In this case no executable file is produced, but an object file is created.

Function Arguments and Return Values

The usual way for functions to communicate is for the calling function to provide an *argument* (or *parameter*) list of values that are handed over to the called function. The called function, in turn, can "return" a value to the calling function. The definition of the called function should indicate the number and data type of the arguments it takes, and the function itself should be declared to be of the same type as the desired return value. Also, the calling function should declare, by type, the functions it uses. A function whose type is undeclared is taken to be type int. Here is a brief example:

```
#include <stdio.h>
main()
{
  int i;
  long factorial, fact();   /* declare the fact() function */

  for ( i = 1; i ≤10; i++)
     {
     factorial = fact(i);  /* i is an "actual argument" */
     printf("%2d factorial = %ld\n", i, factorial);
     }
}
long fact(n)             /* declare function type in definition */
int n;                   /* takes one argument of type int */
{                        /* n is a "formal argument" */
     long ans;

     for( ans = 1 ; n > 1; n--)
     ans *= n;
     return ans;         /* return value */
}
```

Here is the output:

```
 1 factorial = 1
 2 factorial = 2
 3 factorial = 6
 4 factorial = 24
 5 factorial = 120
 6 factorial = 720
 7 factorial = 5040
 8 factorial = 40320
 9 factorial = 362880
10 factorial = 3628800
```

As the output suggests, the function calculates factorials. As the code suggests, 4 factorial, written 4! by mathematicians and publicists, is the product of the positive integers up through 4. Let's look at some points more closely now.

Actual and Formal Arguments—The arguments used in the function call are termed *actual arguments*. In our example, i is the actual argument. The arguments used in the function definition are termed *formal arguments*. In this example, n is the formal argument. Note that the formal argument is declared *before* the opening braces of the function body. Other variables used by the function are declared after the braces, as usual.

C functions pass arguments "by value." This means the value of the actual parameter is assigned to the formal argument. That is, when i is 4, the value 4 is passed along to fact() and assigned to the new variable n. Figure 2–7 illustrates this process.

Figure 2–7
Actual and Formal Arguments

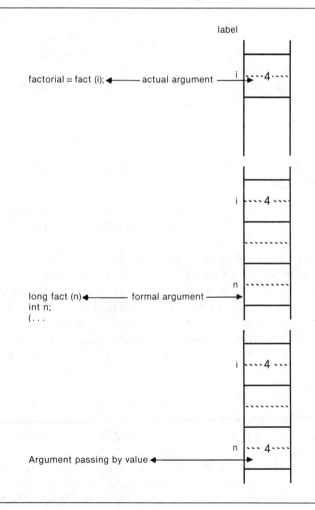

In Chapter 11, we'll look at the assembly language mechanism used by IBM C to pass arguments.

Because the `fact()` function uses its own variable n rather than the original i, there is no danger that `fact()` will accidentally alter i. This is one of the great strengths of passing arguments by value. There is a second method of passing arguments called passing "by reference." Under that system, which is not used in C, the formal argument would become a synonym for the actual argument, and the function would use (and possibly abuse!) the original variable in the calling program.

To see an example of the sort of trouble passing by reference can cause, recall the coding in `fact()`:

```
for( ans = 1 ; n > 1; n--)
    ans *= n;
```

It decreases n from the original value down to 1. If C used argument passing by reference, then i in the calling program would have been left at 1 after each function call. That would make it impossible for i ever to reach a value big enough to end the loop in `main()`.

Another advantage of the passing by value approach is that an actual argument can be an expression. For instance, the call

```
factorial = fact( 2*i + 1);
```

would evaluate the expression and assign the numerical result to the formal argument n.

☐ *Question 2-4* Why can't you use the passing by reference approach to treat an expression like `2*i + 1` as an argument?

Structures as Arguments—With one exception, each argument to a C function must be single-valued. A recent extension to C, however, allows a structure to be passed as an argument. The formal argument must be a structure of the same type. Its individual fields then are initialized to the fields of the structure that is the actual argument.

Prior to this extension, C functions that processed structures worked by passing the address of a structure to a formal argument that was a pointer to a structure.

Return Values and Function Types—Just as variables are typed according to what data type they are to store, C functions are typed according to what data type they return. Thus, in the factorial example, `fact()` is declared to be `long`, the same type as `ans`.

The return value is indicated by the keyword `return` followed by the value to be returned. We used the variable `ans`, but `return` can be followed by more general expressions. The following function, for example, returns the sum of the squares of two integer numbers:

```
int sqr(x,y)
int x,y;
{
    return x*x + y*y;
}
```

In this example, the expression x*x + y*y is evaluated, and the numerical value is returned. More specifically, the numerical value is placed in one of the CPU registers; the calling program then can use the value in that register. Thus, the return mechanism is much like the argument mechanism; only values are transmitted. Figure 2–8 illustrates this point.

Figure 2–8
A Return Value

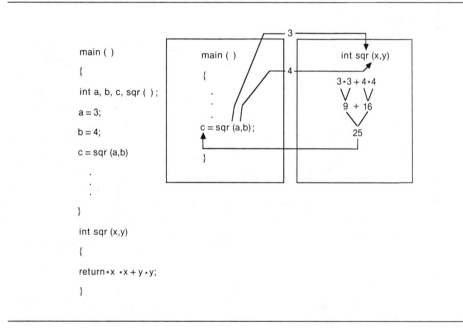

Declaring Function Types—The function type should be declared in two places: in the definition of a function and in the calling program. In our example, for instance, main() needs the return value type so that it will read the proper number of bytes and interpret them properly. The function type can be any single-valued type. This includes, of course, the standard types: char, int, float, and so on. It excludes arrays. This is less limiting than may appear, for a pointer is a single-valued type, and thus a function can return a pointer to an array.

IBM C does allow a function to return a structure.

C assumes that a function whose type is undeclared is type int. Since many functions are of that type, this convention reduces the number of required declarations considerably. However, current usage tends towards a more systematic approach, and many programmers recommend declaring all functions, including type `int`s. To avoid fostering lazy habits, all remaining examples of functions (other than `main()`) in this book will be declared explicitly.

Type Void—Some functions, like our `printpluses()` example, have no return value. Historically, no type was declared for such functions, so they were taken to be type `int` by default. This, however, is logically inconsistent. How can a function have an `int` return type if it doesn't return anything? This inconsistency may not bother you, but it does bother strict program checkers. The solution to this inconsistency is to introduce a new type to describe functions with no return value: type `void`. We'll use this type for the remainder of the book.

Pointers as Arguments

The main reason behind C's argument-by-value system is to insulate one function from another. Since each function uses its own private variables, it won't inadvertently interfere with some other function's variables. But sometimes it's necessary for one function to affect another's variables. The `scanf()` function, for example, places values in the calling program's variables. C deals with this situation by passing the address of a variable as an argument. This tells the called program exactly where the original variable is, so the called program then can manipulate that variable.

The technique is simple. Suppose we want to alter the value of an `int` variable called x. We pass as an argument the address of x, which is &x. Like any other argument, it should be assigned to a formal argument variable of the same type. Thus, the formal parameter should be an `int` address, that is, a pointer-to-`int`. It would be declared, say, like this:

```
int *ptr;
```

Then &x is assigned to `ptr`, and the function can use `*ptr` to represent the original x variable.

Let's redo the factorial example using this approach. First, here is the original version:

```
#include <stdio.h>
main()
{
    int i;
    long factorial, fact();    /* declare the fact() function */

    for ( i = 1; i <=10; i++)
        {
```

```
        factorial = fact(i);
        printf("%2d factorial = %ld\n", i, factorial);
         }
}
long fact(n)                /* declare function type in definition */
int n;                      /* takes one argument of type int */
{
     long ans;

     for( ans = 1 ; n > 1; n--)
     ans *= n;
     return ans;            /* return value */
}
```

Next comes the pointer version. Instead of using a return value, the factp() modifies the variable factorial directly. Hence we provide it with two arguments: the number whose factorial is to be calculated, and the address (&factorial) in which the result will be placed.

```
#include <stdio.h>
main()
{
  int i;
  long factorial;
  void   factp();    /* new type for factp() function */

  for ( i = 1; i <=10; i++)
     {
     factp(i, &factorial);     /* new argument list */
     printf("%2d factorial = %ld\n", i, factorial);
      }
}


void factp(n, plong)  /* void because there is no return value */
int n;
long *plong;        /* plong is assigned address of a long value */
{

     for( *plong = 1 ; n > 1; n--)
        *plong *= n;
}
```

Note that the type is void. A function has a return value only if it uses the return keyword.

☐ *Question 2-5* Since `factp()` alters a variable in the calling program, is it an example of passing arguments by reference?

Return Values versus Pointers

Now we have seen two ways to provide values from a called function to the calling function. You can use the return mechanism, or you can pass the address of a variable to be altered. Which should you use? If the intent of the function is to produce a single value, use the return value if you can. It better protects the integrity of program variables.

Sometimes address arguments are required. The `scanf()` function, for example, may be called to provide a string, a floating point number, a char, or other data, so we can't fit all those types to a single return type. Also, `scanf()` may be asked to provide more than one value, and the return mechanism can only provide one.

If you do design a function using pointer arguments, keep in mind the following:

1. The actual argument must be an address. It can be of the form &x, where x is a variable; it can be a pointer variable, or it can be a pointer expression. Don't use an ordinary variable. A mistake that nearly everyone has made is to do something like the following:

```
scanf ("%d", players);   /* oops! forgot the & */
```

The usual result is that the program attempts to stuff data into an inappropriate place.

2. The formal argument must be declared as a pointer.
3. Within the function, use the * operator to use and modify the value of the original variable.

Array-Processing Functions

One common category of functions requiring pointers are those that process arrays. Since each function argument is a single number (or, occasionally, a structure) the only way to pass an entire array directly is to have as many arguments as there are array members. That approach is not worth pursuing. The usual approach in C is to pass as arguments the name of the array to be processed and the number of elements to be processed. Since the name of an array is a pointer to the first element, this tells the function where to find the first element and how many elements to process, starting there.

Suppose, for example, we want to write a function that multiplies each element by a given value. Let the calling program contain these lines:

```
#define ITEMS 112
   ...
float yencost[ITEMS];
float adjust;
void revalue();


   ...
 scanf("%f", &adjust);
 revalue( yencost, ITEMS, adjust);
   ...
```

The `revalue()` function receives three arguments: an array name, which is a pointer-to-`float`; an integer giving the number of elements; and a floating-point value to be used as a multiplier. Thus, what the function heading must declare is:

```
void revalue( pf, n, mult)
float *pf;              /* pointer-to-float */
int n;
float mult;
```

Next, if `pf` points to the first element (subscript 0) of the array, then `pf + i` points to the subscript i element, and we can use the `*` operator to get the corresponding element:

```
{
   int i;

   for ( i = 0; i < n; i++)
     *(pf + i) *= mult;             /* multiply old value by mult */
}
```

We've used C's "multiply-and-assign" operator. The left-hand value is multiplied by the right-hand value, and the result is assigned to the left-hand quantity.

This version emphasizes the fact that we have passed a pointer, not the array itself, but it is not the way most people would write the program. There are two better options.

The first option will use notation emphasizing that we are working with arrays. We can use the following two facts. First, for formal argument variables *only,* we can use [ ] (empty brackets) to declare a pointer. Second, in C, the array notation `pf` is equivalent to the pointer notation `*(pf + i)`. This is true if `pf` is an array name, and it is still true if, as in this case, `pf` is a pointer variable. Using these conventions, we can rewrite the function this way:

```
void revalue( pf, n, mult)
float pf[];              /* pointer-to-float */
int n;
float mult;
{
    int i;

    for ( i = 0; i < n; i++)
      pf[i] *= mult;              /* multiply old value by mult */
}
```

The declaration form emphasizes that although pf is a pointer-to-float, it also is a pointer to the beginning of an array of floats. Many find the array notation easier to read than the pointer forms.

The second improved approach is to take fuller advantage of pointer possibilities. Since pf is a variable, we can apply the increment operator to it. (A regular array name, being a pointer constant, can't be used with that operator.) Continued incrementing of pf makes pf point to each element in succession. Because incrementing is a more efficient process than ordinary addition, this approach speeds the function up. Here is the implementation:

```
void revalue( pf, n, mult)
float *pf;              /* pointer-to-float */
int n;
float mult;
{
    while ( n-- )         /* for   n elements */
      *pf++ *= mult;         /* multiply old value, move pointer */
}
```

The n variable initially is set to the number of elements. It is decremented each loop after its value is checked. When the checked value is 0, the while loop quits (0 being the same as false), having gone though n iterations. Changing from a for loop to a while loop eliminates the need for the i variable.

The statement *pf *= mult would multiply the pointed-to location by mult. Including the postfix increment operator then increases pf so that it points to the next array member. Note: the C precedence rules make *pf++ mean *(pf++). This means the ++ operator attaches to the pointer pf and not to the value *pf. Because it is the postfix increment operator rather than the prefix operator, the incrementation doesn't take place until after the current value of pf is used. Thus, *pf++ means, "use the current value pointed to by pf, then increment pf itself."

☐ *Question 2-6* What would (*pf)++ mean? What about *++pf?

Functions and Strings

Strings are a special form of array, because C uses the null character (ASCII code 0, or `'\0'`) to mark the end of the string. This enables string-handling functions to dispense with an array-size parameter; the function simply need look for the terminating null character. Here, for example, is a function that counts the number of times a given character appears in a string:

```
int c_in_str( c, s)    /* returns number of times c is in s */
char c, *s;    /* character c, string s */
{
    int n = 0;

    while ( *s )    /* check for null character */
     if ( c == *s++)         /* compare, advance pointer */
            n++;
    return n;
}
```

This function uses a common string-handling idiom: `*s` as a test condition for a `while` loop. The pointer `s` initially points to the first character in a string, then is incremented to point to successive characters. When the pointer reaches the null character, the pointed-to character (`*s`) has the numerical value 0, and that terminates the loop. Note that the `if` condition compares the value `*s` with `c`, but increments the pointer `s`.

Functions and Two-Dimensional Arrays

Writing functions involving two-dimensional arrays can be frustrating if you don't have a clear conception of the exact types involved. To see what can happen, let's look at a programming task that often engenders confusion.

Here is the task: write a program that reads in several strings, then offers the user a menu of several choices. Menu choices should include printing the list of strings in the original order and printing it in some sort of sorted order. Rather than look at the entire program, we'll concentrate on some of the data types required and on creating functions to deal with those data types.

First, we need a place to store the strings. Since a single string is an array of `char`, we can use an array of strings, which would be an array of arrays of `char`:

```
#define MAXLEN 81
#define MAXSTRS 10
```

```
    ...
char strings[MAXSTR][MAXLEN];
```

Here we've created space for 10 strings, each of which can hold a maximum of 80 characters, not counting the terminating null character.

For sorting purposes, it is simplest to leave the original strings alone and to sort pointers to the strings instead. It is much simpler to swap pointers than to swap entire strings. For this, we need one pointer variable for each string:

```
char   *ptstr[MAXSTR]; /* an array of pointers */
```

Note that each element of the `ptstr` array is a pointer-to-char. That is because a pointer to a string points to the first element of a string, which is a `char`.

Initially, the first pointer will point to the first string, the second to the second string, and so on. The program would contain code to the following effect:

```
for ( i = 0; i < count; i++)
    ptstr[i] = strings[i];
```

Here `count` would be the total number of strings actually entered. Note that there is type agreement. First, `ptstr` has the declared array element type: pointer-to-char. Second, `strings[i]` is the name of an array, so it is a pointer to its first element, a `char`. Thus, is a pointer-to-char, too.

We then could write routines that sort the array `ptstr` by comparing the strings the elements point to. Sorting involves assigning new values to the pointers; this is why a pointer variable must be used instead of `strings[i]`, which are pointer constants. You can write such a routine yourself soon as an exercise, but let's look at a simpler problem: writing a function to print the strings pointed to by the pointers of the `ptstr` array.

Functions Using an Array of Pointers

First, what information should we provide for the function? Mainly, we should provide `ptstr`, the name of the array. The name of an array is a pointer to its first element, and each element of this array is itself a pointer-to-char. Thus, the type for `ptstr` is pointer-to-pointer-to-char. That, then, should be the declared type for one formal argument. For a second argument, we can supply the number of strings to be printed. Here is a simple implementation. The main points to notice are the argument types and how the formal arguments are used in the function.

```
void prstrings( ps, n)      /* prints n strings */
char *ps[];        /* pointer-to-pointer-to-char */
int n;
{
```

```
        int i;

        for (i = 0; i < n; i++)
            printf("%2d: %s\n", i+1, ps[i] );
    }
```

This function numbers the strings as it prints them. The `printf()` function expects a pointer to a string when the `%s` format is used, and that is what `ps[i]` is. Note that `ps` is used exactly as `ptstr` would have been used in the calling program. Both point to the first element of the `ptstr` array, which would be the address of the first string to be printed.

As we discussed earlier, the equivalent declaration

```
    char **ps;        /* pointer-to-pointer-to-char */
```

could have been used instead.

☐ *Question 2-7* How would you rewrite `prstrings()` using pointer notation?

To use `prstrings()`, use a function call like this:

```
    prstrings(ptstr, count);
```

The variable `count` would equal the actual number of strings entered, which might be less than the limit `MAXSTR`.

Functions and Arrays of Strings

Suppose we want to print the strings in the original order. Can we use the same function, but with `strings` as an argument?

```
    prstrings(strings, count);
```

The answer is *no*. Strangely enough, although `ptstr[i]` is the same type as `strings[i]`, `ptstr` is *not* the same type as `strings`! Let's look at the two declarations again:

```
    char strings[MAXSTR][MAXLEN];
    char *ptstr[MAXSTR];
```

Both `strings` and `ptstr` are the names of arrays with `MAXSTR` elements; hence, both are pointers. They point, however, to different kinds of things. More technically, they point to different types of data objects. For `ptstr`, as we have seen, the pointed-to data object is an address, a pointer-to-`char`. So `ptstr` points to a 2-byte object. For `strings`, the pointed-to data object is an array of `MAXLEN` characters. Since `MAXLEN` is 81, this means `strings` points to an 81-byte object. More succinctly, `ptstr` is an array of addresses, while `strings` is an array of strings. Figure 2-9 shows how this works.

How, then, can we print out `strings`? One approach is to declare a second array of pointers, assign it the string addresses, and to leave it alone in the sorting process. Then we can use `prstring()` with that array.

The second approach, which we will take now, is to write a separate printing function. The key is to declare the formal argument properly so that `strings` can be passed as an argument. The name `strings` is a single address, the address of an array of 81 characters. Thus we have to declare a pointer to an array. Will this do?

```
char *psa[81];
```

Figure 2-9
Strings and Ptstr

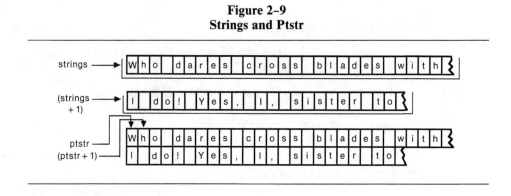

No. The brackets have a higher precedence than the * operator, so this says `psa` is an array of 81 pointers to `char`, whereas we want 1 pointer to an array of 81 characters. We need to use parentheses to give the * operator first precedence. Here is a working version of the function:

```
void prstrarr( psa, n)      /* prints n strings */
char (*psa) [MAXLEN];       /* pointer-to-array-of-MAXLEN chars */
int n;
{
      int i;

      for (i = 0; i < n; i++)
          printf("%2d: %s\n", i+1, psa[i] );
}
```

The only changes we made were in some names and in the formal argument declaration. The declaration also could have been written this way:

```
char psa[][81];
```

Remember, when we are declaring formal arguments, an empty bracket pair to the right is equivalent to the * operator on the left.

☐ *Question 2-8* How would you write a function that sorted an array of string addresses in order of increasing length of the pointed-to strings?

Storage Classes

We have one more major topic to cover in this review/extension of C basics: storage classes. C gives you explicit control over many program facets. For example, the types char, short, int, and long give you a choice storage size for integer values. The unsigned modifier further expands these choices. With storage classes, C gives you control over which functions can work with which variables, and over the duration of variables. C offers four storage classes: automatic, static, external, and static external. There also is an automatic variant called a *register variable*. We'll look at them in turn.

The Automatic Storage Class

Nearly all the variables we've used so far are automatic. *Automatic variables* are defined within a function; that includes formal arguments. Their scope is confined to the function in which they are defined. This means they are *local* variables, known only to the containing function. If you define a variable y in two separate functions, they are two separate variables, each with its own memory location. The storage for automatic variables is allocated when a function is called and freed when the function terminates. In the fact() example, for instance, the variables n and ans would be created and discarded each cycle of the containing loop in the calling program.

Automatic variables help implement the programming goal of isolating the workings of one function from another. You don't have to worry, for example, about accidentally reusing a variable name and having one function mess up another function's variable of the same name. For such reasons, variables defined within a function are automatic variables by default. The keyword auto can be used to make the choice explicit:

```
auto int plooko;
```

Normally, the auto keyword is used to clarify the programmer's intent; we'll see an example shortly.

In Chapter 11, we will see how the compiler sets up automatic variables in assembly language.

Static Variables

Occasionally it's useful for a function to retain memory of a variable's value between function calls. Including the keyword static in the variable's definition will cause the variable to be assigned "static storage." In C terms, this means the variable will be retained in memory for the duration of the whole program, even between calls to the function containing it. It is static in the sense of staying put.

As an example, here is a function that maintains a running total:

```
int runtot(n)
int n;
{
     static int tot = 0; /* define, initialize static variable */
     tot = tot + n;
     return tot;
}
```

There are four points to note here. First, storage for `tot` is allocated before the program starts running. Automatic variables, as we noted, are allocated only when the containing function is invoked. Second, static variables are initialized only once, when storage is allocated. Thus, `tot` starts out at 0, but is *not* reset to 0 each time the function is called. Instead, it retains its current value between calls. Third, the scope of `tot` is still local; only the `runtot()` function knows of and uses it.

Finally, formal arguments must be automatic; we could not, for instance, make `n` in `runtot()` a static variable.

☐ *Question 2-9* Many C programmers delight in condensing code. Can you condense the final two statements of `runtot()` to one? How?

Chapter 11 will provide an inside look at how the compiler sets up static variables.

External Variables

External variables are those defined outside of any function definition. They last for the duration of the program, and they can be shared by several functions, even functions in separate files. Here is an example of the format:

```
int status;   /* an external variable */

main()
{
     ...
}

lepto()
{
```

```
        ...
}
```

The `status` variable would be known to both `main()` and `lepto()`. Either could change the value of `status`, and any change made would carry over to the other function.

External definitions are overridden by local definitions. Consider this bit of code:

```
int big, massive, quitebig;        /* external variables */
main()
{
     ...
}

fitter()
{
   int big;        /* automatic variable--a new big */
   ...
}

sizer(big)
int big;        /* automatic variable--a third big */
{
   static int massive;   /* local, static massive */
   ...
}
```

The first declaration sets up three external variables: `big`, `massive`, and `quitebig`. The `quitebig` variable is recognized by all three functions. The `big` variable, however, is overridden by locally defined bigs in `fitter()` and in `sizer()`. That is, any reference to `big` in `fitter()` will refer to the variable created in that function and not to the external `big`. Similarly, the external `massive` is shared by `main()` and `fitter()`, while `sizer()` interprets `massive` to be a different variable.

The keyword `extern` is used to identify external variables defined elsewhere. The preceding code could be written this way:

```
int big, massive, quitebig;        /* external variables */
main()
{
   extern int big, massive, quitebig;   /* explicitly declaring
                                           external variables used */
   ...
}

fitter()
```

```
{
    int big;        /* automatic variable--a new big */
    extern int massive, quitebig;
      ...
}

sizer(big)
int big;            /* automatic variable--a third big */
{
    static int massive;   /* local, static massive */
    extern quitebig;
      ...
}
```

In this example, it is not necessary to use the `extern` keyword, but its presence clarifies and documents the programmer's intentions.

Defining and Declaring Variables—A *declaration* announces what variables a program or a particular part of a program will use, while a *definition* allocates storage and identifies it with the variable name. The declarations we have been using for automatic variables are also definitions. With external variables, however, we can have declarations that are not definitions. For example, declarations using the keyword `extern` are not definitions because they do not lead to the creation of new variables. Instead, they announce that the named variables have been defined elsewhere.

Consider this fragment, for example:

```
int webster;                /* webster declared and defined */
main()
{
    int funk;               /* funk declared and defined */
    extern int webster;     /* webster declared */
      ...
}
```

Each definition is a declaration, but not every declaration is a definition.

Initializing External Variables—External variables are initialized automatically to 0. You can initialize them explicitly, too, but only when they are defined:

```
int legs = 100;             /* okay */
main()
{
    extern int legs = 98;       /* no good */
      ...
}
```

The Scope of External Variables

The scope of a variable is the range of program in which the variable is recognized. When an external variable is defined in a file, its scope runs from the point of definition to the end of the file; if the variable also is declared using the keyword `extern` in a function within the file, the scope is extended to the whole file, even if the variable is not defined at the beginning.

C permits and encourages multifile programs. Suppose you define an external variable in one file. To use the same variable in a second file, declare it there using the keyword `extern`. Once again, we encounter the distinction between a definition and a declaration. There can be only one definition of an external variable; it will not use the keyword `extern`. It causes the storage space to be allocated and labeled. Functions in the same file as the definition *may* use `extern` to declare that they will use the original variable. Other files using that variable should declare the variable using `extern`. These additional declarations ensure that the functions and files will use the same variable.

IBM C stretches the C standard somewhat. External declarations that initialize a variable are taken to be definitions, and there can be only one definition. That is in accordance with the standard. But IBM C allows more than one noninitializing external declaration, even if the keyword `extern` is omitted. All references to the same name are assumed to refer to the same variable, and the first such declaration is taken to be the definition.

Compiler-Generated External Variables—The IBM C compiler produces several external variables that can be used by your program if you choose. For example, when certain kinds of errors are made, an error code is placed in the external variable `errno`. If a program fails to open a file, for example, you can use the value of `errno` to determine the reason for failure. Another external variable, `_fmode`, determines whether files will be opened in text mode or binary mode. The `environ` variable points to an array of strings containing information about the DOS environment.

We'll talk more about these system external variables as we need them.

The External Static Class

Sometimes you may wish to restrict a variable to one particular file. To do this, declare the variable externally (that is, outside of any function), but with the keyword `static`:

```
static int secrets;
plenk()
{
  ...
}
{
plonk()
{
```

```
    ...
}
```

The functions `plenk()` and `plonk()` can use the `secret` variable, but it is invisible to functions found in other files. This is true even if the files are linked in compilation, and even if those other files contain the line

```
extern int secret;
```

in them.

The Register Storage Class

Normally, variables are stored in a computer's random-access memory (RAM). With the C register storage class you can request that a variable be placed in one of the central processing unit's registers instead. This permits swifter manipulation. Otherwise, the register storage class is the same as the automatic class.

The request is accomplished using the keyword `register`:

```
main()
{
    register int quickie;
    ...
}
```

You can't specify which register you want, and you can't even be sure your request will be honored. The computer has other uses for the registers, so none may be available. IBM C allows for up to two register variables.

The register types are limited by the fact that an IBM PC register is a 16-bit device. Thus, `int`, `char`, and pointer types can be represented by a register variable, but a `float` could not.

Storage Class Summary

To restrict a variable to one function, make it an automatic variable. Formal arguments for a function are always automatic variables, and variables declared in the body of a function are automatic by default.

To share a variable among several functions while restricting its scope to one file, define it externally in the file (outside of any function) and use the keyword `static` in the declaration.

To share a variable over several files, define it externally in one file and declare it using the keyword `extern` in the other files.

Function Scope

By default, functions are external. This merely restates the fact that C functions are defined separately in a file, never inside another function. By using the keyword `static` in a function definition, you can restrict the scope of a function to its own file. Suppose, for example, one of your files contains:

```
static char fendostic(s,n)
char *s;
int n;
{
    ...
}
```

Only functions in that particular file could use the `fendostic()` function. Another file then could use the same name for a different function.

Pointers to Functions

The name of a function is a pointer to that function. This means the function name represents the beginning address of the function code. If you use a function name as a pointer, you should make sure the function is declared first so that the compiler will recognize the name as a function name. Let's see how that works. Here is a simple example in which we print out the addresses of some functions:

```
main()
{
   void prfun();

   prfun();
   printf("main() is at %u, and prfun() is at %u\n", main,prfun);
}

void prfun()
{
   printf("We proudly present the following addresses:\n");
}
```

Here is the output:

```
We proudly present the following addresses:
main() is at 2, and prfun() is at 32
```

As with data pointers, these address values are offsets. With IBM C, the function code and data codes are stored in separate segments. In the small-memory model, a function pointer is the offset from the beginning of the code segment, while a data pointer is the offset from the data segment. Thus, function pointers and data pointers don't measure offsets from the same location.

More typically, a function pointer is used as an argument to another function. This lets the second function use whatever function the argument points to.

Here, for instance, is a program that passes the name of two functions to another function:

```c
#include <math.h>
main()
{
    double cube();
    double fratio();
    double x, dx, r1, r2;

    x = 1.0;
    dx = 0.05;
    r1 = fratio (cube, x, x + dx);
    r2 = fratio (sin, x, x + dx);
    printf("r1 = %.4f, r2 = %.4f\n", r1, r2);
}

double cube (y)
double y;
{
    return y * y * y;
}
```

The sin() function is part of the IBM C library, and cube() is defined in the program. In one case, the fratio() function will use the cube() function, and in the other case, fratio() uses the sin() function; cube and sin are pointers.

How do we write fratio() so that it can use these functions? As usual, one of the first steps is to declare the formal arguments properly:

```c
double fratio( pf, a, b)
double (*pf) ();                /* pf is a pointer to a function */
double a, b;
```

Declaring a and b is straightforward. To declare pf as a pointer to a function, we use *pf to indicate that pf is a pointer. The parentheses enclosing *pf override the higher precedence of the function parentheses. The function parentheses reveal that pf points to a function. Finally, the double indicates that the pointed-to function returns a type double value.

Note what happens if we omit certain parentheses:

```
double   *pf1();     /* a function that returns pointer-to-char */
```

Here the higher precedence of the function parentheses asserts itself.

Next, we need to use the pointed-to function in the program. The declaration indicates that the combination (*pf)() is a function, so that is the combination used in the program. We merely need place the proper arguments in the function parentheses:

```
double fratio( pf, a, b)
double (*pf) ();
double a, b;
{

    return ( (*pf)(b) - (*pf)(a) ) / ( b - a );
}
```

The fratio() function evaluates the pointed-to function using arguments a and b, then divides the function value differences by the difference between b and a. If you know a little calculus, you'll recognize this ratio to be an approximation to the derivative of the pointed-to function, an approximation that approaches the derivative as b approaches a.

When you pass a function pointer as an argument, you should make sure that the pointed-to function takes the number and type of arguments that the called program expects. In our case, for instance, (*pf) uses one double argument. Also, the return value of the pointed-to function should agree with the declared type of return value for the function pointer.

Summary

A pointer is used to indicate an address. A pointer constant has a fixed value, while a pointer variable can be assigned an address of your choice. The address operator (&) can be used to obtain the address of a variable; for example, &santa is the address of the santa variable. The name of an array is another pointer constant; it points to the first element of the array. Similarly, the name of a function is a pointer to the function.

The value stored at the address a pointer points to can be obtained using the indirect value operator (*). Thus, if pt points to (is the address of) the variable santa, then *pt is the value of santa. The indirect value operator also is used to declare pointers. The following declaration says that pt points to a type-int quantity:

```
int *pt;     /* *pt is an int, so pt is a pointer-to-int */
```

One address looks pretty much like another, so a pointer declaration must establish explicitly what type of data object is pointed to. This ensures that the * operator will yield correct values and that pointer arithmetic will be executed properly.

Pointer arithmetic consists of adding or subtracting integers from pointers and of subtracting one pointer from another. C converts all such operations into units the size of the pointed-to object. For example, if ps points to a type float variable, then ps + 1 points to a location one float-size (four bytes) greater.

C array notation is a disguised form of pointer arithmetic. An expression like elves[i] really means *(elves + i). The latter expression can be paraphrased this way: "Find the location pointed to by elves, move i units further, and take the value found there."

Functions are the building blocks of C programs. Functions can be compiled separately, then linked into a larger program. When a program needs to be changed, only the affected functions need be recompiled.

Communication between functions usually is handled using function arguments and function return values. The arguments used in a function call are termed actual arguments. The arguments used in the function definition are termed formal arguments. Formal arguments represent variables that are created when a function is called. At that time, each actual argument in the function call is evaluated, and its numerical value is assigned to the formal argument variable. This process is called argument passing by value. Each argument must be a single number or a structure name. The single number can be a pointer to an aggregate data object, such as an array.

A function can return a single value or a structure using the return keyword. The function should be declared to be the same value as the type of its return value. Functions without return values should be declared type void.

Sometimes it is necessary for a function to modify values in the calling program. To do this, the function can be set up using a pointer variable as a formal argument. The function call is used to provide a particular address as the actual argument. This is assigned to the pointer variable. The function then can use the indirect value operator in conjunction with the pointer to use and alter the value stored at the original address.

One common use of this technique is with array-handling functions. The calling function provides an array name, which is a pointer to the array, and the called function uses a corresponding pointer variable to manipulate the array.

Several storage classes are available for variables. Variables declared inside a function are, by default, automatic variables. Such variables are local to the defining function. They are allocated when the function is called and deallocated when the function terminates.

External variables are defined outside any function definition. They are shared by all functions following the variable definition. The extern keyword can be used to extend the scope of an external variable to more than one file. An external variable persists for the duration of the whole program.

A static variable is defined inside a function by using the keyword static. It is local to that function, like an automatic variable. However, it persists for the duration of the entire program, like an external variable. Its value is not lost between function calls.

An external static variable is defined by applying the keyword static to an external definition. It is similar to an ordinary external variable, except its scope is limited to one file.

A register variable is defined by applying the keyword register to a variable defined inside a function. It is similar to an automatic variable, except that it may be kept in a register rather than in regular memory. This allows faster processing. However, because the number of registers is limited, there is no guarantee that a register will be available.

The name of a function is a pointer to the function. Typically, a function pointer is passed to another function to tell it which function it should use.

Answers to Questions in the Chapter

■ *2-1.* 3620.

■ *2-2.* Both spaces are the same; each variable is allocated sufficient space to hold the address of a byte of memory. The total number of addressable bytes in memory determine how big a pointer memory unit should be.

■ *2-3.* &pt would be the address in which pt is stored, 3618 in this case.

■ *2-4.* When you pass an argument by reference, the formal argument is a synonym for the original variable; that is, it is merely an alternate name for an existing variable, for a particular address location. The expression 2*i + 1, however, is not a variable and has no address.

■ *2-5.* No. The factp() function still uses the argument by value approach. The plong variable is a brand new variable, which is assigned the address of factorial. The address is the passed value. It is the indirect value operator (*) that the function uses to alter factorial. A true argument by reference call would have used factorial, not &factorial, as its argument.

■ *2-6.* (*pf)++ would mean, "use the current value pointed to by pf, then increase that *value* by 1." *++pf would mean, "move the pointer to the next floating-point number and use the value found there."

■ *2-7.*

```
        void prstrings( ps, n)       /* prints n strings */
        char **ps;          /* pointer-to-pointer-to-char */
        int n;
        {
              int i;
```

```
        for (i = 0; i < n; i++)
            printf("%2d: %s\n", i+1, *ps++ );
    }
```

Or you could use `*(ps + i)`. The chief point to bear in mind is that since ps is a pointer to a pointer, that *ps is itself a pointer.

■ *2-8.* The function can look at strings pointed to by two different pointers. The C library function `strlen()` takes a pointer to a string as an argument, and returns the length of the string; use it to decide which of the two compared strings is longer. If the strings are in the wrong order, swap pointers.

```
void sortstr( ps, n)
char *ps[];
int n;
{
    int top, seek;
    char *tempaddr;

    for ( top = 0; top < n -1; top++)
     for ( seek = top + 1; seek < n; seek++)
            if ( strlen( ps[seek] ) < strlen( ps[top] )
            {                /* swap addresses */
            tempaddr = ps[top];
            ps[top] = ps[seek];
            ps[seek] = tempaddr;
            }

}
```

■ *2-9.* The function should increment tot by n:

```
return tot += n;
```

a. The additive assignment operator adds the value to its right to the variable to the left.

b. The value of a C assignment expression is same as the value assigned to the left-hand term, so the value of tot is returned.

Exercises

1. Write a function that takes the name of an array of int as its first argument and the number of elements as its second argument, and that returns the sum of the elements.

2. Suppose we have a structure type defined as follows:

```
struct name {
        char firstname[12];
```

```
    char lastname[12];
}
```

a. Write a function that takes a structure of type `struct name` as its argument and that prints the contained name last name first.

b. Repeat 2a, but write the function so it uses the address of a structure as the function argument.

3

Binary and Text File I/O

- Binary and text data forms
- Binary and text file formats
- Low-level I/O
- The standard I/O package
- Buffers
- Command line arguments
- Standard files
- Redirection

Binary and Text File I/O

Computers manage information, and often information is stored in files. With personal computers, the floppy disk has become the most prevalent storage form for files, but the hard disk is rapidly increasing its share of total bytes. Programs that work with files must transfer information to and from these devices. C offers a multitude of I/O functions for this purpose, and we will look at them in this chapter.

There are two distinctions to make here. First, the DOS (PC-DOS or MS-DOS) environment supports two forms of files: text (or ASCII) files and binary files. This makes file handling more involved than, say, on a UNIX-like system, which has just one kind of file. Second, C offers two levels of I/O operations: "low-level" I/O and the "standard I/O package." Both have important roles in programming, so we will take a good look at the C functions used with each level. We'll enlarge upon the distinctions between file types and between levels as we proceed.

Text Files and Binary Files

Each operating system can—and does—create its own standards for the structure of a file. DOS has two forms: text and binary. Each stores information in binary form, but the bits are interpreted differently. You can think of a text file as having the bits organized into bytes, with each byte using ASCII code to represent a particular character. A *text file,* then, is a series of ASCII codes. The *binary file* is less restricted; for example, bits may be organized into:

- ☐ single bytes representing a character
- ☐ two bytes representing an integer
- ☐ four bytes representing a floating-point number
- ☐ 68 bytes representing a structure

There are additional formats for the bits as well. The text file has two other requirements that a C program should recognize. One is how it handles the end of a file, and the second is how it represents starting a new line. Let's look at those points.

Text Format versus Binary Format

First, we should distinguish between text and binary *formats* on the one hand, and text and binary *files* on the other. The format refers to the method used to store data. It is determined by the particular I/O functions used, not by the file type. The difference between file types, in turn, is in how the files are structured. Normally, you would use the text format in a text file and the binary format in a binary file. C does not restrict you to these choices, but you can get into trouble using binary formats with text files.

Let's look at the format differences now. Suppose you want to store the phrase "stuffed cabbage leaves." The natural choice would be a text file. One byte would contain the ASCII code for S, the next byte would hold the code for T, and so on.

Now suppose you wanted to store the number 9.8696. You can store it as text. This means storing it as a sequence of 6 characters: 9 . 8 6 9 6. That is, 6 successive bytes would hold the ASCII code for these 6 characters. Using the fprintf() function (see later in the this chapter), for example, would accomplish that.

Using the binary format, on the other hand, means storing the four-byte binary floating-point representation of the number. That is, the same sequence of bits used to represent the number in program memory is also used in the file. The write() and fwrite() functions (described later in this chapter) can accept this form of representation, as shown in Figure 3–1.

Figure 3–1
Text and Binary Representation of a Number

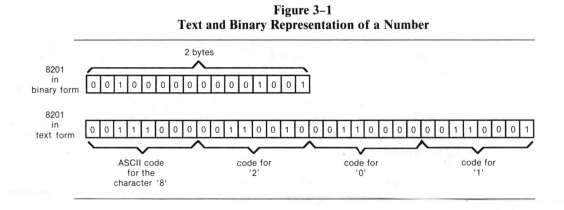

The text representation of a number uses a number of bytes equal to the number of characters in the number, while a binary representation uses a number of bytes equal to the size, in bytes, of the data type. Thus all int values occupy 2 bytes in binary form, but can occupy from 1 byte (the number 5) to 6 bytes (the number − 21446) in text form. A character is represented in the same way in either format, by a byte of ASCII code.

The binary format is more precise, particularly for floating-point numbers, which suffer from round-off errors in text form. It usually is more compact. On the other hand, the text format is more accessible; for example, it can be read using a text editor or the DOS `type` command. It is more portable, since binary representations of numbers may vary from one system to another, while ASCII code is an industry standard.

☐ *Question 3–1* Isn't the text format still a binary format?

Now let's turn to some of the differences in how the two types of files are structured.

The End of File

How does a computer system know where a file ends? One method is to use a special character to mark the end. This is the system used for text files, and the special character is CTRL-Z, ASCII code 26. (Other representations are ^Z and C's `'\032'`; 032 is the octal equivalent of 26.) When a program processing a text file encounters a byte containing 26 in binary form, it should stop. This method has the advantage of simplicity, but it has one defect: the CTRL-Z character cannot be one of the characters *in* a file.

This loss may not trouble you greatly, since the CTRL-Z character is not a common one. If we need to talk about it, we can always spell it out. But the limitation is a severe one for binary data. After all, the value 26 may appear as part of the data to be stored in a file. A program that uses CTRL-Z as a stop sign would see the 26 in binary form and think it to be a CTRL-Z. Thus, another method is needed to locate the end of a binary file.

One way is to maintain a record of the size of the file. A program reading the file can keep track of how many bytes it has read. When a number of bytes equal to the size of the file has been read, the program knows it has reached the end. This is the method used for binary files. (It also is the system used with UNIX.) C's I/O functions, in cooperation with the operating system, keep track of the number of bytes read themselves, so you don't have to program that task explicitly.

End of File for Keyboard Input

Using redirection, which we will discuss soon, your program can run using either keyboard or file input. How, then, does the end-of-file concept work with keyboard input? In the text mode, you enter a CTRL-Z to indicate the end of input. With binary input, you have a problem, because the operating system cannot know in advance how many bytes will be entered. There is no end-of-file indicator for binary keyboard input, so you must supply your own explicit test for identifying end of input.

If you have worked on a UNIX system, you probably are familiar with using CTRL-D to indicate end of file from the keyboard. From that, you might conclude that CTRL-D plays the same role in UNIX that CTRL-Z does in DOS. Well, it doesn't—quite. In UNIX, CTRL-D is a request to the operating system to flush (send on) the input. If it is typed at the beginning of a line, it sends on 0 characters, and that is interpreted to mean end of file. In other words, with UNIX the operating system determines the end of file; the CTRL-D character never reaches the program.

Line Separators in Text Files

In C, the newline character, represented by the escape sequence '\n', is used to indicate a new line of text is to be started. It normally is translated to the line-feed character, also known as LF or ASCII 10 (012 in octal). DOS text files, however, use two characters in sequence for this purpose: the carriage return ('\r', CR, or ASCII 13) followed by the line-feed (LF). We'll refer to this combination as CR-LF.

C Adjustments to Text and Binary Files

C evolved in an environment (UNIX) that maintained just one kind of file, one corresponding more or less to the DOS binary file. Therefore, transporting C to the DOS environment involves some adjustments. Of course, the C language itself need not be changed, for I/O is not actually part of C. Instead, each vendor is free to design its own I/O functions, which then become part of the C library for that implementation.

In practice, most implementations emulate the C I/O library developed for UNIX, providing a de facto standard for I/O. But hardware and operating system differences may require some deviations from the UNIX original. Thus IBM C uses the same I/O function names as UNIX C, but some of the functions' details differ in their usage.

In particular, the DOS functions need to do these three things:

Distinguish between text and binary files

Recognize different end-of-file criteria for the two file types

Handle the text file newline convention

Let's see how these goals are reached.

Distinguishing between File Types—Before a file can be read or written to, it must be *opened*. This can be done through the open() and fopen() functions we will discuss later in this chapter. If the file doesn't exist, it can be created through the creat() or open() or fopen() commands. In IBM C, these commands create and open files in the text mode by default. To open a file in binary mode, you have several choices:

1. When you link your program, link in the file *binmod.obj*. This makes the binary mode the default.

2. When your program is compiled, the compiler creates an external variable called _fmode. Its value determines the file mode. In your program, you can include the file *fcntl.h*, then do this:

```
_fmode = O_BINARY;     /* make binary file mode the default */
```

O_BINARY is a constant defined in fnctl.h. Another constant defined there is O_TEXT; it can be used to reset _fmode so that the text mode is the default. (Appendix A discusses the C preprocessor and how it is used to include files and to define constants.)

3. You can provide an argument to the fopen() or open() function to override the default mode when opening a specific file. We'll discuss the details when we get to those functions, but you'll see a short example before then.

Any one of these choices suffices to set the file mode. The mode in which a file is opened then determines how the I/O functions interpret end of file and newlines.

End-of-File Interpretation—C input functions typically return a special sign when they encounter the end of a file. You most likely are familiar with this C idiom:

```
int ch;

while ( (ch = getchar() ) != EOF)
    ...;
```

Here the getchar() function chugs along until it encounters the end of a file. It then returns the value EOF, defined in the file *stdio.h* as (-1). A more general version of getchar(), called getc(), works in the same manner, but reads a specified file instead of keyboard input. The ch variable is declared int rather than char for reasons of compatibility. Some versions of C implement type char as an unsigned type, which means a negative number like -1 cannot be assigned to a char. IBM C does use a signed char, so we could get away with using a type char ch for the idiom.

An important point to understand is that EOF does not represent a value found in a file. Rather, it is a signal sent by getchar() or getc() when the function encounters something it recognizes as the end of the file.

When a file has been opened in the binary mode, getc() identifies the end of file by keeping track of the file size and of the number of characters read. When the two become equal, getc() returns the EOF signal next time it is called.

When, however, a file has been opened in the text mode, getc() also looks for the CTRL-Z character. The function returns the EOF signal when it first encounters a CTRL-Z or when it runs out of characters, whichever comes first, as Figure 3–2 indicates. (The figure shows several CTRL-Z characters because some text editors and word processors, such as WordStar, pad the end of files with them.)

Figure 3–2
Text and Binary Modes End of File

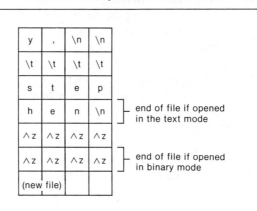

□ *Question 3–2*   Is **EOF** for a text file different from **EOF** for a binary file?

Newlines—When a file has been opened in the text mode, the input functions translate the CR-LF sequence to a simple line-feed (\n). Similarly, the output functions translate a simple '\n' to the sequence CR-LF.

When a file has been opened in the binary mode, input and output functions transmit the exact sequence of characters they find.

An Illustrative Example

A C program can use either the text or binary mode for a given file. For example, a file that was created as a text file can be examined in either mode. How the contents are processed, however, will depend on the mode chosen. We'll look at a program that opens a particular file first in the text mode, then in the binary mode. In each case, it prints out the contents of the file, one character to a line. We'll discuss the file opening process more fully soon, but here is the program:

```
/* ascbin.c-reads a file in text, then binary mode */
#include <stdio.h>
#define CNZ '\032'        /* CTRL-Z */
main()
{
  int ch;
  FILE /*fp;                /* file identifier used in program */
```

```
if ( (fp = fopen ("kate","r") ) == NULL) /* r is read mode */
    exit(2);    / quits if can't open the kate file */
printf("Text Mode:\n");
do
  {
  ch = getc(fp);           /* get character from file */
  switch(ch)
    {
    case '\n' : printf("LF : ");
                break;
    case '\r' : printf("CR : ");
                break;
    case CNZ  : printf("^Z : ");
                break;
    case EOF  : printf("EOF: ");
                break;
    default   : printf("%c : ", ch);
                break;
    }
  printf("%3d\n", ch);
  } while ( ch != EOF);  /* go to EOF */
fclose(fp);
printf("Binary mode:\n");
 if ( (fp = fopen(argv[1],"rb") ) == NULL)
    exit(2);        /* rb is binary read mode */
 do
   {
   ch = getc(fp);
   switch(ch)
     {
     case '\n' : printf("LF : ");
                 break;
     case '\r' : printf("CR : ");
                 break;
     case CNZ  : printf("^Z : ");
                 break;
     case EOF  : printf("EOF: ");
                 break;
     default   : printf("%c : ", ch);
                 break;
     }
   printf("%3d\n", ch);
   } while ( ch != EOF);
 fclose(fp);
}
```

At the insistence of Kate the cat, the author used the EDLIN editor to create the following *kate* text file:

```
top
cat
```

Here is an annotated output of the program:

```
Text Mode:
t  : 116
o  : 111
p  : 112
LF :  10          ←— newline character
c  :  99
a  :  97
t  : 116
LF :  10
EOF:  -1          ←— found a ^Z
Binary mode:
t  : 116
o  : 111
p  : 112
CR :  13          ←— sees the carriage return
LF :  10
c  :  99
a  :  97
t  : 116
CR :  13
LF :  10
^Z :  26          ←— reports ^Z as just another character
EOF:  -1          ←— now finds true end of file
```

The binary mode reveals the true contents of the file. The text mode condensed the CR-LF combination to simple line-feed. Also, the text mode stopped at the CTRL-Z, while the binary mode read that character.

Using WordStar in the N (nondocument mode) to create the same text produces an interesting variation. WordStar creates files in multiples of 128 bytes. When the text uses only a portion of the final block, the remaining bytes are filled with CTRL-Z characters. The text mode processing stops at the first CTRL-Z, but the binary processing mode prints all of them, stopping only when reaching the end of the 128-byte block.

☐ *Question 3-3* Suppose we added a counter to keep track of the number of characters in the last program. How many characters would each part of the program find in the test program?

We're going to take a brief side trip now before looking at the I/O functions. One limitation of the *ascbin.c* program is that it works only with the *kate* file. Often we want a program to operate on some file that we specify when the program is run.

In C this most often is accomplished by using *command line arguments*. You probably know about them, but we'll take a closer look at the mechanics.

Command Line Arguments

In DOS systems, machine-language programs, such as those produced by compiling and linking a C program, are kept in files with the *.exe* or the *.com* extension. A program is run by typing the name without the extension; that is the command line. Other items on the same line constitute the command line arguments. For example, consider the following DOS command

```
copy goya b:nagoya
```

The terms goya and b:nagoya are command line arguments. A C program can be set up so that its command line arguments are made available, as strings, to the program. The technique is to declare them as arguments to main(). Also, you need to declare an integer variable that gets assigned the number of arguments. Here is a brief example; when run, it prints its arguments in reverse order:

```
/* recho.c-reverse echoes arguments */
#include <stdio.h>
main(argc, argv)      /* list formal arguments */
int argc;             /* number of arguments */
char *argv[];         /* the argument strings */
{
   while ( argc-- > 1)
      printf("%s ", argv[argc]);
   putchar('\n');
}
```

The Argument Count and Argument Values

Here argc (*arg*ument *c*ount) is the number of arguments on the command line. The count includes the command name itself. Next, argv (*arg*ument *v*alues) represents an array of strings, one argument per string. You can give these variables any names consonant with C rules and good taste, but argc and argv are common choices. The first string is argv[0], and in DOS 3.0 and later, it contains the command name. In earlier versions of DOS, the command name is not available this way, and argv[0] corresponds to a couple of null characters. Then `argv[1]` (in all versions) is the first argument, and so on. The final argument, then, is `argv[argc — 1]`, reflecting the fact that C arrays start with a zero subscript.

The `argv` argument is, in fact, a single number. Its declaration, recall, is this:

```
char *argv[];
```

In declaring a formal argument, the construction `[]` to the right of an identifier is the same as using `*` to the left; both identify a pointer. Thus, the declaration we used is equivalent to the following:

```
char **argv;
```

Both state that `argv` is a pointer to a pointer to a `char`.

Unraveling Argv

Let's see how this works. Suppose we place the *recho* program in the file *recho.exe* and run it:

```
A> recho man mashes potato
potato mashes man
A>
```

The essence of what happens is clear: the program "remembers" and labels the words in the command line, then it prints them in reverse order. Going through the mechanisms used, however, is a tortuous—perhaps even torturous—route. The tricky part is how C keeps track of the command line strings, for it uses a double pointer. That is, it uses a pointer to the pointers to the strings. We'll go through the process step-by-step now.

When the program is run, four strings are placed in memory. In DOS Version 3 and later, the first string is "recho", and it will require six bytes of memory. (Remember that C strings use a terminal null character to mark the string end.) With earlier DOS versions, the first string consists of two null characters. Next, the "man" string will occupy four bytes, "mashes" will take seven bytes, and the "potato" requires seven bytes. Then, to keep track of these three strings, three consecutive memory locations are assigned the beginning addresses of these three strings. Each of these new locations, then, is a pointer to a `char`, the first character of the pointed-to string. Finally, `argv` is assigned the address of the first of these three pointers, making `argv` a pointer to a pointer to a `char`. Figure 3–3 illustrates this process.

In this example, `argv` points to the address 3742, so `*argv` has the value 3753, which is the value contained in the pointed-to address. Following C array notation conventions, we can also refer to `*argv` as `argv[0]`.

Since `argv` is a pointer to the pointer at location 3742, then `argv + 1` points to the next pointer over, which is the one at location 3744. (A PC

Figure 3–3
Argv —A Pointer to a Pointer

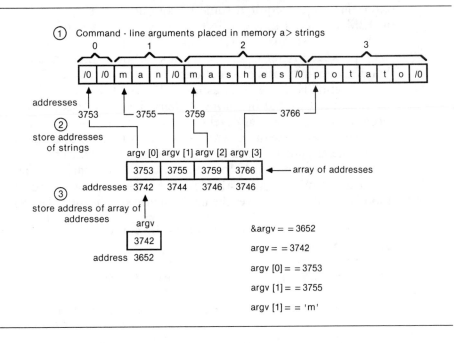

pointer is two bytes.) We can represent the value stored at 3744 by
`*(argv+1)` (using pointer notation) or by `argv[1]` (using array notation).
Either is the address of the beginning of the string "man", which is stored
at location 3755.

How do you print a string? You provide the address of the string as an
argument. Thus, the statement

```
printf("%s", argv[1]);
```

would print the string "man".

Individual characters in a command line argument can be accessed by
going one level further. For example, `argv[1][2]` would be the third character of the "man" string.

□ *Question 3-4* How could you represent the n in "man" using asterisks
instead of brackets?

The default compilation produces a program that does not recognize
DOS's wildcard characters `*` and `?`. If you want a program to recognize
them, you need to link in an object file provided with the compiler. For
the small-memory model, the file is *ssetargv.obj*. For the medium- and
large-memory models, the corresponding files are *msetargv.obj* and
lsetargv.obj.

Low-Level I/O

Now that we've acquired some background, let's see how files are handled in IBM C. Recall that C offers a low-level package of I/O functions and a higher-level "standard I/O" package. First, we will look at the low-level I/O package. Afterward, we'll look at how the standard I/O package handles the same sorts of situations.

Essentially, in IBM C, as in UNIX, the low-level I/O functions are the routines used by the operating system. They are used, for example, in the programming of the high-level routines we discuss later.

Suppose we wish to write a program that takes a filename as a command line argument and counts the number of characters in the file. The program should open the file for reading, count the characters, and close the file when done. We'll start with a fairly simple approach, then make a simple modification that improves the performance significantly. Here's version 1:

```
/* count1.c-counts characters in a file, 1 at a time */
main(argc,argv)
int argc;
char *argv[];          /* use command line to get filename */
{
    char ch;           /* place to hold each character as read */
    int fd;            /* file descriptor-identifies file */
    long count = 0;

    if ( argc != 2)    /* quit if wrong argument count */
        {
        printf("Usage: count1 filename\n");
        exit(1);
        }
    if ( ( fd = open(argv[1],0) ) < 0 )
        {
        printf("count can't open %s\n", argv[1]);
        exit(1);
        }
    while ( read(fd, &ch, 1) > 0 )
        count++;
    close(fd);
    printf("File %s has %ld characters\n", argv[1], count);
}
```

Running it successfully would look like this:

```
A> count1 zeus
File zeus has 356 characters
```

We've used the open(), close(), read(), and exit() functions. Let's go through the program and explain each function as it appears.

The Exit() Function

The program is designed to be used with one filename as an argument. The program checks to see if `argc` is two (the command name and the filename). If it isn't, the program uses the `exit()` function to quit. This function closes up any open files first. The argument is a status report. Normally 0 is used to indicate normal termination, while a non-0 value indicates abnormal termination. You may wonder who or what gets the status report. In a simple program like ours, it isn't used. However, IBM C allows you to set up a program *(parent process)* that launches another program *(child process),* then resumes running when the child terminates. In that case, the parent process can use the child's *exit status,* as provided by the `exit()` function. We'll return to this topic in Chapter 7.

The Open() Function

Next, the `open()` function is used to attempt to open the command line file for reading. The function takes two arguments. The first is a string representing the filename. You can give the string explicitly, as in `"datafile"`, or you can use a string variable, as we do here with `argv[1]`. The second argument is an integer giving the desired mode. The basic values are 0 for *read mode,* 1 for *write mode,* and 2 for *read/write mode.* IBM C has added a few more choices and formalized them with defined constants; we'll see more about that soon.

   If you use an explicit name like *datafile*, the program looks for a file in the current directory. More often, you can specify a particular directory so that the same file is used no matter what directory you are in when you run the program. You can do this by specifying a complete pathname, such as *c:\rain\datafile*. There is one catch: in C, the backslash character is used for special characters. For instance, \n is the newline character, and \r is the carriage-return character. If a backslash character combination has no particular meaning, such as \d, then it is interpreted to mean the character alone. Thus, the string `"c:\rain\datafile"` would be interpreted to be `"c:CARRIAGE-RETURNaindatafile"`, which is not the greatest choice for a filename. Fortunately, a double backslash is interpreted to be a single backslash, so the correct representation of the filename is this: `"c:\\rain\\datafile"`.

   The `open()` function returns an integer called a *file descriptor* or a *file handle.* It, and not the filename, is used to identify the file for the other low-level I/O functions. If the function fails to open the named file, it returns a value of − 1. The `if` statement in the program combines obtaining a value of `fd` with comparing it to − 1. If the file was opened, then `fd` is positive, and the program continues.

The Fcntl.h File—The *fcntl.h* file contains several defined (or *manifest*) constants representing possible choices for `open()`'s second argument. Think of each of them as a flag that can be set. The C bitwise OR operator (see Chapter 4) can be used to set more than one flag. Before seeing how to do that, let's look at the choices, which are shown in Table 3-1.

Table 3-1
Choices of Constants

Constant	Purpose
O_APPEND	Reposition the file pointer to the end of the file before every write operation.
O_CREAT	Create and open a new file; this flag has no effect if the specified file already exits. open() requires a third argument when this flag is used.
O_EXCL	Return an error value if the specified file already exists; only applies if O_CREAT is set.
O_RDONLY	Open file for reading only.
O_RDWR	Open file for reading and writing.
O_TRUNC	Open and truncate an existing file to 0 length; the file must have write permission, and the contents of the file are destroyed.
O_WRONLY	Open file for writing only.
O_BINARY	Open file in binary mode.
O_TEXT	Open file in text mode.

If you include the *fcntl.h* file, you can use these defined (or manifest) constants as arguments. For example, to open the file `pigettes` in the read-only mode, you can use this call:

```
open("pigettes", O_RDONLY);
```

We say that this "sets" the O_RDONLY flag.

To set more than one flag, use the bitwise OR operator: ¦. For example, to open the `pigettes` file in the read-only mode and in the binary mode, do this:

```
open("pigettes", O_RDONLY ¦ O_BINARY);
```

As common sense suggests, some combinations are not allowed. For example, don't try to use the read-only mode simultaneously with the write-only mode.

Setting the O_CREAT flag requires that you supply a third argument indicating the read/write permissions for a file. You can, for instance, specify that a file has only read permission. This protects it from accidental modification, and an attempt to open it in a writing mode will fail. We'll return to this topic later. Now let's return to the other functions in our program.

The Read() Function

The read() function takes three arguments. The first argument is the file handle that specifies the file to be read. In our program, we use fd, the file handle previously returned by the open() function. The second argument is the address of the memory location where the read data is to be placed. The third argument is the number of bytes to be read. Thus, the call

```
read(fd, &ch, 1);
```

tells the system to open the file identified by fd, read one byte of data, and place it at the address &ch. The first call to read() starts at the beginning of the file, and each subsequent call begins where the previous call left off. (This order can be altered by using the lseek() function that we discuss later.)

The read() function returns the number of bytes it read. If it has reached the end of file, it returns a 0, and if there is a reading error, it returns a value of − 1. Thus the loop

```
while ( read(fd, &ch, 1) > 0 )
    count++;
```

normally cycles until the end of file is reached, incrementing count once for each character encountered.

By default, a file is opened in the text mode. Thus the line-feed and carriage-return combination is counted as a single character. If we want to count every character, we could set the O_BINARY flag when calling open().

The Close() Function

The close() function is used to close a file when the program is finished with it. It takes one argument, the file handle of the file to be closed.

Improving the Program

If you compile and run this program, you will find that it is slow, especially if the file to be counted is on a floppy disk. The reason is that the program reads one byte at a time. Each read involves finding the file, searching for the proper location, and reading what is there. We can improve the speed of the program immensely by reading larger chunks of data. To do this, we need a larger storage area in which to place these larger chunks.

For example, we can use an array of 512 characters and read in blocks of data 512 bytes large. Such a block of memory is termed a *buffer*. We can use the return value of read() to tally up the total number of bytes read. Here is a version that does just that:

```
/* count2.c-counts characters in a file, uses a buffer */
#include <fcntl.h>        /* use manifest constants */
#define SIZE 512
main(argc,argv)
int argc;
char *argv[];
{
    char buffer[SIZE];    /* temporary storage */
    int fd;
    int n;
    long count = 0;

    if ( argc != 2)
       {
       printf("Usage: count filename\n");
       exit(1);
       }
    if ( ( fd = open(argv[1], O_RDONLY) ) < 0 )
       {
       printf("count2 can't open %s\n", argv[1]);
       exit(1);
       }
    while ( (n = read(fd,buffer,SIZE)) > 0 )
       count += n;
    close(fd);
    printf("File %s has %ld characters\n", argv[1], count);
}
```

Recall that the name of an array is the address of the first element, so the argument buffer does specify an address.

Try comparing the speed of this version with the first one. You'll find the second version to be faster. However, the difference is smaller than it might be. The reason is that DOS already uses a buffer system of its own when doing disk I/O. So the single byte I/O actually reads from an operating system buffer rather than directly from the disk.

This modification was pretty easy, but suppose we wanted the program to count lines as well as bytes. Then the program would have to examine each byte to see if it was a newline character. At first glance, this would seem to require reading the file byte-by-byte in the aggravatingly slow fashion of the first version. A better approach, however, is to read in a bufferful, as in the second version, then examine the buffer contents for newline characters. When the buffer is fully examined, get the next bufferful. Since the buffer is part of program memory, it can be examined much more rapidly than a file on a floppy disk. However, more programming is required.

Fortunately, we don't have to do that programming. The high-level I/O functions that we discuss soon implement that approach automatically, without any special effort on your part. Before looking at high-level I/O, however, let's look at some more common low-level functions.

The Write() Function

The output counterpart to read() is write(), and the two share a similar syntax. Here is the general form:

```
write(fd,address,bytes)
```

The fd is a file handle identifying which file to write on. The address is the address of the first byte in program memory holding the series of bytes to be copied, and bytes is the number of bytes to be copied. The function also has a return value, the number of bytes actually written. This can be less than bytes if, for instance, the target disk runs out of space. If there is an output error, then the return value is − 1.

The read() and write() functions complement each other. For instance, we could use this programming as the core of a file copying program:

```
#define SIZE 512
   ...
int fold, fnew;
char buffer[SIZE];
   ...
while ( (n = read(fold,buffer,SIZE)) > 0 )
      write(fnew,buffer,SIZE);
```

Here fold and fnew are file handles for the old and new files. The read() function copies 512 bytes to the temporary buffer in program memory, and the write() function copies those bytes to the target file.

It's important to realize that read() and write() are binary I/O functions. We used a type char buffer, but that is just because each element of a char array is just one byte. The actual contents of the files could be text, or they could be binary data, or executable code. As long as the files have been opened in the binary mode, this code fragment copies the exact sequence of binary numbers from file to memory and then to file.

To illustrate the binary nature of write(), suppose you want to store a particular floating-point number in a file. You can do something like this:

```
float num;
   ...
write(fh, &num, sizeof (float) );
```

The C `sizeof` operator yields the size of its operand in bytes. In IBM C, the float type is four bytes long, so this statement directs the computer to find the beginning address of the `num` variable and to copy four bytes worth of data from there to the file specified by `fd`. To avoid problems, the file referred to by `fd` should be opened in the binary mode.

The IBM C compiler offers the option of performing type checking on function arguments. That is, it can check to see if the argument you provided is of the same type as the formal argument used in the function definition. Our last example would fail such checking, for `&num` is type pointer-to-`float` while `write()` is defined as using a pointer-to-`char` argument. This kind of circumstance is fairly common with arguments that are addresses. The solution is to use C's type cast facility:

```
float num;
   ...
write(fh, (char *) &num, sizeof (float) );
```

The `(char *)` preface "casts" `&num` to type pointer-to-`char`.

The `read()` and `write()` functions move in an orderly fashion through their respective files. Each function call resumes where the preceding call quits. You can think of each as maintaining a pointer to a current position in a file. Each call to `read()` or `write()` advances the corresponding pointer appropriately. You can, however, move the pointers without reading or writing.

The Lseek() Function

With this function you can set a file pointer to any place in the file. Here is how the function is used:

```
long pos, offset, lseek();
int fd, mode;
   ...
pos = lseek(fd, offset, mode);
```

Here `fd` identifies the file, `offset` tells how many bytes to shift, `mode` specifies the starting point for the `offset`, and the return value, here assigned to `pos`, is the position of the file pointer after the function is executed. This position is measured in bytes from the beginning of the file. A negative return value indicates the seeking failed.

The return value and `offset` both should be type `long`. This means your program should declare `lseek()` to be type long. You can do that explicitly or by including the file *io.h*, which contains type declarations for this and certain other I/O functions.

The Lseek() Mode—The `mode` argument has three possible values, summarized in Table 3–2.

**Table 3–2
Values of the Mode Argument**

Mode	Meaning
0	Offset is from the beginning of the file
1	Offset is from the current position
2	Offset is from the end of the file

In mode 0, the offset is measured from the beginning of the file. Note that the first byte of the file has an offset of 0L, not of 1L.

In mode 2, the end of the file is located one byte past the last byte in the file. Thus, in this mode, the last actual byte has an offset of −1L. Note that a positive offset moves the file pointer forward, while a negative offset moves it back.

Text Mode, Binary Mode, and Lseek()—Recall that the behavior of read() and write() depends on which mode, text or binary, a file is opened in. In the text mode, for example, read() will count the CR-LF combination as a single character and will recognize CTRL-Z as an end-of-file indicator, while in the binary mode it won't. Does lseek() exhibit similar behavior? No! For either mode, lseek() counts the CR-LF combination as two bytes, and the end of file is the true end, not the first CTRL-Z.

If you think about it, you'll see that it would be difficult to implement lseek() effectively if it were to emulate read() in the text mode. Suppose, for example, we ask lseek() to move ahead 100 bytes. If it had the text mode mentality, lseek() would have to examine all the intervening bytes to see how many times the CR-LF combination shows up. That would defeat the purpose of speedy relocation. Thus, regardless of the mode in which the file is opened, lseek() acts as if the binary mode prevails. This suggests that a program that uses lseek() on the one hand and read() or write() on the other should be opened in the binary mode so that all functions will be using the same interpretations.

A Backward Example

Here is a program that uses write() and lseek(). It prints out a file in reverse order. It does have a defect: it reads and writes one character at a time, which is slow. This fault can be fixed with additional programming, but that would obscure the main point of the this program: illustrating lseek().

```
/* reverse.c-prints file in reverse */
#include <fcntl.h> /* used by open() */
#define CNTL_Z '\032' /* text mode EOF */
```

```
main(argc,argv)
int argc;
char *argv[];
{
    char ch;
    int fd;
    long count, last, lseek();

    if ( argc != 2)
        {
        printf("Usage: reverse filename\n");
        exit(1);
        }
    if ( ( fd = open(argv[1],O_RDONLY | O_BINARY)) < 0 )
        {                               /* read-only and binary modes */
        printf("reverse can't open %s\n", argv[1]);
        exit(1);
        }
    last = lseek(fd,0L,2);    /* go to end of file */

    for ( count = 1L ; count <= last; count++)
        {
        lseek(fd, -count, 2);  /* go backwards */
        read(fd, &ch, 1);
        if ( ch != CNTL_Z && ch != 'r')
            write(1, &ch, 1);  /* 1 is the screen */
        }
    close(fd);
}
```

Remember that C uses the L suffix to indicate an integer is type long. As indicated, the value 1 is the file handle for the standard output, which, by default, is the screen. We'll come back to this and other standard files soon. Here is a sample run:

```
B> reverse katenew

.tnemrepmet teews a htiw
tac kcalb dna etihw
ytterp a si etaK
B>
```

You should be able to reconstruct the original file and guess at its inspiration.

One bit of code requires further comment:

```
if ( ch != CNTL_Z && ch != '\r')
        write(1, &ch, 1);
```

The comparison with `CNTL_Z` causes writing to be delayed until any terminal CTRL-Z characters have been skipped. The comparison with `'\r'` (the C notation for the carriage-return character) causes the carriage-return character in the CR-LF combination to be ignored.

Suppose we wish to modify this program to write the reversed file to new file. Then the program must first create the new file. Let's see how that is done.

Low-Level File Creation

The classic C function for creating a new file is `creat()`. In IBM C, however, the responsibilities of `open()` have been expanded to include file creation. The `creat()` function is retained for compatibility, but the IBM C manual recommends using `open()` for new code. We'll follow that advice.

Recall that the second argument to the `open()` function specifies the file mode. If a file is to be created, the `O_CREAT` flag should be set. Two other flags, `O_EXCL` and `O_TRUNC`, can be used to modify the `O_CREAT` flag; all are defined in the `fcntl.h` file. When the `O_CREAT` flag is used, you must supply an additional argument, called the *permission mode,* to `open()`. Let's look at these points in turn.

File-Creation Flags

If the `O_CREAT` flag is set, and the specified file does not yet exist, then the `open()` function creates and opens the file. If the file already exists, then this flag is ignored. Thus the mode `O_WRONLY ¦ O_CREAT` will cause a file to be created and opened in the write-only mode if nonexistent and to be opened for writing if it already exists. Note that the `O_CREAT` flag merely opens a file; another flag is used to specify the read or write mode.

The other two flags modify the behavior of `open()` if `O_CREAT` is used when the file already exists. If the `O_EXCL` flag is included in the mode, then the file will be opened only if it doesn't exist. Otherwise, `open()` will return a value of −1, indicating failure. The `O_TRUNC` flag truncates an existing file, that is, removes its contents. It ensures that your program starts off with a clean slate.

File Permission Modes

The third argument specifies the permission modes for the file. On UNIX systems, files have nine separate permissions that can be turned on or off. With DOS, there are just two possibilities: read and write, and read only. If, for instance, a file has read-only permission, then an attempt to open the file for writing will fail. This gives a measure of file protection.

DOS uses manifest constants to set the permission mode; to use them, include the *sys \ types.h* and *sys \ stat.h* files. Table 3–3 lists the constants:

Table 3–3
Constants to Set the Permission Mode in DOS

Constant	Meaning
S_IWRITE	Writing permitted
S_IREAD	Reading permitted

To set both, use `S_IREAD ¦ S_IWRITE`. Actually, under DOS, all files are readable, so `S_IWRITE` has the same effect as setting both flags. The apparent option of turning off read permission is maintained for compatibility with other operating systems.

The `open()` function combines the specified permission mode with a *permission mask*. We'll take this up in a later chapter, when we look at `umask()`. The default setting of this mask, however, lets you set the permissions as we described.

Another Backward Example

To see how file creation looks, let's modify *reverse.c* so that the reversed text is put into a second file. We need to decide which mode to use. The `O_CREAT` mode alone will cause the program to write over an existing file. That seems rather harsh, so we will also set the `O_EXCL` flag and have the program abort if the target file already exists.

```
#include <stdio.h>
#include <sys\types.h>
#include <sys\stat.h>
#define CNTL_Z '\032'              /* text mode EOF */
main(argc,argv)
int argc;
char *argv[];
{
    char ch;
    int fold, fnew;
    long count, last;

    if ( argc != 3)
        {
        printf("Usage: reverse file1 file2\n");
        exit(1);
        }
    if ( ( fold = open(argv[1],O_RDONLY ¦ O_BINARY) ) < 0 )
```

```
        {                           /* read-only and binary modes */
        printf("reverse can't open %s\n", argv[1]);
        exit(1);
        }
    if ( ( fnew =
            open(argv[2],O_CREAT ¦ O_EXCL ¦ O_WRONLY, S_IWRITE))
                                                            < 0 )
        {
        printf("reverse can't open %s\n", argv[2]);
        exit(1);
        }
    last = lseek(fold,0L,2);    /* go to end of file */

    for ( count = 1L ; count <=  last; count++)
        {
        lseek(fold, -count, 2); /* go backwards */
        read(fold, &ch, 1);
        if ( ch != CNTL_Z && ch != '\r')
            write(fnew, &ch, 1);
        }
    close(fold);
    close(fnew);
    }
```

One odd point is that the original copy is opened in binary mode, while the reversed copy is opened in text mode. The reason for the first choice, as we saw, is to facilitate use of `lseek()`. The second choice is so that the copy will be in standard text format, with the LF obtained by the `read()` converted to the standard CR-LF and a CTRL-Z placed at the end of the file.

□ *Question 3-5*   Commonly, a program that creates a new file prompts you whether you wish to overwrite if you happen to enter the name of an existing file. Can you include this feature in the preceding program in the backward example? List the code. To simplify matters, assume that the only possible cause of file-opening failure is the pre-existence of the file.

The Creat() Function

As we said, the IBM C manual recommends using `open()` to create files. The older `creat()` function looks like this in use:

```
fh = creat("whatafile", pmode);
```

The first argument is the filename, and the second argument is the per-mission mode, which is the same as `open()`'s third argument. The effect of a creat() call is the same as using open() with a O_CREAT ¦ O_TRUNC creation mode.

Buffered I/O and the Standard I/O Package

The strength of the low-level I/O functions is that they offer excellent control, particularly when used with binary files. If you have a special I/O need (whatever that might be), you can use the low-level I/O functions to create the exact I/O package you need.

The standard I/O package is one such creation. It is designed to provide fast buffered I/O, primarily for text situations. To add to programming convenience, it supplies several special-purpose I/O functions. For many applications, using the standard I/O package is simpler and more effective than using simple low-level output. The essential feature is its use of automatic buffering. Buffered I/O, recall, means reading and writing data in large chunks from a file to an array and back. Reading and writing data in large chunks greatly speeds up the I/O operations, while storing it in an array allows access to the individual bytes. The advantages of this approach are so noteworthy that the C library contains a large number of related functions that implement it. Collectively, these functions are termed the *standard I/O package.*

One key element to using this package is to open files with the fopen() function instead of open(). When fopen() is used, several things happen. The file, of course, is opened. Second, an external character array is created to act as a buffer. The *stdio.h* file sets the buffer size to 512. Third, a structure is created to contain information about the buffer and the file. When an I/O function from the standard package, such as getc(), is invoked, the buffer is filled with data from the file. When getc() reaches the end of the buffer, the buffer automatically is filled with the next block of data. You need not even be aware of the buffer, and you can program as if the I/O functions worked directly with the file.

The functions of the standard package share several definitions and variables. They are set up in the *stdio.h* file, so normally you should include this file when using any of the functions. Here, for example, is the definition of the structure used to describe a file and its buffers; we've added comments:

```
#define  FILE      struct _iobuf     /* FILE is a structure */
extern FILE {
        char *_ptr;          /* ptr to current char in buffer */
        int   _cnt;          /* bytes left in buffer */
        char *_base;         /* ptr to beginning of buffer */
        char  _flag;         /* assorted file information */
        char  _file;         /* file handle */
        } _iob[_NFILE];
```

Individual bits of the _flag member indicate such things as read and write permission and if the end of file has been reached.

Streams

Because the I/O functions work with a file and with a buffer, you need to tell the functions the characteristics about the file and buffer. The fopen() function, we said, creates a structure describing both, and its return value is a pointer to that structure. This pointer, often called a *stream,* then is used by other members of the standard I/O package, much as the integer file handle is used by the low-level I/O functions. Figure 3–4 illustrates the process.

Figure 3–4
Fopen() at Work

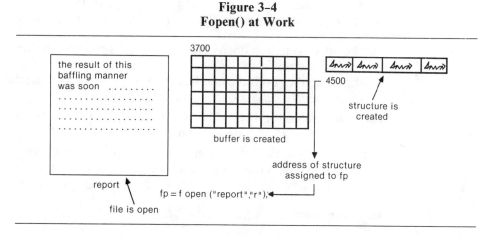

The *stdio.h* file defines FILE to identify the structure type used to hold the file and buffer information. This means that the fopen() function and the stream assigned its return value both should be declared type pointer-to-FILE. The *stdio.h* file itself takes care of the declaration for fopen(), but you need to declare the stream. The stream, then, is used as an argument for the other I/O functions. Here is a simple example, a program that copies to the screen a file whose name is given as a command line argument:

```
/*   kat.c--show a text file on the screen */
#include
<stdio.h>
main(ac,av)
int ac;
char *av];
{
      FILE *fp;      /* fp is a stream   */
      int ch;

      if ( ac != 2)
         {
```

```
                    printf("Usage: kat filename\n");
                    exit(1);
                    }
           if ( (fp = fopen(av[1], "r") ) == NULL )
                    {                           /* opening a stream */
                    printf("For you, %s is unattainable\n", av[1]);
                    exit(1);
                    }
           while ( (ch = getc(fp) ) != EOF)   /* fp identifies file */
                    putchar(ch);
           fclose(fp); }
```

We used ac and av instead of argc and argv to illustrate the mutability of main()'s argument names. The main points, again, are these:

- The fopen() function opens the specified file, creates a buffer to hold blocks of data from the file, and creates a structure of type FILE that describes both file and buffer. The "r" indicates the file is opened in the read mode.
- The return value for fopen() is a pointer to the FILE-type structure; it is designated as a stream and is assigned to fp.
- The stream fp is used as an argument to getc(fp) to indicate which file and which buffer to use and as an argument to fclose() to indicate which file to close and which buffer to dispose of.

There are some minor points to note, too:

- NULL is a special value, defined in *stdio.h*, used by fopen() when it fails to open a file. It is, in fact, the address 0, which is not a valid pointer value in C. In IBM C, NULL is not the absolute address 0; it is the beginning of the data segment.
- EOF is a special value, defined in *stdio.h*, used by getc() (and other functions) to indicate that the end of file has been reached. In IBM C, it has the numerical value −1.

Incidentally, NULL is not the same as the null character. Both have the same numerical value, but NULL is an address while '\0' is an ASCII code. That is, they are different types.

Now let's look in more detail at a few members of the standard I/O package.

The Fopen() Function

The standard I/O packages only work with files opened using fopen(). As we've seen, it returns a pointer to a FILE structure, so its type is pointer-to-FILE. It takes two arguments. The first is a string pointer, such as av[1] or "gooddata". The second argument indicates the type of access desired, and it, too, is a string. Table 3–4 lists the possible choices.

Table 3–4
Choices for Opening a File with Fopen()

Argument String	Purpose
"r"	Open for reading (the file must exist).
"w"	Open for writing; if the file exists, its contents are destroyed.
"a"	Open for writing at the end of the file; create the file if it does not yet exist.
"r+"	Open for both reading and writing (the file must exist).
"w+"	Open for both reading and writing; if the file exists, its contents are first destroyed.
"a+"	Open for reading and appending; create file if it does not exist.

Note that although the final three modes all are read and write, they differ from one another. The "r+" mode only works for an existing file, and the contents are preserved except for any changes made by overwriting parts of the file. The "w+" mode wipes out the contents of the file, if any, so it ensures that you start with a clean slate. The "a+" mode works whether or not the file exists already, and it preserves the original file, if any. It will not let you overwrite existing data in the file.

Indeed, both "a" and "a+" preclude overwriting existing data. Using the rewind() and fseek() functions, (described later in this chapter), you can position the file pointer anywhere you like in the file. However, in these two modes, write operations will always move the pointer to the end of the file before writing begins. (The file pointer referred to here is the one that keeps track of the current I/O location; it is not the pointer-to-FILE mentioned earlier.)

When using one of the combined read/write modes, you must make a call to fseek() or rewind() between a read call and a write call.

To specify the type of file explicitly, you can append t to the mode to indicate text mode or append a b to indicate binary mode. Otherwise, the type is determined by the external variable _fmode, which, we saw near the beginning of this chapter, is set to the text mode by default.

The Fclose() Function

A file opened by fopen() should be closed using fclose(), and not close(). The fopen() function takes the stream returned by fopen() as its argument. Besides closing the file, this function flushes the buffers and frees the buffer space.

The Fflush() Function

Normally, the contents of a buffer are not sent on to the final destination until the buffer is full or until the associated file is closed. (I/O from your terminal, however, is sent on *[flushed]* whenever a newline is encountered.) The fflush() function lets you explicitly force the current contents of a buffer to be sent on. As an argument, this function takes the stream value returned by fopen().

The Getc() Function

This function works just like getchar() except that you must provide it with a stream as an argument to indicate which file is read. (Actually, getchar() is just getc() used with the standard input as its "file.") It is type int. It returns the ASCII value of the byte currently pointed to by the buffer pointer and advances the pointer to the next byte. If the buffer is empty, it causes the next buffer-load to be read in from the file. It returns a value of EOF when it reaches the end of the file.

The Putc() Function

This function inserts the indicated character into the indicated file. (Actually, it inserts the character into the buffer and periodically flushes the buffer into the file.) Its first argument is the desired character, and its second argument is a stream indicating the target file. For example, a program that copied bytes from one file to another could use this code:

```
FILE *old, *new;
int ch;
    ...
while ( ( ch = getc(old) ) != EOF )
        putc(ch,new);
```

The fopen() function, of course, would have been used to provide values for old and new.

Don't forget the distinction between text and binary files. This code could be used with files opened in either mode, but the end-of-file test would operate differently in the two modes. In particular, you would not use this code on a file opened in the text mode but containing binary data.

The Fprintf() and Fscanf() Functions

The fprintf() and fscanf() functions are the file counterparts to printf() and scanf(). Each takes as its first argument a stream indicating the desired file; the remaining arguments are as for `printf()` and `scanf()`. Your familiarity with `printf()` and `scanf()` functions should make the transition to the new functions easy. We will discuss some aspects more fully later.

A File-Conversion Example

Let's use some of these functions to do a useful chore. WordStar, the popular word processing program, uses a nonstandard form for its document-mode files. In general, the WordStar format conforms to the standard text format, but terminal letters to words and intraparagraph newlines are "marked" to facilitate reformatting. The marking consists of adding 128 to the ASCII value. Since the standard ASCII code encompasses the values 0 through 127, adding 128 still keeps the resulting value in the range (0 to 255) assignable to a single byte. Not all words get marked, but we won't go into WordStar details.

This marking makes it inconvenient to use, for example, the standard DOS command `type` with a WordStar file, for the marked characters are interpreted by `type` to represent characters in the augmented list recognized by the IBM PC. Also, the CR-LF translation gets scrambled. Or you may accidentally write or re-edit a C program in the document mode and produce characters confusing to the C compiler. (WordStar's nondocument mode should be used for programs.)

The next program has the modest goal of converting marked characters back to the original ASCII values. We've used the simple approach of looking at the ASCII value and subtracting 128 if the original value is 128 or greater. In the chapter on bitwise operators we'll see a better approach.

A second feature of the program is that it handles the selection of input and output files in a forgiving manner. In fact, most of the program concerns this aspect. If you just give the command with no command line arguments, you are prompted for the input and output filenames. If you provide one command line argument, it is taken to be the input filename, and you are prompted for the output filename. If you provide two command line arguments, they are taken to be the input and output files. If you respond to the prompt for an output file by pressing the RETURN key with no other input, the output is sent to the screen. In short, if you forget how to use the program, it helps you.

A third feature is minimal error-protection. (Not all features are positive!) For example, the program doesn't check to see if you want to overwrite an existing file; it just overwrites it. The `fopen()` function does not have `open()`'s system of mode flags to handle that problem. In a later chapter we'll see other library functions that we can use to make the program safer; meanwhile, we will be careful.

A fourth feature is the use of the special streams `stdout` and `stderr`. Both represent the terminal screen; one can be redirected, and one can't. We'll discuss them and other special streams after the program.

Here, then, is the program:

```
/* ws_dos.c--converts WordStar to DOS format */
#include <stdio.h>
#define SIZE 128
main(ac,av)
int ac;
char *av[];
{
    FILE *fpsource, *fptarget;
    char sfile[SIZE], tfile[SIZE]; /* holds prompted input */
    char *sname,*tname; /* pntrs to source, target file names */
    char *gets();
    int ch;

    switch ( ac )
     {
       case 1 :   /* no command line arguments */
                fprintf(stderr, "File to convert? >");
                sname = gets(sfile);
                fprintf(stderr,
                    "Target file? (or RETURN for screen) > ");
                tname = gets(tfile);
                break;
       case 2 :   /* one command line argument */
                sname = av[1];
                fprintf(stderr,
                    "Target file? (or RETURN for screen) > ");
                tname = gets(tfile);
                break;
       case 3 :   /* two command line arguments */
                sname = av[1];
                tname = av[2];
                break;
       default :  fprintf(stderr,
                "Usage: ws_dos [source file] [target file]\n");
                exit(1);
     }
    if ( (fpsource = fopen(sname,"rt") ) == NULL)
        {
        fprintf(stderr,"ws_dos can't open %s\n", sname);
        exit(1);
        }
    if ( tname[0] == '\0')      /* empty string */
        fptarget = stdout;
    else if ( (fptarget = fopen(tname,"wt") ) == NULL)
        {
        fprintf(stderr,"ws_dos can't open %s\n", tname);
        exit(1);
```

```
        }
     while ( (ch = getc(fpsource) ) != EOF )
        {
        if ( ch > 127 )              /* convert funny characters */
             ch -= 128;
        putc(ch,fptarget);
        }
     fclose(fpsource);
     fclose(fptarget);
  }
```

As you can see, most of the program is concerned with obtaining the filenames. The pointers sname and tname are set to point to the command line arguments (av[1] and av[2]) or to the character array filled at run time (sfile and tfile) as circumstances dictate. Then the appropriate names are used as arguments for fopen(). If tfile points to an empty string, then the stream is assigned the predefined stream stdout instead of an fopen() return value. The actual file transformation is handled by a short while loop.

Let's look further at stdout, stderr, and their companions.

Standard Files and Redirection

C programs in general automatically open three files when run. They are called the *standard input,* the *standard output,* and the *standard error.* These three files are assigned the file handles 0, 1, and 2, respectively. The *stdio.h* file assigns three streams for these same files: stdin, stdout, and stderr. Your program can use these handles and streams to use the associated files. Normally, these files actually are devices. On a PC the standard input is, by default, the keyboard, while the standard output and standard error both are the screen. The getchar() and scanf() functions, for example, read the standard input, while the putchar() and printf() functions write to the standard output.

These assignments, however, can be altered by using redirection. Suppose, for instance, *brie* is a C program that normally takes keyboard input and sends output to the screen. The command

```
A> brie < feta
```

causes the file *feta* to become the standard input. That is, now the file handle 0 and the stream stdin refer to this file instead of to the keyboard, and read(0,buf,SIZE) or getchar() will read the file instead of the keyboard. The < symbol indicates this redirection. The output, in this case, still is directed to the screen.

Similarly, the > symbol causes the filename following it to become the standard output:

```
A> brie > edam
```

In this case, the input would come from the keyboard. If you like, you can use both forms of redirection simultaneously:

```
A> brie < feta > edam
```

In DOS, you can also use a *pipe* (¦) to connect the standard output of one program to the standard input of a second program. That is, if *brie* normally takes input from the keyboard and *cheddar* normally sends output to the screen, then the combination

```
A> cheddar ¦ brie
```

routes *cheddar*'s output to *brie* instead of to the screen.

What about the standard error? When the standard output is redirected, the standard error remains unchanged. Thus, you can write programs that send error messages to the screen even if the rest of the output gets redirected. The *ws_dos.c* program uses fprintf() in this way.

To these three files opened by C programs in general, IBM C adds two more, the standard auxiliary and the standard print. These have the file handles 3 and 4 and the predefined stream names stdaux and stdprn. These files usually represent a port and a printer, but the exact assignments depend on the machine configuration. Given the usual assignments, you could use stdprn, for example, to have fprintf() send output to the printer.

See Figure 3–5 for an illustration of standard files.

With DOS Versions 2 and 3, redirection is part of the operating system. Version 1 doesn't provide redirection, so many C compilers written for DOS Version 1 provided redirection as part of the compiler packages. This can cause problems if you compile a C program under Version 1 and try to run it under a later DOS version. The operating system and the compiled program each try to effect redirection, leading to unsettling results.

More Functions from the Standard Package

As we have seen, including the *stdio.h* file and using fopen() to open files sets up the necessary apparatus for using buffered I/O. We've mentioned getc() and putc() as examples of standard I/O functions, but there are several other members. For example, there are fgets() and fputs(), which are line-oriented I/O functions. Then there are fprintf() and fscanf(), which offer formatted I/O. These all are intended primarily for text-oriented files. The fread() and fwrite() add binary I/O to the standard package.

Standard I/O functions that use the same stream share the same buffer. Since they use the same stream, they also share the same file

Figure 3–5
Standard Files

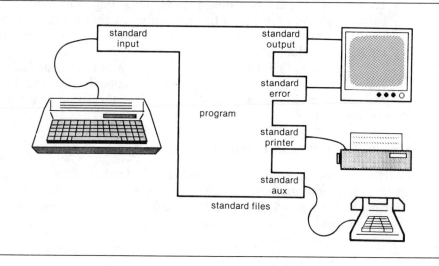

standard files

pointer. As a result, you can use all the I/O functions cooperatively in the same program. If you follow a call to fscanf() with a call to getc(), the second function will begin reading where the first left off. However, you shouldn't mix standard I/O calls with low-level I/O calls. Since one reads from a buffer and one reads directly from the file, they would not coordinate with one another.

The Fgets() and Fputs() Functions

These are line-oriented I/O functions. The combined manual descriptions look like this:

```
#include <stdio.h>
char *fgets(string, n, stream);
int fputs(string, stream);
char *string;
int n;
FILE *stream;
```

The fgets() function reads from the indicated stream. It takes up to n characters or through the newline, whichever comes first. It adds a terminating '\0' to convert the sequence into a character string and places the string in memory at the location given by the pointer string. Note that it is not enough just to declare a string pointer, as done in the manual entry. The string pointer must point to available memory. This usually is accomplished either by using the name of a declared character array as the string pointer or using a memory allocation function to provide a value for a string pointer variable.

Perhaps you have used `gets()`; it reads a line from the standard input. `Fgets()` differs from `gets()` in three respects. First, you have to specify a stream for `fgets()` while `gets()` uses the standard input. Second, `fgets()` lets you set a limit to the number of characters read, while `gets()` does not. Third, `fgets()` includes the newline, if read, as part of the string, while `gets()` does not.

The `fputs()` function serves to write a string to the indicated stream. The terminating null character (`\0`) is not copied. The function returns the last character of the output. It returns 0 if the string is empty and `EOF` if there is an error.

More on Fprintf() and Fscanf()

Here we will take a more advanced look at `fprintf()` and `fscanf()`.

It is important to realize that these two functions act as conversion functions when working with numerical data. Suppose, for example, we have the following code fragment:

```
FILE *fp;
int sects = 6;
float agoat = 10.25;
    ...
fprintf(fp,"%2d %f5.2 ", sects, agoat);
```

In program memory, `sects` is stored as a two-byte binary integer, and `agoat` in four-byte floating-point binary form. The `fprintf()` function then converts the contents of `sects` to the one-byte code for the character 6. Similarly, it converts the contents of `agoat` to 5 bytes of ASCII code for the characters   1   0   .   2   5.

The `fscanf()` function makes the opposite conversions; collections of ASCII characters are converted to binary integer and binary floating-point forms.

A Fprintf() Tidbit—You're probably quite familiar with the use of format width specifiers. For example, consider the following:

```
fprintf(fp,"%2d %5.2f ", sects, agoat);
```

It prints `sects` in a field width of two and `agoat` in a field width of five. In addition it prints just two places to the right of the decimal point.

Suppose, however, you want the program to determine the field widths during run time. Then you can use asterisks for the field widths and use variables in the argument list to provide actual values. That is, a call would look like the following, where n, m, and k are integer variables assigned values during run time:

```
fprintf(fp,"%*d %*.*f ", n, sects, m, k, agoat);
```

Here, n would be the field width used for the %d specifier, m would be the field width for the %f specifier, and k would be the number of digits to the right of the decimal. Note that each asterisk requires a corresponding value in the argument list, with the arguments in the same order as the various format specifiers in the control string. The same technique can be used with printf(), of course.

Secrets of Fscanf()—The fscanf() function, like scanf(), reads input as a sequence of characters. The format specifiers then dictate how given sequences of characters are interpreted. The %d, %f, and %s formats all skip over whitespace (blanks, tabs, and newlines) looking for a sequence of characters containing no whitespace. In the %s format, the sequence of characters is converted to a string by appending a null character, and the string is stored at the indicated location:

```
FILE *fp;
char name[20];
  ...
fscanf(fp,"%s", name);
```

A field width specifier, as in

```
FILE *fp;
char name[20];
  ...
fscanf(fp,"%19s", name);
```

limits the input to the specified width or to the first terminating white-space, whichever comes first. If the reading terminates before the input sequence of characters is entirely read, the next call to read input resumes where the last left off.

When the field specifier indicates a numeric format, such as %d or %f, the sequence of characters is converted to the appropriate binary representation of the numerical value; text format in input is converted to binary format in memory.

What happens if you have, say, a %d format specified, but the input consists of alphabetic characters? Then fscanf() halts and reports failure. The next input read will resume at the same location.

And how does fscanf() report failure? By its return value. Normally, the function returns the number of items successfully read. If it tries to read a single number and fails, the return value is 0. If fscanf() encounters the end of file, it returns a −1.

Also useful is the fact that inserting an asterisk in the format specifier causes fscanf() to skip over the indicated input type. This, together with examining the return value, can let your program verify input and flag or perhaps skip over unwanted input. Here, for instance, is a program fragment that reads all the floating-point numbers in input while skipping over alphabetic material:

```
#include <stdio.h>
    ...
float number;
FILE *fp;
int status;
    ...
while ( (status = fscanf(fp,"%f", &number) ) != -1 )
    if ( status == 0 )          /* bad input */
        fscanf(fp,"%*s");       /* skip over it */
    else
        /* process number */
        ...
```

The "bad" input would be some character sequence not recognizable as a number, but that still meets %s standards, since it is some sequence of characters terminated by whitespace.

Standard I/O and Text Format

Suppose you wish to store an array of floating-point numbers in a file. You could use fprintf():

```
#define SIZE 100
    ...
FILE *fout;
float ratios[SIZE];
int n = 0;
    ...
while ( n < SIZE )
    fprintf(fout,"%5.2f ", ratios[n]);
```

If accuracy is the goal, this approach is poor, for fprintf(), in general, will not store the exact values in the array. The reason is that, as we saw, fprintf() is a conversion function. It converts the floating-point numbers in ratios to *text* form. For instance, the value 1.3593750 would be converted to the *character* sequence 1   .   3   6. We could have specified more decimal places, but we still face the possibility of round-off error.

Similarly, if we used fscanf() to recover the information from the file, there is further margin for error, for in that case, fscanf() converts a character string to the closest equivalent binary value.

Or suppose you wish to write a structure full of data into a file. The fprintf() function doesn't have a format for structures, and you would have to specify individual formats for each structure member.

One way to meet these problems is to use a binary format for writing and reading such data. With the low-level functions, this is done using read() and write(). If fh is an appropriate file handle, for example, we could write the array into the file with this call:

```
write(fh, ratios, sizeof (ratios) );
```

Here ratios tells write() where in memory to find the information, and sizeof (ratios) tells it how many bytes to read. The same form can be used with structures, too. Just use the address of the structure and its size as arguments. A similar approach can be used with read() to recover binary data from a file.

The Fread() and Fwrite() Functions

The standard I/O package has a similar pair of functions. They are called fread() and fwrite(). Like their low-level counterparts, they transfer chunks of binary data to and from files. The chief difference is that they use the buffers set up for the standard I/O package. The combined manual definitions look like this:

```
#include <stdio.h>

int fread(buffer, size, count, stream);
int fwrite(buffer, size, count, stream);
char *buffer;
int size;
int count;
FILE *stream;
```

The buffer argument is the beginning address of the memory location to be used in the program. The size argument specifies how big of a chunk to read or write, while count indicates how many chunks to process. Finally, stream indicates which file to use. To write the ratio array, for example, we could use either of these calls:

```
fwrite(ratio, sizeof (ratio), 1, fp);
fwrite(ratio, sizeof (float), SIZE, fp);
```

That is, we could write in one chunk of 400 bytes or in 100 chunks of four bytes.

We'll use these functions in later chapters, so don't be amazed when they reappear.

The Fseek(), Rewind(), and Ftell() Functions

These functions are concerned with the position of the buffer pointer. The fseek() function works much like its low-level counterpart, lseek(). Its usage is as follows:

91

```
#include <stdio.h>
  ...
int mode, status;
long offset;
FILE *stream;

  ...
status = fseek(stream, offset, mode);
```

The `stream` argument identifies the file. The `offset` argument tells how many bytes to move, and the `mode` specifies whence to measure the offset. As for `lseek()`, a mode of 0 means measure from the beginning of the file, 1 means measure from the current position of the file pointer, and 2 means measure from the end. The return value is 0 if `fseek()` successfully repositions the pointer and − 1 if it fails.

The `rewind()` function takes a single argument, a stream. It relocates the file pointer at the beginning of the file. In that respect, `rewind(stream)` has the same effect as `fseek(stream,0L,0)`. In addition, it clears the end of file and error indicators for the stream. What does that mean? Suppose you used a loop like this:

```
while ( ( ch = getc(old) ) != EOF )
      putc(ch,new);
```

When the end of file is reached by the loop, an external flag is set indicating that end of file has been reached. (The flag is one of the bits in the _flag member of the `FILE` structure.) Subsequent attempts to read from that file will fail unless the eof flag is cleared to zero; `rewind()` clears that flag as well as the read error flag.

The `ftell()` function returns the current position of the file pointer measured from the beginning. It takes a stream as an argument to indicate the file. It is type `long()`. If a file has been opened in the text mode, the returned value may not be the true offset because of the CR-LF to LF translation.

Yet Another Backward Example

To show how these functions are used, here is the standard I/O version of the file-reversing program, which, you may recall, copies one file backwards into another file:

```
/* stdrev.c--uses standard I/O to reverse a file */
#include <stdio.h>
#define CNTL_Z '\032'
main(argc,argv)
int argc;
char *argv[];
{
```

```
char ch;
FILE *fp;
long count, last, ftell();

if ( argc != 2)
    {
    printf("Usage: stdrev file\n");
    exit(1);
    }
if ( ( fp = fopen(argv[1],"rb") ) == NULL )
    {                             /* read-only and binary modes */
    printf("stdrev can't open %s\n", argv[1]);
    exit(1);
    }
fseek(fp,0L,2); /* go to end of file */
last = ftell(fp); /* get byte position of end */
for ( count = 1L ; count <= last; count++)
    {
    fseek(fp, -count, 2); /* go backwards */
    ch = getc(fp);
    if ( ch != CNTL_Z && ch != '\r')
        putchar(ch);
    }
fclose(fp);
}
```

Note that fseek(), unlike lseek() does not return the byte count; hence we had to use ftell() for that purpose. Otherwise, the program follows the low-level version very closely.

Is it any faster than the low-level version? We ran both on a 6-kilobyte file. The screen display speed conceals the true program speed, so we redirected the output to a disk file. The new version took 26 seconds, while the first version took 68 seconds. The savings in time is noticeable but not remarkable. The problem is that using fseek() every byte slows the program.

Usually, a program that does much seeking back and forth *(random access)* can be handled better using low-level I/O. There is no advantage to using a buffer if the program gets a new buffer every I/O call. Where buffering shines is in *sequential access,* in which each byte is processed in order.

The reversing program falls between random access and sequential access. There is seeking, but the data still are contiguous. Probably the most efficient way to handle the reversing program is to use low-level I/O along with an explicit buffer. The idea is to go to the end of the file, fill a buffer, print the buffer in reverse, and then seek back one buffersworth in the file. This greatly reduces the numbers of seeks used. A fairly simple-minded attempt along these lines reduced the run time for the same test conditions to 13 seconds.

☐   *Question 3–6*   Can you implement a program along the lines just described? Try it.

We've examined many aspects of file I/O, but we have not come close to exhausting the IBM C library's resources in this area. Still, you probably would welcome a change of pace by now, so in the next chapter we'll take on a new topic, C's bitwise operators. In the meanwhile, here is a summary of what we've covered in this chapter.

Summary

PC-DOS and MS-DOS maintain two kinds of files. One is called a text, or ASCII, file. In it, each byte is assumed to be the ASCII code for a character. The second type is called a binary file. In it, no particular interpretation is assumed for the bytes. They may represent characters, binary representation of integers and floating-point numbers, structures, machine instructions, graphic instructions, and so on.

The two types differ in how they handle newline characters and the end of file. In a text file, the newline character (' \ n') is represented by the combination CR-LF (a carriage-return and a line-feed). In a binary file, the newline character is represented by just LF. In a text file, the end of text is marked by using a CTRL-Z character. The binary end of file is determined by maintaining a record of the file size.

In C a file can be opened in either mode, regardless of the mode in which it was created. The mode in which a file is opened then determines how it handles newlines and end of file. By default, files are created and opened in the text mode, but IBM C offers several ways to open a file in the binary mode instead. Opening a binary file in text mode is asking for trouble, but sometimes it is advantageous to open a text file in binary mode.

C offers two levels of I/O functions. The more basic level is called low level. The other level is called the standard I/O package, and it sets up automatic buffering of input and output.

In low-level I/O, files are opened with the open() function, which returns an integer file handle. The file handle is used by the other low-level functions to identify which file to use. The read() and write() functions handle the I/O, the lseek() function provides random access to a file, and the close() function closes the file.

In the standard I/O package, files are opened with the fopen() function, which returns a pointer to a FILE-type structure. The structure contains information about the file and about the associated buffer to be used for I/O. Both buffer and structure are created by fopen(). The pointer to the structure is called a stream, and it is used by the other members of the package to identify which file and which buffer to use. Standard I/O functions include getc(), putc(), fscanf(), fprintf(), fgets(), fputs(), fread(), and fwrite(). Random access is implemented using fseek(), rewind(), and ftell(). Figure 3–6 summarizes the two levels of I/O.

Figure 3–6
Some I/O Functions

	FILE OPENING	FILE CREATION	FILE CLOSING	POSITION SEEKING	BINARY I/O	CHARACTER I/O	LINE I/O	FORMATED I/O
low-level	open ( )	open ( ) creat ( )	close ( )	l seek ( )	read ( ) write ( )			
standard I/O	f open ( )	f open ( )	f close ( )	f seek ( ) f tell ( ) rewind ( )	f read ( ) f write ( )	get char ( ) get ( ) put char ( ) put ( )	gets ( ) f gets ( ) puts ( ) f puts ( )	scan f ( ) f scan f ( ) print f ( ) f print f ( )

Typically, the low-level functions are used with binary files and the standard I/O package with text files. However, the fread() and fwrite() functions enable the standard I/O package to deal with pure binary files. The chief advantage of the standard I/O package is that it combines the speed of buffered I/O with the ability to examine individual bytes. This advantage shows up best in programs that read and write files sequentially.

Answers to Questions in the Chapter

■ *3–1.* Yes, the text format is binary, since the ASCII code for the various characters is stored in binary form. The difference is that the text format is restricted to only ASCII codes, while the binary format can use other binary forms.

■ *3–2.* No. The means of detecting the end of file is different, but the **EOF** signal used to announce the end of file is the same for both file types.

■ *3–3.* The text version would count 8 characters, with each newline counting as 1 character. The binary version would count 11 characters, 2 for each line separator, and 1 for the CTRL-Z.

■ *3–4.* This one is a little messy, so let's do it in steps:

  a. argv is a pointer to the address of argument 0.

  b. argv + 1 is a pointer to the address of argument 1.

  c. *(argv + 1) is the address of the "man" string; in particular, it is the address of the m.

  d. Adding 2 to the address of m gives us the address of n: *(argv + 1) + 2.

  e. Use the * operator to the value stored at that address: *(*(argv + 1) + 2); this is equivalent to argv[1][2].

■ *3-5.*

```
char response[10];
...
if ( ( fnew =
        open(argv[2],O_CREAT | O_EXCL | O_WRONLY,
                                    S_IWRITE)) < 0 )
    {
    printf("%s exists--do you wish to overwrite? <y/n>\n",
          argv[2]);
    scanf("%s", response);
    if ( response[0] == 'y' || response[0] == 'Y' )
      {
      if ( ( fnew = open(argv[2],
          O_CREAT | O_TRUNC | O_WRONLY, S_IWRITE)) < 0 )
          {
          printf("Can't open %s\n", argv[2]);
          exit(1);
          }
      }
    else
        exit(1);
    }
```

■ *3-6.* This is a bit kludgy in that it replaces CR's and CTRL-Z's with null characters. A classier approach would be to not copy them at all into the reversed array and to modify the array index and number of bytes written accordingly. The main point, however, is the use of buffers and lseek().

```
#include <fcntl.h>
#define SIZE 512
#define CNTL_Z '\032'
main(argc,argv)
int argc;
char *argv[];
{
    char buffer[SIZE];     /* holds input data */
    char rbuf[SIZE];       /* holds buffer in reverse order */
    int fd;
    int i;
    long count, last;

    if ( argc != 2)
        {
        printf("Usage: reverse filename\n");
        exit(1);
        }
    if ( ( fd = open(argv[1], O_RDONLY | O_BINARY) ) < 0 )
        {
        printf("reverse can't open %s\n", argv[1]);
```

```
            exit(1);
            }
    last = lseek(fd,0L,2);
    while ( last > SIZE)   /* more than SIZE bytes remain */
        {
        last = lseek(fd,-(long) SIZE, 1);
        read(fd, buffer, SIZE);
        for ( i = 0; i < SIZE; i++)   /* reversing process */
            if (buffer[SIZE-1-i] == CNTL_Z ||
                buffer[SIZE-1-i] == '\r')
                    rbuf[i] = '\0';
            else
                    rbuf[i] = buffer[SIZE - 1 - i];
        write(1,rbuf,SIZE);      /* write whole buffer */
        if ( last > SIZE )
            last = lseek(fd,-(long) SIZE, 1);
        }
    if (last > 0)   /* less than a full buffer remains */
        {
        lseek(fd,0L,0);
        read(fd,buffer,last);
        for ( i = 0; i < last; i++)
            if (buffer[last-1-i] == CNTL_Z ||
                buffer[last-1-i] == '\r')
                    rbuf[i] = '\0';
            else
                    rbuf[i] = buffer[last - 1 - i];
        write(1,rbuf,last);
        }
    close(fd);
    }
```

Exercises

1. As we mentioned, DOS itself uses buffers for disk I/O. Thus, even unbuffered C programs read from a buffer set up DOS. Buffered C programs read from the DOS buffer to their own buffers. You can change the number of buffers used by DOS through the *config.sys* file, which is checked by DOS at boot time. The system starts off with two disk buffers of 512K each. A line like this:

        BUFFERS=4

adds four more buffers to the existing two. The actual number of buffers does not change until the system is booted with the altered *config.sys* file. Try increasing the number of buffers and see if it affects the running speed of programs such as `count2.c`.

2. Write a program to convert a text-format file to a binary-format file.

3. The tab character (\t, in C) is generated by the tab key. It usually is interpreted to mean, "move the cursor to the next tab stop." The tab stops usually are located every 8 columns. Thus, if the first column is labeled 1, the next few tab stops are at 9, 17, and 25. Write a program that replaces each tab stop in a file by the correct number of spaces to move the cursor to the next tab stop. (Note: WordStar, in its document mode, spaces tabs by 5 instead of 8; it also substitutes the proper number of spaces for the tab character.)

4

Integer Forms and Bit Operations

- One-byte, two-byte, and four-byte integers
- Signed and unsigned integers
- Decimal, octal, hexadecimal, and binary representations
- Integer conversions
- Bit manipulations
- Bit fields

Integer Forms and Bit Operations

One of C's strengths is that it allows you to be selective about how data is stored and manipulated. Using IBM C, for example, you can choose among three sizes of integers: four-byte (`long`), two-byte (`int` and `short`), or one-byte (`char`). In addition, with the `unsigned` modifier you can alter the exact range of numbers represented. Even more remarkably (for a high-level language), using C you can manipulate individual bits within an integer. Bit manipulations are the highlight of this chapter. You can use them, for example, within an integer as separate flags that can be set and unset individually. But to understand them, you need to know how integers are represented in binary form. Therefore, we'll begin with a review of the integer types.

Integer Types

The basic integer type in C is the `int` type. In IBM C, the `int` type occupies two bytes. It is a signed type, meaning it can hold either positive or negative values. The range is −32,768 to 32,767. In general, the number of bytes used can be modified by the keywords `long` and `short`. The type identifiers `long int` and `long` are equivalent; each denotes a four-byte signed integer. On the IBM, `short int` or `short` is the same as `int`. Some systems, however, have `long` and `int` the same, with `short` shorter. The `char` type is a one-byte integer. Its name derives from the fact that `char` most often is used to store a one-byte ASCII code for a character, but it can be used to store any one-byte integer, whether it represents a character or not. With IBM C, `char`, too, is a signed integer.

The `unsigned` modifier can be used to convert any of these types to an unsigned integer; `unsigned` by itself is taken to mean `unsigned int`. Table 4-1 summarizes the integer types and their ranges. Some types, such as `unsigned char`, are newer extensions to C.

Table 4-1
IBM C Integer Types

Type	Bytes	Range
char	1	−128 to 127
int	2	−32,768 to 32,767
short	2	−32,768 to 32,767
long	4	−2,147,483,648 to 2,147,483,647
unsigned char	1	0 to 255
unsigned	2	0 to 65,535
unsigned short	2	0 to 65,535
unsigned long	4	0 to 4,294,967,295

Integer Constants

With C you can select among three number bases when writing an integer constant: decimal (base 10), octal (base 8), and hexadecimal (base 16). To indicate a decimal integer, just write it in the usual way, for example, 27 or −199. To indicate an octal integer, insert a 0 (the digit, not the letter O) before the number. Thus, 0132 is an octal number, equivalent to decimal 90 (1 64 plus 3 8's plus 2 1's). To indicate a hexadecimal number, use a 0x or 0X (again, use the digit, not the letter O) prefix before the number. The values 10 through 15 are represented by the letters a through f or A through F. Thus, 0x8B is hexadecimal for decimal 139 (8 16's plus 11 1's.) See Figure 4-1. Appendix B contains a more detailed discussion of number bases.

You should realize that these choices are offered as a convenience to you as a programmer. No matter what form you use, the number will be stored internally in binary form.

One important distinction is that octal and hexadecimal constants are considered to be unsigned quantities, while decimal values are not. This becomes important in type conversions and with the right-shift operator, both of which we will discuss later in this chapter.

C has ways to indicate if a written integer constant is to be stored as an int, a long, or a char. An integer constant normally is stored as an int. If it is too large to be stored as an int, it is stored as a long, and if it is too large for that, it is stored as unsigned long. If you wish to force an integer to be stored as a long, give it an l or L suffix. (The uppercase L is recommended, because it is less likely to be mistaken for the digit 1.) Thus 25 would be stored in 2 bytes as an int, while 25L would be stored in 4 bytes as a long.

To indicate that just one byte of storage is to be used, you can use the C ASCII code convention. With this convention, a character can be represented by its octal ASCII code preceded by a backslash and enclosed in single quotes. For example, the ASCII code for the character A is 65, or 0101

Figure 4–1
Different Number Bases

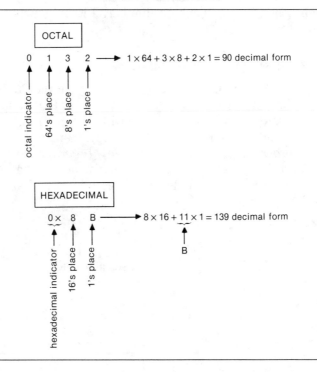

in octal. In C you can represent this value by the notation '＼101', with the backslash indicating that an octal character code is to follow. In this case, a 0 prefix is not required to indicate octal. The distinction between 0101 and '＼101' is that the former occupies two bytes of memory (the upper byte is all 0's), while the latter occupies just one byte. Figure 4–2 diagrams this system.

Figure 4–2
One-Byte Constants

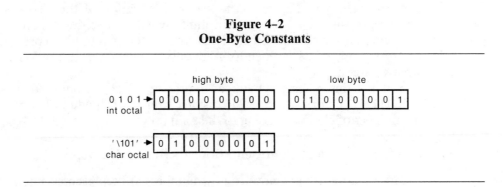

IBM C offers an extension to these standard C representations. With IBM C you can represent a one-byte pattern with a hexadecimal modification of the ASCII code method. Just follow the backslash with an x. For example, 65 in hexadecimal is 0x41, so we can use the notation '\x41' to represent 65 as a one-byte number. Either uppercase or lowercase can be used for the x.

Binary Representation of Integers

To understand the bitwise operators, you should know something about how integers are stored in binary form. For simplicity, let's consider a 1-byte integer. A byte contains 8 bits. We can think of the bits as numbered left to right, from 7 through 0. See Figure 4–3. The left bits are termed *high-order bits,* and the right bits *low-order bits.* Bit 7 is called the *most significant bit,* and bit 0 the *least significant,* just as in the decimal number 284, the 2 is more significant (representing 2 100's) than the 4 (representing 4 1's).

Figure 4–3
Bits in a Byte

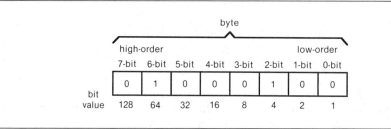

Each bit either can be "set" to 1 (or "on") or "cleared" to 0 (or "off"). Also, each bit is considered to represent a power of 2. The 0 bit is the 0th power (or 1), the first bit is the first power (or 2), and so on. You may refer again to Figure 4–3 to see an illustration of this. To obtain the value represented by a bit pattern, multiply each bit setting by the power of 2 it represents, and add them. Thus, the pattern 01000100 represents 1 × 64 + 1 × 4, or 68. Appendix A discusses binary representation in somewhat greater detail.

Using this scheme a byte can represent integers from 0 (00000000) to 255 (11111111), or a total of 256 distinct values. Each additional bit doubles the number of choices, leading to the total ranges shown in Table 4–1.

Octal and Hexadecimal Representations of Binary Numbers

Binary notation is very close to how numbers are represented internally in a computer. It uses two voltage values instead of 0's and 1's, but the method is the same. Binary notation is cumbersome, and C doesn't offer us a binary format for writing numbers. Yet sometimes the exact binary form is important. For example, the individual bits in an integer can be used as separate flags or as on-off switches. If we want to assign a particular bit pattern to an integer, however, we have to write out the decimal, octal, or hexadecimal equivalent. This is not an impossible task in decimal, but it is much simpler in octal or hexadecimal. Let's look at octal first.

Octal-Binary Conversions—The UNIX environment in which C developed is octal-oriented. Several UNIX commands, such as chmod, have manual descriptions that refer to octal values. Octal values are easily converted to binary format and back again. The key point is that each octal digit represents exactly 3 bits; this stems from the fact that 8 is the third power of 2. To be more specific, the largest 3-bit binary number is 111. This has the value 7, which is the largest octal digit. Thus, the octal values 0 through 07 represent the total range of the first 3 bits. The next 3 bits are represented by the next octal digit. To convert an octal number to binary, convert each octal digit to its 3-bit binary equivalent. To convert a binary number to octal, subdivide it from the right into subgroups of 3 bits, then convert each 3-bit pattern to the equivalent octal digit. Table 4–2 shows the conversion.

Table 4–2
Octal-Binary Conversions

Octal Digit	3-bit Pattern
0	000
1	001
2	010
3	011
4	100
5	101
6	110
7	111

Let's try the scheme on an example. First, let's express 0123 as a binary number. The 1 is 001, the 2 is 010, and the 3 is 011. Stringing them together gives 001010011. If we then discard the leftmost 0, we reduce the number to an 8-bit pattern: 01010011.

Now let's convert 01110100 to octal. First, add a 0 to the left to give 9 bits. This makes the number 001 110 100, which reduces to octal 0164.

☐ *Question 4–1* Two bit patterns commonly used in programming are 011111111 and 11111111. What are their octal equivalents?

Hex-Binary Conversions—The microcomputer community is hex-oriented. The *IBM Technical Reference* manual, for example, gives addresses in hex. Also, in some ways, hex is better than octal for representing binary values. One problem with the octal conversions is that an eight-bit byte doesn't correspond exactly to three octal digits; we had to add or delete an extra 0 in the conversions. Hexadecimal (hex for short) conversions give a better fit because each hexadecimal digit corresponds to exactly four bits. Thus, two hex digits correspond exactly to one byte. Table 4–3 gives the conversions.

Table 4–3
Hex-Binary Conversions

Hex Digit	Binary Pattern
0	0000
1	0001
2	0010
3	0011
4	0100
5	0101
6	0110
7	0111
8	1000
9	1001
A (10)	1010
B (11)	1011
C (12)	1100
D (13)	1101
E (14)	1110
F (15)	1111

Conversions work as with octal, except that you must use 4-bit groups instead of 3-bit groups. Thus 077 represents 6 bits, while 0x77 represents 8 bits. Figure 4–4 shows examples of hex and octal numbers converted to binary and shows the corresponding decimal numbers.

☐ *Question 4–2* The two bit patterns you converted to octal numbers in Question 4–1 were 011111111 and 11111111. Can you now convert them to hex equivalents?

Negative Numbers in Binary Form

To represent negative numbers, we have to reserve a bit to indicate a sign. The simplest way would be to use the leftmost bit as a sign bit, with a one

Figure 4-4
Hex and Octal Conversions to Binary

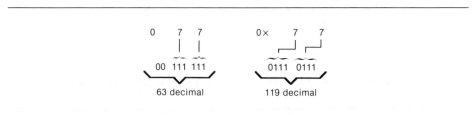

indicating a minus sign. However, that method has some computational problems, as well as having two forms of 0: positive and negative. Instead, IBM C uses the "two's complement" method. It, too, winds up with negative numbers having the leftmost bit set to one, but the interpretation of the other bits needs some comment.

The way the method works for a 1-byte integer is this. For the numbers up to 127, which is consists of 7 1's, the scheme is as described earlier. Let's take up from there with Table 4-4, which helps us to see how the byte is interpreted as an unsigned quantity and as a signed quantity.

Table 4-4
Unsigned and Signed Values for Sample Bit Patterns

Bit Pattern	Unsigned Value	Signed Value
00000001	1	1
01111110	126	126
01111111	127	127
10000000	128	-128
10000001	129	-127
. . .	. . .	. . .
11111110	254	-2
11111111	255	-1

It's a bit like a car odometer. There, the number just before 00000 is 99999; here the number just before 0 is 11111111, or -1. One way to calculate the value of a byte with the 7-bit set is to convert it to an unsigned number, then subtract 256 from it. Thus, 11111110 is 254; subtract 256 to get -2.

A way to change signs for a signed integer is convert each 1 to a 0, each 0 to a 1, and then add 1. Let's apply this method to 00000010, or 2. First, bit conversion changes it to 11111101. Adding 1 converts it to 11111110, or -2.

Two-byte and four-byte numbers use the same method to represent negative numbers. In each case a leftmost bit set to one indicates a negative number, and an integer that is all ones represents a negative one.

Binary Arithmetic

The rules of binary addition and subtraction are pretty simple, for there are only two digit values to contend with. Here is a sample calculation:

$$
\begin{array}{r}
1 \\
+1 \\
\hline
10
\end{array}
$$

As usual, 1 plus one is 2, but you have to remember that 2 is written "10." Of course, when the sum is two, you need to carry the one to the next binary place. For example, consider the next sum:

$$
\begin{array}{r}
011111111 \\
+000000001 \\
\hline
100000000
\end{array}
$$

What happens if you run out of bits? That is, suppose you have to carry a one over to the ninth bit? It is discarded; then we have the following:

$$
\begin{array}{r}
11111111 \\
+00000001 \\
\hline
00000000
\end{array}
$$

It is interesting to note how these last two examples would be interpreted in signed and unsigned arithmetic. In the first example, 00000001 is 1 and 011111111 is 127 for both signed and unsigned cases. But the sum, 10000000, is 128 in unsigned notation and -128 in signed notation. Thus, 127 + 1 is 128 for unsigned char, while 127 + 1 is -128 for char.

Similarly, the second example says that 255 + 1 is 0 for unsigned char, while -1 + 1 is 0 for char. The actual binary arithmetic is the same for both forms, but the interpretation of the binary patterns differs.

Integer Conversions and Sign Extension

In C you can convert from one integer form to another. Some conversions occur automatically when you use mixed-type arithmetic, when you assign one type to a variable of another type, or when you use certain types in an expression. Also, you can use type casts to force conversions. Usually you won't run into problems in going from a smaller type to a larger one, but you can lose data going the other way. There also are potential problems with conversions between signed and unsigned types. To understand type conversions you should know two things: when conversions take place and what happens when they do. Let's look into those two questions.

When Conversions Take Place

Conversions take place when one type is assigned to a variable of a second type, when different types are combined, when certain types are used in expressions, when a type cast is made, and when arguments are passed by function calls. The assignments and type casts are straightforward; the value is converted to the type of the variable or as indicated by the type cast. The arithmetic conversions normally follow the following set of rules.

1. Any `float` operands are converted to `double`.
2. If one operand is double, the other operand is converted to `double`.
3. Any `char` or `short` operands are converted to `int`.
4. Any `unsigned char` or `unsigned short` operands are converted to `unsigned int`.
5. If one operand is `long`, the other operand is converted to `long`.
6. If one operand is of `unsigned int`, the other operand is converted to `unsigned int`.

The list includes floating-point types for completeness. Note that `float` is converted to `double` whenever it appears. This means all calculations are done using double precision. The main reason for using `float` instead of `double` is to save storage space. One consequence of this automatic conversion is that functions that return floating-point values should be declared `double`. Declaring a function `float` results in a `float` value being converted to `double` anyway, so it's better to declare the function `double` and avoid the need for conversion.

Similarly, `char` is converted to `int` in an expression even if the only types present are `char`.

These are general rules. For IBM C, `short` is the same as `int`, so in our case, that conversion doesn't take place. Note that these rules are applied in order. That is, if you add a `long` to an `unsigned int`, rule 5 is applied first, making rule 6 inapplicable.

☐   *Question 4–3*   Suppose that c1, c2, and c3 all are type `char` variables. Do any conversions take place in the following statement?

```
c3 = c1 + c2;
```

In function calls, these same rules apply, unless you are making use of IBM C's argument type-checking process.

What Happens During Conversion

There are several possibilities in the conversion process. We can change small types to larger ones, or larger ones to smaller ones. We can convert signed to signed, unsigned to unsigned, signed to unsigned, and unsigned to signed.

Conversions from Unsigned Types—First, suppose you go from an unsigned type to a signed type of the same size. In this case, the bits are unchanged, but the interpretation may change, because now the high-order bit is a sign bit. For example, suppose you are going from unsigned char to char. The value 64 would remain 64, since the high order bit of 010000000 is 0. But 255 (11111111) would become −1, since that is how that bit pattern is interpreted by the two's complement method.

Next, suppose you go from an unsigned type to a larger type (signed or unsigned). Then more 0's are added to the left; this is called *zero extension*. So assigning an unsigned char of 255 to an int produces the bit pattern 00000000 11111111, which is still 255. Figure 4–5 shows how the 0's are added at the left.

Figure 4–5
Zero Extension

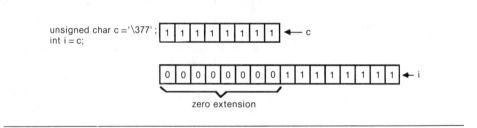

Finally, going from an unsigned type to a smaller type preserves as many of the low-order bits as can fit. The excess high-order bits are dropped. For example, the int value 257 (00000001 00000001) becomes 1 (00000001), while 256 (00000001 00000000) becomes 0 (00000000). Note that this example boils down to taking the int value modulus 256.

Conversions from Signed Types: Sign Extension—First, suppose you wish to convert a signed type to an unsigned type of the same size. The bit pattern is unaltered, but the high-order bit now is interpreted as part of the number instead of as a sign bit. Thus, the char −2 becomes the unsigned char 254.

Next suppose we convert from a signed type to a larger signed type. Here something must be done to keep track of the sign. If the number is positive, the sign bit is 0, and extra 0's are added to the left, just as for unsigned quantities. But if the number is negative, the sign bit is 1. In this case, extra 1's are added to left. This makes the new leftmost bit a 1, indicating a negative number, and it also preserves the proper numerical value. For instance, 11111110, which is a `char` −2, becomes 11111111 11111110 as an `int`, again a −2. This process of filling in the new bits with the value of the sign bit is called *sign extension*. Figure 4–6 shows how the value 1 is used in sign extension.

Figure 4–6
Sign Extension

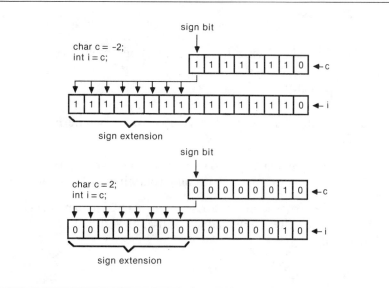

Going from a signed type to larger unsigned type takes two steps. First, the signed type is sign extended to the larger signed type, then that is converted to the unsigned type. For instance, converting a `char` −2 to `unsigned int` would convert to the bit pattern 11111111 11111110, as in the last example. This would then be interpreted as the number 65534.

Finally, going from a signed type to a smaller type, either signed or unsigned, results in saving the low-order bits and discarding the extra high-order bits.

Bit Operations

Now we are in a position to appreciate C's bit operations. C offers six bit-oriented operators: the bitwise COMPLEMENT operator (˜), the bitwise AND operator (&), the bitwise OR operator (¦), the bitwise EXCLUSIVE

OR operator (^), the LEFT SHIFT operator (<<), and the RIGHT SHIFT operator (>>). We'll summarize what each does and provide some examples.

The COMPLEMENT Operator: ~

The COMPLEMENT operator takes a single integer operand and yields a value with each 1 converted to 0 and vice versa. The resulting type is the same as that of the original operand. Suppose, for example that c is type char, while uc is type unsigned char. Also suppose each is assigned the value 2. In binary, both look like this:

    00000010

Then ~c and ~uc each have the binary representation

    11111101

This means that ~c has the value −3, while ~uc has the unsigned value of 253.

☐ *Question 4-4* How can you express an int with all bits set to 1 without concerning yourself with the number of bits?

The expression ~c does not in itself change the value of c; it merely makes the value ~c available for use. If you truly wish to change c, you can do this:

    c = ~c;

The Bitwise OR Operator: |

This operator takes two integer operands and produces a new integer. The usual type conversions we discussed earlier are first applied to the two operands, and the resulting value has the same type as the final type of the operands.

The bitwise OR operator makes a bit-by-bit comparison of its two operands. The 0-order bits of the two operands are combined to produce the 0-order bit of the result. The two first-order bits yield the first-order bit of the result, and so on. The rule used for each comparison is this: if both bits are 0, the resulting bit is 0; otherwise the resulting bit is one. Thus, if either or both bits are one, the result is one.

For example, suppose c1 is 00011001 and c2 is 01010101. Then c1 | c3 is 01011101, as in Figure 4-7. (Actually, the operands are converted to type int, so the actual value is 00000000 01011101, but in the interests of brevity, we will ignore the leftmost byte in this and in the following examples.)

Figure 4–7
ORing Two Integers

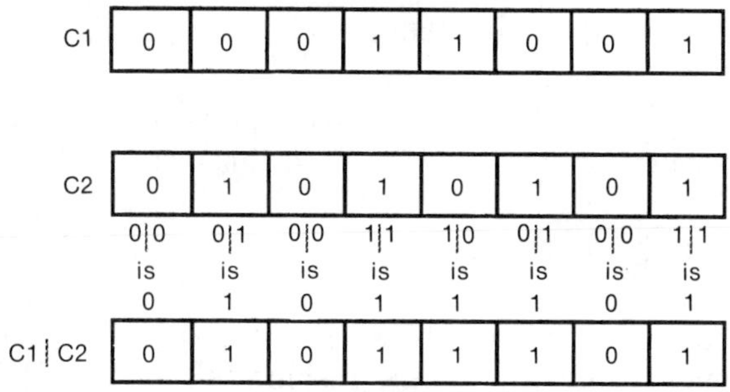

C1	0	0	0	1	1	0	0	1

C2	0	1	0	1	0	1	0	1

	0|0 is 0	0|1 is 1	0|0 is 0	1|1 is 1	1|0 is 1	0|1 is 1	0|0 is 0	1|1 is 1
C1 | C2	0	1	0	1	1	1	0	1

Now we are in a better position to understand how ¦ was used in creating the file-opening mode for the open() function. Let's look at an annotated version of the *fcntl.h* file.

```
/* fcntl.h--annotated and abbreviated */
                          /* binary value */
#defineO_RDONLY    0x0000    /* 00000000 00000000 */
#defineO_WRONLY    0x0001    /* 00000000 00000001 */
#defineO_RDWR      0x0002    /* 00000000 00000010 */
#defineO_APPEND    0x0008    /* 00000000 00001000 */

#defineO_CREAT     0x0100    /* 00000001 00000000 */
#defineO_TRUNC     0x0200    /* 00000010 00000000 */
#defineO_EXCL      0x0400    /* 00000100 00000000 */

#defineO_TEXT      0x4000    /* 01000000 00000000 */
#defineO_BINARY    0x8000    /* 10000000 00000000 */
```

With the exception of O_RDONLY, each manifest constant in the file corresponds to exactly one bit being set to one. This was accomplished by using exact powers of two for the values, for each bit represents a particular power of two.

An expression such a O_RDWR ¦ O_CREAT ¦O_BINARY creates the bit pattern 10000001 00000010, since the presence of a 1 in any bit position yields a 1 for that position in the result. Each bit position, then, acts as a flag which can be *set* to 1 or *cleared* to 0. An int can hold up to 16 flags, but fcntl.h doesn't use them all.

Note that bit 0 acts as toggle for read-only versus write-only. That ensures these two choices are mutually exclusive; the bit can't be 0 and 1 simultaneously.

Using the OR operator to set flags is one of its commoner uses. As a variation, suppose the int variable mode already has been set to a particular mode combination and you want to set one more flag. You could do something like this:

```
mode = mode | O_TRUNC;
```

Like most of C's binary operators, however, **OR** can be incorporated into an assignment operator, so we can do this instead:

```
mode |= O_TRUNC:
```

The other binary bitwise operators also can be combined with the assignment operator in this fashion. (Binary in this context means having two operands.)

□ *Question 4–5*   Suppose **mode** already had the **O_TRUNC** flag set. What then would be the result of the preceding assignment statement?

You may be wondering why | is called the bitwise OR operator. Think of a bit value of 1 being true and 0 being false. Then the rules for combining the two bits reduces to the result being true if one *or* the other contributing bits are true. So | (the bitwise OR operator) works on the bit level as || (the logical OR operator) works on the whole integer level.

□ *Question 4–6*   Suppose **c1** and **c2** are **char** variables set to 0 and 1, respectively.

   a.   What is the value of c1 | c2?
   b.   What is the value of c1 || c2?
   c.   Suppose c1 is reset to 2. What would the answers to a and b be now?

The Bitwise AND Operator: &

The bitwise AND operator takes two operands, just like the OR operator. Like the OR operator, it combines the two integers on a bit-by-bit basis. The only difference is the rule it follows for determining the result. The rule is this: the resulting bit is set to one only if *both* corresponding bits in the operands are 1. Or, looking at each bit as true or false, the resulting bit's value is "true" only if the first *and* the second contributing bits are "true." Thus, 00011001 & 01010101 is 00010001. Figure 4–8 shows how the AND operator works. Only the 0 bit and the 4 bit are set to 1 in both operands, so only those bits get set to 1 in the result.

The AND operator often is used in conjunction with a *mask,* a bit pattern used to blot out, or mask, parts of another bit pattern. For an example, recall the WordStar conversion program from Chapter 3. There, we subtracted 128 from characters whose code was 128 or greater. The programming looked like this:

Figure 4-8
ANDing Two Integers

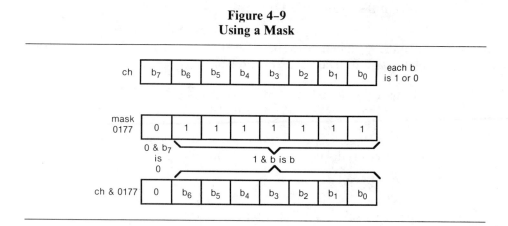

```
while ( ( ch = getc(fsource) ) != EOF)
   {
   if ( ch > 127 )
       ch -= 128;
   putc(ch, ftarget);
   }
```

What we were really trying to do was set the 7 bit to 0, while leaving the rest of the bits unchanged. Since 128 is 10000000 in binary, that is what the code did. But the AND operator can do it more efficiently. The rules for ANDing tell us the following: a 0 AND any bit value is 0; and a 1 AND any bit value is that bit value. This follows from the relations 1 AND 0 is 0, and 1 AND 1 is 1.

If, then, we AND ch with a bit pattern having the last 7 bits set to 1 and 7 bit set to 0, the resulting pattern will have its 7 bit set to 0 and the final seven bits the same as ch's. The required mask, then is 01111111, or 127, or 0177, or 0x7F. Figure 4-9 illustrates this mask.

Figure 4-9
Using a Mask

We can replace our earlier code with this:

```
while ( (ch = getc(fsource) ) != EOF)
    putc( ch & 0177 );
```

If you are feeling hexy, use 0x7F.

We don't have to check to see if `ch` is greater than 127, for this code sets the 7 bit to 0 regardless or whether `ch`'s 7 bit is 0 or 1.

The EXCLUSIVE OR Operator: ^

This operator works in the same fashion as AND and OR. As its name suggests, its rules are more restrictive than those of the standard OR. If 2 bits are operated upon by the EXCLUSIVE OR operator, the resulting bit is 1 only if one or the other, but not both, contributing bits are 1. Thus 00011001 ^ 01010101 is 01001100. Figure 4–10 illustrates this. As we'll see soon, this operator can be used to toggle a bit value on and off.

Figure 4–10
EXCLUSIVE ORing Two Integers

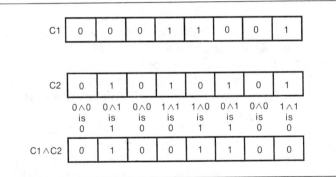

The Left- and Right-Shift Operators: << and >>

These two operators produce a bit-pattern that is shifted to the left or right from the original pattern. A second argument tells the operator how many bytes to shift. The general form is:

```
integer >> shift    ◄─ right shift
integer << shift    ◄─ left shift
```

Here, "integer" is the value to be shifted, and "shift" is the number of bits the pattern is displaced. For example, the expression

```
c2 << 2
```

represents shifting c2's bit pattern two bits to the left. What happens to the vacated bit positions? In a left shift, the vacated right bits are filled with 0's. Any bits shifted past the left end are lost. Figure 4–11 illustrates how the leftmost bits are lost.

Figure 4–11
Left Shift of Bits

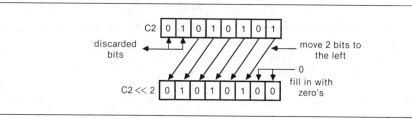

Note that each bit of displacement to the left corresponds to multiplying by two, since each bit-place is worth twice the one just to its right. So a two-bit shift is the same as multiplying by four. Similarly, each bit of right shift corresponds to division by two.

Figure 4–12 shows a right-shift example.

Figure 4–12
Right Shift of Bits

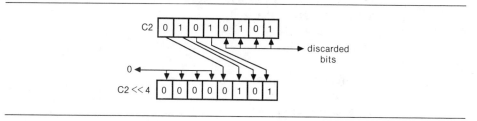

The rightmost four bits are displaced into oblivion, and the vacated left bits are filled with 0's.

There is a complication for right shifts. Unsigned quantities are shifted as described, with the vacated bits filled with 0's. For signed integers, however, vacated bits are filled with the value originally in the sign bit. Thus, if c is signed and uc is unsigned, we have the following relations:

```
c           10001101        ←  Signed value
c >> 3      11110001        ←  Filled in with 1's
uc          10001101        ←  Unsigned value
uc >> 3     00010001        ←  Filled in with 0's
```

This convention preserves the sign of negative numbers and also retains the equivalence to dividing by powers of two.

One common use of the shift operators is obtaining the high and low bytes of a two-byte integer. This is required, for example, in sending information to some of the IBM PC ports. Suppose, for example, that `portset` is an `unsigned int` and we want the high-order byte assigned to `unsigned char hibyte` and the low-byte assigned to `lobyte`. We can use the following code.

```
hibyte = portset >> 8;    /* shift 8 bits to right */
lobyte = portset;         /* rely on truncation */
```

If we don't wish to rely on truncation or if, for some reason, `portset` is signed `int`, we can amplify as follows:

```
hibyte = (portset >> 8 ) & 0377;   /* mask high byte */
lobyte = portset & 0377;           /* ditto */
```

Using Bitwise Operators

The `printf()` function provides for decimal, octal, and hexadecimal formats, but it doesn't give us a binary format. We can use bitwise operators to create a string containing the binary equivalent of a given integer. Here is one approach:

```
/* dectobin.c--displays integers in binary */
#include <stdio.h>
#define BITS 16
main()
{
    int lower, upper;
    char binstr[BITS + 1];
    char *itob();

    printf("To see integers in many forms, please enter ");
    printf("a lower limit: ");
    scanf("%d", &lower);
    printf("Now enter an upper limit: ");
    scanf("%d", &upper);
    printf("%8s %8s %8s %12s\n\n", "decimal","octal",
                "hex", "binary");
    while ( lower <= upper)
      {
      printf("%8d %8o %8x ", lower, lower, lower);
      printf("%18s\n",   itob(lower,binstr,BITS) );
      lower++;
      }
}
```

```
char *itob(num, pb, isize)
int num;
char *pb;
int isize;
{
    int i;

    for ( i = isize - 1; i >= 0;   i--, num >>= 1 )
            pb[i] = (01 & num) + '0';
    pb[isize] = '\0';
    return pb;
}
```

Before looking at the details, let's see a sample run:

```
A>dectobin
To see integers in many forms, please enter a lower limit: 100
Now enter an upper limit: 109
```

decimal	octal	hex	binary
100	144	64	0000000001100100
101	145	65	0000000001100101
102	146	66	0000000001100110
103	147	67	0000000001100111
104	150	68	0000000001101000
105	151	69	0000000001101001
106	152	6a	0000000001101010
107	153	6b	0000000001101011
108	154	6c	0000000001101100
109	155	6d	0000000001101101

The work is done by the itob() function. The main program provides it with three parameters: the number to be converted, the address of the string array in which to place the 1 and 0 characters, and the number of bits to be used. The itob() function returns the address of the string, so the return value can be used as an argument to printf(). Let's look at the details.

The line that produces the appropriate character for the string is this:

```
pb[i] = (01 & num) + '0';
```

The combination 01 & num masks all but the 0-order bit of num; thus its value is 0 or 1, whichever the 0-order bit is set to. The '0' is the *character* 0, that is, ASCII code 48. The entire right-hand expression, then, has the value 48 (the code for the character 0) if the 0-order bit of num is 0, or the value 49 (the code for the character 1) if the 0-order bit is 1. The first time through the loop, i has the value 15, so pb[15] (the 16th element of the string) is set to the character that represents the final bit of num.

Then the program proceeds to fill in the rest of the array, working from right to left. Here is the control segment:

```
for ( i = isize - 1; i >= 0;   i--, num >>= 1 )
```

The index i decreases by 1 each cycle, so that takes care of specifying each array element in turn. Next, the expression

```
num >>= 1
```

is equivalent to the following:

```
num = num >> 1
```

It serves to shift the bits in num one bit further to the right each cycle. Thus the former 1st-order bit becomes the 0-order bit, and its character equivalent is assigned to pb[14]. The process continues until the original 15th-order bit is assigned to pb[0]. Finally, to terminate the string, the null character is assigned to the last element, pb[16].

☐ *Question 4-7* Suppose we'd used num >> 1 instead of num >>= 1 in the for loop control. What would happen?

Flag Work

We already have seen how the OR operator can be used to set a particular bit to one. The bitwise operators also can be used to turn a particular bit off, to check to see if a bit is turned on, and to toggle a bit on and off. These are useful skills for working with some of the library functions and with some devices.

Turning a Bit On

The simple, naive bit is easily turned on. If THE_BIT is a constant defined as the integer that is all 0 bits except for the desired bit, then this idiom turns on that bit for the mode variable:

```
mode |= THE_BIT;      /* turns THE_BIT on in mode */
```

If the bit already is on, this statement leaves it on. All other bits in mode are left unaltered, since 0 OR any bit is just that bit. As we saw with open(), several bits can be set by using OR repeatedly.

Turning a Bit Off

The suggestible bit also is easy to turn off. To turn a bit off, we want to combine an integer with a bit mask in such a way as to leave every other bit unaffected. The OR operator won't work, because it won't set an on bit off. (A one OR any bit is still one). But 0 AND any bit is 0, while one AND any bit is that bit. Thus we need to AND the integer with a mask that is all ones except for the bit in question. The `THE_BIT` pattern is just the opposite, 0 everywhere but the bit. Reversing `THE_BIT` would give the correct mask, and that is what the complement operator does. So this is how to turn a particular bit off:

```
mode &= ~THE_BIT;        /* turns THE_BIT off in mode */
```

Toggling a Bit

Sometimes you may wish to *toggle* a bit, that is, to turn it off if it is on, and on if it is off. For instance, you may wish to toggle the bit that controls the speaker on and off in order to produce some noise. You can do this with the EXCLUSIVE OR operator:

```
mode ^= THE_BIT;         /* toggles THE_BIT in mode */
```

How does this work? First, look at the other bits in `mode`. They are exclusively ORed with 0's in `THE_BIT`. Since $1 \wedge 0$ is 1 and $0 \wedge 0$ is 0, these bits are left unchanged. Next, suppose the bit corresponding to `THE_BIT` originally is 0. Since `THE_BIT` is 1 in that bit position, we have $0 \wedge 1$, or 1. But if the original bit is one, we have one $\wedge$ one, or 0. So this code turns the bit on if off, and off if on.

Checking a Bit Value

Suppose you wish to find the value of a particular bit. For instance, the C library contains a `stat()` function, which fills a structure with information about a given file. One structure member is an integer bit pattern describing the file's read and write permissions. You might need to check if a certain bit is set in that pattern.

To see how this is done, let's use `mode` and `THE_BIT` again. Say we want to do something only if `THE_BIT` is set. It is not enough to compare `mode` with `THE_BIT`, for `mode` may have other bits set, too. One approach is to mask `mode` with `THE_BIT` by using AND. This produces a bit pattern that is 0 everywhere except (possibly) at the `THE_BIT` position. That position is set to whatever the corresponding `mode` was set; one and any bit is that bit. Figure 4-13 illustrates this process.

The next step is to compare the masked `mode` with `THE_BIT`. Both are 0 everywhere other than at the tested bit. If that bit is one in the masked `mode`, then the masked `mode` will equal `THE_BIT`. Here, then, is the idiom we can use:

```
if ( (mode & THE_BIT) == THE_BIT)   /* test if THE_BIT is set /*
     ...
```

Figure 4–13
Masking Off Extraneous Bits

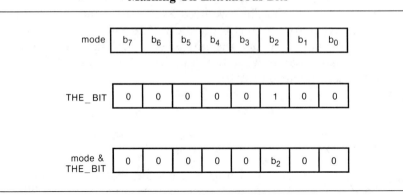

☐ *Question 4–8* Suppose that instead of having a single-bit pattern, such as `THE_BIT`, we use a pattern with more than one bit set. Will these techniques still work?

Bit Fields

C offers one other bit-handling technique. You use it to create named storage units of one-bit size or larger, called *bit fields,* as part of a structure. Figure 4–14 shows bit fields for the icon, color, underline, and blink. Here is an annotated example from the IBM C manual:

```
struct {
        unsigned icon : 8;    /* icon is a field 8 bits wide */
        unsigned color : 4;   /* a four-bit field */
        unsigned underline : 1;   /* yes, a one-bit field */
        unsigned blink : 1;
} screen[25][80];
```

Each element of the two-dimensional `screen` array is a structure containing information about the video screen. To turn underlining on for a particular bit, for instance, you can do this:

```
screen[i][j].underline = 1;
```

This approach is an alternative to using the bitwise operators. In declaring a bit field, you should use the type `unsigned`. Then, as you probably noted, you follow the field name with a colon and the number of bits to be allotted.

Figure 4–14
Bit Fields

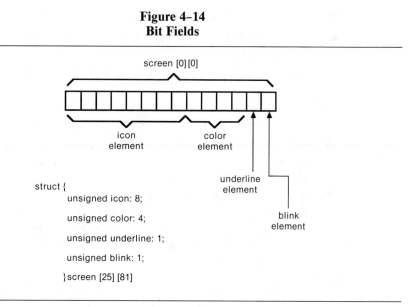

Summary

C integers come in many varieties. In IBM C, long occupies 32 bits, int and short occupy 16 bits, and char occupies 8 bits. Each of these is a signed integer, using the two's complement method of representation. Each has an unsigned counterpart, produced by using the prefix unsigned.

C offers decimal, octal, and hexadecimal notation. The L or l suffix denotes a long constant, and the '\ddd' and '\xdd' forms, where d is a digit, can be used to represent single-byte constants in octal and in hex.

Internally, integers are represented by bit patterns of 0's and 1's using binary code. The bitwise operators provide ways of manipulating the individual bits within an integer.

A structure using bit fields offers a second way to deal with individual bits.

Answers to Questions in the Chapter

■ *4–1.* 01111111 can be grouped as 001 111 111, which becomes 0177. 11111111 can be grouped as 011 111 111, which becomes 0377.

■ *4–2.* 01111111 can be grouped as 0111 1111, which becomes 0x7F. 11111111 can be grouped as 1111 1111, which becomes 0xFF.

■ *4–3.* Yes, by rule 3, each char operand (here c1 and c2) is converted to int before addition. That means the two values are copied into 16-bit registers. Then the resulting type int sum is converted back to char because it is assigned to a char variable.

- *4-4.* Use ˜0; since 0 is an int of all 0's, ˜0 is all ones.

- *4-5.* The flag remains set. Whether the original value is 0 or 1, ORing it with 1 produces a 1.

- *4-6.* *a.* c1 is 00000000 and c2 is 00000001, so c1 ¦ c2 is 00000001, or decimal 1.

- *4-6.* *b.* c1 is 0, or "false," while c2 is non-0 or "true." Since at least one is true, the expression c1 ¦¦ c2 is true, or decimal 1.

- *4-6.* *c.* Now c1 is 00000010 and c2 is 00000001, so c1 ¦ c2 is 00000011, or decimal 3. Also, c1 is non-0, or "true," so the expression c1 ¦¦ c2 is true, or decimal 1.

- *4-7.* The >> operator in itself does not change the value of its operands. Thus, every cycle, the original num would be shifted one bit, and array elements pb[0] through pb[14] would be filled with the character equivalent of the first-order bit. On the other hand, the expression

  ```
  num >>= 1
  ```

  updates num each cycle to the shifted pattern. Another approach would have been to use the following expression:

  ```
  num >> (16 - i)
  ```

  This time, num retains its original value, but it is shifted by more bits each cycle of the loop.

- *4-8.* Yes. The bit operations deal with each bit separately. If, say, TWO_BITS is 00001001, then

  ```
  mode ¦= TWO_BITS
  ```

  turns on bits three and 0 individually. What is happening to bit three is not influenced by what is happening to the other bits.

Exercise

Assembly language has a left-rotate operation that works like a left shift, except that the bits shifted off the left end are inserted back at the right end. Write a function using C's bit operations that accomplishes the same task.

5

Common I/O Problems and Solutions

- Buffered and unbuffered I/O
- Console I/O
- Problems with buffered input in interactive programs
- Menus
- Problems with numeric and non-numeric input
- Modular programming
- Problems with string I/O
- The Ansi.sys escape sequences
- BIOS, DOS, Interrupts, and C

Common I/O Problems and Solutions

The advent of personal computers and of time-sharing terminals on larger computers ushered in the age of interactive programs. Programs that carry on a dialog with the user are much more convenient to use than the old batch programs that communicated through punched cards and printed output. They have opened the world of computer use to many who once found computers too technical or abstruse to use. But interactive programs do require more programming effort. It may not be that difficult to write a program that works well when the user responds properly. But users have an uncanny ability to confound the sensible expectations of a program. Meeting the challenge of improper and peculiar input often becomes one of the more difficult and involved aspects of programming. Also, users now have more sophisticated expectations, and that increases the programmer's burden. In this chapter, we'll look at some common problems in interactive programming and at solutions to them.

Buffers and Echoes

Keyboard input as provided by the standard input in IBM C is buffered and echoed. By buffering, we mean (as mentioned in Chapter 2) that input is saved in an intermediate memory before being sent on to the program. With keyboard input, the buffer is flushed (sent on) when you press the RETURN key; this is called *line-buffering*. *Echoing* means that each keystroke is sent to the screen as well as to the buffer. Each character you type, then, is echoed on the screen.

In contrast, nonbuffered input would transmit each character to the program as it was generated. Nonechoed input would be sent to the program but would not appear on the screen. The concepts are shown in Figure 5-1.

Normally, buffering and echoing are desirable attributes. With buffering you can back up and correct mistakes before transmitting a line of information. Echoing lets you see what you have written. Sometimes, however, nonbuffered and nonechoed input is better. For example, a secret

Figure 5–1
Buffered and Unbuffered Input

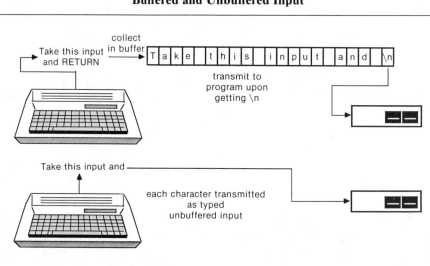

password should not be echoed. And keys used to issue word processor commands should be acted on immediately without waiting for a RETURN key to be pressed.

Different implementations of C have different methods of meeting the need for nonbuffered and nonechoed alternatives. IBM C offers a set of functions, called *console I/O* functions, which deal directly with the console. In particular, the `getch()` function reads a single character from the console. The input is neither buffered nor echoed. One character (CTRL-C) is intercepted if typed; it causes the system to terminate the program. The remaining characters are delivered to the program. Another function, `getche()`, is similar to `getch()` except that it does echo the input character. Include the *conio.h* file when using the console I/O functions; it provides the compiler information about them.

Let's put `getch()` to use in a program to view files. Of course, PC-DOS already has two programs for that purpose. The `type` command shows files, but you have to read fast enough to keep up with it; it doesn't stop each screenful. The `more` command does let you view a screen at a time, but it is more inconvenient to use, as it was designed as a filter. (A *filter* takes input from the standard input, processes it, and passes it on to the standard output.) Both stumble over the special character codes in WordStar files. So there is room for another viewing program, one that lets you view a screen at a time and that renders WordStar files intelligible.

We'll call the program *show*. You can provide it a list of filenames, and it uses the file-handling functions of Chapter 3 to open the file and to send the contents to the screen. It can be used with WordStar files because it uses a bitwise operator to mask the high-order bit in each byte. And it halts after showing about a screenful.

Where does console I/O come in? To indicate that we are done with one screenful and that we want to see the next one, we have to send a signal to the program. If we used getchar(), we would have to press a key, press RETURN, and accept that the struck character gets displayed on the screen. With getch() we avoid those problems; RETURN is not needed, and the pressed key's character does not show. To keep things simple, the program offers two possibilities for text advancement. Pressing the space bar puts a new screen (with some overlap); pressing any other key advances the text one line. Here is the programming:

```
/*  show.c--view files a screen at a time */
#include <stdio.h>  /* used with getc() */
#include <conio.h>  /* used with getch() */
#define LINES 22
#define SPACE ' '
main(ac,av)
int ac;
char *av[];
{
    FILE *fp;
    void show();

    if ( ac < 2 )     /* not enough arguments */
        fprintf(stderr, "Usage: show file(s)\n");
    else while ( ac > 1 )   /* process argument list */
        {
        if ( (fp = fopen(av[1],"rt") ) == NULL )
            fprintf(stderr,"show can't open %s\n", av[1]);
        else
            {
            show(fp);
            fclose(fp);
            if ( ac > 2)     /* if one or more names left */
                getch();        /* wait for keystroke */
            }
        av++;    /* advance to next argument */
        ac--;    /* one argument less left */
        }
}

void show(stream)
FILE *stream;
{
    int ch, response;
    int lc = 0;  /* line count */

    while ( ( ch = getc(stream) ) != EOF )
```

```
    {
    ch &= 0177;          /* clear high-bit to 0 */
    if ( ch != '\n')
        putchar(ch);
    else if ( ++lc < LINES)
        putchar('\n');
    else
        {
        response = getch();
        if ( response == SPACE )
            lc = 0;                /* next LINES lines */
        else
            lc = LINES - 1;    /* one more line */
        putchar('\n');
        }
    }
}
```

The two main programming tasks are arranging for the program to view multiple files and arranging for advancing the display. Main() takes care of the first task, and show() handles the second.

Here is the essence of the scheme for handling several command line arguments:

```
while ( ac > 1)   /* process argument list */
    {
    .../* process av[1] */
    av++;     /* advance to next argument */
    ac--;     /* one argument less left */
    }
```

The while test causes the loop to continue as long as the argument count exceeds one. Remember that the original argument count includes the command name, so a command with one command line argument has an argument count of two. Also recall that array indexing begins with 0, so av[1] refers to argument two, which is the first command line argument. So the loop begins by processing the first command line argument.

The variable av, as you saw in Chapter 3, is a pointer to a pointer to a string. Incrementing it makes av point to the next pointer so that av[1] now refers to the next command line argument. Meanwhile, ac is decremented to keep track of the number of arguments remaining. Figure 5–2 illustrates the process used to go through the command line argument. The loop continues until no arguments are left.

It would be convenient for the program to recognize the DOS wildcard substitution symbols ? and *. The IBM C package includes a file called *ssetargv.obj*; link this file to the program when you compile, and the program will recognize these wildcards.

Figure 5-2
Going through Command Line Arguments

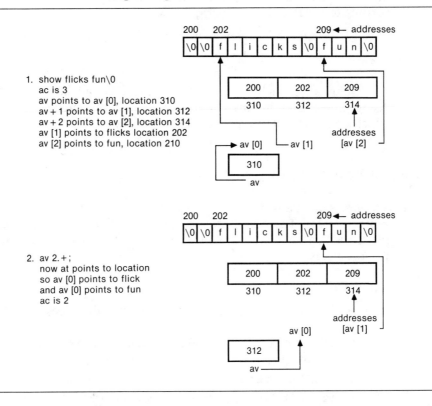

The core of the line-advancement programming is this:

```
if ( ch != '\n')
    putchar(ch);
else if ( ++lc < LINES)
    putchar('\n');
else
    {
    response = getch();
    if ( response == SPACE )
        lc = 0;              /* next LINES lines */
    else
        lc = LINES - 1;    /* one more line */
    putchar('\n');
    }
```

When a non-newline character is read, it is printed. A newline character is printed (a new line is started on the screen) if the current line count (lc) is less than the limit LINES. Otherwise the program awaits a user response. This is where `getch()` is used; the response is sent to the programming without delay and without echoing. Then the line count is reset according to the response.

☐ *Question 5-1* Suppose we want the first pass to show 24 lines and subsequent uses of the space bar to advance 20 lines. How could we change the programming?

Some keys, such as the DOWN ARROW, advance the text two lines. As we'll see later in this chapter, certain keys generate a two-byte code, which `getch()` will interpret as two keystrokes.

Interactive Programming

The last example is only minimally interactive. Let's look at a more typical representative. To concentrate on the interactive aspect, we'll use an example for which the actual program work is simple but which raises several input problems.

A Typical Task

The task is this. Write a simple payroll program that does the following:

1. Offers the user a menu from which to choose a payrate or else the option of quitting.
2. Gets the user's response.
3. Prompts the user to enter the hours worked that week.
4. Gets the user's response.
5. Calculates and displays the total earnings.
6. Displays some degree of fool-resistivity.

Here is a first, rather imperfect attempt, a program whose failings may serve to enlighten us:

```
/*   pay1.c--a mediocre pay program */
#include <stdio.h>
main()
{
    char choice;
    float rate, hours;

    printf("Here is a list of pay rates and actions:\n");
    printf("a) $ 6.00 / hr          b) $ 8.50 /hr\n");
    printf("c) $10.00 / hr          d) $12.50 /hr\n");
    printf("e) quit\n");
    printf("Please enter your choice now.\n");
```

```
      choice = getchar();
      while ( choice < 'a' || choice > 'e' )
          {
          printf("Sorry, that is not a choice. ");
          printf("Please enter an a, b, c, d, or e.\n");
          choice = getchar();
          }
      while ( choice != 'e' )
          {
          switch(choice)
              {
              case 'a' : rate = 6.00;
                          break;
              case 'b' : rate = 8.50;
                          break;
              case 'c' : rate = 10.00;
                          break;
              case 'd' : rate = 12.50;
                          break;
              default  : rate = 0.00;
                          printf("Program error\n");
              }
          printf("Enter the hours worked during the week.\n");
          scanf("%f", &hours);
          printf("Earnings for %.2f hours at $%.2f/hr are $%.2f\n",
                            hours,          rate,   rate * hours);
          printf("Here is a list of pay rates and actions:\n");
          printf("a) $ 6.00 / hr           b) $ 8.50 /hr\n");
          printf("c) $10.00 / hr           d) $12.50 /hr\n");
          printf("e) quit\n");
          printf("Please enter your choice now.\n");
          choice = getchar();
          while ( choice < 'a' || choice > 'e' )
              {
              printf("Sorry, that is not a choicc. ");
              printf("Please enter an a, b, c, d, or e.\n");
              choice = getchar();
              }
          }
      printf("Bye now\n");
  }
```

What are the failings? First, there are failings in style. The program should use defined constants for the payrates; that will make updating the program much simpler. (Appendix A discusses defining constants.) The program should be modularized by using functions; the programming for printing the menu need not have been typed twice. Then there are failings in performance. But before looking at them, let's note some virtues. (In the meantime, you might try to figure out what the performance failings will be.)

In particular, consider this portion of the programming:

```
printf("Please enter your choice now.\n");
choice = getchar();
while ( choice < 'a' || choice > 'e' )
    {
    printf("Sorry, that is not a choice. ");
    printf("Please enter an a, b, c, d, or e.\n");
    choice = getchar();
    }
```

This shows two positive features that enhance error handling. First, the response to the menu selection is read as a character rather than a number. (The choices were letters, of course, but we could have used numbers.) What's wrong with numeric input? Unless special precautions are taken, scanf("%d", &num) will balk if the user accidentally types a letter instead of a digit. But when getchar() is used, an accidental digit is just another character, and getchar() is not impeded in its appointed task.

Still, a digit or a character other than one of the official choices is not what the rest of the program needs. In a burst of protectiveness, the program screens out bad choices. If the choice is less (has a smaller ASCII code than) than 'a';or is greater than 'e', the user is prompted to try again.

Now let's see turn over the program to a user and see what happens. (*User* is a rather dry term, so let's assume the user is named Bonzo; if you prefer a more feminine touch, just read "Bonza" for "Bonzo".)

```
A>pay1
Here is a list of pay rates and actions:
a) $ 6.00 / hr             b) $ 8.50 / hr
c) $10.00 / hr             d) $12.50 / hr
e) quit
Please enter your choice now.
c
Enter the hours worked during the week.
40
Earnings for 40.00 hours at $10.00/hr are $400.00
Here is a list of pay rates and actions:
a) $ 6.00 / hr             b) $ 8.50 / hr
c) $10.00 / hr             d) $12.50 / hr
e) quit
Please enter your choice now.
Sorry, that is not a choice. Please enter an a, b, c, d, or e.
q
Sorry, that is not a choice. Please enter an a, b, c, d, or e.
Sorry, that is not a choice. Please enter an a, b, c, d, or e.
```

```
e
Bye now
A>
```

Well, it does work in a fashion. But there do seem to be some extraneous error messages appearing. They stem from differences in how scanf() and getchar() process input and from the buffering of the input.

Problems with Buffered Input—First, look at what happened when Bonzo mistakenly typed q to quit. The program said Bonzo made two wrong choices. This has a simple explanation. To enter q, Bonzo had to type q, then press the RETURN key. Pressing RETURN flushes the buffer and sends the q to the program; it also generates a newline character and sends it on to the program. The while loop rejects the q as bad input, then it rejects the newline character as bad input; hence the two error messages.

Buffered input also produced the first error message, the one that appeared before Bonzo typed q. When Bonzo responded to the request for hours worked, he typed 40, then pressed the RETURN key to flush the input. The 40 was read by scanf(), and the newline character remained in the input queue until the next input function (getchar()) processed and rejected it.

Why, then, did the very first RETURN Bonzo pressed not cause problems? Look at the sequence of events. Bonzo typed a c, then pressed RETURN. The input was sent to the program. There, getchar() processed the c, which was accepted as valid input. The newline character remained in the program input queue. In this case, the next input function was scanf(), and scanf() (except in the %c format) *skips over* whitespace—newlines, spaces, and tabs.

So the nub of the matter is that scanf() skips over whitespace, while getchar() does not. One solution to our problems, then, is to have the program skip over RETURN-generated newlines before the getchar() loop processes them. We can do this by inserting this programming after the usual input read:

```
while ( getchar() != '\n')
          ;              /* null statement */
```

It reads characters up through the first newline and does nothing else. The characters are not assigned to any variable, so they are discarded.

This programming is particularly suited to interactive programs that expect one response to a line. The regular input function reads the desired response, and the loop skips over garbage on the rest of the line.

Before we make that change, let's look at one more problem.

```
A>pay1
Here is a list of pay rates and actions:
a) $ 6.00 / hr          b) $ 8.50 / hr
```

```
c) $10.00 / hr              d) $12.50 / hr
e) quit
Please enter your choice now.
c
Enter the hours worked during the week.
two
Earnings for 0.00 hours at $10.00/hr are $0.00
Here is a list of pay rates and actions:
a) $ 6.00 / hr                    b) $ 8.50 / hr
c) $10.00 / hr              d) $12.50 / hr
e) quit
Please enter your choice now.
Sorry, that is not a choice. Please enter an a, b, c, d, or e.
Sorry, that is not a choice. Please enter an a, b, c, d, or e.
Sorry, that is not a choice. Please enter an a, b, c, d, or e.
Sorry, that is not a choice. Please enter an a, b, c, d, or e.
e
Bye now


A>
```

Here the irrepressible Bonzo entered two instead of 2 for the hours worked. Obviously, this did not sit well with the scanf("%f", &hours) statement, but what really happened? First, scanf() skipped over whitespace to the first nonwhitespace character. It expected to find a digit character, but instead it found a t. At this point it recoiled in horror, put the t back in the input queue, and returned control to the program. No new value was placed in the hours variable, so the program used the current value, which happened to be 0. The program went on normally, calculating the gross pay and displaying a new menu. Then the getchar() loop encountered and processed the four characters t, w, o, and \n, which had remained in the input queue, and printed an error message for each.

To fix this problem, we need to inspect the return value of scanf(). If it finds a number, the return value will be 1 (the number of items successfully read). If it finds nondigits, the return value is 0, and if it finds end of file, the return value is −1. Here we can use the technique we described in Chapter 3. That is, we can use programming along these lines:

```
while ( scanf("%f", &hours) != 1 )
    {
    printf("Please use numeric input; try again.\n");
    scanf("%*s");
    }
```

The scanf("%s") call is essential. It skips over the non-numeric input. Without it, the loop would repeatedly try to digest the same indigestible input. This code ignores the possibility of an end of file showing up; we'll leave that for the next refinement.

A Second Attempt

This time we will make better use of the preprocessor, implement a more modular approach, and install the input verification programming we just discussed. Here is the new version:

```c
/* pay2.c--a better pay program */
#include <stdio.h>
#define RATE1  6.00    /* use defined constants */
#define RATE2  8.50
#define RATE3 10.00
#define RATE4 12.50
main()
{
    char choice;
    double rate, hours;
    int getchoice();    /* obtains an acceptable menu response */
    double gethours(); /* obtains hours worked */

    while ( (choice = getchoice()) != 'e' )   /* quit on 'e' */
        {
        switch(choice)
            {
            case 'a' : rate = RATE1;
                       break;
            case 'b' : rate = RATE2;
                       break;
            case 'c' : rate = RATE3;
                       break;
            case 'd' : rate = RATE4;
                       break;
            default :  rate = 0.00;    /* defensive programming */
                       printf("Program error\n");
                       break;
            }
        hours = gethours();    /* returns time */
        printf("Earnings for %.2f hours at $%.2f/hr are $%.2f\n",
                        hours,         rate,   rate * hours);
        }
    printf("Bye now\n");
}

int getchoice()
{
    int choice;

    printf("Here is a list of pay rates and actions:\n");
    printf("a) $ %5.2f / hr            b) $ %5.2f / hr\n",
```

```
                    RATE1,                     RATE2           );
         printf("c) $%5.2f / hr              d) $%5.2f / hr\n",
                    RATE3,                     RATE4           );
         printf("e) quit\n");
         printf("Please enter your choice now.\n");
         choice = getcharln();    /* gets 1st char on input line */
         while ( choice < 'a' || choice > 'e' )
            {
            printf("Sorry, that is not a choice. ");
            printf("Please enter an a, b, c, d, or e.\n");
            choice = getcharln();
            }
         return choice;
      }


      /* gets 1st input char, disposes of rest of line */
   int getcharln()
   {
      int ch;

      ch = getchar();
      if ( ch != EOF )
            while ( getchar() != '\n')
                ;
      return ch;
   }

   double gethours()
   {
      double time;

      printf("Enter the number of hours worked during the week.\n");
      while (scanf("%lf", &time) != 1)
            {
            scanf("%*s");      /* skip unwanted input */
            printf("Please use numeric input; try again.\n");
            }
      while ( getchar() != '\n')
                ;
      return time;
   }
```

Using the preprocessor #define directive makes it simpler to update the program. Just change the value there, and its use elsewhere in the program is modified for you.

The getcharln() function incorporates the while loop that disposes of the potentially troublesome newline. The gethours() function also uses that loop. In addition, it uses the scanf("%*s") approach to skipping over non-numeric input. Meanwhile, the use of functions gives the program a more streamlined appearance. The getchoice() function makes sure that only acceptable input choices are forwarded to the main program. The main program itself is built around a while loop set up like this:

```
while ( (choice = getchoice()) != 'e' )   /* quit on 'e' */
   {
     /* process info */
   }
```

This loop is modeled in form after this standard C construction:

```
while ( (ch = getchar() ) != EOF )
   {
        /* do things */
   }
```

The response loop keeps cycling through menu choices until e is entered. One point of interest is the *default* choice in the switch in the loop. Conceivably, you could add another choice to the menu and forget to add it to the list of switch choices. This bit of defensive programming would help you catch what might otherwise prove to be a mysterious error.

Well, let's turn over the program to Bonza this time. (Those of you preferring a more masculine presence can read "Bonzo" for "Bonza".)

```
A>pay2
Here is a list of pay rates and actions:
a) $ 6.00 / hr          b) $ 8.50 / hr
c) $10.00 / hr          d) $12.50 / hr
e) quit
Please enter your choice now.
a
Enter the number of hours worked during the week.
thirty
Please use numeric input; try again.
30
Earnings for 30.00 hours at $6.00/hr are $180.00
Here is a list of pay rates and actions:
a) $ 6.00 / hr          b) $ 8.50 / hr
c) $10.00 / hr          d) $12.50 / hr
e) quit
Please enter your choice now.
^Z
Sorry, that is not a choice. Please enter an a, b, c, d, or e.
Sorry, that is not a choice. Please enter an a, b, c, d, or e.
Sorry, that is not a choice. Please enter an a, b, c, d, or e.
```

```
Sorry, that is not a choice. Please enter an a, b, c, d, or e.
Sorry, that is not a choice. Please enter an a, b, c, d, or e.
Sorry, that is not a choice. Please enter an a, b, c, d, or e.
Sorry, that is not a choice. Please ent^C

A>
```

First, the good news. The improper entry of thirty was handled adroitly. There was no superfluous error message after the menu was re-printed. In short, the program remedies the flaws we noted in *pay1.c*.

The bad news is that when Bonza pressed CTRL-Z in response to the menu, the error messages came pouring out until the ever-alert Bonza pressed CTRL-C to interrupt the program. Two questions may spring to your mind. What does CTRL-Z do? Why did Bonza press it?

First, recall that the CTRL-Z character is used to mark the end of the file in text mode files. Pressing CTRL-Z simulates an end of file for key-board input.

Second, it must be noted that nowhere in the program is the faintest suggestion made that the user press CTRL-Z. Despite that, many users are accustomed to using CTRL-Z to terminate programs, and a number of them undoubtedly would try it here. (An explicit warning not to use CTRL-Z would only increase the number!) Also, it is possible that a user might use redirection to feed in data from a file. The file might not have an e for quit in it, but, if it is a text file, it will have a CTRL-Z.

So Bonza offered the program a CTRL-Z, and the program failed. The next level of refinement, then, should have the program respond prop-erly (that is, quit) when it encounters CTRL-Z. This is not that simple using the present structure, for our uncooperative user might spring a CTRL-Z in response to the menu *or* in response to the request for hours worked. We could sprinkle a few calls to `exit()` through the program wherever input is sampled, but that is poor programming style. A better approach is to re-think the overall program structure.

Making the World Safe from CTRL-Z

Conceptually, the pay program performs two general tasks. First, it gathers information from the user. Second, it processes the information. The *pay2.c* program was organized along those lines, but it did not go far enough in consolidating the data-gathering process. The main `while` loop was controlled by the value of the menu selection, but a better approach would to be control the loop with a function that reported back on the en-tire data-gathering process. That is, we want the main program to look something like this:

```
while ( getdata(&rate, &hours) != QUIT )
    {
    printf("Earnings for %.2f hours at $%.2f/hr are $%.2f\n",
                        hours,          rate,   rate * hours);
```

```
        }
     printf("Bye now\n");
```

Here the getdata() returns a value of QUIT (suitably defined) if the user enters e or CTRL-Z. Because the function's return value is used to signal continuation or quitting, the other required information (rate) and (hours) is communicated by using addresses, as discussed in Chapter 2. All the information gathering is delegated to the getdata() function and to the functions it calls upon. As you can see, this structure makes for a very simple main program.

Some of the other functions become more complicated, however. A user might press CTRL-Z on the same line but following a menu choice, for example. Our original programming discards the rest of the line, so a CTRL-Z pressed there would be lost. So we need to modify getcharln() so that it stops at a newline or at a CTRL-Z. If the latter, the function should put the CTRL-Z back in the input queue so that the next input test will catch it. Since the input is in a buffer to begin with, putting a character back in the queue is not that difficult. Indeed, the ungetc() function of the standard I/O package does just that. Here is the C code:

```c
int getcharln() /* returns first character on line */
{
    int c, ch;

    if (   ( ch = getchar() ) != EOF) /* ch is 1st char */
        {
        while ( (c = getchar()) != '\n' && c != EOF )
                ;    /* skip remaining input on line */
        if ( c == EOF )   /* make noninitial EOF initial EOF */
            ungetc(c, stdin);
        }
    return ch;
}
```

Figure 5–3 illustrates how getcharln() performs.

Let's step through the logic. Suppose the very first character is CTRL-Z. Then EOF is assigned to ch. Next, the body of the if statement is skipped; this keeps the program from trying to read past end of file. Then EOF (the value of ch) is returned to the calling program, which can act upon it.

Next, suppose the first character is not CTRL-Z. It is assigned to ch. Then the rest of the characters on the same line are examined. If none of them is a CTRL-Z, all the characters through the newline are discarded, and the value of ch is returned. If one of them is a CTRL-Z, no more input is read. (No reading is extended past the end of file.) The CTRL-Z, which already has been read, is placed back in the input queue, and, once again, the value of ch is returned. The very next input call, then, will find the

Figure 5–3
Getcharln() at Work

	Input queue	ch	discarded
1. (typed input ──▶}	tulip in	undefined	
2. ch = get charln ( );	-------	t	ulip\n
3. (new typed input ──▶}	frog ^z \n	t	
4. ch = get charln ( );	^z \n	f	rog
5. ch = getcharln ( );	-------	EOF	

Getcharln ( ) reads first character of a line, and discards the rest, except a^z, which becomes the first input item for the next input.

CTRL-Z sitting there, waiting to be read. That call, then, can detect the end of file. In the meantime, the initial character of the original input line was not lost. Another approach would be to have the function return EOF if a CTRL-Z appeared anywhere on the line, but that would result in discarding the rest of the information on the line.

Handling CTRL-Z is probably the trickiest part of the program, and part of it gets reproduced in the function that obtains the time. Here is the whole program:

```
/*  pay3.c--the best of three pay programs  */
#include <stdio.h>
#define RATE1  6.00
#define RATE2  8.50
#define RATE3 10.00
#define RATE4 12.50
#define CONTINUE 1
#define QUIT (-1)
/* functions called in this program */
int getdata();    /* obtains data, returns quit status */
int getchoice();  /* obtains user's menu choice */
int getcharln();  /* returns first character on line */
int gethours();   /* obtains hours worked, skips bad input */
int ungetc();     /* library function, puts character */
                  /* back in input queue */
main()
{
    float rate, hours;

    while ( getdata(&rate,&hours) != QUIT)
        printf("Earnings for %.2f hours at $%.2f/hr are $%.2f\n",
                    hours,          rate,    rate*hours);
```

```
        printf("Bye now\n");
}

int getdata(pr, ph)    /* returns QUIT when it's time to stop */
float *pr, *ph;     /* addresses of rate, hours */
{
    int choice;
    int status = CONTINUE;

    printf("Here is a list of pay rates and actions:\n");
    printf("a) $ %5.2f/hr              b) $ %5.2f/hr \n",
                   RATE1,                    RATE2 );
    printf("c) $ %5.2f/hr              d) $ %5.2f/hr \n",
                   RATE3,                    RATE4 );
    printf("e) quit\n");
    printf("Please enter your choice now.\n");
    choice = getchoice();
    switch(choice)
        {
        case 'a'  :  *pr = RATE1;
                     break;
        case 'b'  :  *pr = RATE2;
                     break;
        case 'c'  :  *pr = RATE3;
                     break;
        case 'd'  :  *pr = RATE4;
                     break;
        case 'e'  :  status = QUIT;
                     break;
        case EOF  :  status = QUIT;
                     printf("EOF encountered\n");
                     break;
        default   :  status = QUIT;
                     printf("Program error\n");
        }
    if ( status != QUIT)
        status = gethours(ph);
    return status;
}

int getchoice()
{
    int ch;
    ch = getcharln();
    while ( ( (ch < 'a' || ch > 'e') && ch != EOF )
        {
        printf("Sorry, that is not a choice. ");
```

```
        printf("Please enter an a, b, c, d, or e. \n");
        ch = getcharln();
        }
    return ch;
}


int getcharln() /* returns first character on line */
{
    int c, ch;

    if (    ( ch = getchar() ) != EOF) /* ch is 1st char */
        {
        while ( (c = getchar()) != '\n' && c != EOF )
                ;    /* skip remaining input on line */
        if ( c == EOF )    /* make non-initial EOF initial EOF */
            ungetc(c, stdin);
        }
    return ch;
}


int gethours(ph)
float *ph;      /* address of hours */
{
    int status, c;

    printf("Enter the number of hours worked during the week.\n");
    while ( (status = scanf("%f", ph) ) == 0)
        {
        scanf("%*s");
        printf("Please use numeric input; try again.\n");
        }
    if ( status == 1)
        {
        while ( (c = getchar()) != '\n' && c != EOF )
                ;
        if ( c == EOF )
            ungetc(c, stdin);
        }
    else      /* status is -1 */
        printf("End of file encountered instead of hours worked\n");
    return status;
}
```

Here are some points to notice. First, at the top of the program, we declared and described the functions used in the program. These functions can be declared in main(), but it is neater to declare them this way. Also, the declarations can be used by all the functions in the file, in case more than `main()` uses one of them. Second, because determining the continue-or-quit status had high priority, we altered the `gethours()` function to return a status and used an address argument to provide the `hours` value.

Does it work? Let us call upon the services of Bonzo once again:

```
A>pay3
Here is  list of pay rates and actions:
a) $ 6.00 / hr             b) $ 8.50 / hr
c) $10.00 / hr             d) $12.50 / hr
e) quit
Please enter your choice now.
^Z
EOF encountered
Bye now

A>pay3
Here is  list of pay rates and actions:
a) $ 6.00 / hr             b) $ 8.50 / hr
c) $10.00 / hr             d) $12.50 / hr
e) quit
Please enter your choice now.
b^Z
Enter the number of hours worked during the week.
End of file encountered instead of hours worked
Bye now

A> pay 3
Here is  list of pay rates and actions:
a) $ 6.00 / hr             b) $ 8.50 / hr
c) $10.00 / hr             d) $12.50 / hr
e) quit
Please enter your choice now.
d
Enter the number of hours worked during the week.
^Z
End of file encountered instead of hours worked
Bye now

A>
```

In the second example, the CTRL-Z was passed on and picked up by the `gethours()` function.

There is one oddity to note. This program ran as described under DOS 3.1. But under DOS 2.1, the final example required pressing the RETURN key twice after the CTRL-Z instead of once. This appears to be due to a small glitch in the DOS 2.1–IBM C interface.

Interactive String Input

So far we have dealt with problems with character as well as numeric input, but we haven't discussed strings. We'll remedy that now. Once again, in order to concentrate on the input aspect, we'll set up a rather modest programming goal. This time we want to write a program that reads in a small list of names and then prints them out.

The scanf() function has a string format specifier, but it only reads up to the first whitespace once the string is started. Thus, for reading names, which may contain spaces, the gets() function is more suitable, since it reads up to the first newline.

☐ *Question 5-2* You can provide scanf() with an optional field-width specifier. Can you not, then, use scanf("%20s", name) to read strings with up to 20 characters, including spaces?

Using Gets() for String Input

Here is our first version:

```
/* names1.c--reads names using gets() */
#include <stdio.h>
#define MAXNUM 5    /* maximum number of names */
#define MAXLEN 12   /* maximum array size */
main()
{
int i = 0;
int count;
char names[MAXNUM][MAXLEN]; /* array of strings */
char *gets();

printf("Enter up to %d names:\n", MAXNUM);
while ( i < MAXNUM  && gets(names[i]) != NULL )
        i++;
printf("Here are the %d names you entered:\n", i );
for ( count = 0; count < i; count++)
   puts( names[count]);
}
```

The gets() function places the input line in the indicated array, replacing the newline with a null character to terminate the string. Also, it returns a pointer to the beginning of the array. Thus, the first time through this program, gets() would return the address of names[0][0]. Hence we declare gets() as type pointer-to-char. However, if gets() encounters the end of file, it returns NULL. As you may recall, this is defined in *stdio.h* as a pointer to the 0 address, which never would be used by a C program to store data. Thus, the comparison can be used as a test for end of file. The loop quits, then, when all the arrays are filled, or when end of file occurs, whichever comes first.

Here is a sample run:

```
A>names1
Enter up to 5 names:
king kong
joe young
bonzo
bonzetta
cheeta
Here are the 5 names you entered:
king kong
joe young
bonzo
bonzetta
cheeta

A>
```

That looks fine. But what happens if we type names longer than the allotted array size? Let's try it:

```
A>names1
Enter up to 5 names:
vicki gar
al tuna
cap cuttlefish
ed squid
nancy crab
Here are the 5 names you entered:
vicki gar
al tuna
cap cuttlefied squid
ed squid
nancy crab

A>
```

The results are odd, but explainable. The gets() function does not check to see if you have allocated enough space. It just puts the first character at the beginning of the address you gave it and keeps going. If it has to overwrite other array members or data, it will. In this case, cap cuttlefish started out in names[2] and overflowed into names[3]. Then ed squid was read into names[3] and, in turn, overwrote the sh that had wound up there. Figure 5–4 shows how the overwriting occurs.

Figure 5-4
A Gets() Gaffe

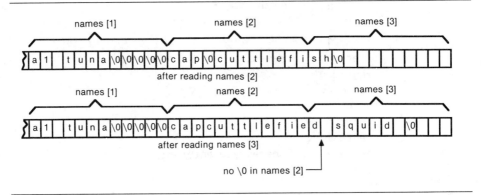

Why, then, didn't the printing loop just print cap cuttlefi instead of cap cuttlefied squid? Because `printf()` locates the end of a string by the terminating null character. There was no null character in `names[2]`, so `printf()` kept going until it reached the null character in `names[3]`.

Using Fgets() for String Input

Most programmers find the thought of user input overwriting data to be amusing in the programs of others and disquieting in their own programs. What is needed is a string input function that will take only up to a pre-scribed number of characters. The simplest solution to this is to use the library function `fgets()`. We discussed its properties in Chapter 3. In review, it takes three arguments: the address of the location to be used to store the string, a maximum size parameter, and a stream identifying the file to be read. Like `gets()`, it returns the address of the string location if successful and `EOF` if not. The limit to the number of characters read is one less than the size parameter; this leaves space for the terminal null character that `fgets()` appends.

Let's see what substituting `fgets()` for `gets()` produces:

```
/* names2.c-uses fgets() carelessly */
#include <stdio.h>
#define MAXNUM 5
#define MAXLEN 12
main()
{
int i = 0;
int count;
char names[MAXNUM][MAXLEN];
char *fgets();

printf("Enter up to %d names:\n", MAXNUM);
```

```
while ( i < MAXNUM   && fgets(names[i], MAXLEN, stdin) != NULL )
        i++;
printf("Here are the %d names you entered:\n", i );
for ( count = 0; count < i; count++)
    puts( names[count]);
}
```

The header comment may lead you to suspect the program is less than perfect. Let's check it out:

```
A>names2
Enter up to 5 names:
vicki gar
al tuna
cap cuttlefish
ed squid
Here are the 5 names you entered:
vicki gar

al tuna

cap cuttlef
ish

ed squid

A>
```

Now you can see that the fgets() function includes the newline generated by the RETURN key as part of the string. Because puts() already adds a newline, this results in an extra blank line. It also leaves one less character element to use for the name. And why did it count four names as five? The cap cuttlefish entry went beyond the limit, so fgets() just read in the characters through the f. In this case, the newline hadn't been reached yet, so it was not part of the string. As usual for C input functions, the next call to fgets() began where the preceding call ended, and the rest of the name (ish) was read as the next entry. See Figure 5–5 for the effects of the fgets function on the data.

To remove these anomalies takes additional programming. If the call to fgets() is terminated by the RETURN key, we would like to remove the newline from the names array. But if the call is terminated by reaching the character limit first, there is no newline to remove. Also, in this second case, we would like to dispose of the rest of the line so that the next call will start at the next line.

One approach is to use the C library function strchr(). It takes two arguments: the address of a string and a character. It searches the string for the character. If it finds it, it returns the address of the character; other-

Figure 5–5
The Effects of Fgets()

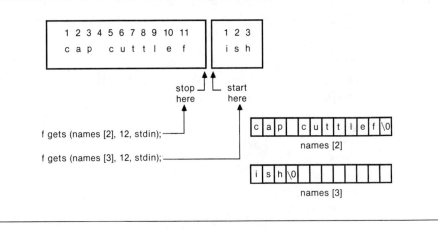

wise, it returns a pointer to **NULL**. We will use it to see if the string just read in has a newline in it. If it does, we will replace the newline with a null character. If it doesn't contain a newline, the input string was too long, and we will clear the rest of the line. Here is the code:

```
/* names3.c--a more careful use of fgets() */
#include <stdio.h>
#define MAXNUM 5
#define MAXLEN 13      /* increase by 1 because of \n */
main()
{
int i = 0;
int count;
char names[MAXNUM][MAXLEN];
char *nlptr;
char *strchr(), *fgets();   /* declare function types */

printf("Enter up to %d names:\n", MAXNUM);
while ( i < MAXNUM && fgets(names[i], MAXLEN, stdin) != NULL )
   {
   if ( ( nlptr = strchr (names[i], '\n')) != NULL )
       *nlptr = '\0';
   else
       while ( getchar() != '\n' )
           ;
   i++;
   }

printf("Here are the %d names you entered:\n", i );
```

```
   for ( count = 0; count < i; count++)
      puts( names[count]);
}
```

Notice that we've increased the array size by one to compensate for fgets() including the newline in the character count. Also note how strchr() is used. It returns a *pointer,* which is assigned to the pointer variable nlptr. This makes nlptr the address of the newline if the search is successful. That, in turn, makes *nlptr refer to the value stored at the location, and the assignment statement makes that value the null character.

Here is a sample run using the same input:

```
A>names3
Enter up to 5 names:
vicki gar
al tuna
cap cuttlef
ed squid
nancy crab
Here are the 5 names you entered:
vicki gar
al tuna
cap cuttlef
ed squid
nancy crab

A>
```

One anomaly in this program is that a name terminated by reaching the character limit holds one more character than a name terminated by the RETURN key, for the second uses up a space with the newline, later replaced by a null character. Another problem with both fgets() and gets() is that they hang up if you enter a CTRL-Z in the middle of the line. One solution is to write a new input function that combines fgets()'s count limit with gets() handling of the newline and which has increased sensitivity to CTRL-Z.

☐ *Question 5-3* How can you use getchar() to accomplish these goals?

Further Refinements

We can add some conveniences for the user. First, the current version is terminated by typing five names or by pressing CTRL-Z at the beginning of a line. (The fgets() function, you will recall, does not respond well to a midline CTRL-Z.) It would be preferable to terminate input by pressing RETURN at the beginning of a line. The program should explain these options to the user. Also, it should show a line count. Many users will be able to keep track of five input names, but MAXNUM could be increased to, say

300. Another enhancement would be some sort of on-screen guide to the maximum length of the input line.

To terminate on an initial RETURN, the program can look at the first character in the input string. If it is a newline, terminate the input loop.

To show line numbers, add a `printf()` statement or two to provide a numbered prompt.

To show the extent of acceptable input, print out an appropriate number of underline characters, then backspace to the beginning. The C representation of the backspace character is \b.

Here is one implementation:

```
/* names4.c--making the program easier to use */
#include <stdio.h>
#define MAXNUM 5
#define MAXLEN 13
#define ULINE '_'
void nchars();
char *strchr(), *fgets();    /* standard I/O functions */
main()
{
int i = 0;
int count;
char names[MAXNUM][MAXLEN];
char *nlptr;

printf("This program reads in names until you reach the ");
printf("program limit\n or press either RETURN or ");
printf("CTRL-Z at the beginning of a line.\n");
printf("Enter up to %d names:\n1> ", MAXNUM);
nchars(MAXLEN - 2, ULINE);
nchars(MAXLEN - 2, '\b');
while ( i < MAXNUM && fgets(names[i], MAXLEN, stdin) != NULL
                                  && names[i][0] != '\n' )
    {
    if ( ( nlptr = strchr(names[i], '\n')) != NULL )
        *nlptr = '\0';
    else
        while ( getchar() != '\n' )
            ;
    if (++i < MAXNUM)
        {
        printf("%d> ", i + 1);          /* print entry number */
        nchars(MAXLEN - 2, ULINE);   /* print underlines */
        nchars(MAXLEN - 2, '\b');   /* backup to beginning */
        }
    }
printf("Here are the %d names you entered:\n", i );
```

```
for ( count = 0; count < i; count++)
    puts( names[count]);
}

void nchars ( n, ch)    /* prints ch n times */
int n;
char ch;
{
    while (n--)
        putchar(ch);
}
```

Note that we've introduced a separate function to print a given character a specified number of times. We could have used a string constant such as "_ _ _ _ _ _ _ _ _ _" to produce the underlines, but the use of a function lets us key the number of underlines to the value of **MAXLEN**. Also, we then can use the same function to put in the backspacing.

The prompt will look like this:

    1> _ _ _ _ _ _ _ _ _ _

The cursor will return to the first underline, and characters typed by the user will replace the underlines. Here is a sample run:

```
A>names4
This program reads in names until you reach the program limit
or press either RETURN or CTRL-Z at the beginning of a line.
Enter up to 5 names:
1> rick nodal_
2> sue trope_ _
3> doug latoad
4> ann land_ _ _
5> _ _ _ _ _ _ _ _ _ _    ◄─ RETURN pressed
Here are the 4 names you entered:
rick nodal
sue trope
doug latoad
ann land

A>
```

☐ *Question 5-4* As it stands, the program truncates overly long entries. How could you modify the program so that it lets you make a reentry if the original entry is too long?

Cursor Control

So far, our I/O examples have pretty much been in a teletype mode, with each input or output line appearing below the preceding one on the screen. To many users, that approach is rather pedestrian. They expect the screen to clear at the start of the program, and perhaps they expect repeated input to be typed on the same line on the screen. The first step to these more sophisticated uses of I/O is to assume control over the cursor.

IBM C offers three methods of cursor control. All begin with using the console I/O functions, since character input must be examined immediately. You don't want to have to press the RETURN key when using an arrow key to move the cursor. The simplest method, which can be used with DOS Versions 2.0 and later, is to use *escape sequences*. These are sequences of characters that, when sent to the console, initiate activities such as cursor movement and clearing the screen. The second method involves using *interrupts* to access subroutines built into the computer's ROM. The third method is to use *direct memory access* to place data in the video display memory. We'll look at the first two methods in this chapter, starting with the simplest one.

Extended Screen Control through Ansi.sys

The *ansi.sys* file is provided with DOS Versions 2.0 and later. It contains code that transforms escape sequences to the proper subroutine calls. To make use of it, you should have this in your *config.sys* file:

```
DEVICE=ANSI.SYS
```

This will increase the size of DOS in memory by the size of the file.

Suppose you wish to clear the screen and send the cursor to the home position in the upper left corner. The *IBM Technical Reference* manual says the code for this command is `ESC [2J`, where `ESC` represents the character generated by the ESC key; its ASCII code is octal 033. To transmit this sequence we can use the console output function `putch()` four times. Like console input, console output is unbuffered, so the characters are transmitted at once. It may be more convenient to use `cprintf()`, which is the console version of `printf()`. The main difference is that `cprintf()` is unbuffered. For instance, we could do this:

```
cprintf("%c%s", '\033', "[2J");
```

The simpler

```
cprintf("\033[2J");
```

also works, but is, perhaps, a little more confusing to read.

Table 5-1 lists some of the other escape sequences available. In this table, ESC represents the ESC key, and # represents a decimal number whose exact value is chosen by the user. Unless otherwise stated, the # parameter can be omitted, in which case it is taken to have a value of 1.

Given these sequences, we still have a problem: how does our program identify when, say, an arrow key is pressed? To deal with this problem, we need to know about "scan codes" and IBM's extended character code.

Scan Codes and Extended Character Codes—The mechanics of getting a keyboard entry from the keyboard to a program are more involved than they have seemed to this point. For instance, we have talked about pressing CTRL-Z. For the computer to recognize that this character is being transmitted, it first determines that the CTRL key has been pressed, has not been released, and that the Z key has been presssed. Clearly, this involves some analysis on part of the computer. Another complication is that the total number of keystroke combinations goes beyond the limits of the standard ASCII code. Let's see how a PC deals with these matters.

First, there is a keyboard processor that determines when a key has been pressed and when a key has been released. If a certain key, say Q, has been pressed, it transmits an identifying scan code to the central processing chip. The code is not an ASCII code; instead it is governed by the key's geometrical position on the keyboard. The ESC key has a code of 1, the 1 key a code of 2, and so on. The Q is the 16th key in order (the function keys and numeric keypad come after the "typewriter keys" of the keyboard), so the Q's scan code is 16 when the key is pressed. When a key is released, a second scan code is sent. It consists of 128 added to the key-pressed code. Thus, when the Q is released, a scan code of 144 is sent.

Altogether, there are 83 keys, so the key-pressed codes range from 1 to 83, and the key-released codes range from 129 to 211, with room for expansion.

These codes then must be converted to a suitable ASCII code, if possible, or to an extended code, if necessary. This is done in the BIOS.

BIOS stands for *basic input/output system*. (This is *basic* as in fundamental, not as in the computer language.) It consists of fundamental subroutines stored in the computer's ROM (read-only memory). The *IBM Technical Reference* manual contains the assembly language code for these routines for those interested. In particular, subroutine 9 provides a keyboard service routine that translates scan codes into program-usable codes.

Suppose, for instance, the Q key is pressed and released. The scan code sequence 16 (key pressed), 144 (key released) is converted to the ASCII code for lowercase Q (113) and placed in a register so that a program can use it. If the Q is held down, successive Q's are transmitted at fixed intervals until the key is released. If it is determined that the right SHIFT key is held down (scan code 54), the ASCII code for uppercase Q is produced instead.

The ASCII code includes representations for uppercase Q, lowercase Q, and CTRL-Q, so these pose no coding problems. But then there are

Table 5-1
Ansi.sys Escape Sequences

CURSOR CONTROL SEQUENCES	
Sequence	**Effect**
ESC [#A	Moves the cursor up # lines without changing columns.
ESC [#B	Moves the cursor down # lines without changing columns.
ESC [#C	Moves the cursor forward # columns in the same line. The sequence is ignored if the cursor is already in the rightmost column.
ESC [#D	Moves the cursor left # columns in the same line unless the cursor already is in the leftmost position.
ESC [#;#H	Moves the cursor to the specified position. The first # represents the line number, and the second # represents the column number. If no parameters are given, the cursor is moved to the home position.

ERASE SEQUENCES	
Sequence	**Effect**
ESC [2J	Erases whole screen and homes the cursor.
ESC [k	Erases from (and including) cursor through the end of the line.

combinations such as ALT-Q and F6 and HOME. Here IBM uses an extended code. The extension is accomplished by using two bytes instead of one for the code. To distinguish a two-byte code for a single character from two one-byte codes for two characters, the first byte of the extended code is set to 0. None of the regular keystrokes generates the null character, so the occurrence of a 0 byte serves to mark the beginning of a two-byte code.

For the alphabetic characters used with ALT, the extended code is just the scan code for the letter with the prefix added. Thus, the extended code for ALT-Q is 00 16. Extended codes for the other keys are given in the *IBM BASIC Manual* and the *IBM Technical Reference* manual. (This is BASIC as in the language, this time.) Table 5-2 lists them for you; keep in mind that in each case, the first byte is 0.

Table 5-2
Extended Codes

Second Byte	Meaning
3	(null character) NUL
15	(SHIFT-TAB) ←
16–25	ALT- Q, W, E, R, T, Y, U, I, O, P
30–38	ALT- A, S, D, F, G, H, J, K, L
44–50	ALT- Z, X, C, V, B, N, M
59–68	function keys F1–F10
71	HOME
72	Cursor Up
73	PG UP
75	Cursor Left
77	Cursor Right
79	END
80	Cursor Down
81	PG DN
82	INS
83	DEL
84–93	F11–F20 (SHIFT-Function Keys)
94–103	F21–F31 (CTRL-Function Keys)
104–113	F31–F41 (ALT-Function Keys)
114	CTRL-PRT SC
115	CTRL-Cursor Left (Previous Word)
116	CTRL-Cursor Right (Next Word)
117	CTRL-END
118	CTRL-PG DN

Table 5–2 (cont.)

119	CTRL-HOME
120–131	ALT-1, 2, 3, 4, 5, 6, 7, 8, 9, 0, −, =
132	CTRL-PG UP

Controlling Your Cursor

We now have the two necessary techniques for cursor control. Using the extended codes, we can identify certain keys, such as the arrow key. Using the *ansi.sys* program we can produce instructions to move the cursor. Now we merely need link the two techniques together.

A straightforward approach is to use getch() to read keyboard input. (This function, in turn, ultimately uses the BIOS services to obtain code values.) If a 0 byte turns up, we can examine the next byte to see if, say, one of the cursor control keys was struck. If so, then we can issue a command in the form of an appropriate escape sequence. The next program does just that. It clears the screen, gives a prompt, and accepts characters you type. Regular text appears where you type it. You can use the cursor control keys to move the cursor where you want, and the F10 key is programmed to clear the screen and home the cursor. Here is the code:

```
/*  cursor.c--lets you type text, move cursor, clear screen */
#include <conio.h>      /* for console I/O */
#define STOP '\032'     /* ctrl-z */
#define ESC '\033'
#define HOME "[H"
#define UP "[A"
#define DOWN "[B"
#define RIGHT "[C"
#define LEFT "[D"
#define CLEAR "[2J"
#define CURSOR(X) cprintf("%c%s", ESC, X)
main()
{
    int ch;

    CURSOR(CLEAR);
    cprintf("Please begin:\n");
    while ( (ch = getch() ) != STOP)
      {
       if ( ch == 0)   /* 0 code */
          {
          ch = getch();
```

```
        switch ( ch )
            {
            case 68 : CURSOR( CLEAR ); break;
            case 71 : CURSOR( HOME ); break;
            case 72 : CURSOR( UP ); break;
            case 75 : CURSOR( LEFT ); break;
            case 77 : CURSOR( RIGHT );   break;
            case 80 : CURSOR( DOWN ); break;
            }   /* end switch */
        }          /* end 0 code test */
    else if ( ch == '\r')
        cputs("\r\n");          /* binary-text translation */
    else if ( ch < 040 )      /* control characters */
        {
        putch('^');
        putch ( ch | 0100 );   /* turn on 6-bit */
        }
    else
        putch ( ch );
    }
}
```

There are some points to note. First, the console I/O functions work in the binary mode rather than the text mode. Thus, getch() does not recognize CTRL-Z as an end-of-file marker. Therefore, we explicitly tell the program to stop on CTRL-Z. Secondly, in the binary mode, the RETURN key generates a carriage-return character (\r). The program converts that to the CR-LF combination so that the cursor returns to the beginning of the line and advances to the next line.

Second, to transmit the escape sequence, we used these macro definitions:

```
#define ESC '\033'
#define CURSOR(X) cprintf("%c%s", ESC, X)
```

The first defines ESC as the code for that character. The cprintf() function prints ESC followed by whatever character sequence X represents. Appendix A discusses macro definitions such as this.

Finally, we print control characters such as CTRL-A in the ^A format. The conversion is simple to make, for the code for a control character differs from the code of the regular, uppercase character only in bit number six. This bit is set to 0 for control characters and to one in the standard characters. The bitwise OR operator offers a quick method to set the bit to one.

Clearly, we could identify other keys and assign duties to them, but let's look at the second approach to cursor control instead.

Cursor Control and Interrupts

The *ansi.sys* program acts as a filter to convert certain character sequences into requests to the BIOS to perform particular tasks. With IBM C we can activate BIOS routines directly through the use of *interrupts*. But before looking into the interrupt technique, let's take a quick glance at the computer resources available to a program.

The Basic I/O System

The basic I/O system (BIOS), as we have said, consists of I/O related subroutines built into the computer's random access memory. They handle I/O not only for the keyboard and the screen, but for disk drives, tape drives, printers, communications, and the like. The BIOS calls ultimately do the work requested by, say, `printf()` in a program or by a `copy` command.

The Disk Operating System

The disk operating system provides a higher level of services than the BIOS. That is, it provides services such as opening and closing files, setting the time, and many others. It may use BIOS calls to perform larger scale tasks. DOS is loaded into the computer memory when the system is booted.

Interrupts

Since the BIOS and DOS contain many powerful routines, it is desirable to be able to access them through a program. Of course, we do so indirectly when using C's I/O calls, but direct access would free us from being limited to the particular uses made by the C library.

We can view these routines as being much like C functions. We call a C function to do a particular task, and when it finishes, program control passes back to the calling function. The hidden mechanics involve telling the calling program the address in memory at which the function is stored. Control transfers to that address; meanwhile the address of the next instruction in the calling program is saved, so the program will know where to return to.

We can't use this exact method to access BIOS and DOS routines. A C program knows the addresses of its own functions because that is part of the compiler's job. It is not the compiler's job to keep track of the memory addresses holding the BIOS and DOS routines. Indeed, these addresses may change. For instance, sometimes routines are modified as bugs are found or as new circumstances develop.

Any program or device that uses the BIOS and DOS routines faces this same problem: the actual addresses may vary from system to system. The solution offered by Intel's designers resembles the use of pointers in C. Certain locations in memory, called *interrupt vectors,* are set aside to hold the addresses of the subroutines. If we want to use subroutine number 5, say, we go to the fifth interrupt vector, find the address stored there, then go to that address to find the routine. Another system may have the subroutine stored at a different location, but the interrupt vector storing the subroutine address will be at the same interrupt vector location. Figure 5-6 shows this correspondence.

Altogether, there are 256 interrupt vectors, although not all of them are used. Some contain addresses of BIOS subroutines, some contain addresses of DOS routines, and you can use some to store addresses of your own routines. Each interrupt vector consists of four bytes, because that many are required to specify an address completely. Interrupt vector 0 is at memory location 0, interrupt vector 1 is at memory location 4, and so on. The routine referenced by, say, interrupt vector 9, is called "interrupt service routine 9," or simply "interrupt 9."

Figure 5-6
Interrupt Vectors

System A		System B	
interrupt memory location	interrupt vector	interrupt memory location	interrupt vector
. . . . . .			
3 0012	F5 116	3 0012	F5 220
2 0008	F4 6A2	2 0008	F4 712
1 0004	F5 006	1 0004	F5 22B
0 0000	F4 ι12	0 0000	F4 112

interrupt 2 means look at location 0008, find F46A2, use routine at F46A2

interrupt 2 means look at loction 0008, find F4712, use routine at F4712

The address values used here are heuristic

One difference between these interrupt routines and functions that you write is that interrupts need not be invoked from a program; some can be generated by hardware. When you make a keystroke, for example, the keyboard processor issues a type 9 interrupt to inform the central processor that it has something to communicate. We will concentrate on the software use, however.

Interrupts, Assembly Language, and Registers

How do you use an interrupt? The system was developed for assembly language use, and to understand the contortions a C program must go through to use interrupts, we need to look at assembly language usage first. Our discussion will be in general terms, so you don't need to know assembly language to follow it.

The basic call in assembly language is quite simple. For instance, the following call invokes a type 9 interrupt:

```
int 9
```

But this is not the whole story. In general, additional information will have to be communicated between the calling program and the interrupt routine. This is done using registers.

Registers are the CPU's workspace. The 8088, for example, has four general purpose registers, four registers usually used for specifying addresses, four "segment" registers for keeping track of blocks of memory known as segments, and a "flag" register that keeps track of various status settings. Each register is 16 bits, and each of the 4 general-purpose registers also can be considered to be composed of 2 separate 8-bit registers.

An INT call usually requires that specific information be placed in specific registers before the call is made. Thus, the registers play the same role that arguments play in a C function call. Some INT calls place values in specific registers. This is like the C return facility except that the multiplicity of registers means an INT call can return more than one value.

The registers are named. The ones most often used in interrupt calls are the general registers AX, BX, CX, and DX. When working in the 8-bit mode, the AX register is subdivided into two parts: the AH, or high-byte register, and the AL, or low-byte register. Similar nomenclature holds for the other three registers. Figure 5–7 shows the registers' names.

For example, let's look at code to clear the screen. It makes use of the type 10h (0x10, or 16) interrupt. (The h suffix is used in assembly language

Figure 5–7
General Registers

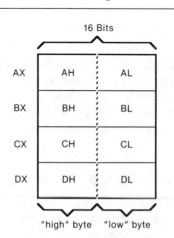

162

to indicate hexadecimal values.) This subroutine performs several screen-related functions, so first we have to specify which particular activity we want it to do. This is accomplished by placing a sub-subroutine number, or *function number,* in the AH register. We will use the scrolling function, which is number 6. So the assembly program will contain this line:

```
mov ah,6            ;scroll up function
```

The mov (for "move") command places the specified number into the named register. The semicolon marks a comment in assembly. We will instruct the function to scroll the entire screen (lines 0 through 24 and columns 0 through 79), using blank lines. An *attribute value* selects a "normal" blank. (A different value could be used to produce inverse video. We'll talk more about attributes in later chapters.) This information is provided to the interrupt function via other registers, as indicated next:

```
mov al,0            ;a blank screen
mov ch,0            ;upper row is row 0
mov cl,0            ;left column is column 0
mov dh,24           ;lower row is row 24
mov dl,79           ;right column is column 79
mov bh,7            ;blank line attribute
```

Finally, the interrupt request is made:

```
int 10h             ;video ROM call
```

In this case, no information is returned, so no further use is made of the registers.

Interrupts from IBM C

To make an interrupt request from C, we have supplied the same information to the registers that an assembler programmer would. This is difficult, for C does not give direct access to registers. But you can write a function in assembly language designed to take values from a C program and place them in the appropriate registers. The trick is to place the information in a C structure and then let the assembly language function transfer the information from the structure to the registers. We'll show you how later in the book, but IBM C already offers a selection of functions that do just that.

The Int86() Function—The function we'll use is called int86(). The *IBM C* manual summarizes it:

```
#include <dos.h>

int int86(intno, inregs, outregs)
int intno;
```

```
union REGS *inregs;
union REGS *outregs;
```

The *dos.h* file contains definitions used by the function. The `intno` variable is the number of the desired interrupt service, and `inregs` and `outregs` are pointers to memory areas used to hold ingoing and returned register values. The actual setup and use of the function to call an interrupt type 10h service would look something like this:

```
#include <dos.h>
    ...
union REGS in, out;
    ...
    /* fill in register values */
int(0x10, &in, &out);
```

In particular, note that the final two actual arguments consist of the address operator applied to appropriate unions.

The Regs Union—We can check the *dos.h* file to see how the `REGS` union is defined. Some of you, however, may want a quick review of unions first.

A *union* allows you to store more than one type of data in the same memory space. The syntax for creating unions is the same as for structures. The following, for example, creates a union capable of holding a `float` or a `char`:

```
union twotype {
              float somenumber;
              char zotcode;
              } ferret;
```

The portion within the brackets establishes a template describing the union. The `ferret` identifier creates a specific variable fitting this template. The identifier `twotype` is called a "tag" and can be used to declare other variables of the same type. That is, we now can do this:

```
union twotype weasel, *p;
```

This establishes a variable `weasel` of the `union twotype` type and a pointer variable p that can be assigned the address of such a union.

Access is by the membership operator. For instance,

```
ferret.somenumber = 10.2;
```

assigns the number 10.2 to the union, while

```
ferret.zotcode = 'B';
```

places the character B in the union.

The difference between a structure and a union is that if we defined a structure along the preceding lines, `somenumber` and `zotcode` would be assigned separate storage, and both values could be stored simultaneously. With a union, the same storage area is used; the size of the union is the size of the largest component member. Usually, then, it would be used to hold one or the other value, not both.

What would happen then, if we did the following?

```
ferret.somenumber = 28.3;
putchar( ferret.zotcode );
```

In this case, the number 28.3 would be stored in four-byte floating-point form in the union. The reference `ferret.zotcode` would refer to the first byte of the four, and `putchar()` would interpret whatever bits happened to be present in that byte as an ASCII code.

Obviously, the preceding example illustrates what not to do, since there is no meaningful correspondence between the two types of data stored in the union. Yet sometimes it is very convenient to do something very similar. Consider this set of definitions:

```
struct twobyte {
                unsigned char lowbyte;
                unsigned char highbyte;
                } ;
union twoway    {
                unsigned int n;
                struct twobite tb;
                };
union twoway data;
```

This union consists of two equal-sized possibilities: an `int` and a two-byte structure. Suppose we make this assignment:

```
data.n = 0x1230;
```

Then the integer 0x1230 is stored in the two bytes. On an IBM PC, the low-order byte is stored first, then the high-order byte. That is, the actual order of storage is 0x30,0x12. Now, to access the separate bytes, we can use the `twobyte` notation:

```
abyte = data.tb.highbyte;
```

This is an example of a data type *overlay*. The same data object, here 16 bits, can be subjected to two different data interpretations: a 16-bit integer, or two 8-bit integers. See Figure 5–8, which also shows another way to make the declarations.

Figure 5–8
A Union Overlay

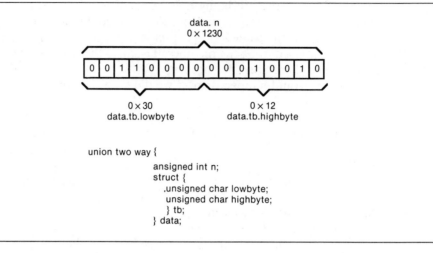

```
union two way {
        ansigned int n;
        struct {
           .unsigned char lowbyte;
           unsigned char highbyte;
           } tb;
        } data;
```

We mention overlays because the *dos.h* file includes definitions of this nature. Here they are, slightly annotated:

```
struct WORDREGS {    /* 16-bit registers */
        unsigned int ax;      /* AX register */
        unsigned int bx;
        unsigned int cx;
        unsigned int dx;
        unsigned int si;
        unsigned int di;
        unsigned int cflag;
        };

struct BYTEREGS {    /* 8-bit registers */
        unsigned char al, ah;    /* the AL, AH register pair /
        unsigned char bl, bh;
        unsigned char cl, ch;
        unsigned char dl, dh;
        };

union REGS {                    /* partial overlay */
        struct WORDREGS x;
        struct BYTEREGS h;
        };
```

This creates space to hold information for 7 16-bit registers. The space corresponding to the first four registers can be used either in the 16-bit mode by using the x member or in the 8-bit mode by using the h member.

A Clear-Screen Routine—Let's see how to use this union by writing a function to clear the screen. First, here is the original coding, in assembly language:

```
mov ah,6            ;scroll up function
mov al,0            ;a blank screen
mov ch,0            ;upper row is row 0
mov cl,0            ;left column is column 0
mov dh,24           ;lower row is row 24
mov dl,79           ;right column is column 79
mov bh,7            ;blank line attribute
int 10h             ;video ROM call
```

Here is a C function to do the same work:

```
#include <dos.h>
void clear()
{
    union REGS inreg, outreg;

    inreg.h.ah = 6;    /* initialize the registers */
    inreg.h.al = 0;
    inreg.h.ch = 0;
    inreg.h.cl = 0;
    inreg.h.dh = 24;
    inreg.h.dl = 79;
    inreg.h.bh = 7;
    int86(0x10, &inreg, &outreg);  /* request interrupt */
}
```

Note the close parallel to the assembly language version. Since this particular interrupt call provides no return values, no use was made of outreg other than completing int86()'s argument list.

More Cursor Control

The way to cursor control is clear now. All we need to do is to find which interrupt routine controls the cursor and what register values it requires. Then we can use int86() to invoke the interrupt. But where do we find the required information?

The primary source of information is the *IBM Technical Reference* manual. As we mentioned earlier, it contains the assembly language code for the BIOS routines. Embedded in the code are comments outlining the required information. Interrupt 10H turns out to be the one we want. It performs several functions. Table 5–3 outlines some of the functions and the register requirements. For the present, we'll go into just enough detail to let us do some cursor control.

Some Functions of the Interrupt 10H Service Routine

In each case in Table 5-3, which summarizes the Interrupt 10H functions, the number of the desired function is placed in register AH.

Table 5-3
Interrupt 10H Service Routine Functions

Function 0: Setting the Display Mode	
Register setup:	place 0 in AH
	place mode in AL
Mode	Interpretation
0	40 × 25 B/W
1	40 × 25 Color
2	80 × 25 B/W
3	80 × 25 Color
4	320 × 200 Color
5	320 × 200 B/W
6	640 × 200 B/W
7*	80 × 25 B/W

*Mode 7 is the monochrome adapter; the other modes use the color/graphics adapter.

Function 1: Setting the Cursor Type	
Register setup:	place 1 in AH
	place scan-line start in bits 4–0 CH
	place scan-line end in bits 4–0 CL

Function 2: Setting the Cursor Position

Register setup: place 2 in AH

place row number in DH

place column number in DL

place page number in BH

Function 3: Getting the Cursor Position

Register setup: place 3 in AH

place page number in BH

Returns: row number placed in DH

column number placed in DL

cursor type (see #1) placed in CH,CL

Function 5: Setting the Active Page

Register setup: place 5 in AH

place page value in AL

Function 6: Scrolling the Active Page Up

Register setup: place 6 in AH

place number of lines to scroll in AL

0 in AL produces a blank window

place blank line attribute in BH

place upper left row number in CH

Table 5–3 (cont.)

place upper left column number in CL

place lower right row number in DH

place lower right column number in DH

Function 15: Obtaining the Display Mode

Register setup:	place 15 in AH
Returns:	current mode is placed in AL
	number of columns placed in AH
	current active page placed in BH

These descriptions introduce a new concept, the "page." A page is a screen's worth of information. Many of the modes can store more than one page in video memory; Function 5 makes it simple and quick to switch from one display page to another. The monochrome mode, however, has just one page, page 0.

More Cursor Control

With this information at our disposal, we can construct additional cursor control functions. In particular, let's create C functions that can locate and position the cursor. With the aid of int86(), this is simple work:

```
#include <dos.h>
void setcurs(row, col, page)
unsigned char row, col, page;
{
    union REGS inreg, outreg;
    inreg.h.ah = 2;        /* interrupt 16 function #2 */
    inreg.h.dh = row;
    inreg.h.dl = col;
    inreg.h.bh = page;
    int86(0x10, &inreg, &outreg);
}

/* obtain cursor position */
void getcurs(pr, pc, page)
unsigned char *pr, *pc, page;
{
```

```
        union REGS inreg, outreg;

        inreg.h.ah = 3;       /* interrupt 16 function #3 */
        inreg.h.bh = page;
        int86(0x10, &inreg, &outreg);
        *pr = outreg.h.dh;    /* row number */
        *pc = outreg.h.dl;    /* column number */
}
```

With these functions, we can rewrite the cursor control program using interrupts instead of the *ansi.sys* escape sequences.

□ *Question 5–5* How would you rewrite the cursor control example using interrupts?

We have discussed interrupts in the context of cursor control, but clearly the scope of the interrupt technique is much greater. We'll return to this topic later as needed.

Ansi.sys versus BIOS Cursor Control

Which of the two methods should you use? The BIOS approach is a bit faster, and it doesn't require adding size to the operating system. The *ansi.sys* approach is easier to use. Perhaps a more important consideration is portability. The *ansi.sys* approach works with any DOS-compatible system. That is, it works with computers running under PC-DOS Versions 2.0 and later, or under MS-DOS Versions 2.0 and later. Note, however, that the *config.sys* file must contain the line

```
        device=ansi.sys
```

for the approach to work. The BIOS approach works with any ROM-compatible system. That is, it works with any computer using the IBM PC ROM or a compatible ROM.

Summary

Writing interactive programs poses many I/O problems. The buffered input provided by the standard I/O package is easy on the user, for it allows him or her to correct input before transmitting it. However, buffered input is flushed by pressing the RETURN key, and this adds a newline character to the input. Some functions, such as scanf() in its numerical modes, skip over empty space and newlines, but getchar() doesn't. Therefore, you should be attentive to what happens to these newlines.

Using scanf() to read numerical input can lead to problems when the input turns out to be non-numerical. But noting scanf()'s return value lets you trap non-numerical input and skip over it.

The standard I/O package functions `gets()` and `fgets()` are useful for reading string input. However, `gets()` offers no protection against overrunning allotted memory. The `fgets()` does offer protection but poses some programming problems of its own.

Using IBM's console I/O gives you more precise control over input. It is unbuffered, so keystrokes are acted upon immediately. If you wish to grant the user the ability to correct input, however, you must supply appropriate programming yourself.

With console I/O you can implement cursor control by using the *ansi.sys* program to translate certain escape sequences of characters to cursor instructions.

A much more powerful approach is to access directly the routines provided by the BIOS and by DOS. These routines are reached by using interrupts, which transfer program control to the routines. The interrupt technique was developed with assembly language in mind, but IBM C has several functions designed to use interrupts explicitly.

Answers to Questions in the Chapter

■ *5-1.* One way would be to redefine `LINES` to 24. Then, when the SPACE BAR is pressed, reset `lc` to 4 instead of to 0.

■ *5-2.* No. The `scanf("%20s", name)` call stops after 20 characters or the first whitespace, whichever comes first.

■ *5-3.* Here is one approach:

```
#include <stdio.h>
char *getline(str, n)
char *str;
int n;
{
  int ch;
  int ct = 0;

  while ( ct < n — 1 && (ch = getchar()) != EOF) && ch !='\n')
     str[ct++] = ch;
  str[ct] = '\B0';
  if ( ct == n — 1 ) /* if stopped because count exceeded */
  while ( (ch = getchar() ) != EOF && ch != '\n' )
        ;                /* skip to newline or EOF */
  if ( ch == EOF)
     {
  if ( ct != 0 )        /* EOF not first character */
        ungetc(ch,stdin); /* put it back */
     else
        return NULL; /* EOF found at beginning of line */
```

```
       }
   return str;
}
```

If you have a different version, try it out in the following test program:

```
#include <stdio.h>
#define SIZE 10
main()
{
  char stuff[SIZE];
  char *getline();

  while ( getline ( stuff, SIZE ) != NULL )
     puts(stuff);
  puts("bye");
}
```

Does your version do the following?

a. Echo the first nine characters of each input line on the next line.

b. Ignore characters after the first nine.

c. Stop if CTRL-Z is pressed at the beginning of a line.

d. If a CTRL-Z is, say, the sixth character, print the first five, then stop.

e. If a CTRL-Z is, say, the fifteenth character, print the first nine characters, then stop.

You may wish to analyze how our version meets these tests.

■   *5-4.*   The program can tell if the count was exceeded by noting whether or not the input string contains a newline. If it doesn't, then fgets() must have stopped because of the number limit. The program already tests for the newline, so we need to augment the else section, which deals with the case of of no newline. If the user wants to repeat, we back up by decrementing the index i.

```
#include <stdio.h>
#define MAXNUM 5
#define MAXLEN 13
#define ULINE '_'
void nchars();
char *strchr(), *fgets();
main()
{
int i = 0;
int count;
char names[MAXNUM][MAXLEN];
char *nlptr;
```

```c
printf("This program reads in names until you reach the ");
printf("program limit\n or press either RETURN or ");
printf("CTRL-Z at the beginning of a line.\n");
printf("Enter up to %d names:\n1> ", MAXNUM);
nchars(MAXLEN - 2, ULINE);
nchars(MAXLEN - 2, '\b');
while ( i < MAXNUM    &&
fgets(names[i], MAXLEN, stdin) != NULL
                              && names[i][0] != '\n' )
    {
    if ( ( nlptr = strchr(names[i], '\n')) != NULL )
        *nlptr = '\0';
    else
        {
          while ( getchar() != '\n' )
              ;
        printf("Too many letters--your entry was truncated. If ");
        printf("this is okay, press RETURN.\Otherwise, first ");
        printf("press the r-key to repeat your entry:\n");
          if ( getchar() != '\n')
              {
              i--;                /* back up an array */
              while ( getchar() != '\n')
                    ;             /* discard rest of response */
              }
        }
    if (++i < MAXNUM)
          {
          printf("%d> ", i + 1);
          nchars(MAXLEN - 2, ULINE);
          nchars(MAXLEN - 2, '\b');
          }
    }
printf("Here are the %d names you entered:\n", i );
for ( count = 0; count < i; count++)
   puts( names[count]);
}

void nchars ( n, ch)
int n;
char ch;
{
    while (n--)
        putchar(ch);
}
```

■ 5-5. Note that we can use the getcurs() and setcurs() functions to implement the more specific demands of the program. Also, we assume that just page 0 is used.

```c
/* intrpt.c--using interrupts for cursor control */
#include <conio.h>
#define STOP '\032'
#define PAGE 0
void clear(), getcurs(), setcurs(); /* in a separate file */
void home(), cursup(), cursl(), cursr(), cursdn();
main()
{
    int ch;

    clear();
    home();
    cprintf("Please begin:\n");
    while ( (ch = getch() ) != STOP)
      {
      if ( ch == 0)    /* 0 code */
         {
         ch = getch();
         switch ( ch )
             {
             case 68 : clear(); home; break;
             case 71 : home(); break;
             case 72 : cursup(); break;
             case 75 : cursl(); break;
             case 77 : cursr();   break;
             case 80 : cursdn(); break;
             }         /* end switch */
         }             /* end 0 code test */
      else if ( ch == '\r')
         cputs("\r\n");
      else if ( ch < 040 )
         {
         putch('^');
         putch ( ch | 0100 );
         }
      else
         putch ( ch );
      }
}

void home()
{
    setcurs(0,0, PAGE);
}
```

```
void cursup()
{
   unsigned char row, col;
   int status = 1;

   getcurs(&row,&col, PAGE);
   if ( row > 0 )
      setcurs(row -1, col, PAGE);
   else
       {
       setcurs(row,col, PAGE);
       status = 0;
       }
return status;
}

void cursl()
{
   unsigned char row, col;
   int status = 1;

   getcurs(&row,&col, PAGE);
   if ( col > 0 )
      setcurs(row, col - 1);
   else
       {
       setcurs(row,col, PAGE);
       status = 0;
       }
return status;
}

void cursr()
{
   unsigned char row, col;
   int status = 1;

   getcurs(&row,&col, PAGE);
   if ( col < 79 )
      setcurs(row, col + 1);
   else
       {
       setcurs(row,col, PAGE);
       status = 0;
       }
   return status;
```

```
        }

        void cursdn()
        {
            unsigned char row, col;
            int status = 1;

            getcurs(&row,&col, PAGE);
            if ( row < 24 )
                setcurs(row + 1, col, PAGE);
            else
                {
                setcurs(row,col, PAGE);
                status = 0;
                }
        return status;
        }
```

Exercises

1. Modify *show.c* so that in the multiple file case, it prints the name of a file before printing the file.

2. Write C functions that return and set the video mode; the setting function should take the mode as its argument. Also write a C function that returns the page number.

3. Start with string-reading program such as that in Question 5-4. Using *ansi.sys* escape sequences, modify the program so that the program begins by clearing the screen and so that the prompt and input always occur on the same line.

4. Repeat Exercise 2, using BIOS calls instead of *ansi.sys* escape sequences.

6

Using Your PC's Memory

- Memory models
- Static memory
- Stack memory
- Recursive functions
- Dynamic memory
- Linked lists
- Memory segments
- Far pointers
- Direct memory access to video display memory

Using Your PC's Memory

The computer's capability for remembering things is crucial to its success. Program code, text data, video screen representations, and more are stored in the computer's memory. In this chapter we will focus on how C programs use memory to store data.

Programs have several strategies at their disposal. External and static variables use *static* memory. Automatic variables use a form of *dynamic* memory called the *stack*. The memory allocation functions of the C library offer a second form of dynamic memory, one that a program can use to assign and free memory blocks from a memory pool. We'll look into all these approaches.

The IBM PC is based on the 8088 microprocessor chip. The architecture of this chip makes some parts of memory more difficult to access than others. We'll look at the PC's segmented memory structure and at how distant memory can be accessed by far pointers. We'll apply this technique to the video display.

Memory Models and Segments

The IBM C compiler offers several memory models for using the PC's memory. The 8088 chip breaks up memory into separate segments, and the memory models differ in the number of segments they can handle.

First, why are there segments? The 8088 chip uses processing elements called registers to hold data and addresses. The registers have 16 bits, a fact that limits the range of addresses a single register can hold to 64K. (A K equals 1 kilobyte, or 1024 bytes.) It is convenient, then, for the computer to work with blocks of memory no larger than 64K; for then the entire block can be accessed using a single address register. Such a block is called a *segment*. The 8088 has four *segment registers*. Each can locate the beginning of a segment, enabling the processor to use up to four segments of memory at a time. Other registers, called *pointer registers* and *index registers,* keep track of locations within a segment. These registers are said to hold "offset'' addresses, for they measure the offset of an address from the beginning of the segment. If more than four segments are needed, it becomes necessary to change the contents of the segment registers.

Memory models are plans for organizing the segments. IBM C, by default, uses the small-memory model. In it, one segment, called the *code segment* or the *text segment,* is used to hold the program code. A second segment, called the *data segment,* holds the program's data. This scheme limits a program to 64K of code and 64K of data. Other memory models allow the use of more code and data, but with the cost of additional running time. We'll discuss these other models later in the book, but for now we will stick to the small-memory model.

In the small-memory model, the location of the beginning of the code segment is kept in the CS (code segment) register. The beginning of the data segment is kept in the DS (data segment) register. The two segments can overlap. For example, if the code only needs 4K of code, the data segment can start 4K after the beginning of the text segment, giving a 60K overlap, as Figure 6-1 indicates. This poses no problem, because the code is not increasing or requiring additional memory. It does mean that the same physical memory location can be specified differently in the two segments.

Figure 6-1
Text and Data Segments

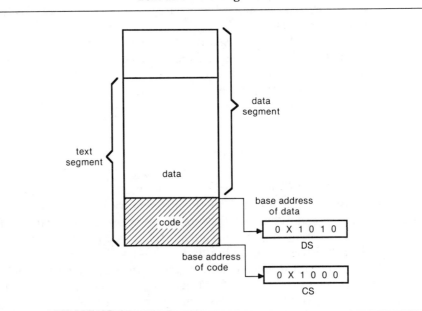

With the small-memory model, the various forms of memory that we will discuss all go into the same segment. Let's start with a look at static memory.

Static Memory

Static memory is the simplest to understand. When you declare a variable so that it is an external or a static variable, the compiler assigns it a particular storage space in memory. When the program is loaded into memory, the storage for the variable is created. As long as the program continues to run, that memory assignment remains in effect. Such memory is called static because it is stationary and stays put.

IBM C places static memory near the bottom (at the low address end) of the data segment. This means it comes just after the program code (but conceptually in a different segment).

Stack Memory

It is not always feasible or desirable to assign memory locations in advance. Consider automatic variables, for example. As you recall, an automatic variable is created when the function containing it is called, and it is allowed to die when the function call ends. One advantage of this approach is that memory is used only when it is needed. Also, as we will see, it makes recursive function calls possible. With automatic variables, in essence, a section of memory is set aside as a scratch pad; the same memory location can be used successively for different variables.

The tool used to implement this scratch pad approach is the stack. The stack imposes an order on the creation and expiration of variables. Conceptually, it works like this. Part of the memory is specified as the stack segment. The beginning address is stored in the SS (for stack segment) register. A second register, called the *stack pointer,* or *SP,* stores an "offset" from the base address. That is, if SP holds the value 4000, then it refers to an address 4000 greater than the stack base. The first item placed in the stack is put in the address indicated by SP. The next item added to the stack is put in the next location, and so on. The last item added is said to be at the "top of the stack." The stack pointer is always set to point to the top item.

When elements are removed from the stack, they are removed from the top. Thus, the last item added is the first item removed. This pattern is termed *LIFO,* for "last in, first out." This sequence makes splendid sense in terms of function calls, for if function A() calls function B(), and function B() calls C(), the automatic variables for these functions are created and placed on the stack in the order that the functions are called. Furthermore, function A() cannot quit until B() returns to it, and B() cannot quit until C() returns to it. Thus, the automatic variables have to be disposed of in the opposite order of their creation: last created, first destroyed. Again, the sequence corresponds to that of stack operations.

The stack implementation has one peculiarity; it is upside down. That is, the stack pointer starts at a relatively high address and additional items are placed at progressively lower addresses. See Figure 6–2.

In the small-memory model, the stack segment (SS) and data segment (DS) registers are set to the same value. This is convenient, because it places

183

Figure 6–2
A Stack

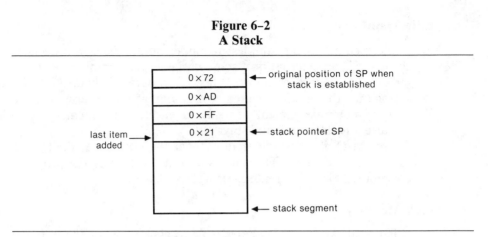

both kinds of data in the same segment. On the other hand, there is the possibility of the stack expanding into the static data area. To handle the problem, IBM C's linker determines the amount of static memory needed, then it sets up the stack. By default, it allocates 2048 bytes to the stack, and the stack pointer (SP) is set to an address high enough (as represented in Figure 6–3) that a 2048-byte stack won't extend into static memory.

Figure 6–3
Stack and Static Memory

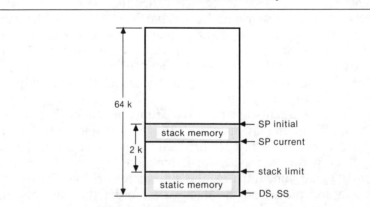

An internal library function call _chkstk() is incorporated into a C program; when more stack space is needed, it checks to see that the limit is not exceeded. If it is, the program halts and lets you know that you have run out of stack space.

You can use the linker **/STACK** option to override the default size. It can be used with clink or with cc:

```
clink /STACK:4000 porf
cc /STACK:1024 pingo
```

The first creates a 4000-byte stack, and the second creates a 1024-byte stack.

Recursive Functions

One of the best illustrations of the stack is the recursive function. In C, a function can call itself; that is what is meant by recursion. Each time a function calls itself, a new set of automatic variables is created and added to the stack. At some point (we hope), the sequence of recursive calls ends. Then each version of the function should return to the version that called it. Every function call must be balanced by a function return; control does not suddenly pass from the final call back to the original call. Similarly, the automatic variables created must be removed from the stack in the usual LIFO order. Understanding stack operations helps us to understand recursion.

An Exercise in Recursion

We can make these concepts more visible with an example. The recur() function will create an automatic variable and print out its value and address. It will call itself repeatedly until a certain test is met, printing the value and address of its automatic variable. To add a little spice, we'll also print the address of an external variable and of the function. Here is the code:

```
/* recur.c--demonstrates properties of recursion */
long level = 1;     /* an external variable */
main()
{
      long n;               /* an automatic variable */
      void recur();

      printf("Enter number of recursions >> ");
      scanf("%ld", &n);
      printf("recursion limit of %ld stored at %u\n", n, &n);
      printf("recursion level stored at %u\n", &level);
      printf("recur() function starts at %u\n", recur);
      recur( n - 1 );
      printf("Done\n");
}

void recur ( n )
long n;                 /* another automatic variable */
{
      printf("down recursion level %ld: n = %ld; &n = %u\n",
```

```
                                                level++, n, &n);
            if (n)
                recur ( n - 1);       /* a recursive call */
            printf("up recursion level %ld: n = %ld; &n = %u\n",
                                                --level, n, &n);
            return;
        }
```

The overall plan is to request from the user the number of recursions desired. This number is the argument for the first call to recur(). Then recur() subtracts one from its original argument for each subsequent call. When the argument reaches 0, recursion ends, and the various levels of recur() calls begin returning.

Note that the name of a function is a pointer to the function. We used this fact to print out the location of the beginning of the recur() function.

Perhaps we should point out that each call to recur() uses the same section of code; merely the variables change. That is, the program is stored in the code segment. Each call to the function runs the program through the same set of instructions in the code segment. But each call also adds a new n to the stack in the data segment.

Here is a sample run:

```
Enter number of recursions >> 5
recursion limit of 5 stored at 4050
recursion level stored at 220
recur() function starts at 106
down recursion level 1: n = 5; &n = 4046
down recursion level 2: n = 4; &n = 4038
down recursion level 3: n = 3; &n = 4030
down recursion level 4: n = 2; &n = 4022
down recursion level 5: n = 1; &n = 4014
down recursion level 6: n = 0; &n = 4006
up recursion level 5: n = 1; &n = 4014
up recursion level 4: n = 2; &n = 4022
up recursion level 3: n = 3; &n = 4030
up recursion level 2: n = 4; &n = 4038
up recursion level 1: n = 5; &n = 4046
Done
```

Let's go through this step-by-step, for it illustrates several important points. First, after responding to the prompt by entering 5, we find that it is stored at location 4050. This is the top of the stack and is labeled n in main(). Next, we find the external variable level is stored at 220 and the beginning of recur()'s code at 106. These addresses are not as close to each other as this sounds. The 220 value is measured from the beginning of the data segment, and the 106 is measured from the beginning of the code section. That is, both are relative addresses, measured as an offset from the beginnings of their respective memory segments.

Much of the space between 200 and 4050 is empty space available for the stack. (The compiler sets up other static sections of memory in addition to the one used to store the level variable, so some of the space is used for them.) Figure 6–4 shows the high address areas for the stack.

Figure 6–4
Memory Use for Recur()

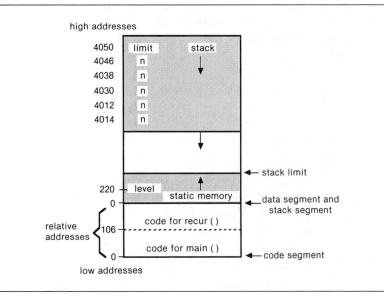

Then we have the first call to recur(), the one made by main(). The argument n − 1 has the numerical value 4, so 4 is passed to the function. The first statement in recur() prints out the level, using the external level variable. Then level is incremented. Next, the program prints the value (4) and address of the formal argument, also called n. We see the address is 4046, which is four bytes less than 4050. This makes sense, because a long variable occupies four bytes. This new n now is at the "top" of the stack.

The next statement calls recur() with an argument of 3, since that is what n − 1 evaluates to. Once again a new variable is created and added to the stack. Now there are three distinct variables called n. Each has its own value and its own address. Once again printf() is called upon. This time the value of level is 2. Because level is an external variable, the incrementing that took place in the previous call to recur() still holds. The rest of the printed line reflects the value and location of the newest n variable.

Note that the new n has an address eight bytes less than the preceding

187

n. Four of those bytes hold the preceding n. The other four bytes are used for bookkeeping purposes when a function call is made; we'll see the details in Chapter 11.

The process continues until the current n reaches a value of 0. At this level of call (level 5) the if test fails, and the level 5 call is able to proceed to the second printf() statement. It prints the n value and the address again, and next the return statement is reached. The level 5 call, then, is the first call to reach completion. Control is transferred to the function that called it, the level 4 call. The level 5 variables are removed from the stack, and the level 4 prints out the value and address of the level 4 n. Then control returns to level 3, and the process continues until control reaches main() once again. Figure 6–5 shows the stack for these changes. (For simplicity, we just show the n values and ignore the other uses made of the stack.)

Figure 6–5
Stack History

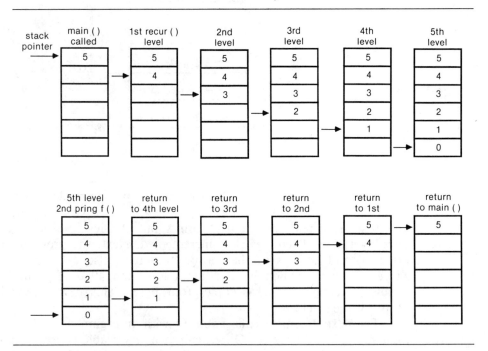

Sometimes recursion is used instead of a loop. The main disadvantage to this approach is that a high level of recursion could run out of stack space. But it does have some advantages. Notice that actions coming between the program beginning and the recursive call are executed in order of the calls. But actions coming between the recursive call and the function return are executed in the opposite order of the function calls. This is because returns are in the opposite order from the calls—LIFO once again.

Using Recursion for Base Conversions

This backward order of operations is appropriate for certain programming problems. Consider, for example, the problem of number base conversions. The usual algorithm for making the conversion calculates the last digit first. A nonrecursive routine would have to store each digit of the conversion process, then print them out in reverse order. Using recursion, however, the calculation can be done before the recursive call and the printing can be done afterward. This would calculate the new digits from right to left, but print them out from left to right, the desired order.

Let's run through the algorithm, then prepare a recursive program. How could we convert 39, for example, to base 8? One method would divide 39 by 8 and note the remainder. For instance, 8 goes into 39 four times, with a remainder of 7. Thus, 39 is 4 × 8 + 7, implying the octal representation is 47. This contains the basis of the algorithm: divide the number by the base. The integer quotient is the number of 8's, and the remainder is the number of ones. Use integer division for the first part, and use the modulus operator to get the remainder.

Suppose there are more than 7 8's? Then repeat the process on the quotient. The remainder will be the number of 8's, and the new quotient the number of 64's, the next power of 8. For example, let's convert 372 to octal:

First Cycle:

372 / 8 = 46   (integer division)

372 % 8 = 4   ➝   the final digit is 4

Second Cycle:

46 / 8 = 5

46 % 8 = 6   ➝   the next digit is 6

Third Cycle:

5 / 8 = 0

5 % 8 = 5   ➝   the next digit is 5

Fourth Cycle:

0 / 8 = 0   no more digits to convert

The final conversion, then, is 564 octal.

We worked through the algorithm in a way to suggest the programming approach. First, divide the number by the base, obtaining the quotient and the modulus. Then apply the same procedure to the quotient, repeating until a 0 quotient is reached. Here is the same idea, worked into a recursive program:

```
/* baseconv.c--driver for the express() function */
#include <stdio.h>
#define TRUE 1
#define FALSE 0
void express();
main()
{
  long number;
  int base;
  int done = FALSE; /* set to true if non-numeric base is */
                                             /* entered */
  puts("This program converts integers to various bases.");
  puts("Use non-numeric input to terminate the program.");
  puts("Enter the number:");
  while ( !done    && (scanf("%ld", &number) == 1) )
     {
       puts("Enter the base: (2-16)");
       if ( scanf("%d", &base) == 1 )
           {
             express(number,base );
             puts("\nNext number:");
           }
       else
           done = TRUE;
     }
}


/* express.c--a recursive function for base changes */
#define RANGE 16
void express ( n, b)
long n;
int b;
{
    static char digits[RANGE+1] = "0123456789ABCDEF";
                /* choice of digit values */

    if (b < 2 || b > RANGE )
        printf("%d is not an acceptable base value\n", b);
    else if ( n < 0 )        /* process negative numbers */
        {
        putchar('-');
        express ( -n, b);
        }
    else
        {
        if ( n >= b )
            express ( n / b, b);
```

```
        putchar ( digits[n % b] ); /* after recursive call */
        }
    return;
}
```

Notice how in the final `else` expression the digit is printed after the recursive call. As we saw, this causes the digits to be printed in the reverse order of calculation. We want to print them this way, because the last digit is found first. Next, note how the expression `n % b` is used as an index for an array. This is a simple method for converting the numerical value 7 to the character 7, the numerical value 12 to the character B, and so on.

□ *Question 6-1* In the `if` statement that checks for negative numbers, the print statement comes before the recursive call. Why?

Here is a sample run:

```
A>baseconv
This program converts integers to various bases.
Use non-numeric input to terminate the program.
Enter the number:
2000000001
Enter the base: (2-16)
2
1110111001101011001010000000001
Next number:
63
Enter the base: (2-16)
16
3F
Next number:
167
Enter the base: (2-16)
11
142
Next number:
q

A>
```

Dynamic Memory Allocation

The stack is an example of dynamic memory, that is, of memory assignments that are determined and changed as a program runs. Often, however, dynamic memory allocation refers to a different strategy of memory management, namely, requesting and disposing of memory as needed. The C library offers several functions to do this, including `malloc()` to allocate memory, and `free()` to release memory back to the memory pool. With this approach, the LIFO dictum need not apply; memory can be freed in any order you desire or not at all.

Memory allocation of this form is more suitable than static or stack memory for many applications. For example, a program may wish to read in sets of data, and the amount of input may not be known in advance. Instead of explicitly declaring enough space to handle the worst expected case, a program can use just what memory it needs. Or a program may need to allocate and free space in some nonstacklike order. For instance, a program that showed multiple windows on a screen would delete window data when a particular window is closed.

In IBM C, the portion of the data segment above the stack is used for this form of dynamically allocated memory.

The Malloc() Function

The primary memory allocation function is `malloc()`. It takes one argument—the number of bytes of memory desired. It returns the address of the beginning of the block. The size of the block may be larger than requested to allow the block to meet maintenance needs and alignment requirements (it can't start and end at arbitrary addresses). The function is declared to be of type pointer-to-`char`, but the return value should be type cast to correspond to the type of data object to be stored. Here is an example:

```
char *malloc();
struct fort {                    /* define a structure */
            int sides;
            long cost;
            char name[20];
            };
struct fort *pf;                 /* create a pointer variable */
   ...
pf = (struct fort *) malloc ( sizeof (struct fort) );
```

Here `sizeof (fort)` is 26 bytes, so `malloc()` returns the address of a free block of memory at least 26 bytes long. The address is type cast into a structure address and assigned to the `pf` pointer. Once this assignment has been made, we can, for example, use `pf->sides` to refer to the `sides` member of the structure.

The Free() Function

If you no longer need this particular structure, you can enter:

```
free(pf);
```

This returns the block to the memory pool, and the bytes now can be assigned new duties by a new call to malloc(). The pf pointer must point to memory previously allocated by malloc() or by its cousins calloc() or realloc().

The calloc() function not only allocates memory, it initializes them to 0. The realloc() function adjusts the size of a previously allocated block. If there is no room to add new memory contiguously, it finds sufficient contiguous memory elsewhere and copies the contents of the old block to the new location. We won't be using these functions, but it's nice to know they are there if we need them.

Important Pointers

Hold on to the pointer returned by malloc(). It is your only guide to where the memory block is.

☐ *Question 6-2* What is wrong with this code?

```
for ( i = 0; i < LIM; i++)
    pf = (struct fort *) malloc ( sizeof (struct fort) );
```

Given that you have a pointer to a block of memory, how do you use the pointer? This is one place the rules you learned about pointer operations come in handy. Let's look at some examples. Suppose you obtained a pointer to one of the basic data types, such as an int. Then use the pointer when an address is needed and use the indirect value operator when a value is needed.

```
char *malloc();
int *pi;
int x,y;
  ...
pi = (int *) malloc( sizeof (int) );
scanf("%d", pi);   /* scanf() needs an address as argument */
y = x * 5 + *pi *2;  /* use value */
```

Note that until malloc() is called, pi is a variable with no value; the call to malloc() assigns it an address. Now pi holds the address of an int-sized block of memory. At this point, that block contains nothing of value. It is up to the program to place something there. That occurs when scanf() reads a value and places it in the location that pi points to. Once that is done, we can use *pi to indicate the value stored there; that occurs in the last line of the program fragment. In short, we must assign an address to the pointer and place data at the address before using *pi.

For a second example, let's create space for an array and initialize its elements:

```
char *malloc();
```

```
int *pai;
int i, size;
  ...
scanf("%d", &size);
pai = (int *) malloc( size * sizeof (int) );
pai[0] = 1;
for ( i = 1; i < size; i++ )
  pai[i] = pai[i-1] * 2;
```

Remember, the name of an array is a pointer to the first element of an array, and a pointer to the first element of an array can be treated as a name of an array.

Let's try a complete, if simple, program. The object is to read in a first and last name and allocate just the right amount of storage to hold each one. We use a large temporary array to read in the names, then use malloc() to create more suitable storage. The strcpy() function takes two string addresses as arguments and copies the string found at the second address to the first address. Our memory allocation ensures there is sufficient memory space to hold the string. Here is the program:

```
/* memname.c--uses malloc() to remember names */
#include <stdio.h>
#define ARSIZE 80
main()
{
    char temp[ARSIZE];
    char *fname, *lname;
    char *malloc();

    printf("Enter your first name >> ");
    gets(temp);
    fname = malloc ( strlen(temp) + 1);    /* extra byte for 0 */
    strcpy(fname,temp);
    printf("Enter your last name >> ");
    gets(temp);
    strcpy( lname = malloc ( strlen(temp) + 1), temp);
    printf("Your fame has preceded you, %s %s\n",
                                        fname, lname);
    printf("I am too amazed to continue. Bye.\n");
}
```

The strlen() function gives the number of characters in a string. We add one to this value since the allocated memory will have to hold a terminating null character as well as the counted characters. Note that for the last name, we combined allocation and copying into one statement. In C, the value of an assignment expression, such as

```
lname = malloc( strlen(temp) + 1)
```

is the value of the left-hand member, here lname, which is the destination address. So

```
strcpy( lname = malloc ( strlen(temp) + 1), temp);
```

allocates the required number of bytes, assigns the address of the block to lname, then copies the contents of temp array to that address.

Here is a sample run:

```
A>memname
Enter your first name >> Bingo
Enter your last name >> Toffle-Twiggens
Your fame has preceded you, Bingo Toffle-Twiggens
I am too amazed to continue. Bye.
```

☐ *Question 6-3* What would happen if we eliminated from the program the statement in which malloc() gives fname an address?

The space we used for temp and for storing the two names probably is less than would have been required by using two predefined arrays of 80 bytes each, but the difference is not great. The real payoff comes when a large amount of input is processed. We wouldn't, for instance, need to declare a thousand 80-byte arrays on the off chance that some one would enter a thousand names.

But using malloc() repeatedly presents a new problem: how do we keep track of all the allocated blocks? Our program used two predefined pointers because it expected two names. What if a hundred or a thousand names are expected. We could create an array of a thousand pointers, and that would let us read and allocate memory for up to a thousand names. But this approach still commits the program to a predefined maximum input. Also, it is not very elegant. A better approach is to use malloc() to create space for new pointers as well as new input. But then how do we keep track of the new pointers? The answer is to use structures.

Structures and Pointers

First, let's review again some properties of structures and pointers. (Chapter 2 also contains such a summary.) A structure definition has three parts: the tag, the template, and the variable list. The template establishes a particular scheme for storing data. The tag establishes an identifier that can be used to declare other structure variables using the same template. The variable list establishes particular variables that use the template. Either the tag or the variable list can be omitted, but not both. Here is a sample declaration:

```
struct vege {
```

```
        char name[20];
        float price;
        int aisle;
        } potato;

struct vege yam, onions, *pv;
```

This establishes `potato` as a structure of the `vege` form; `potato` is an "aggregate variable," meaning it contains more than one item of information. The tag `vege` is used to declare another variable (`yam`), an array of structures (`onions`), and a pointer to a structure (`pv`). Figure 6-6 illustrates the parts of a structure definition.

Figure 6-6
A Structure Definition

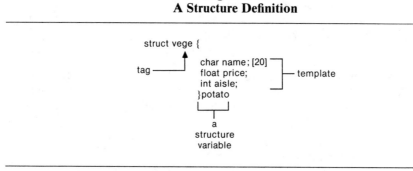

The membership operator (a period) is used to access individual members of a structure. Thus, `potato.aisle` is the `aisle` component, and so on. The type of an expression such as `potato.aisle` is the type of the rightmost member. This means `potato.aisle` can be used like any other `int`. All of the following are valid uses:

```
potato.aisle = 13;
scanf("%d", &potato.aisle);    /* use address of int */
printf("%d %d\n", potato.aisle,  111 % potato.aisle);
```

Similarly, `potato.name` is the name of a 20-`char` array and can be used like other array names. For instance, the following are valid uses:

```
scanf("%s", potato.name); /* array name is an address */
printf("%s is on aisle %d\n", potato.name, potato.aisle);
potato.name[0] = 'P';   /* 1st element of array */
```

Structure members also can be accessed using a pointer to the structure. Suppose we have this assignment:

```
pv = &potato;   /* structure address assigned to pointer */
```

Note that the name of a structure is *not* the address of the structure; we must use the address operator to obtain the address. We have two ways to use the pointer to access, say, the `aisle` member. First, we can use the indirect value operator. If `pv` points to a structure, then `*pv` is the semantic equivalent of a structure name. So we can use `(*pv).aisle` to represent the member. The parentheses are needed to overcome the higher precedence of the membership operator.

The second approach is to use a new operator, the indirect membership operator. The operator is constructed from a hyphen and a greater-than symbol; it looks like this: `->`. To indicate the `aisle` member, we would use this expression: `pv->aisle`. This is simpler than using the `(*pv).` combination. In short, use the membership operator if you are using a structure name; use the indirect membership operator if you are using a pointer to a structure. In either case, as Figure 6–7 shows, the final expression has the same type as the rightmost identifier. Thus, `pv` is a pointer, but `pv->aisle` is an `int`.

Figure 6–7
Direct and Indirect Membership

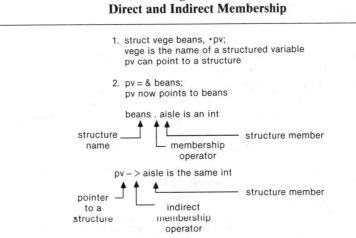

Saving Input in a Linked List

Before this digression on structures we discussed using `malloc()` to create storage not only for data being read in, but also for pointers to that data. One approach is to create a series of structures. Each structure will contain two pointers. One pointer will point to the input item, and the second pointer will point to the next structure. This creates a "linked list," with each structure linked to the next by a pointer. Figure 6–8 illustrates the concept of the linked list.

Figure 6–8
A Linked List

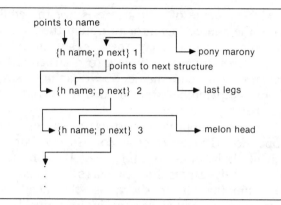

We'll need a way to identify the final structure in the list; a simple way is to assign the NULL pointer to the pointer to the next structure.

To implement this approach, we'll use malloc() twice each input cycle. One call will set up storage for the input, and the second call will set up a structure. Each time a new structure is created, its address will be assigned to the corresponding pointer in the previous structure.

The following shows how this looks:

```
/* horses.c--collects and displays horse names */
#include <stdio.h>
#define ARSIZE 80
char *s1 = "Please enter a horse name. To stop, enter ^Z";
char *s2 = "or press [return] at the beginning of a line.";
char *s3 = "Please enter next name. To stop, enter ^Z";
#define PROMPT(X)   printf("%s\n%s\n", X, s2);
struct horses {
            char *hname;
            struct horses *pnext;
          };
typedef struct horses HORSE, *HORSEPTR;
char *getline();   /* user-defined */
char *malloc();    /* from the library */

main()
{
    char temp[ARSIZE];
    HORSEPTR pfirst, pprev, pnow;
    int count = 0;

    PROMPT(s1);
    pprev = (HORSEPTR) NULL;  /* signifies no input */
```

```
    while ( (getline (temp,ARSIZE) != NULL) && temp[0] != '0')
        {
        pnow = ( HORSEPTR) malloc ( sizeof( HORSE ) );
        if (pprev == (HORSEPTR) NULL )
             pfirst = pnow;     /* remember first one */
        else
            pprev->pnext = pnow;   /* put address in last strct */
        pnow->hname = malloc ( strlen(temp) + 1);
        strcpy(pnow->hname, temp);
        pnow->pnext = (HORSEPTR) NULL;  /* mark current list end */
        pprev = pnow;
        PROMPT(s3);
        }
    if (pprev == (HORSEPTR) NULL )
        puts("No horses--bye.");
    else
        {
        puts("And here they are!");
        pnow = pfirst;
        do {
            printf("%3d> %s\n", ++count, pnow->hname);
            pnow = pnow->pnext;
            } while ( pnow != (HORSEPTR) NULL);
        }
}


char *getline( s, n )
char *s;
int n;
{
    int ch;
    int ct = 0;

    while ( ct < n - 1 && ((ch = getchar()) != EOF) && ch !='\n')
        s[ct++] = ch;
    s[ct] = '\0';
    if ( ct == n - 1 )
        while (   (ch = getchar() ) != EOF && ch != '\n')
             ;      /* process rest of input line */
    if ( ch == EOF)
        {
        if ( ct > 0 )
            ungetc(ch,stdin);
        else
            return NULL;
        }
```

```
        return s;
}
```

Here is a sample run:

```
Please enter a horse name. To stop, enter ^Z
or press [return] at the beginning of a line.
Flying Fool
Please enter next name. To stop, enter ^Z
or press [return] at the beginning of a line.
Pretty Pauper
Please enter next name. To stop, enter ^Z
or press [return] at the beginning of a line.
Grindlestone
Please enter next name. To stop, enter ^Z
or press [return] at the beginning of a line.
Odd Corpuscle
Please enter next name. To stop, enter ^Z
or press [return] at the beginning of a line.
[RETURN]
And here they are!
  1> Flying Fool
  2> Pretty Pauper
  3> Grindlestone
  4> Odd Corpuscle
```

Analyzing the Program

As usual, there are several points to note. First, we've used the preprocessor to define a convenient macro for printing the prompts. To modify the prompts, we merely need to redefine the strings s1, s2, and s3. (See Chapter 2 for a review of the char pointer technique of initializing strings.) Within the program, X is replaced by s1 or s3, as indicated.

Other important points are the definition of the horses structure template, the use of typedef to simplify declarations and type casts, and the techniques used process the linked structures. We'll look at these points in turn.

The Horses Structure—A key feature is this definition:

```
struct horses {
            char *hname;
            struct horses *pnext;
          };
```

Note that it is okay to use a pointer to a structure type as a member of a structure of the same type. That is, the horse structure has a member that is a pointer to a `horse` structure. This feature is what makes the linked structure system work. The `hname` member of the structure will be used to point to the string containing a name, while the `pnext` member will hold the address of the next structure.

Incidentally, the following recursive definition is not allowed:

```
struct thing {              /* NO! A structure cannot contain */
          char *tname;         /* an example of */
          struct thing nthing;    /* itself */
          };
```

Using Typedef—We have used C's `typedef` feature to establish aliases for the types `struct horses` and pointer-to-`struct horses`. This is convenient, because the program uses these types several times. If you are not familiar with `typedef`, here is how it works. Choose the names you want as identifiers. We chose `HORSE` for type `struct horses`, and `HORSEPTR` for a pointer to that structure. Next, declare the identifiers as if they were variables of the intended type. Then prefix the declaration with the keyword `typedef`. That is what we did. As a result, we could use `HORSEPTR` in the program instead of `struct horses *`. The `typedef` facility does not create new types, it just gives a more convenient way of expressing types. We used uppercase letters to indicate that the identifiers were aliases.

Don't confuse `typedef` with the preprocessor `#define`. The latter sets up string substitutions that take place before compilation. It is as if you typed out the `#define` definitions wherever they are used. The `typedef` process is executed by the compiler itself. It is a bit more awkward to use than a `#define` but is more versatile as far as type declarations go.

□ *Question 6-4* How could you use `#define` to establish an alias for the type `struct horses`? Could you also use it for a pointer to that type?

Processing the Linked Structures—It is important to realize that the linking system works only one way. Each structure contains information about the next structure, but not about the preceding one. For this reason we should keep track of the address of the first structure, for that starts us at the correct end of the list. The `pfirst` pointer performs that service.

Also, each structure starts off with its `pnext` member initialized to `NULL`. That way, if no further structures are created, the `NULL` will mark it as the final structure. But when a new structure is created, we have to go back and assign its address to the `pnext` member of the previous structure. To accomplish this, the program maintains one pointer to the new structure (`pnow`) and one to the previous structure (`pprev`). Once the new structure is set up, its address (`pnow`) is placed in the structure pointed to by `pprev`:

```
pprev->pnext = pnow;
```

Thus, the `pnext` component of the structure pointed to by `pprev` now points to the current structure. Once that linkage is accomplished, then `pprev` is updated to point to the new structure in order to ready it for the next cycle:

```
pprev = pnow;
```

This reassignment causes `pprev` to refer now to the latest name, with `pprev->next` pointing to `NULL`. Of course, the first time through there is no previous structure, so `pprev` is initialized to `NULL`. Also, within the read loop, a `NULL` value indicates the first cycle; this tells the program when to initialize `pfirst`.

In the program, we type cast `NULL` to `HORSEPTR` for self-consistency. However, this is not necessary, because the compiler accepts comparisons of pointers of any type with `NULL`.

We can use `malloc()` to allocate memory for the input and for the structures using the methods we discussed with the *memname.c* example earlier in this chapter.

The `getline()` function, which we examined in Question 5-3, avoids some of the problems of `gets()` (overrunning memory) and of `fgets()` (including a newline).

The code for printing out the input is interesting, for it demonstrates how to move through a linked list. Here is the code again:

```
pnow = pfirst;
    do {
        printf("%3d> %s\n", ++count, pnow->hname);
        pnow = pnow->pnext;
        } while ( pnow != NULL);
```

First, `pnow` is initialized to `pfirst`. The `pnow->hname` pointer is used to indicate which string to print, then `pnow` is set to `pnow->pnext`, which is the address of the next structure. This continues until the structure containing the `NULL` pointer is processed. The do `while` loop makes sure the processing goes through and not just to the final structure. The earlier check of `pprev`'s value guarantees that the loop is not entered unless there is at least one structure.

> ☐ *Question 6-5* Couldn't we have used `pfirst` directly in the final loop instead of assigning its value to `pnow`?

The singly linked list is fine for the purposes of this program. If, however, you wish to sort the list or add a deletion capability, you will find a doubly linked list easier to work with. With that data form, each structure would contain a pointer to the next structure and a pointer to the previous one.

Saving the Data

We want to do more with the data than just reprint it! One avenue is to add features such as sorting or deleting. Another fruitful activity is saving the information in a file; certainly that is the essential function of many programs.

Using a Record Separator—There are several ways to save the data. One is to use a regular text file, using `fputs()` or `fprintf()`. That would work fine with our example, for the data are text strings. The chief consideration is storing them in a way that allows for easy retrieval. For instance, this would not do:

```
fprintf(fp, "%s", pnow->hname);
```

The problem here is that one string would run into the next, and a program trying to read the file would not be able to tell where one string ends and another starts. (Neither `fputs()` nor `fprintf()` passes on the terminating null character.)

One solution is to provide a "record separator." Each basic data unit, here a string, constitutes a record. The separator should be a character that would not occur in the string. A null character would be one possibility, but a better choice would be the newline character, since we already have functions that use the newline character to mark the end of a read.

The record separator technique, however, won't work for binary files for the same reason that CTRL-Z fails as an end-of-file marker for them: the ASCII value of any character could be a legitimate item of binary data. Let's see, then, if we can come up with a technique that is more general than the record separator.

Uniform Binary Records—Perhaps the simplest method is to use storage blocks of uniform size. For example, if the file is opened in binary format, we could do something along these lines:

```
strcpy(temp, pnow->hname);
fwrite( temp, sizeof (temp), 1, fp);
```

Recall that the first argument to `fwrite()` is the address from where data writing starts, the second argument is the number of bytes to be read as a block, the third item is the number of blocks to be read, and the final argument is the file identifier provided by `fopen()`. Here `temp` is the 80-character array we defined earlier. Incidentally, we could use the same method with an `open()`ed file and `write()`.

This method has three advantages. First, it is easy to read the material back:

```
fread(temp, sizeof (temp), 1, fp);
```

Because all the blocks are the same size (80 bytes), this can be done repeatedly, reading one record at time. Second, the method is easily generalized to structures: just use the structure address and the structure size. Third, it is simple.

The main disadvantage is that this method potentially wastes storage space.

Variable-Size Records—We'll try a third method, using variable-size records. The idea here is to store the record's size within each record. The reading program will first read the size of the rest of the record, then read a chunk of that size. For simplicity, we've placed the writing and the reading processes in two separate programs. If you are interested, however, you can try combining them into one, writing functions to handle the main tasks.

Following is the code for the file-writing program. It is a slightly altered version of *horses.c*. As usual, we have tried to concentrate on the essentials of the process and have avoided going off on a lengthy error-checking tangent. Note the prime feature—how it uses fwrite() to store first the string size, then the string.

```
/* horsefile.c--puts horse names into a file */
#include <stdio.h>
#define ARSIZE 80
char *s1 = "Please enter a horse name. To stop, enter ^Z";
char *s2 = "or press [return] at the beginning of a line.";
char *s3 = "Please enter the next name. To stop, enter ^Z";
#define PROMPT(X) printf("%s\n%s\n", X, s2);
struct horses {
                char *hname;
                struct horses *pnext;
              };
typedef struct horses HORSE, *HORSEPTR;
char *getline();
char *malloc();

main()
{
    char temp[ARSIZE];
    HORSEPTR pfirst, pprev, pnow;
    int count = 0;
    int recsize;
    FILE *fp;

    if ( (fp = fopen("horse.dat","ab")) == NULL )
        {
        fprintf(stderr,"Can't open horse.dat file\n");
        exit(1);
        }
```

```
                PROMPT(s1);
                pprev = (HORSEPTR) NULL;
                while ( (getline (temp,ARSIZE) != NULL) && temp[0] != '\0')
                   {
                   pnow = ( HORSEPTR) malloc ( sizeof( HORSE ) );
                   if (pprev == NULL)
                        pfirst = pnow;
                   else
                       pprev->pnext = pnow;
                   recsize = strlen(temp) + 1;      /* required space */
                   pnow->hname = malloc ( recsize ); /* allocate space */
                   strcpy(pnow->hname, temp);        /* fill space */
                   pnow->pnext = NULL;
                   fwrite(&recsize, sizeof (int), 1, fp); /* save size */
                   fwrite(pnow->hname, recsize, 1, fp);   /* save string */
                   pprev = pnow;
                   PROMPT(s3);
                   }
             fclose (fp);           /* close data file */
             if (pprev == NULL)
                puts("No horses--bye.");
           else
               {
               puts("And here they are!");
               pnow = pfirst;
               do {
                   printf("%3d> %s\n", ++count, pnow->hname);
                   pnow = pnow->pnext;
               } while ( pnow != NULL);         pnow = pfirst;
               }
   }
char *getline( s, n )
char *s;
int n;
{
    int ch;
    int ct = 0;

    while ( ct < n - 1 && ((ch = getchar()) != EOF)
                              && ch !='\n')
        s[ct++] = ch;
    s[ct] = '\0';
    if ( ct == n - 1 )
        while (   (ch = getchar() ) != EOF && ch != '\n')
             ;      /* process rest of input line */
    if ( ch == EOF)
        {
```

```
            if ( ct > 0 )
                ungetc(ch,stdin);
            else
                return NULL;
            }
        return s;
        }
```

The key section is obtaining the `recsize`, storing it, and writing a record of that size. Note that you cannot obtain the size of the record by using

```
sizeof (*pnow->name)
```

The pointer (`*pnow->name`) points to the first character of a string, so the `sizeof` operator provides a value of one byte. On the other hand, `sizeof (temp)` does provide the size of the whole array, even though `temp` technically also is a pointer-to-`char`. That is because the array is declared to have a specific size, and C takes that into account. But we want the length of the string, so we use `strlen()`. We add one to allow space for the null character. We don't have to use the null string when storing the string in a file, but if we omit it there, we will have to remember to add it back on when we read a string from the file to a program. It's simpler just to include the null character when storing the string, and that is what we did.

We wrote to the file while still in the read loop so that we could use the current value of `recsize` before it was forgotten. If you want to write to the file elsewhere in the program, you will need all the `recsize` values later. One way to obtain these values would be to redefine the structure by adding a `recsize` member to it. Then each structure would locate a string, specify its size, and locate the next structure. A second method would be to use `strlen()` again to recompute the size of each string.

Figure 6-9 illustrates the storage scheme; each string is preceded by its length, including the null character.

Figure 6-9
Storing Strings

| 11 | Andy'sBoy\0 | 16 | Cindy'sDelight\0 | 16 | Ellen's |

One final point: the program opened the file in the append mode, so repeated calls to the program will add data to the file. If the file doesn't yet exist, the `fopen()` append mode creates it, so that base is covered.

Next, here is code to recover the file contents:

```
/* horseread.c--displaces contents of horse.dat */
#include <stdio.h>
struct horses {
                char *hname;
                struct horses *pnext;
              };
typedef struct horses HORSE, *HORSEPTR;
char *malloc();

main()
{
    HORSEPTR pfirst, pprev, pnow;
    int count = 0;
    int recsize;
    FILE *fp;

    if ( (fp = fopen("horse.dat","r")) == NULL )
       {
       fprintf(stderr,"Can't open horse.dat file\n");
       exit(1);
       }
    pprev = (HORSEPTR) NULL;
    while ( fread( &recsize, sizeof(int), 1, fp) == 1 )
       {
        pnow = ( HORSEPTR) malloc ( sizeof( HORSE ) );
        if (pprev == NULL)
             pfirst = pnow;
        else
           pprev->pnext = pnow;
        pnow->hname = malloc ( recsize );
        if ( fread (pnow->hname, recsize, 1, fp ) != 1)
            {
            fprintf(stderr,"File-reading error\n");
            exit(1);
            }
        pnow->pnext = NULL;
        pprev = pnow;
        }
    fclose(fp);
    if (pprev == NULL)
        puts("No horses in file--bye.");
    else
       {
       puts("And here they are!");
       pnow = pfirst;
       do {
            printf("%3d> %s\n", ++count, pnow->hname);
```

```
            pnow = pnow->pnext;
        } while ( pnow != NULL);
    }


}
```

Essentially, we have modified *horses.c* to read from a file instead of the keyboard; much of the two programs are identical.

Here are some sample runs of *horsefile* and *horseread*:

```
A>horsefile
Please enter a horse name. To stop, enter ^Z
or press [return] at the beginning of a line.
Andy's Boy
Please enter the next name. To stop, enter ^Z
or press [return] at the beginning of a line.
Cindy's Delight
Please enter the next name. To stop, enter ^Z
or press [return] at the beginning of a line.
Ellen's Fantasy
Please enter the next name. To stop, enter ^Z
or press [return] at the beginning of a line.
[RETURN]
And here they are!
   1> Andy's Boy
   2> Cindy's Delight
   3> Ellen's Fantasy

A>horseread
And here they are!
   1> Andy's Boy
   2> Cindy's Delight
   3> Ellen's Fantasy

A>horsefile
Please enter a horse name. To stop, enter ^Z
or press [return] at the beginning of a line.
Gerard's Horror
Please enter the next name. To stop, enter ^Z
or press [return] at the beginning of a line.
Isabelle's Jewels
Please enter the next name. To stop, enter ^Z
or press [return] at the beginning of a line.
Ken's Litigation
Please enter the next name. To stop, enter ^Z
or press [return] at the beginning of a line.
[RETURN]
```

```
And here they are!
  1> Gerard's Horror
  2> Isabelle's Jewels
  3> Ken's Litigation

A>horseread
And here they are!
  1> Andy's Boy
  2> Cindy's Delight
  3> Ellen's Fantasy
  4> Gerard's Horror
  5> Isabelle's Jewels
  6> Ken's Litigation
```

Note that each call of *horsefile* adds to the current file.

Clearly there is more to be said about this example, particularly about file handling, but we'll put that off until another chapter. Instead, let's look at another memory-related matter.

Video Memory

In Chapter 5 we discussed two of three methods of screen control. The third, and much the fastest, is direct memory access. For some applications, such as rapid spreadsheet paging or games, fast screens are very desirable. To understand the direct memory access method, we need to know more about how video display works.

On an IBM PC the screen display is represented on a one-to-one basis in memory. For instance, the IBM Monochrome Display monitor features a 2000-character display arranged in a pattern 80 characters wide and 25 characters tall. Each of these positions corresponds to a two-byte memory unit on the Monochrome Display Adapter (MDA) board. One byte holds the ASCII (or extended) code for the character. The second byte holds the *attribute,* which is a collection of bits indicating whether the character should be normal, highlighted, blinking, or reverse video. The processor on the board periodically scans these 2000 memory units (4000 bytes), placing the corresponding character, complete with attributes, on the screen. The Color/Graphics Adapter (CGA) board performs a similar trick for a color/ graphics terminal, but more memory is needed, for the color graphics mode maps each of 64,000 pixel elements to two bits of memory, as represented in Figure 6–10. Thus, the CGA card has 16K of display memory.

When you use putchar() or a DOS call to write characters to the screen, those routines use a BIOS interrupt to do the actual work of placing the proper information in each byte of screen memory. However, it is possible to bypass BIOS and access the screen memory directly. We just need to know the address of the screen memory and how to reach that address.

Figure 6-10
Memory-Mapped Video

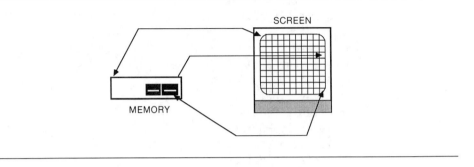

We can get the addresses from the *IBM Technical Reference* manual. The MDA (Monochrome) memory begins at 0xB0000, or decimal 720896. The CGA (color graphics) memory begins at 0xB8000, which is 753664 in decimal.

To specify addresses in C, we use pointers. However, we can't assign an address of 720896 to a regular pointer. The reason is that a regular pointer is a 16-byte object, so the range of values it can hold is 65,536, or 64K or 0x10000. This restriction in pointer size is one reason that the small memory model is restricted to 64K of data and 64K of code.

We seem to be at an impasse, but there is a way around this roadblock. To understand it, we have to look more closely at how the 8088/8086 CPU family deals with memory.

Memory Segments and Offsets

Because 64K is the largest address an 8088/8086 register can hold, memory is organized into segments which can be up to 64K long. Within a given segment, a single register can locate any memory location by giving its relative address, or offset, from the beginning of the segment. If you print the value of a C pointer, for example, it provides the offset of the location from the segment beginning.

The segments are not fixed in memory. The linker assigns the final location of each segment when it loads a program. The processor uses four "segment" registers to hold the starting locations of four segments. The registers are named CS, DS, SS, and ES. The CS register is used to mark the beginning of the code, or text, segment, in which machine language program instructions are stored. The DS register marks the beginning of the data section, in which program data, such as string constants and external variables, are stored. The SS register marks the base of the stack. The ES is used for any extra segments required by a program.

The segments need not be distinct. In the small memory model, for example, the data segment and the stack segment share the same space; thus, DS and SS have the same value. This is convenient, since it means that both external and automatic variables are in the same segment and can be referenced in the same relative address system.

Although a segment is not restricted to any one location, there is a restriction on where it can start. The starting address must be a multiple of 16, or 0x10. This extends the addressing range by a factor of 16 to 1,048,576 bytes (0x100000 in hex).

Segment Values—Let's see how that works. Suppose we want DS to represent a segment base address of 0x200 (512). Since we know the base address has to be multiple of 0x10 (16), we can store the proper multiple of 0x10 (16). That is, we can store 0x20 (32) in the DS register, and the processor will multiply that value by 0x10 (16) to get the actual base address, 0x200 (512). (By now, you probably have noticed that these operations go much more smoothly in hex than in decimal; you just have to drop or add a 0.)

What's gained by this ploy? The largest value a 16-bit register can hold is 0xFFFF (1 less than 0x10000). This is the 64K limit we mentioned. But it gets multiplied by 0x10 when converted to an address, giving a value of 0xFFFFF. This is 1 megabyte (less 1), so now the processor has a 1-megabyte range instead of a 64K range.

Of course, the segment register can't indicate addresses not divisible by 16. But the offset address takes up the slack. If the base is 0x200, then that plus an offset of 0x7 specifies the address 0x207.

In general, then, the processor uses a two-part representation for addresses. One part is a segment value that identifies the segment; the second part is an offset giving the displacement of the address from the segment beginning. The address 0x207 we just mentioned could be written 20H:7H, with 20H representing the segment value and 7H representing the offset. (We're using the assembly language H notation for hex numbers to indicate that the 20H:7H notation is not a C notation.) More generally, the notation DS:SI would indicate that the segment value is in the DS register and the offset value is in the SI register.

It is simple to get an absolute address from a segment-offset pair. Just use this formula:

$$\text{absolute address} = 0x10 \times (\text{segment value}) + \text{offset}$$

Figure 6–11 illustrates this formula.

As long as a program confines itself to one segment, the segment registers stay fixed, and all manipulations are done using offset addresses. If, however, a program needs to access another region in memory, it can reset the appropriate segment register and use offset relative to the new segment base. This slows things down, but it does open up memory to a program.

C and Segments

Handling segments is not part of standard C, so those who have implemented C for the IBM PC have had to develop their own ways to deal with

Figure 6–11
Segment Value, Offset, and Absolute Address

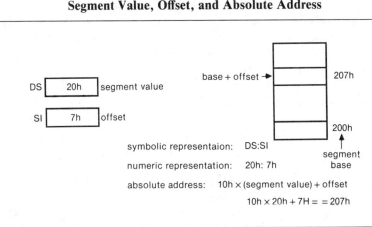

the problem. The simplest method is to ignore it and accept the 64K limitations. Unfortunately, this makes video memory manipulation off limits. IBM C offers a variety of choices. One is to use the large memory model, which uses 32-bit pointers instead of 16-bit pointers. The extra 16 bits are used to indicate the segment. The segment register scheme is used, so the high-order 16 bits hold absolute address of the segment base divided by 16; that is, the high-order word holds what we have called the segment value. Such pointers are called *far pointers.* Figure 6–12 shows how the address and pointer are represented for the far pointer. The 16-bit pointer used in the small memory model is termed a *near pointer.*

Figure 6–12
A Far Pointer

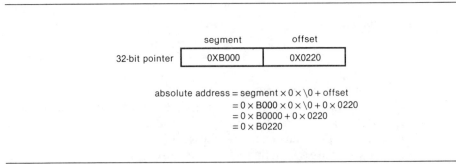

One problem with using the large-memory model is that all its pointers are far pointers by default; that slows down a program. However, with IBM C, it isn't necessary to go to the large model to use a far pointer. The small model can use the keyword `far` to create a 32-bit pointer. And with that kind of pointer, we can access video memory. Pointers declared without using the `far` keyword still are 16-bit pointers in the small-memory model.

Declaring a Far Pointer—Here is how to declare a far pointer to, for example, an `unsigned int`:

```
unsigned int far *pt;   /* pt is a 32-bit far pointer */
```

The two low-order bytes will contain the offset address. The two high-order bytes will contain the segment value, which is the segment base address divided by 10h.

To activate the keyword `far`, you need to invoke the `/Ze` option when compiling a program.

Suppose we want to assign the starting address of the MDA display memory to a far pointer. We would want the segment base to coincide with the beginning of video memory. Since the address is 0xB0000, the segment value would be 0xB000. We would want that to be in the high-order bytes of a 32-bit storage unit. The `L` suffix will make 0xB000L type `unsigned long`; that takes care of having 32 bits. Then we can use the left shift operator to move the pattern 16 bits to the left. Thus the desired value for the 32-bit pointer is this:

```
0xB000L << 16
```

Can we then say this?

```
pt = 0xB000L << 16;
```

We can, but we will get a compiler warning, for `pt` is a pointer, while the constant is an `unsigned long`. A type cast will clear up that problem:

```
pt = (int far *) (0xB000L << 16) ;
```

Direct Memory Access (DMA) to the Screen

Let's try it out. We've put together a program that places a character in memory location 0xB0000. If you use the CGA board, use 0xB8000 instead.

Remember to include the `/Ze` option in the compile command line:

```
cc /Ze vid0
```

Here's the code:

```
/* vid0.c--puts a character in Monochrome video memory */
#include <conio.h>
#define SCREEN   ( (int far *)( 0xB000L << 16 ) )
```

```
#define ATTR ( 0x70 << 8)     /* reverse video attribute */
#define STOP '\032'
main()
{
  int far *fp;    /* a far pointer */
  int char ch;

  fp = SCREEN;      /* assign screen memory address to fp */
  while ( ( ch = getch() ) != STOP )
      *fp = ch | ATTR;      /* place value in memory */
}
```

Not only is this simple, but it works. Each character, as you type it, appears in reverse video in the upper left corner of the screen. There are two matters needing further discussion. One is the use of the attribute and the second is the scheme used to associate particular memory locations with particular screen locations.

The Attribute—The attribute is one byte of data devoted to describing the properties of the character. It is the high-order byte of the two-byte word describing a character, so we left-shifted its value 8 bits before combining it with the character value. Figure 6–13 shows this process.

Figure 6–13
Character and Attribute

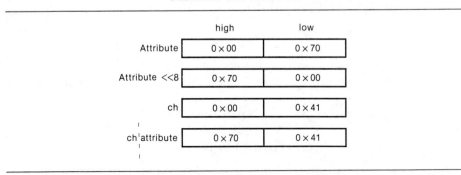

Figure 6–14 shows the meanings of the eight bits. The seven-bit turns blinking on and off, the three-bit turns enhanced intensity on and off, bits zero through two control the foreground, and bits four through six control the background. The R, G, and B labels refer to Red-Green-Blue values. They are more meaningful to the CGA adapter. But for either adapter, turning on red, green, and blue simultaneously indicates white, and turning them all off indicates black. Table 6–1 indicates what different foreground and background combinations produce. Each of these combinations can have the blink and intensity bits set or cleared.

Figure 6–14
Attribute Bits

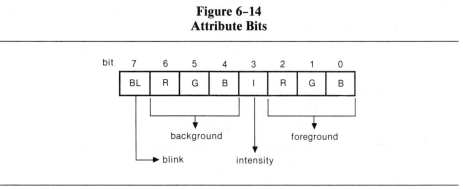

Table 6-1 Monochrome Attribute Combinations

Background	Foreground	Result
0 0 0	0 0 0	nondisplay
0 0 0	0 0 1	underline
0 0 0	1 1 1	bright character, dark background
1 1 1	0 0 0	reverse video

Note that the underline attribute for the MDA card becomes the blue attribute when used with a CGA card.

If we set bits 7 and 4 to 0, the normal display has the value 0x7, and reverse video is 0x70.

Screen Mapping—As you noticed, location 0xB0000 maps to the upper left corner. Successive words in video memory associate with successive screen positions going from left to right. When one row is finished, the association continues with the first character position on the next row. One possibility is to describe the 4000 bytes of Monochrome video memory as an array of 2000 unsigned integers. Array element 0 defines the upper left corner, array element 79 is the upper right corner, element 80 is the first character of the second line, and so on up to element 1999, which would represent the lower right corner.

For greater programming convenience we can describe the video memory as a 25 by 80 array of elements. That would allow specifying elements by row and column. To implement this approach, we need to declare a far pointer to an array of 80 elements. Such a pointer is syntactically the same as the name of an array of 80-element arrays, and that is what is needed. If you are not clear on this point, review the Chapter 2 discussion of using pointers in functions handling two-dimensional arrays. Here is how to make such a declaration:

```
unsigned (far *vidptr) [80];
```

The parentheses are important, since they override the otherwise higher precedence of the braces. You could read this declaration this way: `vidptr` is a `far` pointer to an array of 80 `unsigned` integers.

Using the Whole Screen

Let's use the array concept to fill the whole screen with a typed character. Note that we use the `typedef` facility to create an alias for the far pointer type. We then can use that alias to declare a variable and to type cast the screen address. To add a bit of variety, we put in a loop to add some video reverse. The `kbhit()` function is part of the console I/O package. It returns "true" if there has been a keystroke, and it returns "false" otherwise. Thus the loop it is in runs until you strike a key or until 400 video reverses have taken place, whichever comes first. Here is the program:

```
/* vid1.c--fill screen with characters using DMA */
#include <conio.h>
#define ROWS 25
#define COLS 80
typedef unsigned (far *VIDEO) [COLS];
#define MCSEG   ((VIDEO) (0xB000L << 16) )
#define STOP '\032'
#define NORMAL (0x7 << 8 )
#define REVERSE  (0x70 << 8)
main()
{
  VIDEO scrptr;
  int row, col;
  int ct = 0;
  unsigned char ch;

  scrptr = MCSEG;
  while ( (ch = getch() ) != STOP)
      {
        for (row = 0; row < ROWS; row++)
          for ( col = 0; col < COLS; col++)
              scrptr[row][col] = ch | NORMAL;
        while ( !kbhit() && ct++ < 400 )
              scrptr[ct % ROWS][ct % COLS] = ch | REVERSE;
        ct = 0;
      }
}
```

Try it to see the effect!

☐ *Question 6-6* What purpose does the modulus operator (%) serve in the final loop?

Screen Speed

This mode of screen control is quite a bit faster than going through BIOS. To get an idea of the speed, try the following program. It places a happy face in the middle of the screen. If you press an arrow key it goes off in the direction the arrow points until you press another arrow key to change its direction or a nonarrow key to stop it. It leaves behind a spore to mark its path.

```c
/* fastface.c--face leaves tracks across screen */
#include <stdio.h>
#include <conio.h>
#define ROWS 25
#define COLS 80
typedef unsigned  (far *VIDEO) [COLS];
#define MCSEG   ((VIDEO) (0xb000L << 16) )
#define STOP '\032'
#define NORMAL (0x7 << 8 )
#define REVERSE  (0x70 << 8)
#define UP 72       /* extended code for up arrow key */
#define DN 80
#define LT 75
#define RT 77
#define SP ' '
#define FACE ('\002' ¦ REVERSE)  /* IBM happy face character */
#define TRACK ('.' ¦ NORMAL)
void wait();
main()
{
  VIDEO scrptr;
  unsigned int row, col;
  unsigned char ch;
  unsigned long delay;

  puts("Enter a delay count:");
  scanf("%lu", &delay);
  scrptr = MCSEG;
  for (row = 0; row < ROWS; row++)
     for ( col = 0; col < COLS; col++)
         scrptr[row][col] = SP ¦ NORMAL;
  scrptr[row = 12][col = 39] = FACE;
  while ( (ch = getch() ) != STOP)
```

```
            {
        if (ch == '\0')
            {
            ch = getch();
            switch ( ch )
                {
                case UP : do {scrptr[ row ] [ col ] = TRACK;
                              if ( row == 0) row =ROWS;
                              scrptr[ --row][col] = FACE;
                              wait(delay);
                              } while ( !kbhit() );
                          break;
                case DN : do {scrptr[ row ] [ col ] = TRACK;
                              if (row == ROWS -1) row = -1;
                              scrptr[++row][col] = FACE;
                              wait(delay);
                              } while ( !kbhit() );
                          break;
                case LT : do {scrptr[ row ] [ col ] = TRACK;
                              if (col == 0) col = COLS;
                              scrptr[row][ --col] = FACE;
                              wait ( delay );
                              } while ( !kbhit() );
                          break;
                case RT : do {scrptr[ row ] [ col ] = TRACK;
                              if (col == COLS - 1) col = -1;
                              scrptr[ row ][++col] = FACE;
                              wait (delay);
                              } while ( !kbhit() );
                           break;
                }   /* end switch */
            }       /* end if */
        }           /* end while */
    }               /* end main() */
void wait (ct)
unsigned long ct;
{
    while (ct--)
        ;
}
```

The face hurries about quite quickly, so we included a timing delay that can be set at run time. A value somewhere between 1000 and 5000 slows the face down enough so that you can control its motion. The program looks like a precursor to some video games.

Note the usefulness of the kbhit() function for this type of situation. Each motion loop continues until you press a key.

☐ *Question 6-7* Why does pressing a nonarrow key stop the face?

Direct Memory Access versus BIOS

The main advantages of using direct memory access instead of the BIOS interrupts are increased speed and increased control of the screen. One disadvantage is that you also have more details to attend to. This is more true of the CGA display than of the MDA display. A second disadvantage is that you make a program very equipment-dependent when you start incorporating specific addresses into a program. However, the dominance of IBM is such that most manufacturers follow the IBM lead in such matters.

The BIOS routines, on the other hand, are more standardized. Implementations of the routines may differ from system to system, but they are accessed by the same interrupt number and perform the same basic tasks.

The most portable usage would be to stick to the I/O functions of the standard I/O package, but they don't give the control possible with the other approaches.

Summary

C programs on the IBM use three kinds of memory: static, stack, and dynamically allocated. Each has its own uses. Static memory is useful for data that is to be shared among functions. Stack memory is ideally suited for automatic variables. Allocated memory lets a program adjust its memory requirements to meet its needs.

The principle memory allocation function is `malloc()`. When you use `malloc()`, you identify the number of bytes you want, and the function returns a pointer to a free block of memory. The program's only contact with the allocated memory is through the pointer, so care should be taken to preserve its value.

A common way to keep track of allocated memory is to define structures that point to the data and to other structures of the same type. We investigated a singly linked list, but other possibilities include doubly linked lists, trees, and heaps. We haven't discussed these other forms, but the central idea for all these structures is that each structure holds one or more addresses to link it to one or more other structures.

In some contexts it is important to understand how memory is managed by the IBM's 8088 chip. The inherent limitation of a 16-bit register limits the range of memory addressable by a register to 64K. To get around this limitation, the 8088 maintains a set of four segment registers that hold the base address of four conceptually distinct segments of memory. The actual base address is divided by 0x10. This means that segments can only start at addresses divisible by 0x10, but it extends the addressing range to 1Mb. An actual address, then, can be specified by two 16-bit values. The first is the segment value just discussed. The second is the offset, measured in bytes from the segment base. The actual address is given by

$$\text{address} = 0x10 \times \text{Segment} + \text{Offset}$$

Programs typically confine code to one segment and data to one segment. This allows all calculations and references to be made using just the offset addresses. C pointers in the small memory model are 16-bit pointers holding the offset.

By using the large memory model or by using the keyword `far`, C can implement a full 32-bit pointer. The low-order bytes hold the offset, and the high-order bytes hold the segment value. By using a far pointer, a C program can access the full 1Mb of addressable memory.

IBM Monochrome and Color/Graphics Display Adapters use a memory map of the screen, with specific memory locations dedicated to specific screen locations. A processor scans the video memory periodically and sets the screen display accordingly. By using a far pointer, a C program can access the video memory directly, providing faster and more detailed control of the screen.

Answers to Questions in the Chapter

■ *6-1.* Placing the print statement before the call causes the minus sign to be printed before the recursive call. This means that the minus sign is printed before any digits are printed, which is what we want.

■ *6-2.* At the end of the loop, the only address retained is the address of the last block allocated. The other blocks are there using up memory space, but we are left with no legitimate means of accessing them.

■ *6-3.* The `strcpy()` function would interpret whatever value happened to be in `fname` as an address and would try to copy the string to that location. Always assign address values to pointers before using them.

■ *6-4a.*

```
#define HRST struct horses
```

■ *b.* Can't be done. Yes,

```
#define HRPT struct horses *
```

will work for declaring one pointer:

```
HRPT p1;
```

but the declaration

```
HRPT p2, p3;
```

sets up p2 as a pointer and p3 as a structure, for the preprocessor converts this to

```
struct horses *p2, p3;
```

- *6-5.* Yes, but then the program will forget where the list starts. That's okay if the loop is at the end of the program, but you might want to do something else with the structures.

- *6-6.* It ensures that the row value is never greater than 24 and that the column value is never greater than 79; it keeps the array indices within proper bounds.

- *6-7.* Any keystroke makes kbhit() true, ending the kbhit() loop. That stops the motion. The following break ends the switch and the big if statement, and the program flow returns to the outer while loop. At that time the keystroke that kbhit() detected gets read. If it is a nonarrow character, the entire switch statement is skipped.

Exercises

1. Convert the bitwise binary conversion program in Chapter 4 to a recursive program.

2. Write a recursive program that converts numbers from other bases to base 10.

3. Write a program that inputs a mixture of string and numeric data, such as stock names along with buy and sell values in decimal form. Place each set of information in a suitable structure. Use malloc() and linked structures to store the data. Each linked structure will contain two addresses: the address of a structure containing a stock name and stock values, and the address of the next linked structure. Have the program print out all the stock information at the end.

4. Modify the program from Exercise 3 so that the stock information is stored in a file containing fixed-length records. Create a program to read the file.

5. Modify Exercise 4 to use variable-length records in the file.

6. Modify *horses.c* so that it uses a doubly linked list; that is, each structure should contain a pointer to the preceding structure and a pointer to the following structure. Test the program by having it print the list of horses in the original order and in the reverse order.

7. Use direct memory access to write a program that places typed input on the top line of the screen, going backwards from right to left.

7

Standard Library Functions

- Portable library functions
- File permissions
- File access
- Error handling with `errno` and `perror()`
- Accessing file information
- Time reporting
- Interrupt handling
- Environmental parameters
- Processes
- File deletion
- Conversion functions
- String functions

Standard Library Functions

The IBM C library contains over 200 functions and macros, making it a tremendous resource for the programmer. It provides solutions to many common programming problems, saving you the effort of "reinventing the wheel." Most of the library functions are identical or very similar in use and in effect to functions found in UNIX-like systems. In particular, the IBM C library is designed for compatibility with XENIX and UNIX System V. We'll term these shared functions *standard functions*. Examples include the standard I/O functions and memory allocation functions we have used. Programs using these functions should be very portable from one system to another. Yet there are differences you should know.

Other functions are specific to the PC-DOS operating system. Examples of these are the console I/O functions and int86(). Programs using these functions would not transport to non-IBM-like systems without careful modification.

The various C compilers for the IBM PC supply, by and large, the same standard library functions, because all are based on the UNIX model. Some, however, resemble more closely earlier versions of the UNIX library. There also are differences in how adjustments are made to the DOS environment. For example, the techniques for specifying text and binary files differ from compiler to compiler. Still, the differences are minor. The IBM-specific functions, however, diverge more dramatically.

In this chapter we'll look at many of the standard functions, and the following three chapters will investigate the specialized functions.

Because files are so important to computers, many of the functions concern files. We've already discussed basic file I/O, but there is more territory to cover. Another important topic is string handling. Again, we've used some functions, but we'll take a more thorough look now. Then there are process-related functions, error-handling functions, and other topics. We'll try to provide you with a good background in these areas, and we'll also point out some of the differences between DOS and UNIX implementations.

File Permissions

The C language was created to aid the development of the UNIX operating system. As a result, the C library contains many functions pertaining to operating system matters. One such area is that of file permissions; operating systems keep track of such things as which files are executable programs, which files are read-only, and the like. When we discussed the open() function, we mentioned that we need to provide a permission mode argument when creating a new file. PC-DOS offers just two real choices: read-only and read-write. A read-only file, as the name suggests, can be read but not altered. It can't even be removed. Clearly, that is a useful mode for important data files. We'll take a closer look now at the permission mode and how it can be influenced and altered.

Permission Modes

The *sys\stat.h* file defines two manifest constants that can be used to set up the permission mode:

```
#define S_IWRITE 0000200        /* write permission */
#define S_IREAD  0000400        /* read permission  */
```

S_IWRITE corresponds to the seven bit being set to one, and S_IREAD corresponds to the eight bit being set to one. But as long as you include the *sys\stat.h* file, you can use the manifest constants without knowing their exact values.

Logically, these definitions suggest that S_IREAD specifies a read-only mode, that S_IWRITE specifies a write-only mode, and that the combination S_IREAD¦S_IWRITE specifies a file that can be read and written to. However, PC-DOS currently allows all files to be read, so S_IWRITE has the same effect as S_IREAD ¦ S_IWRITE. Nonetheless, you should use the second form if that is what you mean; that will preserve compatibility with operating systems that do recognize a write-only mode. UNIX and XENIX do, and perhaps some future PC-DOS version will, too.

Using the Permission Mode

In Chapter 3 we saw that the permission mode was used with the creat() function and, when the O_CREAT file mode was specified, with the open() function. Let's look at an example with open():

```
/* rofile.c--creates a read-only file */
#include <stdio.h>
#include <fcntl.h>
#include <sys\types.h>
#include <sys\stat.h>
main()
{
```

```
int fh;     /* file handle */
char *p = "Golden Lab, Collie, St. Bernard\n";

if ( (fh = open("dog.dat", O_CREAT ¦ O_WRONLY, S_IREAD) )
        != -1)
    {
     write(fh, p, strlen(p) );
     close(fh);
    }
  else
     fprintf (stderr, "ERROR!\n");
}
```

Recall that `stderr` is a file stream used for printing error messages on the screen.

You should distinguish between the two modes specified in the `open()` call. The first mode (the second argument) is a file-opening mode. It states in what manner the file will be used this particular time it is opened, and its meaning persists only until the file is closed again. The second mode (the third argument) is a file-creation mode. It is used only when the file is created, and it stays in force until changed explicitly. It is made part of the file record-keeping data. Figure 7-1 differentiates the two modes.

Figure 7-1
Two Types of Open() Modes

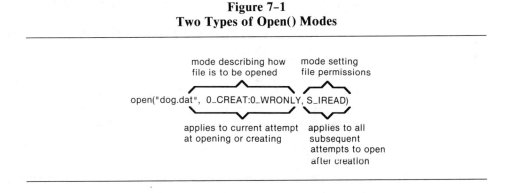

An important point is that the permissions imposed by the file-creation mode do not take effect until after the first time the file is closed. For instance, *rofile.c* creates a read-only mode, yet it writes to the file. But future attempts to open the *dog.dat* file for writing will fail:

```
A>rofile

A>type dog.dat
Golden Lab, Collie, St. Bernard
```

```
A>rofile
ERROR!

A>erase dog.dat
Permission Denied
A>
```

The second attempt to use *rofile* failed because at this juncture the file existed in a read-only mode. The system `erase` command also failed, for removing a file is considered a form of writing. (The actual error message may be different than the one shown here, depending on your version of DOS.)

The Umask() Function

When `creat()` or `open()` uses the permission mode, it is combined with a *creation mask,* using the bitwise operations we discussed in Chapter 4. If a bit in the mask is one, the corresponding bit in the final permission value is set to 0 (off). By default, the mask is 0 for the read and write bits, so the requested permission mode becomes the final mode. With the `umask()`, function, however, you can reset the mask.

☐ *Question 7-1* Suppose `mask` is an integer with key bits set to 1. How would you combine it with a permission-mode value (call it `pmode`) to turn those key bits off while leaving the rest unchanged?

For example, to set the default to read-only, make this call:

```
oldmask = umask(S_IWRITE);  /* disables write permission */
```

The function returns the previous mask value. It's a good idea to assign this value to an `int` variable so that you can restore the default setting when you are finished. Actually, the effects of `umask()` are confined to the program using it. Any changes made end when the program ends. But a large program may require different `umask()` values for different sections.

DOS and UNIX/XENIX

Perhaps this machinery seems rather elaborate to control a single write-permission bit, and there are more elaborations to come. The reason for this apparent overkill is that it represents an adaptation to DOS from a UNIX-like environment. In that multiuser environment, there are three separate permission groups: user, group, and other. Each of these groups must have three independent permissions specified: read, write, and execute. Thus, permission mode and creation mask originally applied to nine bits.

Changing Permissions: Chmod()

Suppose you eventually want to alter a read-only file. Or perhaps you want to set permissions while using `fopen()`, which doesn't use a permission mode. Then you can use the chmod() function. It takes two arguments: a file pathname, and a permission mode. It then assigns those permissions to a file.

Let's write a function that takes a command line list of files and converts them to read-only files:

```
/* nowrite.c--removes write permissions from files */
#include <stdio.h>
#include <sys\types.h>
#include <sys\stat.h>
#include <io.h>
main(argc,argv)
int argc;
char *argv[];
{
    if ( argc < 2)
        {
        fprintf(stderr, "Usage: nowrite file(s)\n");
        exit(1);
        }
    while ( argc > 1 )
        {
        if ( access ( argv[1], 00 ) != 0 )
                fprintf(stderr,"%s does not exist\n", argv[1]);
        else
                chmod ( argv[1], S_IREAD);
        argv++;
        argc--;
        }
}
```

This program uses chmod() just as we described. It also uses the access() function to screen out nonexistent files. The particular call we made to access() returns a non 0 value if the named file does not exist. We'll look at this function soon.

☐ *Question 7-2*   The *nowrite* program calls out for a *yeswrite* program. What would it look like?

One useful application is in creating a data file that can only be modified through using the correct program. The data file can be created in a read-only mode. Then, when the program needs to change the file, it can use chmod() to make the file writable. When finished, it can use chmod() to reset the read-only mode. This protects the file from accidental modification or deletion.

Checking Files and Reporting Problems

Ideally, a program should verify the existence of a file before attempting to use it, and it should check to see if it is writable before trying to change it. If the program encounters difficulties in its attempts to use a file, it should let you know what the problem seems to be. The C library, because of its operating system heritage, has several useful facilities to help with these goals.

The Access() Function and the Errno Variable

The access() function is a useful one. As its name suggests, it provides access information about a file. The access() function takes two arguments. The first is a string representing the file pathname. The second is an integer specifying the modes we wish to test. There are four possibilities; they are summarized in Table 7–1.

Table 7–1
Permission Mode Values

Value	Check for
06	Read and write permission
04	Read permission
02	Write permission
00	Existence of file

Under DOS, 02 and 06 are equivalent, since any file with write permission also has read permission. Also, 00 and 04 are equivalent, since any file that exists has read permission.

The access() function returns a value of 0 if the file has the given mode, and a value of − 1 if it doesn't. In the latter case, access() also assigns a value to the external variable errno.

And what is errno? It is an external variable set up by the C compiler. It's used to store an "error number." Many functions make use of errno, so let's take a closer look. The system maintains a list of error numbers. These are defined symbolically in the file *errno.h*. For example, the symbolic value ENOSPC means no more space is available on a device, and EACCES means that access is denied. When an error occurs during a library call, the corresponding error number is assigned to the external variable errno. Your program can investigate the errno value after a library call fails and use it to decide what to do next.

The access() function sets errno to one of the values in Table 7–2 if it fails.

Table 7-2
Values for Denial of File Access

Value	Meaning
EACCES	Access denied; the file's permission setting does not permit the specified access.
ENOENT	File or pathname is not found.

A program investigating errno should do so immediately upon a library call failure. Otherwise, the value could be altered by an intervening call.

Let's look at a specific example. The next program prints out a message based on the errno value. The program itself has the simple goal of appending a message to a file. It uses access() to see if this is possible and prints an explanatory message if it fails. Note that we include the *errno.h* file and declare errno as an external variable. The first is required for using the symbolic constants. The second is needed so that our program can find errno.

```
/* addtag.c--appends to a file and illustrates errno */
#include <stdio.h>
#include <io.h>
#include <errno.h>
char *claim = "\nThis file is the property of Greed Inc." ;
main(ac,av)
int ac;
char *av[];
{
    extern int errno;    /* the error-number variable */
    FILE *fp;

    if ( ac < 2 )
        {
        fprintf(stderr,"Usage: addtag file(s)\n");
        exit(1);
        }
    while ( ac > 1 )
        {
        if ( access( av[1], 02 ) != 0 )
            if ( errno == EACCES )
                fprintf(stderr, "%s is read-only\n", av[1] );
            else        /* errno == ENOENT */
                fprintf(stderr,"%s does not exist\n", av[1] );
        else if ( (fp = fopen(av[1],"a" )) == NULL )
                fprintf(stderr,"can't open %s\n", av[1] );
```

```
                else
                    {
                    fputs( claim, fp);
                    fclose (fp);
                    }
            av++;
            ac--;
            }
    }
```

Here, `access()` checks for write permission. The two reasons `access()` might fail to find write permission is that the file is read-only and that the file doesn't exist; the `errno` value lets us see which is the cause. If the file passes the test, we go on to try to open the file.

Here is a sample run:

```
A>addtag fox rabbit lettuce hare
rabbit is read-only
lettuce does not exist

A>
```

The other two files were opened for writing and had the line appended.

The Perror() Function

We used the `errno` information to expand the program's error-reporting, but we could have been more ambitious. For instance, the **EACCES** report could be used to initiate a `chmod()` call. If, however, the error message is the only thing needed, we can use the `perror()` function instead of using `errno` explicitly.

This function takes one argument, a string. It then prints that string, a colon, and an error message corresponding to the current `errno` value. Here is *addtag.c* reworked to use `perror()` instead of using `errno` values explicitly:

```
/* addtag1.c--use perror() */
#include <stdio.h>
#include <io.h>
char *claim = "\nThis file is the property of Greed Inc." ;
main(ac,av)
int ac;
char *av[];
{
    void perror();
    FILE *fp;
```

```
    if ( ac < 2 )
        {
        fprintf(stderr,"Usage: addtag file(s)\n");
        exit(1);
        }
    while ( ac > 1 )
        {
        if ( access( av[1], 02 ) != 0 )
                perror(av[1]);
        else if ( (fp = fopen(av[1],"a" )) == NULL )
                fprintf(stderr,"can't open %s\n", av[1] );
                else
                    {
                    fputs( claim, fp);
                    fclose (fp);
                    }
        av++;
        ac--;
        }
}
```

Because perror() uses errno directly, we don't need to include the *errno.h* file. Here is a sample run:

```
A>addtag1 fox rabbit lettuce hare
rabbit: Permission denied.
lettuce: No such file or directory.

A>
```

This time the system messages were used. How does this work? In addition to errno, the compiler creates the external variables sys_nerr and sys_errlist. They have these declarations:

```
int sys_nerr;                /* number of system messages */
char *sys_errlist[sys_nerr]; /* array of error messages */
```

Each member of the sys_errlist array is initialized to a particular error message. The index is just the corresponding error number.

   □ *Question 7-3*   How could you obtain a list of error messages by using a program?

More File Information: Stat()

You may have noticed that the *addtag* programs still checked fopen()'s return value, even though the file supposedly was cleared for access. Can a file fail to open even after winning the access() seal of approval? Yes, it can. There may be a hardware failure. More importantly, we've overlooked a possibility. Consider this sample run:

```
A>addtag fox lion tiger cats
lion is read-only
tiger does not exist
can't open cats

A>
```

The last error message is the one our program generates when fopen() fails. What went wrong? It turns out that *cats* is a directory. We didn't check for that possibility; one reason is that access() doesn't provide that information.

If we want to check whether the pathname identifies a directory and not a regular file, we have to turn to stat(). This function takes two arguments: a pathname and the address of a structure. It then fills the structure with information about the file or directory. A program can then examine the contents of the structure. Figure 7–2 shows stat's actions.

Figure 7–2
The Actions of Stat()

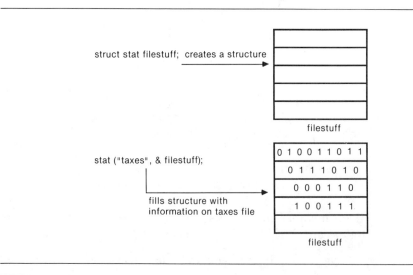

To use stat(), you need to know something about the structure. Because DOS maintains less information about a file than does a UNIX system (where stat() was bred), some of the structure members are unused or redundant. Table 7–3 is a list of those described by the library manual.

**Table 7–3
Structure Members and Their Values**

Member	Value
st_mode	File mode information in bit form
st_dev	Drive number of disk containing file
st_rdev	(Same contents as st_dev)
st_nlink	Number of links (always 1 in DOS)
st_size	File size in bytes
st_mtime	Time of last modification
st_atime	(Same contents as st_mtime)
st_ctime	(Same contents as st_mtime)

With UNIX-like systems, st_atime is time of last access, and st_ctime is time of creation.

The stat() function returns a value of 0 if successful and a value of −1 if it fails. In the latter case, it sets errno to ENOENT in the belief that the file or directory could not be found.

The file mode member needs further discussion. Its type is unsigned short, so it is a 16-bit value. The *sys\stat.h* file contains the following definitions:

```
#define S_IFMT    0170000    /* file type mask */
#define S_IFDIR   0040000    /* directory bit */
#define S_IFREG   0010000    /* regular file bit */
#define S_IREAD   0000400    /* read permission bit */
#define S_IWRITE  0000200    /* write permission bit */
#define S_IEXEC   0000100    /* execute/search bit */
```

If the pathname is that of a directory, the S_IFDIR bit is set, and so on.

Let's see how we would rewrite the *addtag* program using stat() instead of access():

```
/* addtag2.c--use stat() for file information */
#include <stdio.h>
#include <sys\types.h>               /* needed by stat() */
#include <sys\stat.h>                /* needed by stat() */
char *claim = "\nThis file is the property of Greed Inc." ;
main(ac,av)
int ac;
char *av[];
{
    void perror();
```

```
            FILE *fp;
            struct stat stats;     /* declare a structure */

            if ( ac < 2 )
               {
               fprintf(stderr,"Usage: addtag2 file(s)\n");
               exit(1);
               }
            while ( ac > 1 )
              {
               if ( stat (av[1], &stats) != 0 )   /* no file */
                    perror(av[1]);
               else if (( stats.st_mode & S_IFMT) == S_IFDIR )
                    fprintf(stderr,"%s is a directory\n", av[1]);
               else if ( (stats.st_mode & S_IWRITE) != S_IWRITE)
                    fprintf(stderr,"%s is nonwritable\n", av[1]);
               else if ( (fp = fopen(av[1], "a") ) == NULL)
                    fprintf(stderr,"can't open %s\n", av[1] );
               else
                    {
                    fputs( claim, fp);
                    fclose (fp);
                    }
                av++;
                ac--;
                }
        }
```

The `stat` structure is defined in the *sys\stat.h* file. That definition, in turn, uses definitions from the *sys\types.h* file.

An extended `if else` sequence tests for a variety of properties before the actual file writing occurs. The strangest looking parts of the program are where bit values are tested. If you weren't careful, you might think that this is an adequate test:

```
    else if ( stats.st_mode != S_IWRITE)
```

The problem with this is that this compares S_WRITE with the *entire* stat.st_mode. The mode could very well have the write bit set, but it also will have other bits, such is the read bit and the file bit, set. Thus the two values will always be unequal. What we need to do is to mask all but the write bit of the mode; then we can compare that one bit to S_IWRITE. The masking is accomplished by using this expression:

```
    stats.st_mode & S_IWRITE
```

All but one bit of S_IWRITE are 0's, and ANDing any bit with 0 results in 0.

Thus this combination turns all but the write bit off. The write bit in the mode is itself unaffected, since one plus any bit equals the bit. Figure 7–3 shows how the mask works. The result then can be compared with S_IWRITE, as we did in the program.

Figure 7–3
Mode Testing with Stats.st__mode and S__IWRITE

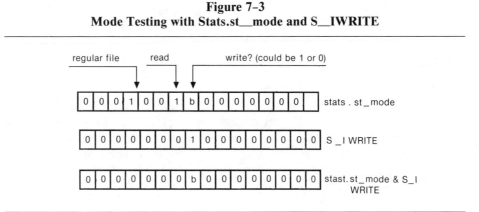

The *sys\stat.h* file contains a predefined mask S_IFMT that can be used for directory or file tests. It sets four bits to one. It isn't really needed for DOS tests, for we can use the same technique we did for S_IWRITE. However, UNIX systems have some file types that set more than one bit; for them a fancier mask is needed. For compatibility, we used S_IFMT.

A File Information Example

Let's look at another example, one that reports back file information:

```
/* finfo.c--use stat() to get file information */
#include <stdio.h>
#include <sys\types.h>
#include <sys\stat.h>
main(ac,av)
int ac;
char *av[];
{
    struct stat finfo;

    if ( ac < 2 )
        {
        fprintf(stderr,"Usage: fileinfo file(s)\n");
        exit(1);
        }
    printf("%-20s %10s %15s\n\n", "File name", "size",
                    "last altered");
```

```
        while ( ac > 1 )
            {
            if (  stat(av[1],&finfo) != 0 )
                        perror(av[1]);
            else
                printf("%-20s %10ld %15ld\n", av[1], finfo.st_size,
                                finfo.st_mtime);
            av++;
            ac--;
            }
    }
```

You may have noticed that we used the **%ld** format in printing the size and time fields. If you check the **stat** structure definition in *sys\stat.h*, you'll find that these members are defined using types defined in *sys\types.h*. The final result is that both are **long** quantities, so we need to use the **long** format. Failing to do so can lead to mysterious errors. Running it, we get output like this:

```
A>finfo tofu fries curd
File name                size    last altered

tofu                     1920        509480988
fries                    1792        506025042
curd                        0        509589960

A>
```

The time is in elapsed seconds from 00:00:00 Greenwich time, 1970, according to the system clock. This is useful, for instance, if you need to determine a time difference, but less useful if you want to read a date. Fortunately, there is a library routine to convert this form to the usual month, day, year, and time form.

Time with Time() and Ctime()

Having discussed the major file functions, let's move on to time functions. The C library contains several time-related functions. The one we need to get the time in a more readable form is **ctime()**.

The **ctime()** function converts time from seconds to a string containing the more usual representation. Here is its declaration:

```
char *ctime( time )
long *time;
```

Declaring the argument as a pointer to **long** really means the actual argument should be the address of a long variable holding the time in seconds. The `ctime()` function then returns a pointer to a character string holding the date in the following format:

```
Tue May 27 08:11:07 1986\n\0
```

The compiler allocates a static memory location to hold this 26-character string. Each call to `ctime()` updates that buffer, obliterating the previous contents. The *time.h* file contains a declaration for `ctime()` as well as information used by some other time-related functions.

Here is the revised file information program.

```
/* finfo.c--revised file info program */
#include <stdio.h>
#include <sys\types.h>
#include <sys\stat.h>
#include <time.h>
main(ac,av)
int ac;
char *av[];
{
    struct stat finfo;

    if ( ac < 2 )
        {
        fprintf(stderr,"Usage: fileinfo file(s)\n");
        exit(1);
        }
    printf("%-20s %10s %15s\n\n", "File name", "size",
                        "last altered");
    while ( ac > 1 )
        {
        if (    stat(av[1],&finfo) != 0 )
            perror(av[1]);
        else
            printf("%-20s %10ld    %s", av[1], finfo.st_size,
                    ctime( &(finfo.st_mtime) ) );
        av++;
        ac--;
        }
}
```

☐ *Question 7-4* Why was the newline in the final print statement of the previous version removed in this version?

And here is a sample run:

```
A>finfo tofu fries curd
```

```
File name               size    last altered

tofu                    1920    Sat Feb 22 10:29:48 1986
fries                   1792    Mon Jan 13 10:30:42 1986
curd                       0    Sun Feb 23 16:46:00 1986


A>
```

The `ctime()` function often is used in conjunction with the `time()` function. This function obtains the time in seconds form, and `ctime()` can be used to convert the result to string form. The syntax is a little unusual; here is the function declaration:

```
long time ( tmpt)
long *tmpt;
```

When you call time, you normally supply it with the address of a `long` variable. The time function then places the time in that location. It also supplies the time as a return value. Thus, if `time1` and `time2` are `long` variables, this call assigns the current time to both variables:

```
time1 = time ( &time2 );
```

If the null pointer is provided as argument, only the return mechanism applies. This is convenient for uses like this:

```
printf("The current time is %s", ctime(NULL) );
```

This produces output along these lines:

```
The current time is Tue Apr 29 13:55:18
```

The IBM C library also offers a more extended time service using the `asctime()`, `ftime()`, `gmtime()`, and `localtime()` functions. They use a structure instead of a `long` to hold the time information and offer a bit more detail. If you believe time is of the essence, you may wish to peruse the descriptions of these functions in the software manual.

Interrupt Handling: Signal()

Let's go on to another area of library support. PC-DOS provides a way for you to interrupt a running program: CTRL-C. Normally, this shuts down a program, closing files, but leaving buffered I/O unflushed. The `signal()` function offers you a way to modify the effect of this interrupt. Again, we will find a method that seems a bit elaborate for handling one condition, and again the reason is that we are using a function that has been scaled down in scope from a more complex system.

The `signal()` function takes two arguments. The first is an integer identifying which interrupt signal is to be handled. With DOS, there is just one choice. Use the manifest constant `SIGINT`. It is defined in the *signal.h* file, and corresponds to a type 23H system interrupt, which is the CTRL-C signal. The second argument is, in principle, a pointer to a function to be called when the `SIGINT` interrupt is detected.

If you write the function yourself, you should make it a type `int` function that takes one `int` argument. The `signal()` function will then pass `SIGINT` as the actual argument to your function. Instead of using your own function, you can use two predefined pointers from the *signal.h* file. They are `SIG_IGN`, which means your program should ignore the interrupt, and `SIG_DFL`, which means your program should go back to the default response, which is to quit.

Once an interrupt has been detected, the specified action (default quit, ignore, or your special function) is executed. If your program chooses to go on, it resumes at the statement it was processing when the interrupt was sent. It also resets the default interrupt response so that the next interrupt will halt the program. Here is an example:

```
/* think.c--mildly headstrong program using signal() */
#include <signal.h>
#include <stdio.h>
main()
{
    char *pc = "Please don't interrupt; I'm thinking.";
    int ifbreak() ;             /* declare the function */

    signal( SIGINT, ifbreak); /* use ifbreak() on ^C /
    for ( ; ; )               /* a forever loop */
        puts(pc);
}
int ifbreak ( sig )           /*interrupt-handling function */
int sig;
{
    puts ("Hey, buzz off!");
}
```

The `for( ; ;)` construction creates an endless loop. The `ifbreak()` function must be declared even though it is the default `int` type. This is so the compiler will recognize the name `ifbreak` to be a pointer to a function.

Here is a sample run:

```
A>think
Please don't interrupt; I'm thinking.
Please don't interrupt; I'm thinking.
```

241

```
Please don't interrupt; I'm thinking.
Please don't interrupt; I'm thinking.
Please don't int^C
Hey, buzz off!
errupt; I'm thinking.
Please don't interrupt; I'm thinking.
Please don't interrupt; I'm thinking.
Please don't interrup^C

A>
```

Notice that the second interrupt stopped the program. If you want the program to continue ignoring interrupts, you must reset signal():

```
/* thinka.c--reset signal handling */
#include <signal.h>
#include <stdio.h>
int ifbreak();
main()
{
    char *pc = "Please don't interrupt; I'm thinking.";
    int i = 10;

    signal( SIGINT, ifbreak);
    while ( i--)
        puts(pc);
    signal ( SIGINT, SIG_DFL);  /* back to normal */
    for( ; ; )
        puts(pc);
}
int ifbreak ( sig )
int sig;
{
    signal ( SIGINT, ifbreak);  /* reset */
    puts ("Hey, buzz off!");
}
```

Here, if there is an interrupt, the ifbreak() function is called. It resets the interrupt condition so that the next interrupt will also invoke the ifbreak() function. If we stopped here, the program would be break-proof, and we would have to reset the computer to stop it. Realizing this, we confined the breakproof feature to the first 10 iterations. After that, we used signal() to reestablish the default service.

This program illustrates that signal() establishes a condition that holds for a certain segment of a program. Think of it as issuing a standing order that is subject to revision.

Here is a sample run:

```
A>thinka
Please don't interrupt; I'm thinking.
Please don't interrupt; I'm thinking.
Please don't interrupt; I'm thinking.
Please don't interrupt; I'm thinking.
Please don't int^C
Hey, buzz off!
errupt; I'm thinking.
Please don't interrupt; I'm thinking.
Please don't interrupt; I'm thinking.
Please don't interrup^C
Hey, buzz off!
t; I'm thinking.
Please don't interrupt; I'm thinking.
Please don't interrupt; I'm thinking.
Please don't interrupt; I'm thinking.
Please don't interrupt; I'm thinking.
Please don't i^C

A>
```

Interrupts in the first 10 iterations were processed by the ifbreak() function, and the first interrupt after the 10 protected iterations was processed normally.

When would you use signal()? One occasion would be when you want to protect a certain crucial section of your program from interruption. You would use an approach like that of the last example. In particular, the called function would reset the interrupt-handling condition you desire, and you would restore the default response after the critical portion of the program ended.

A second, perhaps more common, use would be to augment the program shutdown process. Here is an example:

```
  ...
int closeout();
  ...
signal(SIGINT, closeout);
  ...
int closeout( sig )
int sig;
{
  extern char *file;

  signal(SIGINT, SIG_IGN);   /* don't interrupt closeout */
  chmod ( file, S_IREAD );   /* reset permission */
  exit(0);                   /* now quit */
}
```

Presumably, the main program altered the permission mode of a read-only file; the `closeout()` function resets the read-only permission when you interrupt the program. The `exit()` function flushes all buffers and closes all open files, so we don't have to do so explicitly.

The Environment

DOS, like UNIX, maintains a set of "environmental" variables. These are static variables that can be used by the operating system and by program running under the operating system. To see what the current environmental variables are, give the SET command:

```
A> SET
COMSPEC=A:\COMMAND.COM
PROMPT=$n$g
PATH=A:\BIN
TMP=B:
INCLUDE=A:\INCLUDE
LIB=A:\LIB

A>
```

What are these variables? Where did they come from? Of what use are they?

Some of the parameters, such as `COMSPEC`, were set up when the system was booted, and others here were user-defined using the `set` command. For instance, the command

```
SET TMP=B:
```

was used to create the `TMP` environmental parameter and to assign it the value B:. Note that there are no spaces around the equal sign.

The operating system uses the `COMSPEC` parameter to tell it where to find the *command.com* file; this is the file containing the DOS command-processing program. The `PROMPT` sets up the appearance of the prompt, and `PATH` determines which directories will be searched for command files. The DOS manual describes these parameters and how to set them.

The environment can act as an interface between the operating system and a program. For instance, the IBM C Compiler uses the `LIB` parameter to tell it on which disk and in which directory to look for the library files. The `PATH`, `TMP`, and `INCLUDE` parameters in our example also are used by the C compiler. Some of the time functions use the `TZ` variable, if set, to determine the local time zone. Your program can use an environment parameter to provide or override default values used by your program.

Or you may wish to have your program redefine a parameter. Perhaps it would reset PATH to a particular directory holding files used by your program. In this context, it is important to realize that a C program works with a *copy* of the original environment. Any changes your program makes in the copy will hold for the duration of the program, but when the program ends, the original DOS-set values will again hold.

The C Environment Table

An IBM C program has access to the environment and can inspect individual parameters. When a program is run, the current environment values are copied into a table. Each individual parameter and variable pair is stored as a single string in this form:

```
TMP=B:\0
```

Here TMP is the parameter name, B: is the parameter value, and the null character marks the end of the string. The strings are stored in sequence in the stack. Next, the addresses of these strings are stored in consecutive positions in the stack, one address for each string. The NULL address is appended to the list of addresses to act as an end marker. Finally, the address of the address of the first string is stored in an external variable called environ. Figure 7–4 shows this variable's use as a pointer to a pointer. Using array notation, this makes environ[0] a pointer to the first string, environ[1] a pointer to the second string, and so on. The scheme is very much like the argv scheme, except that a null pointer instead of a count (argc) is used to identify the end of the array of strings.

Accessing and Altering the Environment Table

The preferred method in IBM C to access and modify the environmental parameters is to use the getenv() and the putenv() functions. The getenv() function takes one argument, a string consisting of the name of the environmental parameter. It then returns a pointer to a string consisting of the parameter's value. If it fails to find a parameter by the given name (and it is case sensitive), it returns the NULL pointer. For example, consider this segment:

```
char *getenv();      /* returns a pointer to a string */
char *pc;
   ...
if ( (pc = getenv("LIB") ) != NULL )
    printf("The value of the LIB parameter is %s\n", pc);
else
    printf("LIB is undefined\n");
```

With the environment list we gave at the beginning of this section, this program fragment would produce the following output:

Figure 7-4
Environ—A Pointer to a Pointer

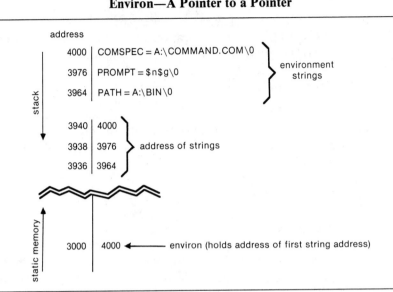

The value of the LIB parameter is A:\LIB

Figure 7-5 shows the action of getenv().

Figure 7-5
Obtaining the Environmental Parameters with Getenv()

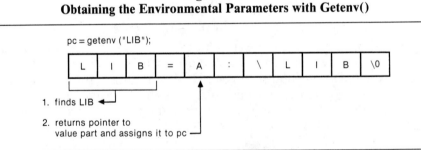

The putenv() is used to redefine an environment parameter or to create a new one. As an argument it takes a string showing name and value separated by an equals sign. It returns 0 if successful, −1 if not. Here is how a simple call would look

```
putenv("USER=toby");
```

Just as with the set command, there should be no spaces around the equals sign. Don't forget that this alters the C programs copy of the environment; the original environment is unaffected.

Accessing the Environment Table Directly

We also can access the table directly using two different methods. Using getenv() and putenv() is preferred, but looking at the other methods provides a bit more insight into how the environment table is maintained.

One method is to make use of the external identifier environ. It, recall, is a static variable holding the address of a pointer to the first string of the table. The second method is to provide main() with a third argument, as in this heading:

```
main(ac,av,env)
int ac;
char *av[];
char *env[];
```

This creates an automatic variable (hence a stack variable) called env and assigns it the address of the address of the first environmental string.

At this point it may seem that the only difference between environ and env is that one is in static memory and one is in the stack. And, at this point, that is the only difference. But, when putenv() is used to modify the environment, environ keeps track of the changes, while env does not. To see what actually happens, let's run an example that investigates env and environ and before and after putenv() is used to modify the environment:

```
/* envir.c--investigating the environment */
#include <stdio.h>
#define PA(X) printf("&X: %u; X: %u; *X: %u\n", &X, X, *X)
#define PV(X,N) printf("X[%d]: %s\n", N, X[N])
extern char **environ;     /* a static variable */
main(ac,av,env)
int ac;
char *av[];
char *env[];               /* a stack variable */
{
   int i;

   printf("Initial values:\n");
   PA(environ); / * print &environ, environ, and *environ */
   PA(env);
   putenv("HASTE=waste");
   printf("Values after first putenv() call:\n");
   PA(environ);
   PA(env);
   putenv("PROMPT=>>");
```

```
      printf("Values after second putenv() call:\n");
      PA(environ);
      PA(env);
      for (i = 0;  environ[i] != NULL; i++)
        PV(environ,i);
      for ( i = 0; env[i] != NULL; i++)
        PV(env, i);
    }
```

The program uses a couple of printing macros; you may wish to refer to Appendix A if you are not familiar with this usage. Here is the output:

```
A>envir
Initial values:
&environ: 402; environ: 3842; *environ: 3856
&env: 3840; env: 3842; *env: 3856
Values after first putenv() call:
&environ: 402; environ: 3958; *environ: 3856
&env: 3840; env: 3842; *env: 3856
Values after second putenv() call:
&environ: 402; environ: 3958; *environ: 3856
&env: 3840; env: 3842; *env: 3856
environ[0]: COMSPEC=A:\COMMAND.COM
environ[1]: PROMPT=>>
environ[2]: PATH=B:\BIN
environ[3]: TMP=A:
environ[4]: INCLUDE=B:\INCLUDE
environ[5]: LIB=B:\LIB
environ[6]: HASTE=waste
env[0]: COMSPEC=A:\COMMAND.COM
env[1]: PROMPT=$n$g
env[2]: PATH=B:\BIN
env[3]: TMP=A:
env[4]: INCLUDE=B:\INCLUDE
env[5]: LIB=B:\LIB

A>
```

There's a lot of information here, but with a little patience we should be able to determine what it means. Initially, we have two pointer variables (environ and env) set to the same address. The PA() macro prints out the address of a variable, the value (or pointed-to address) of the variable, and the value stored in the pointed-to address. Since environ and env are double pointers, this final item will be the address of the first environment string. The first two calls show that environ and env are stored in two separate addresses. This is proper, since they are two separate variables. Both contain the same address, 3842. This is the address of the initial element in the array of string addresses. Finally, the address 3842 contains another address, 3856, that is the address of the first environmental parameter. Figure 7–6 shows this arrangement more simply than words can do.

Figure 7–6
Pointer Variables Env and Environ

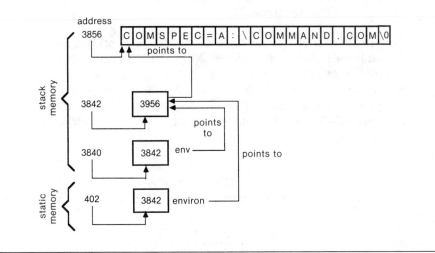

Then the program makes a call to putenv() and adds a new parameter (HASTE) to the list. Again, information is printed about environ and env. The addresses of these two variables remain unchanged, of course, since the variables haven't been moved. But now environ *contains* a different address, 3958 instead of 3842. Meanwhile, the env variable is still 3842. But although now environ is not equal to env, the values *environ and *env are still the same. In short, env and environ now point to different pointers. But those pointers point to the same string.

Here's what happens in this process. The putenv() call added a new parameter to the environment. That means a ncw address has to be added to the list of string addresses. Judging from the address values, the stack is being used to hold the address, and a program can't back up and insert something into the stack. Instead, an entire new array of addresses is added to the stack. The old array is copied into the new array, so that the first member of both old and new array is still 3856, the address of the first string. But the new array is one member longer and holds the address of the new parameter. The env variable still points to the old array of addresses, but environ was updated to point to the new array. Only the addresses were recopied; the strings were left alone. That's why both the first pointer in both the old and new array of pointers have the same value; they point to the original string.

The next call to putevn() changes a parameter but doesn't add any new ones, so no new address array is changed. However, the contents of the address corresponding to the **PROMPT** parameter are changed to the address of the new string. Only the new array is updated in this fashion, as shown by the final part of the program.

To print out the environment, we make use of the fact that the end of the address array is marked by the **NULL** pointer:

```
for (i = 0;  environ[i] != NULL; i++)
    PV(environ,i);
```

This loop marches through the address list, printing the strings at the stored addresses, until it encounters **NULL**. The printout reveals that env still refers to the original environment. Not only does it not include **WASTE**, but it shows the original setting for **PROMPT**. The environ pointer, however, points to the master list of addresses for the current environment string. Figure 7–7 shows the old and new arrays for the addresses.

Figure 7–7
Old and New Address Arrays

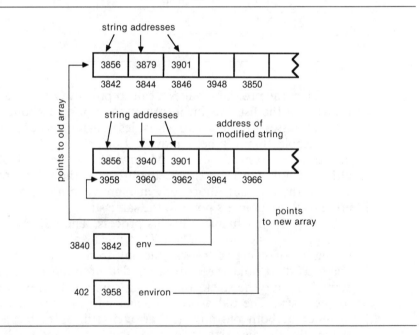

Using the Environment

One possibility we mentioned was using an environment parameter to override program default values. As an example, here is a short program that prints out the first few lines of each file in its command line argument list.

The exact number of lines is taken from an environmental variable called TOPCOUNT. If no such variable is found, the program uses a default value.

```c
/* top.c--examines tops of files */
#include <stdio.h>
#include <stdlib.h>                   /* declares getenv() */
#include <conio.h>
#define DFLT_CT 10                    /* program default value */
main(ac, av)
int ac;
char *av[];
{
    int lc;                           /* line count */
    int lines = DFLT_CT;              /* line limit */
    FILE *fp;
    int ch;
    char *topcount;                   /* ptr to envir. var */

    if ( ac < 2 )
        {
        fprintf(stderr,"Usage: top file(s)\n");
        exit(1);
        }
    if ( (topcount = getenv("TOPCOUNT") ) != NULL )
        lines = atoi(topcount);   /* converts string to int */
    while ( ac > 1 )
        {
        if ( (fp = fopen(av[1],"r") ) == NULL )
            perror(av[1]);
        else
            {
            lc = 0;                   /* initialize line count */
            while ( lc < lines && (ch = getc(fp) ) != EOF)
                {
                putchar(ch);
                if (ch == '\n')
                    lc++;
                }
            fclose(fp);
            if ( ac > 2 )             /* if there is a file left, */
                getch();              /* wait for a keystroke */
            }
        av++;
        ac--;
        }
}
```

The program pauses between files, awaiting a keystroke before continuing. You could, of course add a prompt at that point.

Here is a sample run that illustrates setting the environment parameter. Initially, the program uses the default value:

```
A>top classlist
Roger Ames
Caryn Astal
Penny Banasol
Dick Buffer
Regulus Canape
Tani Chrophulson
Cranefield Dimsum
Evelyn Eaves
Arthur Flintwood
Wilhelmina Gladworthy

A>SET TOPCOUNT=4
A>top classlist
Roger Ames
Caryn Astal
Penny Banasol
Dick Buffer

A>
```

Note that TOPCOUNT was typed using uppercase. DOS is not case sensitive, but C is. Therefore the user had to type the name as it was used in the C program.

UNIX System V and XENIX maintain environments, too. Both maintain the external variable environ and have the getenv() function, but XENIX lacks putenv().

Conversions

Our example made use of a conversion function, so let's look at that topic now. The atoi() function is one of several data conversion routines from the library. It converts a number in string form to integer form. Figure 7-8 shows how the function works. (The name stands for *a*scii-*to*-*i*nteger.) Sometimes numbers come as strings. Environment parameters are one example, since all values—numerical or otherwise—are stored as strings. Another example would be command line arguments, which are passed as strings. For interactive input, it is simpler to use scanf(), but you could design an input function—using, say, getchar() and atoi()—to do the job more efficiently. (Scanf() is a fine function, but since it must handle a variety of formats, it tends to be less efficient than a single-purpose function.)

Figure 7–8
The Atoi() Data Conversion Function

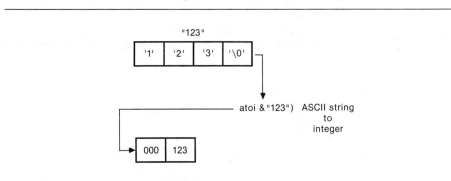

Table 7–4 lists IBM C's data conversion functions.

Table 7–4
Data Conversion Functions in IBM C

Function	Use
atof()	Convert string to float
atoi()	Convert string to int
atol()	Convert string to long
ecvt()	Convert double to e-format string
fcvt()	Convert double to f-format string
gcvt()	Convert double to g-format string
itoa()	Convert int to string
ltoa()	Convert long to string
ultoa()	Convert unsigned long to string

☐ *Question 7–5* In Chapter 6 we wrote a recursive function that performed number base conversions. How could you incorporate it into a program that converts a command line argument base 10 integer to a binary number?

The declaration for atof() is contained in the *math.h* file, and the remaining declarations are found in the *stlib.h* file.

The Sprintf() Function

The `sprintf()` function is another conversion function. As its name suggests, it belongs to the `printf()` family of functions. All of these functions convert arguments as directed into text output. But while `printf()` and `fprintf()` send the text to the screen or to a file, the `sprintf()` function places it in a buffer. This is useful for constructing a string from assorted forms of information.

The first argument should be the address of the buffer, and the subsequent arguments follow the `printf()` format. For example, consider this code fragment:

```
char *pc = "Stodgemeyer";
int acnum = 27777;
char info[40];

printf("The %s account number is %d", pc, acnum);
sprintf(info, "The %s account number is %d", pc, acnum);
```

The `printf()` statement prints the following:

```
The Stodgemeyer account number is 27777
```

It formats the string and the integer variable into standard text format.

The `sprintf()` call places the same sequence of characters in the array `info`; it also appends a null character, thus producing the standard string format. The `info` string could be printed later, perhaps after additional string operations had been performed upon it.

Deleting Files: Unlink()

With `creat()`, `open()`, and `fopen()`, we can create files. To counterbalance these functions, we have `unlink()`, which deletes files. The name comes from UNIX, in which more than one name can be "linked" to a file. There, the `unlink()` function unlinks names from a file. When the last name is unlinked, the file goes too. With DOS, only one link is possible, so a single call to `unlink()` is enough to delete the file. The function takes the pathname of the doomed file as an argument and returns values of 0 if successful and −1 if not.

Here is a program that shows you the top few lines of file, then asks if you wish to delete it. We can use `unlink()` to remove the file, and the *top* program to show it. The most efficient way to use *top* would be to rewrite it as a function, but since we are highlighting the C library, we will use the `system()` function to run the *top* program. Using the `system()` function, you call upon DOS commands and upon other *.com* and *.exe* programs. As an argument it takes the desired command as a string. To construct the string, we bring in two string-handling functions, strcpy() and strncat(). We'll discuss all these functions in due time, but first, here is the program:

```c
/* rm.c--shows file head, inquires about removal */
#include <stdio.h>
#include <string.h>
#define CMD "top "          /* name of EXE command */
#define MAXCH 128
main(ac, av)
int ac;
char *av[];
{
    char cmdstr[MAXCH];
    char response;

    if ( ac < 2 )
        {
        fprintf(stderr,"Usage: rm file(s)\n");
        exit(1);
        }
    while ( ac > 1 )
        {
        if ( access (av[1], 04 ) != 0 )
            perror(av[1]);   /* no read permission */
        else if (access (av[1], 02) != 0 )
            fprintf(stderr,"%s is read only\n", av[1]);
        else
            {
            printf("Top of %s file:\n\n", av[1] );
            strcpy(cmdstr, CMD);
            strncat(cmdstr,av[1], MAXCH - strlen(CMD) - 1 );
            system(cmdstr);  /* run command */
            printf("Remove this file? <y/n>\n");
            response = getchar();
            while (getchar() != '\n')
                    ;
            if ( response == 'y' || response == 'Y' )
                unlink(av[1]);
            }
        av++;
        ac--;
        }
}
```

The strcpy() function copies the string "top " (including the space) into the cmdstr array. The strncpy() function adds the av[1] string to the end of the current string in `cmdstr`. The final argument to `strncat()` specifies the upper limit of the number of characters to be copied. The `system()` command limits the string argument to 128 bytes, so this limit was set accordingly.

Suppose, then, we give this command:

```
A>rm oldnews oldstuff
```

Then, the first time through the loop, `cmdstr` is assigned the string "top oldnews". The `system()` call then passes this on to DOS, and the result is the same as if you had typed this:

```
A>top oldnews
```

When the command finishes, control returns to the calling program. The next cycle through, `cmdstr` will be set to "top oldstuff," and that command will be executed.

This program doesn't check to see if the argument is a directory; you may wish to test your command of `stat()` by fixing the program so that it will screen out directories.

Process Control: System(), Exec(), and Spawn()

The `system()`, `exec()`, and `spawn()` functions are part of a process control package. A process is a program being executed by the operating system, so every time you run a program, you run a process. The concept includes the program's code and data and information relating to the running of the program, such as the number of files open. You may want to run a program from within another program; you can use the process control functions to do so. These functions all launch new processes, but in somewhat different matters.

The `system()` and `exec()` functions also are found in the UNIX/ XENIX environment, but `spawn()` is not.

The System() Command

The `system()` command, we saw, runs a command and returns to the program. Essentially, it transmits the command to the DOS command interpreter, the *command.com* program. This program runs the indicated command as if you had typed its name at the keyboard. Suppose, for example, you wished at some point in your program to copy a file. Instead of writing a file-copying routine, you could do this:

```
system("copy b:prices b:temp");
```

Here we used predetermined file names, but by using the `strpy()` and strcat() string-processing functions, or, perhaps, sprintf(), you could have the program construct a command string during run time.

The Exec() Family of Functions

The system() call returns to the original process when the call is done. The exec() family, however, launches a new process, called a "child" process. This "overlays" the parent process in memory. That means the memory previously used for the "parent" process code is now used to hold the child process's code. As a result, the parent process can not be returned to, since its code no longer is present. Only if the exec() call fails will control return to the parent.

There are six separate functions in the exec() family: execl(), execle(), execlp(), execv(), execve(), and execvp(). These functions differ in how they handle arguments, environment, and pathnames. We'll go into these differences soon. In the meantime, we'll use the term exec() as a general name representing all six functions.

One use of exec() is to set up a chain of programs, each running the next. This can be useful when the amount of memory present is insufficient to hold all the programming at once. (The large memory model is useful only if the system has a large memory.) Each child inherits the open files of the parent in order to facilitate the transition. However, the mode of the file (text or binary) is not transmitted. The setmode() function (see later) can be used to handle that problem.

Another use of exec() is to create a program that acts as a decision maker for what final program is to be run.

Let's look at an example using execl(). The first argument it takes is a string specifying the program to be run. Then come a series of string arguments specifying the command line arguments for the called command. A NULL pointer is used to mark the end of the list. Rather than develop two huge chunks of program code just to show *when* exec() would be used, we'll develop a much shorter example to show *how* it is used. Here it is:

```c
/* step1.c--first of 2 steps */
#include <stdio.h>
main(ac,av)
int ac;
char *av[];
{
    if ( ac < 2)
       {
        fprintf(stderr,"Usage: step1 number\n");
        exit(1);
       }
    puts("This simulates a lot of programming.");
    execl("step2.exe", "step2", av[1],"y", NULL);
```

257

```
        fprintf(stderr,"Exec call failed: ");
        perror("step2");
}
```

This runs the *step2.exe* program as if the following command line were given:

```
step2 av[1] y
```

However, the first command line argument for `step1` would be substituted for `av[1]`; `step1` passes its command line argument on to `step2`. If the call succeeds, `step1` is history; if it fails, control returns to `step1`, and it prints the error messages.

Of course, this program requires the existence of a separately compiled program called *step2.exe*. Here, for testing purposes, is such a program:

```
/* step2.c--continues where step1 ends */
#include <stdio.h>
main(ac, av)
int ac;
char *av[];
{
   int count;

   if ( ac != 3 )
       exit(1);          /* wrong argument count */
   count = atoi (av[1]);
   if ( count < 1 )
       exit(2);          /* improper argument value */
   if ( av[2][0] == 'y')
       while (count--)
           puts("This simulates even more programming.");
   else
       puts("Nothing doing");
   exit(0);
}
```

The *step2.c* program is designed to work with exactly three arguments, which is what *step1.c* provides. Note that the `av[0]` argument is a null string for DOS versions earlier than 3.0.

Here is a sample run:

```
C>step1 3
This simulates a lot of programming.
This simulates even more programming.
This simulates even more programming.
```

```
This simulates even more programming.

C>
```

The arguments 3 and y were passed successfully to step2. Because step2 was launched successfully, there was no return to step1, and the step1 code was replaced with step2 code.

The exec() group falls into two families: those that use an argument list, as execl() did, and those that use an argument array. That is, instead of using several pointers to strings, they use a pointer to an array of strings. Table 7–5 summarizes the differences.

Table 7–5
The Exec() Family

Function	Arguments	Uses PATH?	Environment
execl()	list	no	inherit from parent
execle()	list	no	pass environment pointer as last argument
execlp	list	yes	inherit from parent
execv()	array	no	inherit from parent
execve()	array	no	pass environment pointer as last argument
execvp	array	yes	inherit from parent

Let's go over these differences. First, those functions that don't use the PATH environment variable interpret the command line literally. For instance, the first argument for our example was step2.exe. The execl() call would look for that command file in the current directory only. The execp() call, however, would use the current value of PATH to decide which directories to search for the *step.exe* file.

Next, most of the exec() calls pass on the parent's environment to the child. The execle() and execve() calls, however, add one final argument to the argument list. This is a pointer to an array of environment variables. These variables should be set up just as they are by the set command. That is, the strings should look like this:

```
TOPCOUNT=2
PATH=C:\SPECIAL\BIN
```

The argument itself should be a pointer to an address. Here is a sample setup:

```
char *en[4];    /* an array of 4 ptrs. */

en[0] = "PATH=C:\\SPECIAL\\BIN";
en[1] = "TZ=MST7MDT";
en[2] = "XLIM=320";
en[3] = NULL;


execle("xt.exe", "xt", "200", "G", NULL, en);
```

The child process will use this environment. For the PATH variable, note that in C we have to use \\ in a quoted string to get a single backslash in the stored string. Also note that the final address in the environment sequence should be NULL.

Finally, let's look at the argument lists. To see the differences between functions, we first have to define some individual strings and an array of strings:

```
char *str;       /* ptr to a string */
char *ar[4];     /* array of 4 ptrs to strings */

str = "data3";
ar[0] = "detox";
ar[1] = "data1";
ar[2] = "data2";
ar[3] = NULL;
```

The ''l'' group of exec() calls could use the strings this way:

```
execl("c:\\bin\\detox.exe", ar[0], ar[2], str, NULL)
```

The individual strings can be used as needed.

The ''v'' group, however, would work like this:

```
execv("c:\\bin\\detox.exe", ar);
```

Note that the final member of the ar array should be a pointer to NULL; that marks the end of the list.

The Spawn() Family

This family of functions is specific to the DOS environment, but we will mention it in this chapter because of the close resemblance to the exec() family. The chief difference is that the spawn() functions create a child process that does not overlay the parent process. As a result, control can return to the parent when the child process terminates. Furthermore, the return value of a spawn() function is the value provided by the exit() function in the child. Note that a program using spawn() requires enough memory for both the parent and the child process, since the parent is not overwritten. These functions are not found in the XENIX or UNIX libraries, so they are not portable to those systems. The `exec` and `spawn` functions are illustrated in Figure 7-9.

Figure 7-9
Parent and Child Processes with Exec() and Spawn()

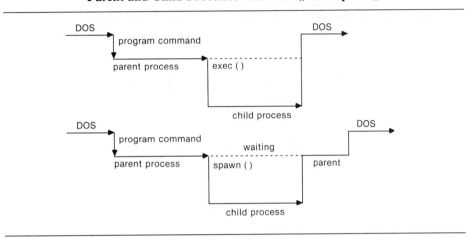

The `spawn()` functions come in the same varieties as `exec()`; that is, there are `spawnl()`, `spawnle()`, `spawnlp()`, `spawnv()`, `spawnve()`, and `spawnvp()` functions. The suffixes have the same import as they do for `exec()`.

The `spawn()` functions take one more argument than their `exec()` counterparts. The first argument should be one of the following manifest constants, which are defined in the *process.h* file:

```
P_WAIT     /* suspend parent process until execution of child is
                                                  complete */


P_NOWAIT   /* execute parent and child processes concurrently */


P_OVERLAY  /* Overlay parent with child, destroying parent */
```

The `P_OVERLAY` choice makes `spawn()` behave like `exec()`. The `P_NOWAIT` option is not yet implemented. Presumably, it awaits a DOS version that supports multitasking.

Here is an example using the `P_WAIT` parameter; it uses the same *step2* program we used earlier:

```
/* stepback.c--launches a child, later resumes running */
#include <stdio.h>
```

```
#include <process.h>   /* used by spawn() */
main(ac,av)
int ac;
char *av[];
{
    int status;

    if ( ac < 2)
      {
       fprintf(stderr,"Usage: stepback number\n");
       exit(1);
      }
    puts("This simulates a lot of programming.");
    status = spawnl(P_WAIT,"step2.exe", "step2", av[1],"y", NULL);
    if (status == -1)
      {
      fprintf(stderr,"Spawn call failed: ");
      perror("stepback");
      }
    else if (status > 0 )
      fprintf(stderr, "step2 terminated by a type %d error\n",
                                                     status);
    else
      fprintf(stderr, "step2 completed successfully\n");
}
```

Note that step2's exit status is assigned to status and used by the calling program.

Here is a sample run:

```
C> stepback 3
This simulates a lot of programming.
This simulates even more programming.
This simulates even more programming.
This simulates even more programming.
step2 completed successfully

C>
```

The spawn() family resembles system() in that both return control to the parent when the indicated command has been run. The system() call, as its name implies, is intended primarily to run DOS system calls, although it works with *.exe* and *.com* files in general. The spawn() family is intended to tie together user-generated programs. Unlike system(), it does not evoke the *command.com* program to run processes; thus, the spawn() family does not run DOS commands like dir or copy.

More File-Related Functions: Setmode(), Fileno, and Fdopen()

The `fopen()` and `open()` functions let us set the file translation mode to text or to binary when the file is opened. But sometimes it is desirable to set the translation mode *after* a file is opened. For example, we mentioned that a child process inherits the parent's open files, but without knowledge of the mode in which they had been opened. Another use is to change the default modes of the standard files *stdin, stdout, stderr, stdaux,* and *stdprn*. By default, the first three usually are opened in text mode, and the rest are opened in binary mode. However, the console I/O functions open *stdin* and *stdout* in the binary mode.

Using `setmode()` is simple. Its first argument is the file handle, and its second is `O_TEXT_` or `O_BINARY`, depending on the mode you want. Don't forget to include the *fcntl.h* file for the definitions of these constants. The function returns a 0 if it is successful and −1 otherwise.

For example, to set the standard input to binary mode, use this statement:

```
setmode( 0, O_BINARY);
```

Why was 0 used instead of *stdin*? Because `setmode()` uses the file *handle,* not the file `stream`. Remember that the handle is an integer, while the stream is a pointer to a structure.

The `setmode()` function is specific to DOS. UNIX-like systems don't need it, because they have only one file type. We mention it in this chapter because it is used in conjunction with more general functions, such as `exec()` and `system()`.

Suppose you opened a file using `fopen()`. You have a stream identifier, but what is the handle? The `fileno()` function takes care of that. If you provide `fileno()` a stream as an argument, it will return the handle. For instance, the last example could be rewritten as follows:

```
setmode( fileno(stdin), O_BINARY);
```

The `fdopen()` function goes the other way. If you provide it with a handle as an argument, it will return a stream. It also sets up the buffering and the structure required for a stream.

Text-Processing with the Ctype Family

Now let's look at another class of functions. The IBM C Compiler provides several routines for classifying characters. These routines tell you if a character is a digit, an uppercase letter, and so on. They are preprocessor macros rather than functions, and they are defined in the *ctype.h* file. They take a character argument and return "true" (non-0) or "false" (0) depending

263

on whether or not the character falls in a specified class. Table 7–6 provides a list of these macros.

Table 7–6
Ctype.h Character Classification Macros

Name	True If Argument Is
isalnum()	alphanumeric (letter or digit)
isalpha()	alphabetic
isascii()	ASCII (0x00 − 0x7F)
iscntrl()	a control character
isdigit()	a decimal digit
isgraph()	a printable character other than space
islower()	lowercase
isprint()	a printable character
ispunct()	a punctuation character
isspace()	whitespace (space, tab, newline)
isupper()	uppercase
isxdigit()	a hexadecimal digit

The isascii() routine produces valid results for all integer values, but the other routines work properly only for standard ASCII values (0–127) and EOF. Therefore, if there is a possibility of non-ASCII values, a program should screen characters with isascii() before applying other tests.

Here is a sample program that performs a simple analysis on the standard input:

```
/* chartype.c--counts characters by type */
#include <stdio.h>
#include <ctype.h>
main()
{
  unsigned long upc = 0L; /* uppercase count */
  unsigned long lwc = 0L; /* lowercase count */
  unsigned long dgc = 0L; /* digit count */
  unsigned long wsc = 0L; /* whitespace count */
  unsigned long cnc = 0l; /* control-character count */
  unsigned long pnc = 0L; /* punctuation count */
  unsigned long nac = 0l; /* non-ASCII count */
  int ch;
```

```
        while ( (ch = getchar() ) != EOF )
            {
            if ( !isascii(ch) )    /* first screen non-ascii */
                    nac++;
            else if ( islower(ch) )
                    lwc++;
            else if ( isupper(ch) )
                    upc++;
            else if ( isspace(ch) )
                    wsc++;
            else if ( isdigit(ch) )
                    dgc++;
            else if ( ispunct(ch) )
                    pnc++;
            else if ( iscntrl(ch) )
                    cnc++;
                }
            }
        printf("non-ascii count = %ld\n", nac);
        printf("lowercase count = %ld\n", lwc);
        printf("uppercase count = %ld\n", upc);
        printf("whitespace count = %ld\n", wsc);
        printf("digit count = %ld\n", dgc);
        printf("punctuation count = %ld\n", pnc);
        printf("control character count = %ld\n", cnc);
    }
```

Here is a sample run:

```
A>type textsamp
"Oh no! I've connected myself to the 100 MW ^BVoltorama!^B"
exclaimed Tom in electrified tones.

A>chartype < textsamp
non-ascii count = 0
lowercase count = 62
uppercase count = 6
whitespace count = 14
digit count = 3
punctuation count = 6
control character count = 2
```

The *ctype.h* file also defines the five conversion macros listed in Table 7–7. Each returns the result of the conversion.

Table 7-7
Ctype Conversion Macros

Name	Converts Argument to
toascii()	ASCII
tolower()	lowercase if initially uppercase
_tolower()	lowercase; undefined if argument not uppercase
toupper()	uppercase if initially lowercase
_toupper()	uppercase; undefined if argument not lowercase

The tolower() routine first ascertains if its argument is an uppercase character. If so, it returns the lowercase value; otherwise it returns the original value. The _tolower() routine does not check to see if its argument is uppercase. Thus, it is slightly faster but will produce unmeaningful results if the argument isn't uppercase. A similar distinction holds between toupper() and _toupper().

The tolower() and toupper() routines also are available as functions. The macro versions are faster but do not handle arguments with side effects correctly. That is, a call like

```
ch = toupper ( *cp++);
```

won't handle the incrementation correctly. See the Appendix A, which describes the preprocessor, for more details.

To use the function versions, don't include the *ctype.h* file. If you need that file for other macros, then use the #undef feature to undefine the tolower() and toupper() macros. This directive is discussed in Appendix A.

Text Processing with String Functions

The IBM C library is rich in functions designed to work with C strings. They perform such tasks as finding the length of a string, copying a string, adding onto a string, finding characters in a string, and converting strings to uppercase or to lowercase. Table 7-8 lists those string functions whose declarations are given in the *string.h* file. In the table, the arguments s, s1, and s2 are strings, n is an integer, and c is a character.

Of this list, all but strcmpi(), strlwr(), strnset(), strrev(), strset() and strupr() are common to IBM C, XENIX, and UNIX System V.

Table 7–8
String Functions

Type (Char *) Functions Returning a Pointer to Their First Argument

Name	Action
strcat(s1,s2)	Appends s2 to s1
strcpy(s1,s2)	Copies s2 into s1
strlwr(s)	Converts s to lowercase
strncat(s1,s2,n)	Appends n characters of s2 to s1
strncpy(s1,s2,n)	Copies n characters of s2 to s1
strnset(s,c,n)	Initializes first n characters of s to c
strrev(s)	Reverses s
strset(s,c)	Sets all characters (but ' \ 0') in s to c
strupr(s)	Converts s to uppercase

Type (Char *) Functions Returning a Pointer
If Successful and NULL Otherwise

Name	Returns a Pointer to
strchr(s,c)	First example of c in s
strdup(s)	Duplicate of s, using malloc()
strbrk(s1,s2)	First example in s1 of any character in s2
strrchr(s,c)	Last example of c in s
strtok(s1,s2)	Next token in s1 using token delimiters from s2

Type Int Functions

Name	Description
strcmp(s1,s2)	Compares s1 and s2 lexicographically
	Returns 0 if the strings are the same, less than 0 if s1 precedes s2 in ASCII sequence, and greater than 0 if s1 follows s2
strmcpi(s1,s2)	Case-insensitive version of strcmp()
strcspn(s1,s2)	Returns index of first character in s1 belonging to s2. Returns length of s1 if there is no match
strlen(s)	Returns length of s, not counting ' \ 0'

Table 7–8 (cont.)
Type Int Functions

strncmp(s1,s2)	Like strcmp(), but limits comparison to first n characters
strspn(s1,s2)	Returns index of first character in s1 not belonging to s2

You can find many uses for these functions, and we'll look at a couple of them now.

Screening Menu Choices

In Chapter 5 we had an example of a menu-driven program. This program rejected invalid selections with this code segment:

```
ch = getcharln(); /* fetch first char on line, discard rest */
while ( ch < 'a' || ch > 'e') && ch != EOF )
    {
    printf("Sorry, that is not a choice. ");
    printf("Please enter an a, b, c, d, or e.\n");
    ch = getcharln();
    }
```

This coding relies on the menu choices being consecutive letters in the alphabet. What if they aren't? One possibility is to check each possibility explicitly, but that is tedious. The strchr() function offers a second choice. We can create a string consisting of the valid choices, then use strchr() to see if the actual choice is in the string. While we are at it, we can convert the response to lowercase so that the menu selection process becomes case insensitive. Here is one possible coding; it assumes the menu choices are a (for append), d (for delete), s (for sort), c (for change), and q (for quit):

```
static char *answers = "adscq";
  ...
ch = tolower ( getcharln() );
while ( strchr( answers, ch ) == NULL  && ch != EOF )
    {
    printf("Sorry, that is not a choice. Please select\n");
    printf("a letter from this list: %s\n", answers);
    ch = tolower ( getcharln() );
    }
```

The answers pointer was made static so that it would be initialized just once instead of each time the containing function was called. Alternatively, we could have used an external string.

One nice feature of the string approach is that if you decide to add more menu choices, you can modify the `answers` string and not have to modify the actual test.

☐ *Question 7-6* How could you get the valid choices printed with spaces between the characters?

Substituting a String for a Character

Our next exercise is to write a function that replaces a given character in a string with the characters of an entire string. To test the function, we'll place it in a program whose objective is to replace the symbol * with the name of a hypothetical magazine. First, here is replacement function:

```
/* replace.c--replaces a character with a string */
#include <string.h>
#define NULL  ((char *) 0 )
char *malloc();

char *replace( s1, c, s2, max)
char *s1;      /* string to be modified */
char *c;       /* ptr to char to be replaced*/
char *s2;      /* string of chars to replace c */
int max;       /* maximum available space in target string */
{
    int len;
    char *temp;

    len = strlen(s1) + strlen(s2) - 1; /* needed length */
    if ( len > max -1 )
        return NULL;          /* stop if not enough room */
    temp = malloc( len + 1);  /* create workspace */
    strcpy(temp, s2);      /* copy replacement string */
    strcat(temp,c   1);    /* add rest of original string */
    strcpy(c, temp);       /* copy into original string */
    free(temp);            /* free workspace */
    return s1;             /* return ptr to beginning of string */
}
```

Here is how the function works. It copies the replacement string into a temporary array. To it, it adds that portion of the original string following the first occurrence of the character to be replaced. This string is copied onto the original string, beginning at the position of the character to be replaced. This step is accomplished by the

```
strcpy(c, temp);
```

statement, for c points to that character. The string pointer arguments to a string function need not point to the first character of a string; this extends the versatility of functions such a strcpy(). Figure 7-10 illustrates the replacement. Most of the remaining program is concerned with keeping the new string within a given size limit.

Figure 7-10
Replace() at Work

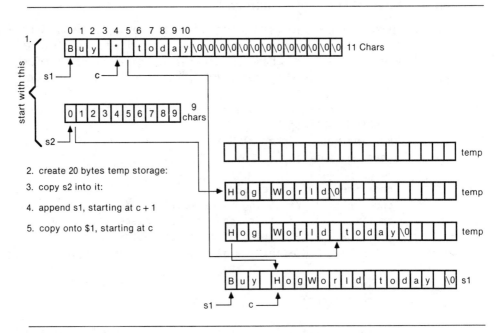

□ *Question 7-7* Can you use the string functions to construct a function that takes a string pointer and a character and returns the number of characters in the string that follow the final occurrence of the given character? Have a return value of −1 indicate that the character is not found in the string.

The function replaces only the first occurrence of the character with the string, but by using it repeatedly until a NULL is returned, it can process all the characters.

Next, here is a program to test the function. It also uses the getline() function we developed in Question 5-3. We assume here that it is a separate object code file.

```
/* hw.c--tests replace.c */
#include <stdio.h>
#include <string.h>
#define MAXNUM 20
```

```
#define MAXLEN 78
#define EXTRA  80  /* extra space for string replacements */
#define ULINE '_'
#define SYMBOL '*'
#define REPLACE "Hog World"
char  *getline(), *replace();
main()
{
int i = 0;
int count;
char lines[MAXNUM][MAXLEN + EXTRA];
char *pc;

printf("Enter up to %d lines:\n1> ", MAXNUM);
while ( i < MAXNUM  && getline(lines[i], MAXLEN) != NULL
              && lines[i][0] != '\0' )
   {
   while (  (pc = strchr(lines[i], SYMBOL) ) != NULL )
       replace ( lines[i], pc, REPLACE, MAXLEN + EXTRA);
   if (++i < MAXNUM)
       printf("%d> ", i + 1);
   }
printf("Here are the %d lines you entered:\n", i );
for ( count = 0; count < i; count++)
   puts( lines[count]);
}
```

Here is a sample run:

```
A>hw
Enter up to 20 lines:
1> Hello *ers! Have we got a * deal for you! Get 14
2> issues of * and a free * teeshirt for $12. Now
3> doesn't that make you shout "*! *! *!"
4> [RETURN]
Hello Hog Worlders! Have we got a Hog World deal for you! Get 14
issues of Hog World and a free Hog World teeshirt for $12. Now
doesn't that make you shout "Hog World! Hog World! Hog World!"

A>
```

Performing Math Operations

IBM C offers several floating-point math functions, including a square root function, several trig functions, log and exponential functions, and a few others. These functions require floating-point support. The 8088 processor

271

in the IBM PC does not do floating-point calculations, so the support must come either from library routines or from a floating-point coprocessor. The IBM C Compiler offers several ways to implement floating-point support. If you make extensive use of floating-point operations, check the manual for details to see which best fits your needs. The default choice uses the co-processor if it is installed and calls upon a library that emulates the co-processor if one is not present. However, the various implementation choices are compile-time options; they don't affect how programs are written.

Let's look at a common kind of calculation: converting between rec-tangular coordinates and polar coordinates. To locate a point on a two-dimensional plane requires two numbers. One approach is to use one number (the x coordinate) to tell how far to the left or right of the origin a point is. A second number (the y coordinate) gives the distance above or below the origin. This is the rectangular coordinate approach shown in Fig-ure 7-11. The same figure also shows the polar coordinate approach; it describes a point by giving its distance and direction from the origin.

Figure 7-11
Rectangular and Polar Coordinates

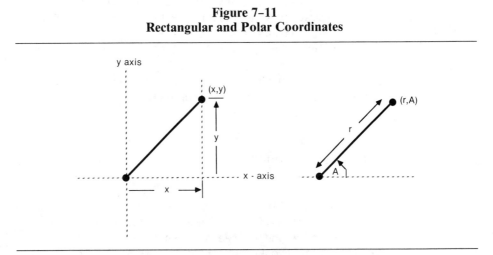

Often one or the other coordinate systems is used to describe a *vector,* which can be visualized as an arrow having a certain direction and magni-tude. In physics and engineering, for example, vectors are used to describe things like motion and forces, where both the direction and size matter. Converting from one type of coordinate system to the other is a common need in these areas. When we speak of vectors, the number pairs are called *components.*

Polar to Rectangular Conversion

Converting from polar components to rectangular components is a straight-forward application of trigonometry, illustrated in Figure 7-12. If we use A to represent the angle and r as the distance, we have these equations:

$$x = r \cos A \qquad \longleftarrow \quad \text{the x component}$$
$$y = r \sin A \qquad \longleftarrow \quad \text{the y component}$$

Figure 7–12
Polar to Rectangular Components

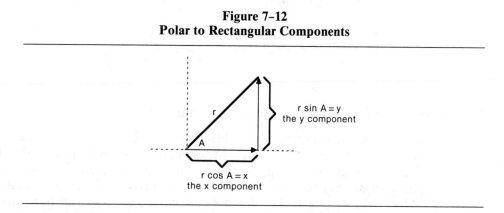

Since the library contains sine and cosine functions (sin() and cos()), we can write a C function to make this conversion. Before writing it, let's consider the form. We need to give the function two values (r and A), and it should provide two values (x and y) to the calling program. One way to do that is to pass four arguments: the values of r and A and the addresses of x and y. But the r and A set describe a single entity, as do the x and y pair. This suggests representing each pair by a structure. Not only does this emphasize that each pair describes one entity, but a structure can be a return value. Thus we can set up the function to accept one structure as an argument and to return a second structure.

There is one more point to make. The library trig functions expect angles to be measured in radians. *Radians* are an angle measure used in mathematics and physics; pi radians equal 180 degrees, so 1 radian is about 57.3 degrees. Our function will assume angles are in degrees, so it will have to make a conversion.

Here, then is the conversion function; note that we must include the *math.h* file:

```
#include <math.h>
struct vectxy {
        float x;        /* x component */
        float y;        /* y component */
        };
struct vectra {
        float r;        /* vector magnitude */
        float a;        /* angle in degrees */
        };
#define PI 3.141592654
#define D_PER_R  ( 180.0 / PI ) /* degrees per radian */
```

```
struct vectxy poltoxy ( v )
struct vectra v;
{
    struct vectxy vc;

    vc.x = v.r * cos ( v.a / D_PER_R );
    vc.y = v.r * sin ( v.a / D_PER_R );
    return vc;
}
```

Rectangular Components to Polar Components

Going the other direction is slightly more involved. Getting r from x and y is simple, for we can use the Pythagorean theorem, which states that r is the square root of the sum of the squares of x and of y. We can use the library function sqrt() for this calculation. A property of the angle is that its sine is the ratio of y to r. There is a function, the arc sine function, that takes the ratio as an argument and returns the angle. In the C library, this function is called asin(). The complication is that the return value of asin() is given as an angle between (after conversion to degrees) −90 degrees and +90 degrees. That is, it gives an answer in the first or fourth quadrants, as Figure 7–13 has graphed it. The problem is that angles in the second quadrant duplicate the sine values of those in the first quadrant. In Figure 7–13, for example, A1 and A2 have the same sine value. Similarly, the third quadrant duplicates the fourth quadrant's values.

Figure 7–13
Quadrants Used by Asin

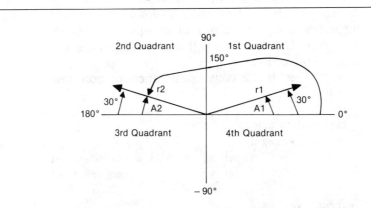

Suppose, then, we have a vector like r2 in Figure 7–13. Using the arc sine function will give us the angle A1. But then we can look at the value of x. If x is negative and y is positive, we know the vector really is in the second quadrant, and we can subtract A1 from 180 degrees to get A2. If both x and y are negative, the vector is in the third quadrant, and we can make a similar adjustment.

Here is a function that makes the conversion:

```c
#include <math.h>
struct vectxy {
                float x;        /* x component */
                float y;        /* y component */
                };
struct vectra {
                float r;        /* vector magnitude */
                float a;        /* angle in degrees */
                };
#define PI 3.141592654
#define D_PER_R   ( 180.0 / PI )

struct vectra xytopol ( vc )
struct vectxy vc;
{
    struct vectra v;
    double arad;     /* angle in radians */

    v.r = sqrt( vc.x * vc.x + vc.y * vc.y);
    arad = asin ( vc.y / v.r );
    if ( vc.x >= 0.0 )        /* 1st and 4th quadrants */
       v.a = arad * D_PER_R;
    else if ( vc.y >= 0.0 )      /* 2nd quadrant */
       v.a = 180.0 - arad * D_PER_R;
    else                         /* 3rd quadrant */
       v.a = -180.0 + arad * D_PER_R;
    return v;
}
```

A Vector-Addition Example

We can use these functions to handle a common engineering and physics problem: vector addition. Often vectors are given in polar form, but adding them is much simpler in rectangular form. In that form, you just add all the x components together to get the x component of the answer. Adding all the y components gives the y component of the answer. A common method, then, for adding vectors in polar form is to convert them to rectangular components, add them, and convert the answer back to polar form. Here is a program that uses the functions we developed to do just that:

```c
#include <stdio.h>
#include <math.h>
```

275

```
struct vectxy {
          float x;       /* x coordinate */
          float y;       /* y coordinate */
          };
struct vectra {
          float r;       /* vector magnitude */
          float a;       /* angle in degrees */
          };
#define TRUE 1
#define FALSE 0
main()
{
   struct vectxy vxy, vxycum, poltoxy();
   struct vectra vra, vracum, xytopol();
   int done = FALSE;

   vxycum.x = vxycum.y = 0.0;
   printf("Enter magnitude: r = ");
   while ( scanf("%f", &vra.r) == 1 && !done )
      {
      printf("Enter angle in degrees: A = ");
      if ( scanf("%f", &vra.a) != 1 )
         done = TRUE;
      else
         {
         vxy = poltoxy( vra );
         vxycum.x += vxy.x;
         vxycum.y += vxy.y;
         vracum = xytopol ( vxycum );
         printf("%20c%10c%10c%10c%10c\n",' ', 'x','y','r','A');
         printf("%20s%10.2f%10.2f%10.2f%10.2f\n",
                                                "Current vector:",
                 vxy.x, vxy.y, vra.r, vra.a );
         printf("%20s%10.2f%10.2f%10.2f%10.2f\n", "Vector sum:",
                 vxycum.x, vxycum.y, vracum.r, vracum.a );
         printf("Enter next magnitude: r = ");
         }
      }
}
```

Here is a sample run:

```
Enter magnitude: r = 5
Enter angle in degrees: A = 36.87
                            x         y         r         A
         Current vector:  4.00      3.00      5.00      36.87
            Vector sum:   4.00      3.00      5.00      36.87
```

```
Enter next magnitude: r = 13
Enter angle in degrees: A = 157.38
                         x          y          r          A
      Current vector:   -12.00      5.00      13.00     157.38
         Vector sum:     -8.00      8.00      11.31     135.00
Enter next magnitude: r = 20
Enter angle in degrees: A = 225
                         x          y          r          A
      Current vector:   -14.14    -14.14      20.00     225.00
         Vector sum:    -22.14     -6.14      22.98    -195.50
Enter next magnitude: r = q
```

Now you can use the PC to duplicate the skills of a scientific hand calculator.

Summary

The IBM C library contains a multitude of useful functions. Many of them are similar or identical to functions found in UNIX, XENIX, and other UNIX look-alike libraries. Using these functions, you can more easily transport C programs from one system to another.

Answers to Questions in the Chapter

■ *7-1.* pmode & ˜mask: The ˜ operator converts 1's to 0's and vice versa. Any bit & 0 is 0, so that turns off the position corresponding to a 1 in mask. Any bit & 1 is the original bit, so the remaining bits are unchanged.

■ *7-2.* Just change the mode-setting argument in chmod().

```
/* yeswrite.c--restores write permissions */
#include <stdio.h>
#include <sys\types.h>
#include <sys\stat.h>
#include <io.h>
main(argc,argv)
int argc;
char *argv[];
{
    if ( argc < 2)
        {
        fprintf(stderr, "Usage: yeswrite file(s)\n");
        exit(1);
        }
    while ( argc > 1 )
        {
```

```
            if ( access ( argv[1], 00 ) != 0 )
                    fprintf(stderr,"%s does not exist\n", argv[1]);
            else
                    chmod ( argv[1], S_IWRITE | S_IREAD);
            argv++;
            argc--;
            }
    }
```

■ 7-3.

```
#include <stdio.h>
main()
{
  extern int sys_nerr;
  extern char *sys_errlist[];
  int n;

  for ( n = 0; n < sys_nerr; n++)
    printf("%3d: %s\n", n, sys_nerr[n] );
}
```

Since we are redeclaring sys_nerr and not actually allocating space, we use empty brackets.

■ 7-4. Because the string provided by ctime() already contains a newline.

■ 7-5. Use atoi() to convert the argument to integer form, and pass the converted form and the base two to the conversion function as arguments.

■ 7-6. One approach is to replace

```
        printf("a letter from this list: %s\n", answers);
```

with this:

```
        printf("a letter from this list: ");
        prspcstr(answers);
```

Of course, this entails writing a new function:

```
#include <stdio.h>
void prspcstr(s)
char *s;
{
    while ( *s )   /*  *s not the null character */
        {
        putchar( *s ); /* print value */
        putchar(' ');
        s++;           /* increment pointer */
        }
}
```

■ *7-7.* We can use `strrchr()` to locate the character and `strlen()` to count the remaining characters.

```
/* ntoend.c--
returns number of characters to end of string */
int ntoend(s, c)
char *s;    /* string to be searched and counted */
char c;     /* character to start count from */
{
    char *pc;

    if ( (pc = strrchr( s, c) ) == NULL )
        return (-1);
    else
        return ( strlen(pc) );
}
```

Exercises

1. Write a program that checks to see if a file exists. If the file doesn't exist, create it with `fopen()` in the write mode. If it does exist, use `chmod()` to make it writable, and use `fopen()` to open it in the append mode. Then have the program place your name, which it reads from the keyboard, and the current date, which it obtains from the system, in the file. After closing the file, use `chmod()` to make it read-only. The first call to the program will create the file and place the first name-date combination into it. Subsequent calls add to the file.

2. Modify Exercise 1 so that the file used can be altered using an environmental parameter.

3. Write a function `getword()` that skips over whitespace to get the next word in an input line; a word is any contiguous set of non-whitespace characters.

4. Write a function `getint()` that uses `getword()` to fetch a word of input and which returns the numerical value of the word if it consists of digits. Make sure it can handle an initial minus sign.

5. Write a function that takes two string pointers as arguments and returns the length of the first string minus the length of the second. Write two versions, one using `strlen()` and one not using it.

8

IBM-Specific Facilities

- Nonportable features
- BIOS interrupts
- DOS interrupts
- I/O Ports
- Controlling the speaker

IBM-Specific Facilities

The IBM PC has many special properties. Some can enhance your programming, and some create programming obstacles. For example, the PC has a built-in speaker, so you can incorporate sound into your programs. The built-in ROM and the disk operating system offer a host of routines to augment the C library. Several of these routines provide interfaces with the keyboard, the screen, and the disk drives. On the other hand, the segmented memory used in the IBM makes accessing the entire memory more complex than with many processors. As programmers, we need to contend with these matters.

Functions designed to be portable must often be too general to take full advantage of the specific features of a particular system. In recognition of this, the IBM C library contains several functions particularly designed to work within the IBM PC environment. We already have encountered some functions of this type, such as the console I/O functions.

Other functions we have mentioned are those that give access to the BIOS routines built into the ROM memory and to the DOS routines provided with the operating system. We'll explore these functions more thoroughly in this chapter.

The 8088 chip in an IBM PC communicates with other processors and devices in the computer through a set of *ports*. IBM C includes functions that let us use these ports from a C program.

The 8088's segmented memory poses special problems to the programmer, and there are special library functions to help resolve them. We'll look at all these areas in this and the following two chapters. We'll draw upon a variety of examples, but we'll place the strongest emphasis on the screen interface.

Perhaps the greatest variation between different C compilers for the IBM PC comes in how these special needs are met. There are no corresponding UNIX functions to provide guidelines, so various companies have gone their own ways. Often the differences are a matter of choosing a different name or argument list for a specialized function. Sometimes different strategies may be involved. Still, the theory and general form of our examples should carry over to compilers with similar capabilities, but you will have to study the appropriate manual to learn how to implement particular ideas.

BIOS Calls

BIOS (basic input/output system) calls provide a close interface with the system hardware. If you need to control a speaker or a video display, the BIOS can help you. You met the BIOS in Chapter 5. Let's review what you encountered there. The BIOS consists of several routines coded into the ROM (read-only memory). These routines are accessed through numbered *interrupts,* which can be generated by hardware or software. The system maintains a table of addresses called *interrupt vectors.* If, say, a type 10H interrupt is generated, control is transferred to the routine whose address is stored in the number 10h interrupt vector. In general, the routines require information to be placed in certain registers, and when the routines finish running, they place results in certain registers.

To instigate a particular interrupt from C, we must provide the interrupt number and set up the registers as required. As you saw in Chapter 5, this can be accomplished by using the int86() call. This function takes three arguments. The first is the number of the desired interrupt, the second is the address of a union holding values for the registers, and the third is the address of the union into which will be placed the resulting register values.

You have a choice of many routines. Table 8-1 lists the BIOS interrupt numbers for software-generated interrupts. Many of these routines, however, have several subroutines, so the total number of choices is greater than might appear from this list. The routines are documented in the *IBM Technical Reference* manual. There, under ROM BIOS Listings, you will find the assembly-language code for the routines. The code contains, as embedded comments, descriptions of each routine and of the registers involved.

Note that the last two interrupts can be set by the user. The first determines what happens when CTRL-BREAK is pressed. By default, nothing happens, but a user can write a routine describing the desired response and place the address of this routine in the appropriate interrupt vector. For example, in DOS that keystroke combination aborts a running program. The second interrupt (1C) relates to the system timer. The timer generates a hardware interrupt 18.2 times a second. Each time it does, one "tick" has elapsed, and the system increases the system clock counter by one. If you create a routine and place its address in the 1C vector location, that routine will be run every tick.

The Tick Counter

Let's take a look at a relatively simple, but useful, interrupt, interrupt 1AH. (The H suffix is one of the commonly used notations for indicating hexadecimal values.) Interrupt 1AH is used to read and reset the system

Table 8–1
BIOS Software Interrupts (Numbered in Hex)

Interrupt	Function
5	Print screen
10	Video I/O
11	Equipment check
12	Memory size check
13	Diskette I/O
14	Communications Port I/O
15	Cassette I/O
16	Keyboard I/O
17	Printer I/O
18	ROM Basic
19	Bootstrap start-up
1A	Time of day
1B	Keyboard break (user settable)
1C	Timer tick (user settable)

clock. As we mentioned, the clock keeps time in units called ticks, with 18.2 ticks to a second. More precisely, there are 1193180/65536 ticks a second. The 1193180 is the basic frequency in Hertz (or cycles per second) of the 8255 timer, one of the peripheral chips found in an IBM PC. The tick count is a 32-bit quantity.

The *IBM Technical Reference* manual reveals that to use this function to *read* the time, we must first set the AH register to 0. To *set* the time, set the AH register to 1. In the reading mode, a call to this routine sets the registers as follows:

high 16 bits of count → CX

low 16 bits of count → DX

0 → AL if less than 24 hours have passed since last read

non-0 → AL otherwise

We can use the `int86()` function to obtain the tick count. First, we have to create two unions of the `union REGS` type, as defined in the *dos.h* file. To refresh your memory, or to save you the effort of thumbing back to Chapter 5, we reproduce the definitions creating the `union REGS` type:

```
struct WORDREGS  {                          /* 16-bit registers */
                 unsigned int ax;           /* AX register */
                 unsigned int bx;
```

```
                    unsigned int cx;
                    unsigned int dx;
                    unsigned int si;
                    unsigned int di;
                    unsigned int cflags;        /*flag register */
                    };

    struct BYTEREGS  {                          /* 8-bit registers */
                    unsigned char al, ah;
                    unsigned char bl, bh;
                    unsigned char cl, ch;
                    unsigned char dl, d;
                    };

    union REGS  {
                    struct WORDREGS x;
                    struct BYTEREGS h;
                    };
```

The union overlays the 16-bit **WORDREGS** representation with the 8-bit representation of **BYTEREGS**. Recall that the first 4 registers can be addressed as 16-bit entities (AX, BX,) or as 8-bit entities (AL, AH, etc.) AL represents the low-order byte of AX, and so on.

Using this structure, it is simple to obtain the tick count. The main problem is recombining the two 16-bit registers CX and DX to get the full 32-bit count. Here is one approach:

```
/* t_counts.c--returns current tick count from clock */
#include <dos.h>
#define INT_TIME 0x1A                  /* the interrupt number */
long t_counts()
{
  union REGS rin, rout;      /* input, output register values */
  long tc;

  rin.h.ah = 0;                     /* choose read clock mode */
  int86(INT_TIME, &rin, &rout);
  tc  = ( (long) rout.x.cx ) << 16; /* high bytes */
  tc += rout.x.dx;                       /* add low bytes  */
  return tc;
}
```

The CX register contains the 2 high-order bytes of the count. We converted this 16-bit quantity to a 32-bit quantity with a type cast, then left-shifted the bits to the high bytes. Next, we added the contents of DX. Since they represent the low-order bytes, they did not need to be left-shifted. We didn't use the 24-hour elapsed information.

The clock is reset to 0 after 24 hours, or after about 1,573,000 ticks. Thus, we don't have to go all the way to unsigned long to accommodate the count.

We can use this function to time program fragments. For instance, we can find out how long a counting loop takes using a regular automatic variable as a counter compared to using a register variable as a counter:

```
/* timeloops.c--compare auto and register variables */
#include <stdio.h>
#define T_PER_S (18.2)    /* ticks per second */
long  t_counts();          /* returns tick count */
main()
{
  int i, n;
  long ts,te;
  register j;

  printf("Enter number of loop iterations:\n");
  while ( scanf("%d", &n ) == 1)
    {
    ts = t_counts();                /* starting tick count */
    for ( i = 0; i < n; i++)
        ;
    te = t_counts();                /* ending tick count */
    printf("Regular variable:  ");
    printf( "%d loops took %lu counts, or %0.2f seconds\n",
              n, te - ts, (te - ts)/ T_PER_S );
    ts = t_counts();
    for ( j = 0; j < n; j++)
        ;
    te = t_counts();
    printf("Register variable: ");
    printf( "%d loops took %lu counts, or %0.2f seconds\n",
              n, te - ts, (te - ts)/ T_PER_S );
    }
}
```

Here is a sample run:

```
Enter number of loop iterations:
10000
Regular variable:  10000 loops took 8 counts, or 0.44 seconds
Register variable: 10000 loops took 4 counts, or 0.22 seconds
20000
Regular variable:  20000 loops took 16 counts, or 0.88 seconds
Register variable: 20000 loops took 8 counts, or 0.44 seconds
```

```
30000
Regular variable:  30000 loops took 24 counts, or 1.32 seconds
Register variable: 30000 loops took 13 counts, or 0.71 seconds
q
```

Using the register variable cut the time in half. Incidentally, the results emphasize that the time resolution is one tick count, or about 0.05 seconds.

A Waiting Function

Sometimes we wish to include a time delay in a program, perhaps to give the user time to respond. We can use the tick count for this purpose. Note that the tick count is set by the 8253 timer, not by the 8284A clock chip used to run the 8088 chip. Running the 8088 at a higher clock rate, as some PC clones and add-on boards do, doesn't affect the 8253 rate. If you use a counting loop like that of the last example to produce a delay, the result will depend on the 8088 clock rate. The tick count, however, is independent of the CPU processing rate, but it will depend on the timer chip used.

```
/* waitsec.c--waits the requested number of seconds */
#define T_PER_S (18.2)   /* ticks per second */
long t_counts();

void waitsec( secs )
double secs;
{
    unsigned long count0, count;

    count0 = t_counts();             /* get current count  */
    count = count0 + secs * 18.2;    /* get stopping count */
    while ( t_counts() < count)
            ;                         /* stop when reached  */
}
```

This program does have the time overhead of calling t_counts() twice, but that is not important for the use we mentioned.

Here is a program to test the function; we can't really show the output.

```
/* waitsome.c--tests waitsec() */
#include <stdio.h>
void waitsec();
main()
{
    double time;

    printf("How long do you wish to wait in seconds?\n");
    while ( scanf("%lf", &time) == 1 && time > 0 )
```

```
        {
        waitsec(time);
        printf("Now how long do you wish to wait?\n");
        }
  }
```

The Int86() Return Value

Besides placing values in a union, the `int86()` function also provides the AX register value as a return value. For some interrupt routines, this is the only value we need examine. For example, consider interrupt routine number 11H. It uses the bits of the AX register to provide equipment information. Figure 8-1 shows the meaning of the various bits.

Let's try this interrupt; interpreting the return value will provide good practice in bit operations. Here is a sample program that examines some of the bits:

```
/*  equip.c--use interrupt 11h */
#include <stdio.h>
#include <dos.h>
#define DSKTE    0x0001    /* diskette drives are present */
#define VID_MASK 0x0030    /* video mode bits */
#define EGA      0x0000    /* ega monitor */
#define BW4025   0x0010    /* bw 40x25 with color card */
#define BW8025   0x0020    /* bw 80x25 with color card */
#define MONO     0x0030    /* monochrome monitor */
#define DRV_MASK 0x00C0    /* drive count bits */
#define DRV_SHFT 6         /* shift drive bits to right end */
#define PRN_SHFT 14        /* printer count shift */
#define EQCK 0x11          /* equipment check interrupt */
main()
{
   union REGS rin, rout;
   unsigned int equip;

   equip = int86 ( EQCK, &rin, &rout);
   if ( equip & DSKTE != DSKTE )
      printf("No disk drives\n");
   else
      printf ("%u disk drive(s)\n",
           ( (equip & DRV_MASK) >> DRV_SHFT) + 1 );
   switch ( equip & VID_MASK )
      {
      case  MONO  : printf("Monochrome monitor\n");
                 break;
      case BW8025 : printf("Color card: 80 x 25 bw\n");
                 break;
```

Figure 8–1
Meaning of the Equipment Check Bits

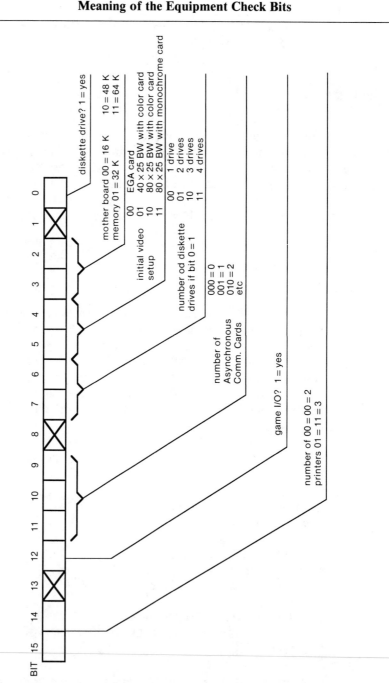

```
    case BW4025 : printf("Color card: 40 x 25 bw\n");
              break;
    case EGA    : printf("EGA card\n");
              break;
    default     : printf("Faulty code");
    }
  printf("%u printer(s) attached\n", equip >> PRN_SHFT );
}
```

Note that for the drive count, 00 means 1 drive, 01 means 2 drives, and so on.

This time we'll ask you a few questions about the program.

☐ *Question 8-1* What does the expression

```
(equip & DRV_MASK) >> DRV_SHFT)
```

accomplish?

☐ *Question 8-2*

a. Suppose we had used

```
printf ("%u disk drives\n",
         ( equip & DRV_MASK) >> DRV_SHFT + 1 );
```

instead of

```
printf ("%u disk drives\n",
         ( (equip & DRV_MASK) >> DRV_SHFT) + 1 );
```

What would have happened?

b. How do you suppose we thought of this question?

☐ *Question 8-3* How does the switch work?

Here is a sample run:

```
A> equip
3 disk drive(s)
Monochrome monitor
1 printer(s) attached

A>
```

One important point to bear in mind is that these values represent *initial* settings. The IBM PC has two sets of DIP switches whose settings are supposed to represent the system configuration. When the system is booted, these settings are read into a specific memory location. The number 11H interrupt reports these settings, but events after booting may have changed some of the actual modes. For instance, the 10H interrupt may have been used to reset the video mode. Such changes are not reflected in the return value for the 11H interrupt.

DOS Interrupts

There are many more BIOS calls, but let's look at another source of useful routines—DOS. The standard DOS commands, of course, provide the user interface with the PC. To do their work, DOS commands use a coordinated set of routines that constitute the DOS interrupts. IBM C makes these available to your programs.

The BIOS interrupts, we saw, activate routines stored in the ROM. The DOS interrupts activate routines placed in RAM memory when DOS is booted. If you were to use a different operating system, the BIOS interrupts would still be available, but the DOS interrupts would be replaced by what the other operating system chooses to supply. On the other hand, a non-PC-compatible computer running under DOS could use DOS interrupts, but not the IBM PC interrupts.

The DOS interrupts are considered "high-level" routines as opposed to the "low-level" BIOS routines. They offer more convenience and services, but they themselves often make use of the BIOS routines to do their work. Because DOS is an evolving system, the DOS interrupt system is evolving and expanding, too. It is described in the *DOS Technical Reference* manual. Table 8–2 lists the DOS 2.1 interrupts.

Table 8–2
DOS 2.1 Software Interrupts

Interrupt (in hex)	Service
20	Program terminate
21	Function request
22	Terminate address (control transfers to this address when a program terminates)
23	Ctrl-Break exit address (performed on Ctrl-Break)
24	Critical error handler
25	Absolute disk read
26	Absolute disk write
27	Terminate but stay resident (leaves program in memory)

The function request interrupt (21H) provides a choice of over 80 functions. You indicate which function you want by setting the AH register to the function number. Table 8–3 lists the main groups into which these calls fall.

The "traditional" group represents services provided by versions of DOS prior to 2.0; many are carryovers from the old CP/M operating sys-

Table 8–3
Interrupt 21H Function Groups

Numbers	Service
0–12	Traditional character device I/O
12–24	Traditional file management
25–26	Traditional non-device functions
27–29	Traditional file management
2A–2E	Traditional non-device functions
2F–38	Extended function group
39–3B	Directory group
3C–46	Extended file management group
47	Directory group
48–4B	Extended memory management group
4C–4F	Extended function group
54–57	Extended function group

tem. The "extended" group represents new functions. Many of the new functions are intended to replace traditional versions. For instance, the extended file management group uses a C-like system of file handles. This provides a simpler interface than the traditional calls, which use something called a *file control block* instead of a handle. However, the extended functions don't run under DOS Versions 1.0 and 1.1.

Let's look at some examples.

DOS Interrupt 21H Calls with Intdos()

The int86() function can be used for DOS interrupts as well as for BIOS interrupts. However, to save some effort, IBM C offers the intdos() function specifically for calling upon interrupt 21H functions. Since the interrupt number is known to be 21H, this function takes just two arguments, the addresses of two REGS unions. To choose a function, use the input union to set the AH register to the desired function number.

For example, function 2A returns the date in month–day–year form. The CX register contains the year (1980–2099), DH contains the month number, and DL contains the day. Here is a function that returns a pointer to a string containing the date:

```
/* getdate.c--returns ptr. to date as "Month xx, xxxx" */
#include <dos.h>
#define GETDATE 0x2A
char *getdate()
{
```

```
            static char *months[12] = {"January", "February", "March",
                            "April", "May", "June", "July"
                            "August", "September", "October",
                            "November", "December"};
            static char date[20];
            union REGS rin, rout;
            unsigned ax;

            rin.h.ah = GETDATE;
            intdos(&rin, &rout);
            sprintf(date, "%s %d, %d", months[rout.h.dh -1],
                    rout.h.dl, rout.x.cx);
            return date;
    }
```

The two static declarations cause storage to be allocated when a program using getdate() is compiled. Subsequent calls to getdate() use the same locations, so the previous contents of date get overwritten. The function uses the month number as an index to provide the month in string form, and the sprintf() function combines the data into a single string.

Here is a program to test the function:

```
/* trydat.c--test the getdate() function */
#include <stdio.h>
char *getdate();   /* include this during linking */
main()
{
    char *pd;

    pd = getdate();
    printf("%s:\n\nI see by my calendar watch that it is %s\n",
            pd , pd);
}
```

Here is a sample run:

```
A>trydat
March 5, 1986:

I see by my calendar watch that it is March 5, 1986

A>
```

Segment Use with Intdosx()

Some of the DOS functions require information about the segment registers. Since those registers are not part of the REGS union, an intdos() or int86() call won't work for such functions. Fortunately, IBM C also supplies the `intdosx()` and `int86x()` functions. These work like their x-less counterparts, but take one additional argument, the address of an **SREGS** structure. This structure, defined in *dos.h*, is used to hold the required segment register information. Here is how it is set up:

```
struct SREGS {
        unsigned int es; /* segment register ES */
        unsigned int cs;
        unsigned int ss;
        unsigned int ds;
        };
```

Let's try it. The DOS interrupt 21H function number 35H returns the address stored in a given interrupt vector. If, for instance, you wish to know where the code for interrupt 5 is kept, you would invoke this function, placing the interrupt number (5) in register AL. Upon return, the address stored in interrupt 5 is placed in ES:BX. This notation means the segment is placed in the ES register, and the offset in the BX register. Here is a sample use:

```
/* getvec.c--check interrupt vectors */
#include <stdio.h>
#include <dos.h>
#define GETVECTOR 0x35
main()
{
   unsigned int intnum;
   union REGS rin, rout;
   struct SREGS segreg;

   printf("Enter interrupt number in hex:\n");
   while ( scanf("%x", &intnum) == 1 )
     {
     rin.h.al = intnum;
     rin.h.ah = GETVECTOR;
     intdosx(&rin, &rout, &segreg);
     printf("segmented address = %x:%x, absolute address = %lx\n",
             segreg.es, rout.x.bx,
             ( (unsigned long) segreg.es << 4) +
rout.x.bx );
     printf("Next interrupt number:\n");
     }
}
```

To get the absolute address, we shift the segment value 4 bits to the left, which is equivalent to multiplying by 16. (See Chapter 6 if you wish to review this point.) Here is a sample run:

```
A>getvec
Enter interrupt number in hex:
5
segmented address = f000:ff54, absolute address = fff54
Next interrupt number:
10
segmented address = f000:f065, absolute address = ff065
Next interrupt number:
16
segmented address = f000:e82e, absolute address = fe82e
Next interrupt number:
21
segmented address = 6a8:180, absolute address = 6c00
Next interrupt number:
q
```

Note that the three BIOS interrupts are all in the same segment (ROM), while the DOS interrupt was loaded into a much lower memory location, one in RAM.

DOS Errors

Sometimes a particular DOS command cannot be carried out successfully. If there is an error, a DOS error number is placed in the AX register, and the carry flag is set to 1. The carry flag is represented by the final member of the REGS union, so we can use it to see if an error occurred. Then we can use the AX value to identify the particular error. The DOS error code also is assigned to the external variable _doserrno.

We'll illustrate this technique with the DOS function 56, which renames a file. According to the *DOS Technical Reference* manual, DS:DX should point to the string containing the drive, path, and filename of the file to be renamed. This means that a segment value should be placed in DS and that the offset of the string from the segment beginning should be placed in DX. Also, ES:DI should point to a string containing the path and filename to be used. Possible error returns are 3, 5, and 17 from the DOS error table provided in the *DOS Technical Reference* manual.

Note that this function uses segment information, so we'll have to use intdosx() rather than intdos(). We'll use the small-memory model (the default). With this model, data addresses are expressed as offsets from the beginning of the data segment. Thus, the addresses of the two strings can be used for the DX and the DI values. The segment value for the data segment is kept in DS, and, by default, ES is set to DS. Rather than relying on this information, however, we can use the library segread() function to obtain the current DS value and then explicitly set ES to it. The segread() function takes one argument, the address of a SREGS structure; when called, it assigns the segment register values to the appropriate structure members.

Here is a program incorporating these ideas:

```
/* chname.c--renames a file */
#include <stdio.h>
#include <dos.h>
#define RENAME_F 0x56     /* DOS function number */
void segread();           /* library function */
main(ac,av)
int ac;
char *av[];
{
   union REGS rin, rout;
   struct SREGS segreg;
   int ax;

   if ( ac != 3)
      {
           fprintf(stderr,"Usage: chname file1 file2\n");
           exit(1);
           }
   if ( access(av[1], 04 ) != 0 )   /* no read permission */
      {
           perror(av[1]);
           exit(1);
           }
   if ( access( av[2], 0 ) == 0 )
      {
           fprintf(stderr,"%s already exists--bye\n", av[2] );
           exit(1);
           }
   rin.h.ah = RENAME_F;
   rin.x.dx = (unsigned ) av[1];  /* type-cast addresses */
   rin.x.di = (unsigned ) av[2];
   segread ( &segreg);            /* find segment values */
   segreg.es = segreg.ds;         /* make sure ES = DS */
   ax = intdosx( &rin, &rout, &segreg);
   if (rout.x.cflag)              /* error indicator */
      {
      fprintt(stderr,"I'm sorry, but there was an error:\n");
      switch ( ax )               /* ax is error number */
         {
         case 3 : fprintf(stderr,"Path not found\n");
                  break;
         case 5 : fprintf(stderr,"Access denied\n");
                  break;
         case 17 :fprintf(stderr,"Not same device\n");
                  break;
         default :fprintf(stderr,"Error in Error Messages\n");
         }
```

```
      }
   }
```

Register values in the REGS union are declared to be unsigned, so we type cast the string addresses to avoid a type clash.

Here is a sample run:

```
A>chname ch112 ch113
I'm sorry, but there was an error:
Access denied

A>
```

How could access be denied when we tested for access? In this case, ch112 was a directory, not a file; and we failed to use stat() to test for that possibility.

You may be wondering how using this function call differs from using system() to run the system rename command. In the latter case, control is turned over to the *command.com* program, and it runs the command. With the current case, the relevant section of DOS code is accessed directly.

The Bdos() Function

The library does have one more function for making DOS calls. It's called bdos(). Like intdos(), it executes an INT 21h call, but it is intended for those functions that use, at most, the DH and/or AL registers. Here is how it is declared:

```
#include <dos.h>

inbdos( dosfn, dosdx, dosal)
int dosfn;                /* INT 21h function number */
unsigned int dosdx;       /* DX register value */
unsigned int dosal;       /* AL register value */
```

It returns the value of the AX register after the call has been completed.

There are, as we saw, many more DOS functions to examine. We have, however, covered the main techniques for using them, so let's move on to another aspect of PC architecture.

Ports: Inp() and Outp()

Do you want to run the speaker? Program the timer? Program a video controller device? Then you will want to use ports. First, let's get a little background. The 8088 processor acts as the brains of an IBM PC, but the system uses several other processors. For example, there is a direct memory access processor, a timer, processors for the video adapters, a keyboard processor, and so on. The 8088 processor must communicate with these processors and others, and with devices such as disk drives, printers, and game controls. To do so, it uses a set of I/O channels called *ports*. There are 64K possible ports, but the IBM PC uses only a small fraction of that total. Communication to and from the ports takes place in single bytes. The concept of using ports is shown in Figure 8-2.

IBM C provides two port-related functions. The first is called `inp()`, and it reads a value from a port. The second function, `outp()`, is used to send values out a port. Both are part of the *conio.h* family, and you can include that file to provide the proper function declarations.

The `inp()` function takes one argument, the port number, which is an `unsigned int`. It reads a byte from the port and returns that value.

The `outp()` unction takes two arguments. The first is the port number, and the second is the byte value being sent to the port. The return value is just the value that it sends.

Figure 8-2
Ports for Input and Output

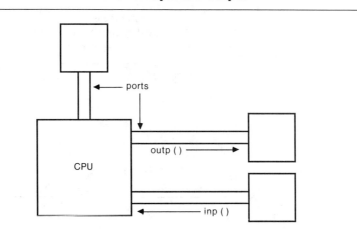

Ports and the Speaker

For many devices, we can avoid using ports directly and let BIOS or DOS interrupts handle the port work. But there are no interrupts specifically designed to run the speaker, so you need to use ports explicitly if you wish to generate sound. That makes the speaker a good choice for illustrating the use of ports.

To make a speaker sound, you need to send it a varying electric signal. The voltages we can apply to the speaker follow the usual binary logic of computers: there are just two values, "high" and "low." The high value causes the speaker cone to move one way, and low causes it to move the opposite way. If you just switch the voltage from low to high, you produce a click. To get a tone, you have to switch the voltage back and forth between the two settings, causing the speaker to oscillate back and forth. If you create 100 oscillations a second, then the speaker produces a tone of that frequency. The rather abrupt on-off method of moving the speaker produces something called a *square-wave tone*; it is rather buzzier than, say, the smoother tones produced by a tuning fork.

Frequencies usually are measured in Hz (or Hertz), which is the modern term for cycles per second. Another unit, used for high frequencies, is the *MHz,* or *megahertz*; that is one million Hz. Sometimes oscillations are described by the *period,* which is the length of time of a single oscillation. The period is the reciprocal of the frequency; a period of 0.02 seconds corresponds to 50 Hz.

Figure 8-3 illustrates the speaker connections. The AND gate is a device that allows the speaker voltage to be high only if input voltage 1 *and* input voltage 2 are high. To make the speaker oscillate, we can keep one voltage high all the time and switch the other voltage high and low at the desired frequency of oscillation.

Figure 8-3
The Speaker and Its Controls

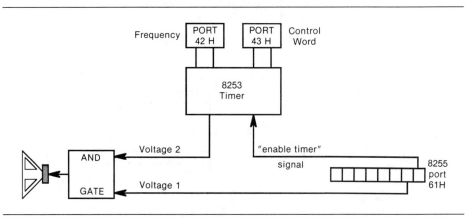

Voltage 1 is the easier to control. Its state is governed by the 8255 Programmable Peripheral Interface (PPI) chip. In particular, we need to set bit 1 in port 61H to 1.

Voltage 2 is more complex. First, we must "enable" the voltage, that is, we first must make it possible to set the voltage to high. The enabling also is controlled via the 8255 PPI and port 61H. In this case, the 0 bit of the port should be set to 1. Once enabling has taken place, Voltage 2 will be controlled by another chip, the 8253 Programmable Interval Timer. This chip is the 1.19 MHz timer used to run the system clock. It has three separate output counters, of which Counter 2 is connected to the speaker AND gate. By using port 43H, we can program Counter 2 to output a square wave, that is, an oscillating voltage like that in Figure 8-4. Then we can use port 42H to select a particular frequency. As long as Voltage 1 is set to high, the speaker will move back and forth with the same frequency as the square wave. If we then turn Voltage 1 to low, the sound will stop, because one of the voltages to the AND gate would then always be low.

Figure 8-4
A Square Wave

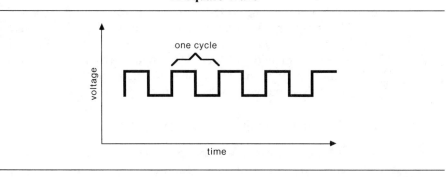

Activating the Speaker with Port 61H

To activate the speaker, we need to turn bits 0 and 1 on in port 61H. But don't rush out and enter an

```
outp( 0x61, 3);
```

statement. The problem is that this port controls the status of more than one device; setting the port to 3 turns the other bits off and changes the state of other devices. Figure 8-5 shows what each bit controls. A "+" indicates that a "high" value, or 1, establishes the indicated state, while a " − " indicates that a "low" value, or 0 is needed. This is the notation used in the *IBM Technical Reference* manual.

The safe approach to take is to use inp() to obtain the current port setting. We then can OR it with three to turn bits 0 and one on, and when we are done, we can restore the current port setting. Here is a simple program that turns on the speaker for a while, then turns it off:

```
/* beep.c--makes a beep */
#include <conio.h>
#define SPKRPORT 0x61        /* speaker port */
#define SPKRON   0x03        /* on bits for speaker */
#define DELAY    10          /* seconds of beep */
```

```
void waitsec();          /* user-defined function */
main()
{
unsigned char port61;

port61 = inp(SPKRPORT);    /* get current setting */
outp(SPKRPORT, port61 | SPKRON);  /* turn speaker on */
waitsec(DELAY);          /* wait DELAY seconds */
outp(SPKRPORT, port61);   /* restore original settings */
}
```

Note that the program uses the `waitsec()` function we developed earlier in this chapter. The code for that function should be linked in.

This program works (most likely) even though we haven't done anything about the timer. The reason is that when DOS is booted, it sets up the 8253 timer to provide a 1000 Hz squarewave for the system error beep. Unless another program has reprogrammed the timer, the timer will still be providing this signal when we run our program.

Setting the Frequency with the 8253 Timer

We can take a more active role and program the frequency ourselves. The first step is to send a one-byte "control word" out through port 43H. This word sets up the counter in the proper state. Figure 8-6 shows the structure of the word.

Figure 8-5
Meaning of the Port 61H Bits

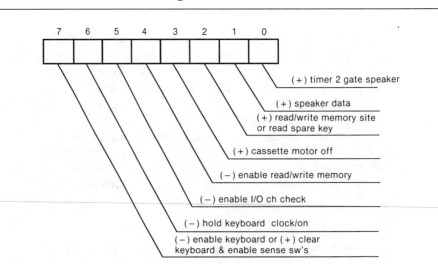

Figure 8-6
The 8253 Control Word

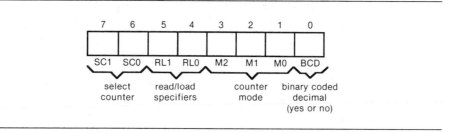

The SC1 and SC0 bits identify which of the 3 counters to use: counter 0, 1, or 2. We want 2, which requires setting SC1 to 1 and SC0 to 0. Next, RL1 and RL0 describe how that counter will read information sent to it. We will be sending 2 bytes of frequency information; that requires that both of these bits be set to 1. This causes the counter to read 2 bytes, the least significant byte first. The M2, M1, and M0 bits express, in binary form, which of 6 modes (numbered 0 to 5) we want. We'll want the square-wave generating mode, which is mode 3. This means bits M1 and M0 should be set to 1. Finally, the BCD bit indicates whether the usual 16-bit binary counter or a *binary coded decimal* counter should be used. A 0 selects the first choice, which is what we want.

Setting the appropriate bits gives us the binary byte 10110110, or 0xB6. This should be sent to port 43H. Next, we set up the frequency by sending a two-byte "divisor," low-byte first, to port 42H, which is the port to counter 2. The counter, remember, is producing 1,193,180 counts a second. The divisor tells it how many counts to make between the beginning of one square wave and the next. For instance, a divisor of 1000 would mean the duration of each square wave cycle is 1000 counts, or 1000/1193180 seconds per cycle. The frequency would be the inverse of this, or 1193180/1000 cycles per second. That is 1193 Hz. The divisor gets its name from the fact that dividing into 1.19 MHz gives the frequency. Remember, send the low byte, then the high byte of the divisor.

☐   *Question 8-4*   What is the largest possible divisor? What frequency does it produce? What is the corresponding period?

A Sound Sampler

Here is a sampler that produces tones of varying pitch and duration. Port 42H controls the frequency, and port 61H controls the duration:

```
/* sound.c--run-down tones */
#include <conio.h>
#define CLOCKFREQ 1193180L    /* timer frequency */
#define SPKRMODE   0xB6       /* set timer for speaker */
#define T_MODEPORT 0x43       /* timer-mode port */
```

```
#define FREQPORT     0x42        /* frequency-control port */
#define SPKRPORT     0x61        /* speaker port */
#define SPKRON       0x03        /* speaker-on bits */
#define FREQ0        0x12C       /* a frequency */
#define FREQ1        0x19F       /* a higher frequency */
#define DIV0         CLOCKFREQ / FREQ0     /* sets frequency */
#define DIV1         CLOCKFREQ / FREQ1
#define CLICK        0.40        /* initial tone duration */
void waitsec();
main()
{
  unsigned char port0;
  unsigned int div0 = DIV0;
  unsigned int div1 = DIV1;
  float delay = CLICK;
  unsigned int ct = 0;

  outp(T_MODEPORT, SPKRMODE);    /* set up timer */
  port0 = inp(SPKRPORT);         /* get old port setting */
  while ( !kbhit() )             /* continue until a key is struck */
    {
        outp(FREQPORT,div0 & 0xFF);  /* send low byte */
        outp(FREQPORT, div0 >> 8);   /* send high byte */
        outp(SPKRPORT, port0 | SPKRON); /* turn on */
        waitsec(delay);                  /* wait */
        outp(SPKRPORT, port0);           /* turn off */
        outp(FREQPORT,div1 & 0xFF);      /* reset frequency */
        outp(FREQPORT, div1 >> 8);       /* finish resetting */
        outp(SPKRPORT, port0 | SPKRON);
        waitsec(delay);
        outp(SPKRPORT, port0);
        div0 *= 1.05;            /* lower the frequencies */
        div1 *= 1.05;
        delay *= 1.05;          /* increase the delay time */
    }
        getch();               /* dispose of keyboard stroke */
}
```

Note the bitwise operations. The expression

```
div0 & 0xFF
```

masks the high-order byte of `div0` to all 0's while leaving the low-order byte unchanged. Thus the result is just the low-order portion of `div0`, as required. Then, the expression

```
div0 >> 8
```

shifts the high byte of div0 into the low-byte position. Since div0 is unsigned, zero extension is used, and the high-order bits are set to 0. Thus, the outp() call just sends the original high-order byte, as required.

A mildly amusing variation is to use 0xB8 instead of 0xB6 as the output to port 43H. The sound then resembles a ticking clock gradually slowing down.

Summary

The IBM PC has many capabilities that can be tapped by using machine-specific features of the IBM C implementation. Some "interrupt" routines are built into the BIOS ROM; these can be accessed through the int86() and int86x() functions. These functions use unions to provide and return register values used by the BIOS interrupts. The x version also uses a structure containing values for the segment registers. Other interrupt routines come with DOS. These, too, can be invoked using the int86() and int86x() calls. The DOS interrupt 21H has so many subfunctions that the intdos(), intdosx(), and bdos() functions were included to handle them.

The CPU communicates with various other components of the computer using ports. The inp() and outp() functions let C programs read from and write to ports.

Answers to Questions in the Chapter

■ *8-1.* The expression

```
(equip & DRV_MASK)
```

turns all but bits seven and six off; these two bit retain their original value. Then,

```
(equip & DRV_MASK) >> DRV_SHFT)
```

shifts everything six bits to the right so that bits seven and six become bits one and 0. The whole expression then has the value 0, 1, 2, or 3, depending on the bit values. Adding one gives the number of drives.

■ *8-2.* *a.* The plus operator has higher precedence than >>, so the one would be added to DRV_SHFT, producing a seven-bit shift instead of six.

b. No comment!

■ *8-3.* The expression equip & VID_MASK turns off all bits but five and four, which are left unaltered. Each of these two bits can be 0 or 1, giving four possible values which correspond to the case labels.

■ *8-4.* Since a 2-byte register is used to hold the divisor, the largest possible divisor is 65535. The corresponding period is 65535/1193180, or 0.0549 seconds, giving a frequency of 1/.0549, or 18.2 Hz. The number is familiar; it's the number of ticks per second. That is because this largest possible divisor is what is used with one of the other counters on the chip to advance the system clock tick by tick.

Exercises

1. BIOS interrupt 16h provides keyboard support. If AH is set to 0, this function returns the next ASCII character struck from the keyboard. The ASCII code is placed in AL and the scan code in AH. Write a program that exhibits the ASCII character and the scan code as each key is pressed.

2. Here is a description of DOS interrupt 21H, function 36H. This is the get disk free space function. AH, as is usual for DOS 21H interrupts, is set to the function number. DL is set to the drive number, with 0 being the default drive, 1 drive A, 2 drive B, and so on. The following values are returned:

BX—the number of available clusters on the drive

DX—the total number of clusters on the drive

CX—the number of bytes per sector

AX—the number of sectors per cluster, or else FFFFH if an invalid drive is specified

Storage on a disk is organized into *sectors,* and sectors are organized into *clusters.*

Use this function to write a program that reads a drive label and returns the number of free bytes. It's your choice whether the program reads the drive label as a command line input or as prompted input.

3. Write a program that causes particular keys to produce particular notes when struck. Have each note persist until another key is pressed.

9

Text and Graphic Displays

- Monitor interfaces
- Color text
- Color graphics

Text and Graphic Displays

One of the most important goals of many programs is to provide an appropriate video display. In Chapter 5 we first looked at using the BIOS 10H interrupt routines for the video display. In Chapter 6 we experimented with direct memory access to the video displays. We return to these topics now, for they provide many good illustrations of the special PC-related facilities of the IBM C compiler.

Revisiting the Video Displays

Let's begin by taking a more thorough look at the IBM PC video interface. First, there are two IBM video adapters that have been in common use for several years. One is the Monochrome Display Adapter (MDA), which is used in conjunction with a special monitor called the Monochrome Monitor. The combination offers excellent text resolution but no real graphics capabilities. (Other manufacturers have developed cards that can be used to create graphics with that monitor.) The second is the Color/Graphics Adapter (or CGA card), which is used with conventional monitors. It provides color support for color monitors and graphics support for color and black-and-white monitors. More recently, IBM has introduced an EGA (Enhanced Graphics Adapter) and an even more powerful professional graphics board, but we won't discuss them.

The Monochrome Display Adapter

This card comes with a Motorola 6845 CRT Controller chip and 4K bytes of display memory. As we discussed in Chapter 6, the memory stores the information to be displayed on the screen. Each character on the screen is represented by two bytes. The first, stored at an even address, holds the character code, and the second holds the attribute, which provides information about how the character is to be displayed. The 80 × 25 display can show 2000 characters, requiring 4000 bytes, so the memory is just large enough to hold one screen's worth of characters.

Regular output functions such as `putchar()` use DOS or BIOS interrupts to place the appropriate code in the display memory. Or, as we saw in Chapter 6, we can place the code directly into the display memory by using the display memory address. The 6845 scans the display memory. Each 2-byte character-attribute pair then is translated into a character on the screen. The entire display memory is scanned and the screen "refreshed" at 50 HZ, that is, 50 times a second.

Images are constructed from tiny display elements on the screen. Some call them *pixels,* but IBM calls them *pels*; either term stands for *picture elements.* The Monochrome Monitor constructs a character from a 7 × 9 array of pels; each character is contained in a 9 × 14 character box. Thus the resolution of the screen is 720 pels across (80 × 9) and 350 pels down (25 × 14). The information needed to construct each character is provided by an 8K *character generator* that holds the fonts for the various characters.

The controller has several ports, many of which should be set to particular values for the Monochrome Monitor. The BIOS power-on routine takes care of that.

If you intend to use direct memory access, you need to know the display memory location and the data format. The display memory starts at 0xB0000; dividing by 0x10 gives the corresponding segment value of 0xB000. Memory locations within the display memory typically are specified by offsets from this base value.

The data format, as we said, consists of character codes in the even bytes and attributes in the odd bytes. If you set aside a 2-byte word to hold the character and its attribute, the character goes into the low byte and the attribute into the high byte. The reason for this is that in a PC the low byte comes first in a word. Figure 9-1 illustrates the attribute layout. Bit 7, labeled `BL` is used to control blinking; a 1 value makes the character blink. Bit 3, labeled `I`, controls the intensity; a 1 value produces heightened intensity. Bits 2-0 control the foreground. A bit pattern of 111 produces a white character, 000 produces a dark character, and the bit pattern 001 produces an underlined character. Bits 6-4 control the background. The pattern 111 produces a white background, and the pattern 000 produces a dark background. The R, G, and B labels come into play for color attributes, which we will discuss later. The standard text attribute is 00000111, or 07 in octal.

Figure 9-1
The Attribute Byte

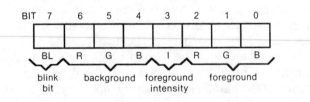

The Color/Graphics Adapter

The CGA also uses a Motorola 6845 CRT Controller and a video display memory that can be accessed both by the controller and by the CPU. It has some important differences from the other card. First, it has more video display memory, 16K instead of 4K. Second, the address of the display memory is 0xB8000, implying a segment value of 0xB800. Third, its memory can be used in two different fashions. One is the same as used by the MDA: a two-byte word is used to hold a character and its attribute. The other, used by the graphics modes, maps the memory to each individual pel on the screen, giving you point-by-point control over the appearance of the screen. The two types of memory use are divided into seven separate modes; individual modes can be selected using the BIOS 10H interrupt. Let's look at the modes more closely.

The Text Modes

There are 4 text modes: 40 × 25 B/W, 40 × 25 Color, 80 × 25 B/W, and 80 × 25 Color. All use the 2-byte character-attribute pair to represent the display in the display memory. Just as with the Monochrome Monitor, the character goes into the low byte, and the attribute into the high byte. On screen, characters are defined by a 5 × 7 pel pattern in an 8 × 8 pel character box. The 40-column modes use wider pels than the 80-column pels. Neither gives as good a resolution as the MDA with its 7 × 9 characters in 9 × 14 boxes. Figure 9–2 compares the pels of the MDA and the CGA.

Figure 9–2
MDA and CGA Character Boxes

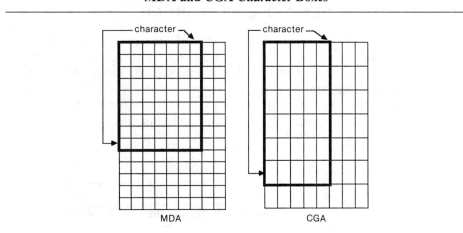

A 40 × 25 display constitutes 1000 characters and requires 2000 bytes of memory. Similarly, the 80 × 25 displays require 4000 bytes. This implies that the 16K display monitor can hold up to 8 screens worth of low resolution text or 4 screens worth of high-resolution text. You can use the BIOS 10H interrupt to specify particular pages, with one page corresponding to one screen of text.

The B/W and Color modes differ in how the attribute is interpreted. The B/W modes use the same attribute settings as the Monochrome Adapter, except that there is no underline mode. In the Color modes, the R, G, and B bits are used to select particular colors for the foreground and the background. We'll explore the details of these modes soon.

The Graphics Modes

The three graphics modes are Low-resolution (160 × 100 with 16 colors), Medium-resolution (320 × 200 with 4 colors), and High-resolution (640 × 200 in B/W). (The BIOS does not support the Low-resolution mode.) There is a trade-off between resolution and the number of colors allowed. This stems from the limited size of display memory. Consider the High-resolution mode. It must specify on-off settings for a 640 × 200 array of pels. That's a total of 128,000 pels. If you map one pel to one bit of memory, that requires 128,000 bits or 16,000 bytes of display memory. Since the display memory is 16K (16,384 bytes), it is just large enough to accomplish this. If you also want to indicate a color, that takes more bits per pel. The Medium-resolution mode uses two bits per pel. Since two bits can be set to four possible combinations, two bits can be used to specify four colors. But using more bits per pel means describing few pels, hence the Medium resolution is just 320 × 200.

Now that we have an overall view of the capabilities of the different video modes, let's get more specific.

More BIOS Calls: Revisiting Interrupt 10H

In Chapter 5, we used interrupt 10H to control the cursor for the monochrome monitor. This time, we'll use it to control a color monitor controlled by the standard color/graphics card. First, let's extend our description of the interrupt 10H subroutines. Table 9-1 reproduces and adds to the table in Chapter 5. In each case, the number of the desired function is placed in register AH. One function (Function 4) relating to the optional light pen is omitted.

Table 9-1
Major Functions of the Interrupt 10H Service Routine

Function 0: Setting the Display Mode

Register setup: place 0 in AH
place mode in AL

Table 9–1 (cont.)

Mode	Interpretation	Mode	Interpretation
0	40 × 25 B/W	4	320 × 200 Color
1	40 × 25 Color	5	320 × 200 B/W
2	80 × 25 B/W	6	640 × 200 B/W
3	80 × 25 Color	7*	80 × 25 B/W

Function 1: Setting the Cursor Type

Register setup:	place 1 in AH
	place scan-line start in bits 4-0 CH
	place scan-line end in bits 4-0 CL

Function 2: Setting the Cursor Position

Register setup:	place 2 in AH
	place row number in DH
	place column number in DL
	place page number in BH

Function 3: Getting the Cursor Position

Register setup:	place 3 in AH
	place page number in BH
Returns:	row number placed in DH
	column number placed in DL
	cursor type (see #1) placed in CH,CL

Table 9–1 (cont.)

Function 5: Setting the Active Page

Register setup:	place 5 in AH
	place page value in AL

Function 6: Scrolling the Active Page Up

Register setup:	place 6 in AH
	place number of lines to scroll in AL
	0 in AL produces a blank window
	place blank line attribute in BH
	place upper-left row number in CH
	place upper-left column number in CL
	place lower-right row number in DH
	place lower-right column number in DH

Function 7: Scrolling the Active Page Down

Register setup:	place 7 in AH
	place number of lines to scroll in AL
	0 in AL produces a blank window
	place blank line attribute in BH
	place upper-left row number in CH
	place upper-left column number in CL
	place lower-right row number in DH
	place lower-right column number in DH

Table 9–1 (cont.)

Function 8: Read Character/Attribute Pair at Cursor Position

Register setup:	place 8 in AH
	place page (alpha modes) in BH
Returns:	character placed in AL
	attribute placed in AH

Function 9: Write Character/Attribute Pair at Cursor Position

Register setup:	place 9 in AH
	place page (alpha modes) in BH
	place character in AL
	place attribute (alpha mode) or color (graphics mode) in BL
	place number of characters in CX

Function 10: Write Character Only at Cursor Position

Register setup:	place 10 in AH
	place character in AL
	place number of characters in CX
	place page (alpha modes) in BH

Function 11: Set Color Palette†

Register setup:	place 11 in AH
to set background	place 0 in BH
	place color code in BL
to set foreground	place 1 in BH

Table 9-1 (cont.)

(320 × 200 mode)	place color code in BL
	0 is green, red, yellow
	1 is cyan, magenta, white

Function 12: Write Dot

Register setup:	place 12 in AH
	place row number in DX
	place column number in CX
	place color value in AL
	If bit 7 of AL is 1, exclusively OR value with current dot contents

Function 13: Read Dot

Register setup:	place 13 in AH
	place row number in DX
	place column number in CX
Returns:	dot color value placed in AL

Function 14: ASCII Teletype Routine‡

Register setup:	place 14 in AH
	place character in AL
	place page (alpha mode) in BH
	place foreground color (graphics mode) in BL

Table 9-1 (cont.)

Function 15: Obtaining the Display Mode

Register setup: place 15 in AH

Returns: current mode is placed in AL

                    number of columns placed in AH

                    current active page placed in BH

*Mode 7 is the monochrome adapter; the other modes use the color/graphics adapter.

†For alpha modes, the background mode sets the border instead.

‡This routine advances the cursor after each write, moving it to the next line, if necessary. Backspace, carriage-return, bell, and line-feed characters are treated as commands rather than as characters to be transmitted.

Using the Color 80 × 25 Text Mode

The behavior of some of the routines depends on the video mode. Let's see how they can be used with one particular mode, the 80 × 25 color text mode.

The first requirement is the proper hardware; the computer should have a color card and a color monitor capable of a display resolution of 80 × 25. Next, we use routine 0 to set the desired mode. We can write a C function using int86() to do just that:

```
/*setmode.c--set the video mode */
#include <dos.h>
void setmode( m )
unsigned char m;       /* mode number to be set */
{
    union REGS rin, rout;

    rin.h.ah = 0;       /* select routine 0 */
    rin.h.al = m;       /* set AL to mode value */
    int86(0x10, &rin, &rout);
}
```

Once we are using that mode, what color options do we have? First, we can use routine 11 to set a border color. This is one of the mode-dependent routines; in the graphics mode it sets the background color and the color palette. (We'll discuss those terms later.) Second, we can use routine 9 to select a background and foreground color for each character sent to the screen. To use either of these routines, we need to know something about how colors are represented.

Character Color Attributes—The 8-bit character attribute is used to indicate the desired foreground and background colors for a given character. Bits 2–0 indicate foreground color, which is the color used for the character. Bit 3, if set to 1, provides extra brightness or intensity for the foreground color. Bits 6–4 indicate background color, and bit 7, if set to 1, provides a blinking character. Figure 9–3 indicates these assignments.

Figure 9–3
The Color Attribute

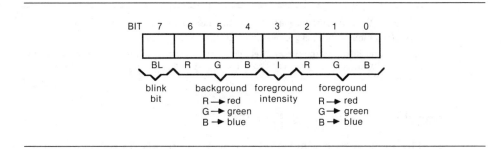

Note that bits 2–0 and 6–4 are labeled R, G, and B, respectively. This is because they activate the red, green, and blue colors, respectively. Thus, to have a blue foreground, you would set bit 0 to 1, and bits 1 and 2 to 0. To get colors other than red, green, or blue, you set more than one bit to 1. The scheme is the same one nature uses. For example, mixing red light with blue light produces magenta light, and the bit pattern 101 corresponds to magenta. (This also is how magenta is produced on a video screen. The screen has red, green, and blue phosphors. To get magenta, the red and blue phosphors are activated.) Table 9–2 gives the complete list of available foreground colors; the I (for intensity) bit produces a brighter version, as indicated.

Table 9–2
Available Foreground Colors

I	R	G	B	Color	Hex
0	0	0	0	black	0x0
0	0	0	1	blue	0x1
0	0	1	0	green	0x2
0	0	1	1	cyan	0x3
0	1	0	0	red	0x4
0	1	0	1	magenta	0x5
0	1	1	0	brown	0x6

Table 9–2 (cont.)

I	R	G	B	Color	Hex
0	1	1	1	light gray	0x7
1	0	0	0	dark gray	0x8
1	0	0	1	light blue	0x1
1	0	1	0	light green	0x2
1	0	1	1	light cyan	0x3
1	1	0	0	light red	0x4
1	1	0	1	light magenta	0x5
1	1	1	0	yellow	0x6
1	1	1	1	white	0x7

Note that brown is actually dark yellow, light gray is dark white, and dark gray is light black.

The background choices use the same RGB bit patterns. There is no equivalent to I for the background portion of the attribute, so the intensified colors are not available for a background to a character.

Using the Write Character/Attribute Routine—Routine 9 prints the character/attribute pair at the current cursor location. That means the character is printed using the foreground and background values from the attribute. The cursor is not repositioned by this routine, so consecutive calls will overwrite the same position unless you arrange to move the cursor. We can put together a C function to print the character/attribute pair and advance the cursor. Here is a simple version:

```
/* putcl.c--print char/color at current cursor, move cursor */
#include <dos.h>
void getcurs(), setcurs();  /* user-supplied functions */
unsigned char getpage();    /* user-supplied */

void putcolor(ch,at)
unsigned char ch, at;  /* character and attribute */
{
  union REGS rin, rout;
  unsigned char row, col, page;

  rin.h.bh = page = getpage();    /* set active page */
  rin.h.ah = 9;    /* write char/attr routine */
  rin.x.cx = 1;    /* print just one character */
  rin.h.al = ch;   /* character to print */
```

```
    rin.h.bl = at;   /* attribute to use */
    int86(0x10, &rin, &rout);  /* print it */
    getcurs(&row, &col, page);      /* find cursor position */
    if (col < 79)
       setcurs(row, col+1, page);  /* move to right */
    else if ( row < 24 )
       setcurs(row +1, 0, page);   /* or to next line */
    else
       setcurs(0, 0, page);         /* or to home position */
}
```

We need to provide the write routine with the active page, and that is what the `getpage()` function does. Here is its code:

```
#include <dos.h>
/* returns current page number */
unsigned char getpage()
{
    union REGS rin, rout;

    rin.h.ah = 15;    /* get mode routine */
    int86(10x, &rin, &rout);
    return rout.h.bh;   /* page value */
}
```

Mode 3 supports 4 pages, numbered 0 through 3. By default, page 0 is used. You could, however, use routine 5 to set different active pages, write on those pages, and use routine 5 to flip back and forth between the pages. If you have the time and interest, try it.

To move the cursor around, we've used the `getcurs()` and `setcurs()` functions we developed in Chapter 5. Here they are again:

```
#include <dos.h>
/*  moves cursor to indicate position */
void setcurs(row, col, page)
unsigned char row, col, page;
{
    union REGS inreg, outreg;

    inreg.h.ah = 2;        /* interrupt 10H function #2 */
    inreg.h.dh = row;
    inreg.h.dl = col;
    inreg.h.bh = page;
    int86(0x10, &inreg, &outreg);
}

/* obtain cursor position */
```

```
void getcurs(pr, pc, page)
unsigned char *pr, *pc, page;
{
    union REGS inreg, outreg;

    inreg.h.ah = 3;      /* interrupt 10H function #3 */
    inreg.h.bh = page;
    int86(0x10, &inreg, &outreg);
    *pr = outreg.h.dh;   /* row number */
    *pc = outreg.h.dl;   /* column number */
}
```

We made putcolor() a wrap-around function, moving the cursor to the upper left corner when it reaches the lower right. Another possibility would be to scroll up one line.

☐ *Question 9-1* How could you make the program scroll up one line?

Setting the Border—The active display does not use the whole screen. Surrounding the active display is a border area normally left black. You can use routine 11 with a color text mode to select a border color from the 16 choices in Table 9-2. Just set the BH register to 0 and the BL register to the numerical value shown in the table. Here's a C function to do the work:

```
/* setbord.c--set border color */
#include <dos.h>
void setborder(color)
unsigned char color;   /* code for color */
{
    union REGS rin, rout;

    rin.h.ah = 11;       /* routine number */
    rin.h.bh = 0;        /* tell it to set border */
    rin.h.bl = color;    /* specify the color */
    int86(0x10, &rin, &rout);
}
```

Play Time

To show how these functions work, we've devised a program that lets you use function keys to reset the border color. It also prints characters with varying attributes so that you can see all the possible combinations. It uses the functions we just developed plus cursor and screen control functions from Chapter 5. The last were modified to use getpage(). We'll list them after the program. The *color.h* file is one we put together to hold color-related definitions. The quotes around it tell the preprocessor to look in the current directory rather than in the *include* directory for it. Similarly, we set up key scan codes in *keys.h*. We'll list these files, too, after the program.

```
/* color.c--demonstrates color text mode 3 */
#include <stdio.h>
#include <conio.h>
#include "color.h"   /* contains definitions of colors */
#include "keys.h"    /* key scan codes */
#define STOP '\032'
#define CL8025 3      /* color, alphanumeric 80 x 25 mode */
int cursup(), cursdn(), cursl(), cursr();
void backspace(), home(), getcurs(), setcurs(), clear();
void setmode(), setborder(), putcolor();
main()
{
   int ch;   /* character value */
   int at = 0;  /* attribute */

   setmode(CL8025);
   setborder(BLUE);
   clear();
   home();
   cprintf("Please begin:\n");
   while ( (ch = getch() ) != STOP)
     {
     if ( ch == 0)  /* 0 code */
        {
        ch = getch();
        switch ( ch )
              {
              case F7 : setborder(RED); break;
              case F8 : setborder(BLUE);break;
              case F9 : setborder(GREEN); break;
              case F10 : clear(); break;
              case HM : home(); break;
              case UP : cursup(); break;
              case LT : cursl(); break;
              case RT : cursr();  break;
              case DN : cursdn(); break;
              }   /* end switch */
        }          /* end 0 code test */
     else if ( ch == '\r')
        cputs("\r\n");
     else if ( ch == '\b')
        backspace();
     else if ( ch < 040 )
        {
        putch('^');
        putch ( ch | 0100 );
        }
```

```
        else
          putcolor ( ch, at++ );
        }
  }
```

Here are the functions we developed earlier in this chapter. We assume they are in a single file so they can share the *dos.h* inclusion.

```
/*setmode.c--set the video mode */
#include <dos.h>
void setmode( m )
unsigned char m;      /* mode number to be set */
{
    union REGS rin, rout;

    rin.h.ah = 0;      /* select routine 0 */
    rin.h.al = m;      /* set AL to mode value */
    int86(0x10, &rin, &rout);
}

/* putcl.c--print char/color at current cursor, move cursor */
void getcurs(), setcurs();  /* user-supplied functions */
unsigned char getpage();    /* user-supplied */

void putcolor(ch,at)
unsigned char ch, at;  /* character and attribute */
{
  union REGS rin, rout;
  unsigned char row, col, page;

  rin.h.bh = page = getpage();     /* set active page */
  rin.h.ah = 9;     /* write char/attr routine */
  rin.x.cx = 1;     /* print just one character */
  rin.h.al = ch;    /* character to print */
  rin.h.bl = at;    /* attribute to use */
  int86(0x10, &rin, &rout); /* print it */
  getcurs(&row, &col, page);     /* find cursor position */
  if (col < 79)
     setcurs(row, col+1, page);  /* move to right */
  else if ( row < 24 )
     setcurs(row +1, 0, page);   /* or to next line */
  else
     setcurs(0, 0, page);        /* or to home position */
}

/* returns current page number */
unsigned char getpage()
```

```
{
    union REGS rin, rout;

    rin.h.ah = 15;     /* get mode routine */
    int86(10x, &rin, &rout);
    return rout.h.bh;    /* page value */
}


/* setbord.c--set border color */
void setborder(color)
unsigned char color;    /* code for color */
{
    union REGS rin, rout;

    rin.h.ah = 11;          /* routine number */
    rin.h.bh = 0;           /* tell it to set border */
    rin.h.bl = color;       /* specify the color */
    int86(0x10, &rin, &rout);
}
```

Next, here are the `setcurs()` and `getcurs()` listings. They are assumed to be in the same file, as the preceding functions, so they share the *dos.h* file:

```
/*  moves cursor to indicate position */
void setcurs(row, col, page)
unsigned char row, col, page;
{
    union REGS inreg, outreg;

    inreg.h.ah = 2;         /* interrupt 10H function #2 */
    inreg.h.dh = row;
    inreg.h.dl = col;
    inreg.h.bh = page;
    int86(0x10, &inreg, &outreg);
}


/* obtain cursor position */
void getcurs(pr, pc, page)
unsigned char *pr, *pc, page;
{
    union REGS inreg, outreg;

    inreg.h.ah = 3;        /* interrupt 10H function #3 */
    inreg.h.bh = page;
    int86(0x10, &inreg, &outreg);
    *pr = outreg.h.dh;    /* row number */
```

```
        *pc = outreg.h.dl;    /* column number */
}
```

Here are the modified cursor control functions; they are assumed to be in the same file, too:

```
/* cursor-control functions */
unsigned char getpage();  /* used by functions in this file */

void home()
{
    setcurs(0,0, getpage());
}

void cursup()
{
    unsigned char row, col;
    int status = 1;

    getcurs(&row,&col, getpage());
    if ( row > 0 )
        setcurs(row -1, col, getpage());
    else
        {
        setcurs(row,col, getpage());
        status = 0;
        }
return status;
}


void cursl()
{
    unsigned char row, col;
    int status = 1;

    getcurs(&row,&col, getpage());
    if ( col > 0 )
        setcurs(row, col - 1);
    else
        {
        setcurs(row,col, getpage());
        status = 0;
        }
return status;
}
```

```
void cursr()
{
   unsigned char row, col;
   int status = 1;

   getcurs(&row,&col, getpage());
   if ( col < 79 )
      setcurs(row, col + 1, getpage());
   else
      {
      setcurs(row,col, getpage());
      status = 0;
      }
return status;
}

void cursdn()
{
   unsigned char row, col;
   int status = 1;

   getcurs(&row,&col, getpage());
   if ( row < 24 )
      setcurs(row + 1, col, getpage());
   else
      {
      setcurs(row,col, getpage());
      status = 0;
      }
return status;
}
```

Next, here is the *color.h* file:

```
/* color.h--color values and macro */
#define BLACK        0
#define BLUE         0x1
#define GREEN        0x2
#define CYAN         0x3
#define RED          0x4
#define MAGENTA      0x5
#define YELLOW       0x6
#define WHITE        0x7
#define INTENSE      0x8
#define BLINK        0x80
#define XORBIT       0x80
#define BACKGROUND(X)     ((X) << 4)
#define SETBKGN      0
```

```
#define SETPLTE     1
#define PALETTE1    0
#define PALETTE2    1
```

☐ *Question 9-2* Suppose you wanted to print the character Q in blinking red on a blue background. What putcolor() call would you give using the *color.h* data?

Finally, here is the initial augmentation of the *keys.h* file. More keys can be added as needed.

```
/* keys.h--keyboard extended scan codes /*
#define F1    59
#define F2    60
#define F3    61
#define F4    62
#define F5    63
#define F6    64
#define F7    65
#define F8    66
#define F9    67
#define F10   68
#define HM    71
#define UP    72
#define PU    73
#define LT    75
#define RT    77
#define END   79
#define DN    80
#define PD    81
```

The display is interesting to watch. The attribute value starts at 0, which is black on black; characters printed with this attribute are a bit difficult to read! But at is incremented each call, so the next attribute is 1, blue on black. Then comes green on black, and so on, with each of the 16 possible foregrounds printed on the black background. The next incrementing sets the 4 bit to 1, producing a blue background, and again all 16 foregrounds are printed. This continues until all 16 foregrounds are printed on all 8 backgrounds, both in Nonblink and Blink mode. When at reaches 256, the pattern recycles. This is because only the final 8 bits are assigned to the function attribute variable, since it is type unsigned char. Meanwhile, you can select one of three border colors at any time by striking a function key. If you like color, you should like running this program.

Using a Graphics Mode

Now let's use one of the graphics modes, the 320 × 200 graphics mode, or mode 4. The setmode() function can be used to start this mode, and routine 11 can be used to set the background and palette.

The *background color* is simply the color assumed by the screen wherever nothing else has been placed. You specify the background with routine 11 by setting BH to 0 and BL to the color code as given in Table 9–2 or in the *color.h* file we created.

Your choice of foreground color is limited to two sets of three colors each. Each color set is termed a *palette*. Palette number 1 consists of green, red, and yellow. Palette number 2 consists of cyan, magenta, and white. (One version of the *IBM Technical Reference* manual provides at least 3 different descriptions of the palettes, but this is the one that seems to match what we see on the screen.) To choose a palette, use routine 11 with BH set to 1 and with BL set to 0 for palette 1 and to 1 for palette 2. You use other functions to specify which of the three palette colors you wish to use.

We can create a C function to handle these choices:

```
/*  sets background and palette for graphics mode 4 */
#include <stdio.h>
#include "color.h"
void setcolor(background, palette)
unsigned char background, palette;
{
   union REGS rin, rout;

   rin.h.ah = 11;                /* routine number */
   rin.h.bh = SETBKGN;           /* set background */
   rin.h.bl = background;        /* background color in BL *
   int86(0x10, &rin, &rout);
   rin.h.bh = SETPLTE;           /* set palette */
   rin.h.bl = palette;           /* palette value in BL */
   int86(0x10, &rin, &rout);
}
```

Memory Considerations—In the text modes, the memory is mapped to the screen on a character-to-character basis; the smallest unit of screen information is a single character. In the graphics modes, however, the screen is mapped on a point-to-point basis. In this case, the smallest unit of screen information is 1 pel, or picture element. The 320 × 200 graphics mode uses 320 × 200, or 64,000 pels. With only 16K of available memory, the system has to describe 4 pels per byte of memory. This leaves just two bits per pel, and that is too few to allow a full range of color selections for each dot.

Figure 9–4 shows how the pel information is arranged in a byte.

Each pel has two color-value bits, C1 and C0. Table 9–3 shows the four possible combinations and their meanings.

The order of colors in palette 1 is green, red, yellow. The order in palette 2 is cyan, magenta, and white.

One way to activate pels is to use the write dot routine, routine 12. Place the row number (0 to 199) in DX and the column number (0 to 319) in CX.

Figure 9–4
Pels in a Byte

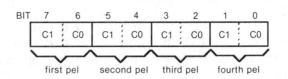

Table 9–3
Pel Information in a Byte

C1	C0	Meaning
0	0	dot is assigned background color
0	1	dot is assigned first color of current palette
1	0	dot is assigned second color of current palette
1	1	dot is assigned third color of current palette

A second way to produce graphics output is to use the write character/attribute routine. It still produces characters in the graphics mode, but in a different fashion. For instance, to print a P in the upper left-hand corner of the screen in the text mode involves putting the ASCII code for P in the first byte of video memory and its attribute in the second byte. The card then converts that information to a particular pattern of pels to place on the screen. In the graphics mode, however, all the pels involved in forming the character must be set individually in video memory. A character occupies several columns and rows of dots, so the necessary information is spread over several bytes of memory, with not all the bytes adjacent to each other. In fact, odd rows are stored in a different memory section from even rows! Fortunately, the write routine takes care of the details.

The register usage for routine 9 in the graphics mode differs from the text usage in two ways. First, the graphics mode does not require setting BH to the page number, because there is only one page. Second, the BL register is set not to an eight-bit attribute, but to the two-bit code we just discussed. There is the possibility of setting bit seven to one. Instead of producing blinking, as it does in the text mode, setting this bit in the graphics mode causes the color value to be exclusively ORed (XORED) with the current color value(s) present at the location.

What does XORing accomplish? Suppose, for example, you print a red character on a red background; the character is unreadable. But RED ^ RED is 0100 ^ 0100, or 0000, or black, so the character becomes readable.

To take another example, magenta on red is tough to see, but MAGENTA ^ RED is 0101 ^ 0100, or 0001, or blue; blue on red is easily read. Using the XOR option makes the result readable, unless you are printing black on black.

Let's try a graphics example. Here is a slight alteration of the last program. You can use the function keys to change the background and palette. To stave off fatigue, we won't relist the supporting functions we've used already.

```
/* grachr.c--characters in the graphic mode */
#include <stdio.h>
#include <conio.h>
#include "color.h"
#include "keys.h"
#define STOP '\032'
#define COLOR1 1
#define COLOR2 2
#define COLOR3 3
#define GR320  4
int cursup(), cursdn(), cursl(), cursr();
void home(), getcurs(), setcurs(), clear();
void setmode(), setcolor(), putcolor();
unsigned char getmode();
main()
{
    int ch, color = COLOR1;;
    unsigned char oldmode;

    oldmode = getmode();
    setmode(GR320);
    home();
    setcolor(RED,PALETTE1);
    cprintf("Please begin:\n");
    while ( (ch = getch() ) != STOP)
      {
      if ( ch == 0)   /* 0 code */
         {
         ch = getch();
         switch ( ch )
             {
             case F4 : color = COLOR1; break;
             case F5 : color = COLOR2; break;
             case F6 : color = COLOR3; break;
             case F7 : setcolor(WHITE, PALETTE2); break;
             case F8 : setcolor(BLUE,PALETTE2);break;
             case F9 : setcolor(RED,PALETTE1); break;
             case F10 : clear(); break;
```

```
                case HM : home(); break;
                case UP : cursup(); break;
              case LT : cursl(); break;
                case RT : cursr();  break;
                case DN : cursdn(); break;
                }   /* end switch */
          }           /* end 0 code test */
      else if ( ch == '\r')
          cputs("\r\n");
      else if ( ch < 040 )
          {
          putch('^');
          putch ( ch ¦ 0100 );
          }
      else
          putcolor ( ch, color );
      }
   setmode(oldmode);
}


unsigned char getmode()
{
   union REGS rin, rout;

   rin.h.ah = 15;
   int86( 0x10, &rin, &rout);
   return rout.h.al;
}
```

There are some interesting things to notice when you run this program. One is that when you change the palette, characters already typed change color. That's because the stored information describes how to use the palette rather than specifying a particular color value. Second, it is interesting to see how some text items move in and out of view as the background is changed. Third, the characters are wider, with 40 characters to a line instead of 80. That's because an 8 × 8 cell of pels is used to form a character, so the 320 pels per row can accommodate only 40 characters.

Rewriting Putcolor( )—Because of the last point, the `putcolor()` function should be changed to start a new row every 40 characters instead of 80. This raises a philosophical point: should `putcolor()` be generalized to include a maximum line width as a parameter, or should separate functions be used for the different modes? Both approaches have drawbacks: one proliferates the number of arguments required, and the other proliferates the number of functions. Another approach would be to use defined constants; this would involve recompiling the function to fit the desired mode. Another possibility would be to establish a default value that can be overridden by an environmental variable. That saves recompilation, but requires remembering to set the variable.

There is another approach that avoids these pitfalls. The read display mode routine provides the number of character columns; the putcolor() function can use this to set the proper value.

☐ *Question 9–3* Can you rewrite putcolor() in the format just suggested?

Nontext Use of the Graphics Mode

Rather than make characters, let's make colored patterns. The key is to use the write-dot routine. Here is a C function to do that:

```
#include <dos.h>
void putdot(row,col,color)
unsigned int row, col;
unsigned char color;
{
  union REGS rin, rout;

  rin.h.ah = 12;            /* the write-dot routine */
  rin.x.cx = col;           /* column number of dot */
  rin.h.al = color;         /* color of dot */
  rin.x.dx = row;           /* row of dot */
  int86(0x10, &rin, &rout);   /* make dot */
}
```

In this case, the possible color values are the integers 0 through 3. A value of 0 means use the background color, while the other choices indicate which of the three palette selections is to be used.

We'll use putdot() to fill in rectangular regions with specified colors. To do that, we'll write a function that takes the row boundaries, the column boundaries, and the color choice as arguments:

```
/* makebar.c--fills a rectangle with color */
void makebar(r1,r2,c1,c2, clr);
unsigned int r1, r2;  /* row r1 through row r2 */
unsigned int c1, c2;  /* column c1 through column c2 */
unsigned char clr;    /* color value: 0-3 */
{
    int row, col;

    for ( row = r1; row <= r2; row++ )
        for (col = c1; col <= c2; col++ )
                putdot( row, col, clr);
}
```

The nested for loops serve to set each dot within the specified rectangle to the indicated color.

To show you many of the possible combinations, the program will let you use function keys F1 through F8 to set the background to the eight unintensified background colors. Function keys F9 and F10 will let you switch back and forth between the two palettes. To do that, we use the same logic we used earlier to activate the cursor movement keys. Here is the program:

```
/* bars.c--draw crossing bars */
#include <stdio.h>
#include <conio.h>
#include "color.h"
#include "keys.h"
#define STOP '\032'
#define ROWS 200
#define COLS 320
#define COLOR1 1      /* the three palette choices */
#define COLOR2 2
#define COLOR3 3
void setmode(), setcolor(), putdot(), makebar();
main()
{
    int ch;
    unsigned char pl = PALETTE1;     /* palette variable */
    unsigned char bg = BLACK;          /* background variable */

    setmode(4);                        /* choose med-res graphics */
    setcolor(bg,pl);                     /* set background, palette */
    makebar(10, 30, 0, COLS, COLOR1 );
    makerow(90, 110, 0, COLS, COLOR2 );
    makerow(170, 190, 0, COLS, COLOR3 );
    makebar(170, 190, 0, COLS, COLOR3);
    makebar(170, 190, 0, COLS, COLOR3);
    makebar(0, ROWS, 10,30, COLOR1);
    makebar(0, ROWS,60,80, COLOR2);
    makebar(0, ROWS,110,130, COLOR3);
    makebar(0, ROWS,190,210, COLOR1 | XORBIT);    /* XOR option */
    makebar(0, ROWS,240,260, COLOR2 | XORBIT);
    makebar(0, ROWS,290,310, COLOR3 | XORBIT);
    while ( ( ch = getch() ) != STOP )
      {
      if ( ch == '\0' )
          {
          ch = getch();
          switch (ch)
          {
          case F1 : bg = BLACK; setcolor(bg,pl); break;
```

```
                    case F2 : bg = BLUE; setcolor(bg,pl);break;
                    case F3 : bg = GREEN; setcolor(bg,pl);break;
                    case F4 : bg = RED;setcolor(bg,pl); break;
                    case F5 : bg = CYAN;setcolor(bg,pl); break;
                    case F6 : bg = MAGENTA;setcolor(bg,pl); break;
                    case F7 : bg = YELLOW;setcolor(bg,pl); break;
                    case F8 : bg = WHITE;setcolor(bg,pl); break;
                    case F9 : pl = PALETTE1;setcolor(bg,pl); break;
                    case F10 : pl = PALETTE2;setcolor(bg,pl); break;
                    }
                }
            }
        setmode(3);
        }
```

This program should be linked to the code for `setmode()`, `makebar()`, and `putdot()`.

There are several interesting things to note as you run this program. The first is how setting the EXCLUSIVE OR bit alters the appearance of two crossing bars. Without using the bit, the color of the intersection is the color of the last bar drawn at that location. With it set, we get the color that results from exclusively ORing both colors, as we described earlier.

Second, you will note it takes time for the program to draw all the bars. Our IBM PC took nearly 30 seconds to do the work. But the changes produced by pressing the function keys take place practically instantaneously. That is because changing the background or palette *does not* alter the video memory. Instead, these changes alter how the CRT controller *interprets* the memory.

Third, it's neat to watch the color changes and to see bars appear and disappear as the background changes.

To speed up the graphics operations significantly, we'll have to go to direct memory access methods. We'll take that up in Chapter 10.

Summary

The Monochrome Display Adapter and the Color/Graphics Adapter both use video display memory to map the screen. The memory is scanned regularly, and the contents are translated into screen images. With the MDA and the text mode of the CGA, the screen is mapped character by character. Each character is represented by two bytes in memory. One byte holds the character code, and the second holds the attribute, a collection of bits describing how to portray the character. You use BIOS interrupts to set the video mode and control the contents of the display memory.

When the CGA is in its graphics mode, the video display memory is used to map individual pels, or picture elements, on the screen. Memory limitations create a trade-off between screen resolution and the number of available colors. The High-resolution B/W mode, for example, uses one bit per pel. The Medium-resolution Color mode uses two bits per pel, allowing a choice of four colors for the pel. With BIOS calls you can set individual pels, but the process is slow.

Answers to Questions in the Chapter

■ *9-1.* Use the interrupt 10H routine 6. Set AL to 1, the number of lines to be scrolled.

■ *9-2.* Use the BACKGROUND macro to shift BLUE into the background bits, then use the ¦ operator to combine background with foreground and the blink bit:

```
putcolor ( 'Q', BLINK ¦ BACKGROUND(BLUE) ¦ RED);
```

■ *9-3.* Here we use routine 15 to get the column width.

```
void putcolor(ch,at)
unsigned char ch, at;
{
    union REGS rin, rout;
    unsigned char row, col;

    rin.h.ah = 15;
    int86(0x10, &rin, &rout);
    rin.h.ah = 9;
    rin.h.bh = rout.h.bh;
    rin.x.cx = 1;
    rin.h.al = ch;
    rin.h.bl = at;
    int86(0x10, &rin, &rout);
    getcurs(&row, &col);
    if (col < rout.h.ah)
        setcurs(row, col+1);
    else if ( row < 24 )
        setcurs(row +1, 0);
    else
        setcurs(0,0);
}
```

Exercises

1. Write a function that sets the page to the value given by its argument. Use it in a program in which you select the viewing page by using a function key; F1 is page 0, F2 is page 1, and so on.

2. Take a function like—for example, the show function of Chapter 5—and modify it so that it displays text with a color and background set by two environmental parameters.

10

Reaching into Memory

- Segmented memory
- Memory models
- Near and far pointers
- Direct memory access

Reaching into Memory

Memory is getting cheaper all the time. Gone are the days when users accepted 64K or even 16K of memory. Newer PCs typically are sold with a minimum of 256K of random access memory, and the total can go as high as 640K. A video card comes with additional memory, which is used to map the screen. But the small-memory model is limited to 64K of code and 64K of data, and the linker decides where to locate these bytes. Thus, the small-memory model cuts you off from much of the system's memory, including the video display memory. Yet a program should be able to tap the resources it needs. In this chapter, we will investigate how to exceed the bounds of the small-memory model. We will discuss three techniques. One is to use *far pointers* within a small-memory model program; we first saw that approach in Chapter 6. The second is to use the large-memory model. The third is to include special memory-related functions in the code. Let's begin by reviewing the 8088's memory architecture.

Segmented Memory

In Chapter 6, we discussed the IBM's segmented memory. In review, we said that a 16-bit register can address only 64K bytes of memory. The 8088 chip gets around this limitation by using two registers to specify a complete address. One register, called a *segment register,* holds the segment value of some base address. The base address must be a multiple of 16, and the segment value is the base address divided by 16. The largest possible segment value, then, is approximately 64K, corresponding to an absolute base address 16 times larger, or about 1Mb. To specify an address fully, you can give a segment value and an offset, which is measured from the segment base.

The 8088 chip has four segment registers: CS, DS, ES, and SS. Usually, the CS segment register holds the segment value for the base of the code segment, which is the segment holding the program code. Data is kept in the data segment, and its segment value is stored in DS. SS is used for the stack segment, and ES is used for the extra segment, if any.

If all the code is confined to one 64K segment, then the CS segment can stay fixed, and all code addresses can be specified just using the code offset value. Similarly, if all the data is confined to a single segment, all the data addresses can be specified using just the data offset value. This simplifies and speeds up programming. If a program needs to access a greater range of code or data addresses, it can do so by using more than one segment. But in that case, 32-bit addresses are required, with 1 16-bit word used for the segment value and 1 word for the offset. Naturally, this slows down programs a bit.

How does IBM C deal with these memory matters? The main tool is selecting the proper kind of pointer. IBM C uses 2 kinds. The near pointer, used by default in the small-memory model, is a 16-bit pointer that holds just the offset portion of an address. Thus, it only can access addresses within a segment. The far pointer, however, is a 32-bit pointer that holds both the offset and the segment value. Such a pointer can access any usable address. To use far pointers for data, we can invoke the large-memory model, which uses them by default. Or we can stay with the small-memory model, but explicitly specify that certain pointers are far pointers. In some situations we don't have to use one of these two methods for creating far pointers; instead, we can use functions that take segment values and offsets as separate values.

First, we'll take a general look at these three approaches to accessing memory; then we can get down to specific applications.

Memory Models

The first method for accessing more data memory is to use the right memory model. Let's see what is available. IBM C offers four standard memory models: small, medium, large, and huge. Their respective code and data pointers are illustrated in Figure 10–1. The small model is the default. It assumes that all code is confined to one code segment and that all data is confined to one data segment. All pointers, by default, are 16-bit near pointers that hold only the offset portion of the addresses.

The medium model still assumes that data is confined to one segment, but it also assumes that code is not. Thus, data pointers are still 16-bit near pointers. The code pointers, however, are 32-bit far pointers holding the segment value and the offset. To use the medium model, use the compiler option /AM.

The large model uses far pointers for both code and for data. Its chief restriction is that no *single* data item can occupy more than one segment. To use the large model, use the compiler option /AL.

Finally, the huge model removes the restriction that no single data item can occupy more than one segment. The /AH option selects this model.

You can construct other memory models with the compiler, but the four we have listed have library support. The compiler comes with a small-model library, a medium-model library, and a large-model library, which also is used by the huge model. You can, for example, use strcpy() with

Figure 10–1
Memory Models and Pointers

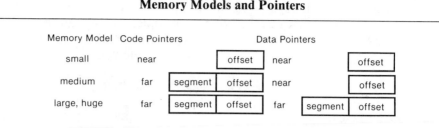

Memory Model	Code Pointers			Data Pointers		
small	near		offset	near		offset
medium	far	segment	offset	near		offset
large, huge	far	segment	offset	far	segment	offset

any of the models, but different versions are provided with the different libraries. The medium- and large-library versions provide code that needn't be in the same code segment as the main program. The large-library version also must cope with far data pointers. The details are concealed from the user. Just specify the desired compiler option, and the correct library version is used.

Creating a Far Pointer in the Small-Memory Model

With the large-memory model, all data pointers are far pointers by default. In the small-memory model, we can create individual far pointers by using the keyword far. This keyword is enabled by the compiler option /Ze.
Consider, for example, this declaration:

```
char *pc;
```

In the small and medium models, pc is a 16-bit pointer by default. In the large model, pc is a 32-bit pointer by default. To make a far pointer, use the keyword far as follows:

```
char far *pfc;
```

This states that pfc is a far pointer. That is, pfc will hold a 32-bit address, which should be the address of an 8-bit char value. The low-order 16 bits hold the offset, and the high-order 16 bits hold the segment value.
Similarly, the near keyword can be used to establish a 16-bit pointer in a large- or huge-model program.
Remember that the far and near keywords are enabled by the compiler /Ze option.

Segment-Related Functions

The third method of coping with segments is to provide functions that specifically deal with segments. For example, we've already used the segread() function, which places the current segment register values into a type SREGS structure.
A second example is the movedata() function, which is used in the

small and medium models to move data between segments. Rather than using far pointers, it uses two arguments (segment and offset) to represent each address. It can be used, for example, to copy an array from the local data segment to the video display memory without using either the large-memory model or a far pointer. For example, look at this call:

```
movedata( ds, array1, 0xB800, 0x00, 160);
```

The first argument—ds—is the segment value of the source array; the second argument is the offset of the source array; the third argument is the segment for the destination; the fourth argument is the destination offset; and the final argument—160—is the number of bytes to be copied. Here ds is the current data segment value, perhaps obtained using segread(). Next, array1 is the name of an array, hence the offset address (in the small- and medium-memory models) of the array. For the destination, we used the video display memory with a zero offset. We'll use similar code in a program later.

Sometimes you can't use segread() to get the proper segment values. Suppose, for example, that the source array was created using an explicit far pointer in a small-memory model. In that case, the pointer would hold both segment and offset values in it. To use movedata(), we would have to extract that data. We could do it with bit operations, but the IBM C library saves us the trouble. The *dos.h* file defines two macros, FP_OFF() and FP_SEG(), which return the segment value and the offset, respectively, of a type far pointer.

Using Far Pointers

Now that we've seen the general methods of dealing with segmented memory, let's get more specific. In particular, let's return to the bar-drawing program of Chapter 9. The slow part of the program was the creation of a color rectangle. To speed it up, we would like to use direct memory access. The video memory is in a different segment from the program memory, so we need to use a far pointer. One approach is to use the large-memory model in which all pointers are far pointers by default. However, our code is rather small, and it would seem wasteful to have to drag in far pointers for the code segment. Hence, it is more efficient to stick to the small model and use an explicit far pointer to access the video memory.

To implement this approach for the *bars.c* program, we can rewrite the putdot() function, leaving everything else the same. We can declare a far pointer and initialize it to point to the beginning of video memory at 0xB8000. Then we can calculate the offset needed to specify a particular pel.

One immediate problem is that each byte contains the information for four pels. The two high-order bits of a byte describe the first pel, the next two bits the next pel, and so on, as shown in Figure 9.4. This means that to set a pel, we need to find the proper byte, then find the proper two bits within the byte. These bits then should be set to the proper two-bit code for the desired color.

There is a further problem to face. The even-numbered lines are stored in an 8000-byte block beginning at 0xB8000, the start of the video memory. The odd-numbered lines are stored in the 8000-byte block starting at an offset of 0x2000 from the beginning of video memory. To locate the proper bits for a pel must take this into account. Figure 10-2 shows how lines on the screen are separated into even and odd storage locations.

Figure 10-2
Memory Mapping of Video Lines

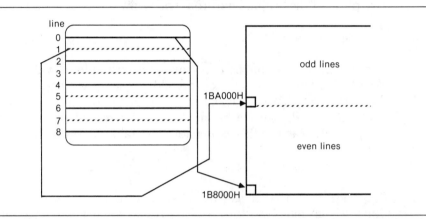

Suppose, then, we wish to place the two-bit color code `color` in the right memory location to describe a pel whose coordinates are `row`, `col`. We start with a pointer called `scrptr` that points to the beginning of video memory. We have to generate an offset from the beginning position to the pel position. The offset has three parts:

$$\text{offset} = \text{even/odd offset} + \text{row offset} + \text{column offset}$$

The even/odd offset is 0 or 0x2000, the row offset locates the beginning of a row, and the column offset is from the row beginning to the pel.

First we have to find the offset of the appropriate memory block. If `row` is even, this offset is 0; if `row` is odd, the offset is 0x2000. One way to test for an odd row is to use the modulus operator:

```
if ( row % 2 )    /* expression is 1, or true, if row odd */
    scrptr += 0x2000;  /* add 0x2000 to the base address */
```

A second and quicker approach is to use a bitwise operator. Consider the the following:

```
if ( row & 01 )
   scrptr += 0x2000;
```

If `row` is odd, then the 0-bit must be a 1; all other bits are multiples of 2, and hence even. The expression `row & 01` has the value 1 if the 0-bit of row is 1 and the value 0 otherwise. Thus, this expression also tests whether numbers are odd.

Once we get the right memory block, we need to calculate the proper offset from the beginning of the block. Since each screen row contains 320 pels and each memory byte describes 4 pels, we can consider each screen row to consist of 80 bytes. Each row, then, produces an offset of 80 bytes. Since just every other screen row goes into a given memory block, the relative offset of the beginning of row `row` is given by this expression:

```
80 * (row / 2)
```

Clearly this works for the even rows. For example, row 2 has a relative offset of 80 bytes. It also works for odd rows, since integer division truncates to an integer. That is, $\frac{1}{2}$ is 0 and $\frac{3}{2}$ is 1, giving the correct relative offsets for the odd rows. Because a bit right shift of 1 is equivalent to integer division by 2, we also can use this expression to obtain the row offset:

```
80 * (row >> 1)
```

Next, we need to get the offset due to the column position. The first four pels go into byte 0 of a given row, the next into byte one and so on. Thus we need to divide the pel column by four to get the byte offset from the beginning of the row. Instead of integer division, we can use a right shift of two bits. Thus, the column offset is this:

```
(col >> 2 )
```

Our program will combine the three expressions just described to locate the address of the byte described a pel at a given row and column.

The next problem is to set the correct two bits within the byte to the correct color code. Consider a byte; pel 0 goes to bits 7 and 6, pel 1 goes to bits 5 and 4, pel 2 goes to bits 3 and 2, and pel 3 goes to bits 1 and 0. If we start with a pattern in bits 1 and 0, pel 0 requires a left shift of 6, pel 2 a left shift of 4, pel 3 a left shift of 2, and pel 3 no shift. We can express the shift size with this expression:

```
shift = 2 * (3 - col % 4 );
```

Here `col` is the pel column number, and the modulus operator gives the remainder upon division by 4. This operator gives its order within a byte. A pel in column 12, for example, would be the 0 pel in byte 3, while a pel in column 13 would be the 1 pel in byte 3.

☐ *Question 10-1*   Can you replace the modulus operation with a bitwise operation?

Finally, we are ready to set the bits. If the XOR option is in effect (bit 7 of color set to 1), we can use XOR on the shifted color code with the current contents of the two bits. Otherwise, we must set the two bits to the new pattern. This can be done by using the & operator to turn both bits off and then using the ¦ operator to turn the desired bits on. Using the ¦ operator alone would cause bits that are already on to be left on. Putting all these moves together produces the following code. Remember that to have the compiler recognize the keyword `far`, you must invoke the `/Ze` option:

```
/* putdot.c--use DMA to place colored dot on screen */
#define BCOLS 80        /* bytes per row */
typedef unsigned char (far *VIDEO); /* far ptr to char */
#define ODDOFST   0x2000L            /* offset for odd rows */
#define GRSEG     ((VIDEO) (0xb800L << 16) )  /* segment value */
#define CLMSK 0x3                    /* 2-bit color mask */
#define REM4 0x3             /* used to get remainder */
void putdot(row,col,color)
unsigned int row, col;
unsigned char color;
{
  VIDEO scrptr = GRSEG;
  unsigned int offset, shift;

  shift = 2 * (3 - col & REM4 );
  offset = BCOLS * (row >> 1) + (col >> 2);
  if ( row & 01 )
      scrptr += ODDOFST;
  if ( color >> 7 )
      *(scrptr + offset ) ^= ( (color & CLMSK) << shift);
  else
      {
      *(scrptr + offset) &=~(CLMSK << shift);
      *(scrptr + offset) ¦= ((color & CLMSK) << shift );
      }
}
```

☐ *Question 10-2*   Explain the following statement:

```
*(scrptr + offset ) ^= ( (color & CLMSK) << shift);
```

How much do we gain by using direct memory access instead of the BIOS calls? In this case, the time to draw the screen on our system is 12 seconds, compared to 28 for the BIOS version. This is noticeably faster, but still a bit slow. How much did using bit operations instead of integer division and the modulus operator help? Substituting those operations for the bit operations increases the time from 12 to 15 seconds, so using the bit operations is worthwhile.

Part of the speed problem is that the program addresses a pel at a time. To draw a horizontal bar in *bars.c* involves calling putdot() nearly 4000 times. The C library offers functions that transfer data in larger blocks. If we give up the exclusive OR feature, we can use these functions to speed up the program immensely.

Buffer Functions

The C library offers several "buffer" functions. They resemble the string functions, but work on arrays—that is, buffers—in general. Instead of using the null character to mark the end of a data string, the buffer functions use an explicit buffer count. The functions we'll use here are memset() and movedata(). The memset() function takes three arguments: the address of the beginning of a destination buffer; a byte value, ch; and a count, cnt. The first cnt bytes of the buffer are set to the value ch. If we use the large-memory model, we can use this function to copy a particular color setting into sections of video memory. Since the makbar() function sets a large number of bytes to one particular value, memset() would be very useful in that context. One drawback is that memset() works with whole bytes, so it is simplest to work with blocks of pels that are multiples of four pels wide and that start at byte boundaries.

Suppose we don't want to use the large model. Then we can set the video memory in two steps. First, memset() can be used to set a scratch buffer to the desired color value. Then the movedata() function we discussed earlier can be used to copy the buffer into video memory. Because the segments and offset are specified separately and explicitly, this function can be used with the small-memory model.

We will rewrite the makbar() function using both approaches, since each has interesting features. Running either version with *bars.c* cuts the drawing time for the screen from 12 seconds to about $\frac{1}{10}$ second! But you are probably tired of *bars.c* by now, so we will put together a new program to test the new functions. But first we have to write the functions.

Using Memset() and Movedata()

This approach retains the small-memory model. Because movedata() uses separate arguments for segment and offset values, we don't even have to use far pointers. We've already worked out the segment and offset values for the video memory, so all we need now are the segment and offset values for the scratch buffer. Suppose we declare an array rw. Then the array name rw *is* the offset from the beginning of the data segment. The segread() function provides the current segment register values, placing them in type SREGS structure defined in *dos.h*. The ds member of the array holds the value of the DS register, which is the base of the data segment.

The other problem we face is setting all the bit pairs in a byte to a color value; we can use the bit operators for that. Here, then, is one implementation. Because it does not use far pointers, you don't need to use the /Ze compiler option:

```
/* makebar0.c--small-memory approach */
#include <memory.h>    /* declarations for buffer functions */
#include <dos.h>       /* used for segread() */
#define ROWS 200
#define COLS 80
#define ODDOFST    0x2000    /* offset for odd rows */
#define GRSEG      0xb800    /* segment value for display mem */
#define CLMSK 0x3            /* color bits mask */

void makebar(r1,r2,c1,c2,color)
unsigned int r1, r2, c1, c2;
unsigned char color;
{
  unsigned int offset;
  unsigned char rw[COLS];  /* scratch buffer */
  unsigned char cv;
  int r;
  int nbytes;
  struct SREGS reg; /* holds segment register values */

  nbytes = (c2 - c1) / 4 + 1;  /* number of bytes needed */
  segread(&reg);
  cv = CLMSK & color;    /* set 1 pel to color */
  cv |= ( cv << 2);      /* set 2 pels to color */
  cv |= ( cv << 4);       /* set all 4 pels to color */
  memset ( rw, cv, nbytes);
  for ( r = r1; r <= r2; r++)
    {
    offset = COLS * (r >> 1) + (c1 >> 2);
    if ( r & 01 )
        offset += ODDOFST;
    movedata(reg.ds, rw, GRSEG, offset, nbytes);
  }
}
```

The largest block of memory that we would copy with one move would be one row of 320 pels, or 80 bytes, so that is the size we used for the scratch buffer.

Using Memset() and the Large-Memory Model

Now let's try the second method. By using the large-memory model, we can use memset() to set bytes in the display memory directly. Here is how that approach looks:

```
/* makbar1.c--large-memory model version */
#include <memory.h>
#include <dos.h>
#define ROWS 200
#define COLS 80
#define ODDOFST   0x2000L
#define GRSEG   ( ( unsigned char *)(0xb800L << 16))
#define CLMSK 0x3

void makebar(r1,r2,c1,c2,color)
unsigned int r1, r2, c1, c2;
unsigned char color;
{
  unsigned long offset;
  unsigned char cv;
  int r;
  int nbytes;
  unsigned ds;

  nbytes = (c2 - c1) / 4 + 1;
  cv = CLMSK & color;
  cv |= (cv << 2);
  cv |= ( cv << 4);
  for ( r = r1; r <= r2; r++)
    {
    offset = COLS * (r >> 1) + (c1 >> 2);
    if ( r & 01 )
       offset += ODDOFST;
    memset( GRSEG + offset,cv, nbytes);
    }
}
```

To use this version you must compile it *and* any other code files of the program by using the /AL large-memory model option. That is, you can't simply link this module with other modules compiled using the small-memory model.

This version is neater looking. It saves time by copying directly to video memory, but it loses time by using far pointers for all its operations. We ran trials using each version to draw 1000 20 × 20 boxes, or over 60 screenfuls. Each took 4.6 seconds, so the two factors canceled each other in this application.

Color Blocks in Motion

We can use either of the new makbar() functions to create a colorful display. The following program sets up a red square (color one of the palette) on a blue background. The cursor arrow keys move the block around on the screen, and as it moves, it leaves a green path (color 2 of the palette) behind. We can use function keys to change the background and the palette, as before, and the HOME, PG UP, END, and PG DN keys to select which palette color is left as a trail. The PG DN key, for example, selects the background color for the trail, effectively changing the moving block into an eraser. The speed of movement is controlled by the keyboard delay time rather than by the screen drawing time. Here is the listing; the code should be linked with the code of the other functions mentioned:

```
/* movsqr.c--bold but primitive graphics */
#include <stdio.h>
#include <conio.h>
#include "color.h"
#include "keys.h"
#define STOP '\032'
#define ROWS 200
#define COLS 320
#define BKGR   0
#define COLOR1 1
#define COLOR2 2
#define COLOR3 3
#define SIDE   20
#define MB(X,Y,C) makeblock(X, X+SIDE-1, Y, Y+SIDE-1, C)
void setmode(), setcolor(), makebar();
main()
{
    int ch;
    unsigned char pl = PALETTE1;
    unsigned char bg = BLUE;
    unsigned int urow = 80;
    unsigned int lcol = 160;
    unsigned char tr = COLOR2;

    setmode(4);
    setcolor(bg,pl);
    MB(urow, lcol, COLOR1);
    while ( ( ch = getch() ) != STOP )
      {
      if ( ch == '\0' )
         {
         ch = getch();
         switch (ch)
            {
            case PU : tr = BKGR; break;
            case HM : tr = COLOR1; break;
```

```
                    case PD : tr = COLOR2; break;
                    case END : tr = COLOR3; break;
                    case F1 : bg = BLACK; setcolor(bg,pl); break;
                    case F2 : bg = BLUE; setcolor(bg,pl); break;
                    case F3 : bg = GREEN; setcolor(bg,pl); break;
                    case F4 : bg = RED; setcolor(bg,pl); break;
                    case F5 : bg = CYAN; setcolor(bg,pl); break;
                    case F6 : bg = MAGENTA; setcolor(bg,pl); break;
                    case F7 : bg = YELLOW; setcolor(bg,pl); break;
                    case F8 : bg = WHITE; setcolor(bg,pl); break;
                    case F9 : pl = PALETTE1; setcolor(bg,pl); break;
                    case F10 : pl = PALETTE2; setcolor(bg,pl); break;
                    case UP : if (urow >= SIDE )
                                    {
                                    MB(urow, lcol, tr);
                                    urow -= SIDE;
                                    MB(urow, lcol, COLOR1);
                                    }
                                    break;
                    case DN : if (urow < ROWS - SIDE)
                                    {
                                    MB(urow, lcol, tr);
                                    urow += SIDE;
                                    MB(urow, lcol, COLOR1);
                                    }
                                    break;
                    case LT : if (lcol >= SIDE )
                                    {
                                    MB(urow, lcol, tr);
                                    lcol -= SIDE;
                                    MB(urow, lcol, COLOR1);
                                    }
                                    break;
                    case RT : if (lcol < COLS - SIDE )
                                    {
                                    MB(urow, lcol, tr);
                                    lcol += SIDE;
                                    MB(urow, lcol, COLOR1);
                                    }
                                    break;

            }
        }
      }
   setmode(3);
}
```

Direct Memory Access in the Text Mode

To bring everything together, let's look at one more example—one that uses BIOS calls, direct memory access using far pointers, and port information all in one program. The goal this time is to put together a program that displays a file a screen at a time. By using direct screen access, we can make a program that is considerably faster than the *show.c* program from Chapter 5. To concentrate on the essentials, we'll not include partial overlap between successive screens or single-line advances.

Let's think about the requirements of the program. First, it should know what kind of device it is using. We can use the BIOS 10H interrupt to determine the mode and to set a text mode if needed. The program should clear the screen; again, we can use the BIOS 10H interrupt. The program should read characters and place each character and its attribute in successive locations in screen memory. It should start a new line when it reaches the end of the screen or when a newline character shows up. It should halt when the screen is full, then resume when a key is pressed. The *IBM Technical Reference* manual says that if the monitor is a color/graphics monitor in the high-resolution text mode, the CPU should access the video memory only during the vertical retrace time (that's when the beam is moving back to the top of the screen). We can use a port to check for that.

The *show.c* program can provide the overall framework, modifying it to fit the new approach. Here is that framework, slightly modified:

```c
/* fastshow.c--using DMA */
#include <stdio.h>
#include <conio.h>
#include "vid.h"        /* defines VID_ADDR type */
main(ac,av)
int ac;
char *av[];
{
    FILE *fp;
    void fastshow();
    void setup();
    VID_ADDR dispmem;    /* display memory addresses */

    setup( &dispmem );              /* get mode information */
    if ( ac < 2 )
        fastshow(stdin, dispmem );
    else while ( ac > 1)
        {
        if ( (fp = fopen(av[1],"rt") ) == NULL )
            fprintf(stderr,"fastshow can't open %s\n", av[1]);
        else
            {
```

```
                    fastshow(fp, dispmem );
                    fclose(fp);
                    if ( ac > 2)
                      getch();      /* halt between files */
                    }
                ac--;
                av++;
                }
        }
```

Now we have to supply a `setup()` function to set up the proper mode, and a `fastshow()` function to put output on the screen. Let's do `setup()` first.

Determining the Mode

We'll check the mode. If it is one of the 80 × 25 modes, we'll leave it be. Otherwise, we'll set to the 80 × 25 B/W mode. The output function will need to know whether to use the Monochrome or the CGA video display memory, so we'll return that information to the calling program. We've set up the *vid.h* header file to define a structure to hold the required information. This file is used with several functions in this program, so let's look at it:

```
/* vid.h--constants for video calls */
typedef unsigned int  (far * VIDMEM);
typedef struct {
                VIDMEM display; /* display segment */
                int  statusport; /* status port number */
                } VID_ADDR;
#define CGSEG 0xB800          /* segment values */
#define MONSEG 0xB000
#define CGMEM   ((VIDMEM) (0xB800L << 16 ) )
#define MONMEM  ((VIDMEM) (0xB000L << 16 ) )
#define BW4025      0       /* modes */
#define CL4025      1
#define BW8025      2
#define CL8025      3
#define CL320       4
#define BW320       5
#define BW640       6
#define MONO        7
#define CGSTAT      0x3DA      /*CG status port */
#define MONOSTAT    0x3BA      /* MONO status port */
```

Next, here's code to check the mode and provide the addresses of the video memory and of the status port.

```
#include "vid.h"
void setmode(), setpage();
int getmode();

void setup(paddr)
VID_ADDR *paddr;
{
    VIDMEM base;

    switch ( getmode () )
        {
        case MONO   :  paddr->display = MONMEM;
                       paddr->statusport = MONOSTAT;
                       break;
        default     :  setmode(BW8025);
        case BW8025 :  paddr->display = CGMEM;
                       paddr->statusport = CGSTAT;
                       setpage(0);
                       break;
        }
}
```

The getmode(), setmode(), and setpage() functions all use BIOS calls, so it is convenient to place them in one file. We'll add a clear screen function to that list, since we will need one later. This set of functions can be used:

```
/* int10h.c--collection of BIOS 10H calls */
#include <dos.h>
#define GETMODE 15
#define SETMODE 0
#define SETPAGE 5
#define SCROLLUP 6
int getmode()
{
  union REGS rin, rout;

  rin.h.ah = GETMODE;
  int86(0x10, &rin, &rout);
  return rout.h.al;
}

void setmode(mode)
unsigned char mode;
{
    union REGS rin, rout;
```

```
        rin.h.ah = SETMODE;
        rin.h.al = mode;
        int86(0x10, &rin, &rout);
    }

    void setpage(page)
    unsigned char page;
    {
        union REGS rin, rout;

        rin.h.ah = SETPAGE;
        rin.h.al = page;
        int86(0x10, &rin, &rout);
    }

    void cls()
    {
      union REGS rin, rout;

      rin.h.ah = SCROLLUP;
      rin.h.bh = 07;          /* attribute used for blank lines */
      rin.h.al = 0;           /* scroll up a blank page */
      rin.h.ch = 0;           /* start at row 0, */
      rin.h.cl = 0;           /* column 0 */
      rin.h.dh = 24;          /* end at row 24, */
      rin.h.dl = 79;          /* column 79 */
      int86(0x10, &rin, &rout);
    }
```

That takes care of initializing the program. Now let's turn to the output phase.

Outputting Text with a Far Pointer

Keep in mind that each character on the screen is represented by a character/attribute pair in memory. The character code goes into the first, or low-order byte of the word, and the attribute goes into the high-order byte. Thus, if ch is the desired character and ATR is the attribute, we wish to place the following combination into memory:

```
(ATR << 8) ¦ ch
```

We can specify the location with a pointer to the beginning of video memory plus an offset. The offset will begin at 0 (the upper left corner of the screen), and we can increment it each time we write a character. Thus we will have code of this form:

```
*( screenpointer + offset++) = (ATR << 8) ¦ ch;
```

Finally, we have to attend to the line count. If a newline character shows up, we should advance the offset to the beginning of the next row, that is, to the beginning of the next block of 80 2-byte character/attribute pairs. The following code does this and incorporates the other features we just discussed.

```c
#include <stdio.h>
#include "vid.h"
#define ROWS 25
#define ATR  07              /* usual attribute */
void cls();
void fastshow (stream, screen)
FILE *stream;
VID_ADDR screen;
{
    unsigned ch;
    int lc = 0;  /* line count */
    unsigned long offset = 0L;

    cls();
    while ( ( ch = getc(stream) ) != EOF )
        {
        ch &= 127;
        if ( ch != '\n')
           *( screen.display + offset++) = (ATR << 8) | ch;
        else
           {
           lc++;           /* one more line */
           offset = (offset / 80 + 1) * 80;
           }
        if (lc == ROWS)
           {
           lc = 0;
           getch();        /* wait for key to be hit */
           offset = 0L;     /* reinitialize */
           cls();          /* clear the screen */
           }
        }
    getch();    /* wait */
}
```

Now we can pull all the pieces together and compile them. Remember to use the /Ze option to enable the far keyword.

The program is quite quick, but it is unrefined. There are several possible improvements we can make. Let's look at some of them.

First, if you run the program with the standard CGA card and a standard monitor, you may get a little "snow," or interference, while a new page comes up. According to the *IBM Technical Reference* manual, we should write in modes 2 and 3 only during the vertical retrace time. This occurs when the monitor's electron beam reaches the lower end of the screen and resets to the top. Writing during this time avoids interference in the display between action of the CRT Controller and the CPU.

To find out when a retrace occurs, we can check one of the ports to the video controller chip. For the CGA card, port 0x3DA has the required information. If bit 0 is set to 1, it is retrace time and okay to write. The Monochrome Display Adapter uses port 0x3BA for the same purpose, but that adapter does not have the snow problem. We can use code like this to wait until the proper time:

```
while ( (inp ( 0x3DA ) & 01) != 0 )
     ;      /* wait until end of current retrace */
while ( (inp ( 0x3DA ) & 01) == 0 )
     ;      /* wait until next retrace */
```

The logic, copied from one of the video BIOS routines, goes like this. If bit 0 is 1, it's retrace time and okay to write. But we might have caught a point 90 percent through the retrace, so we'll wait until it's done. Then we'll wait through the next nonretrace time (bit 0 being 1), and then we'll write, knowing that we're starting at the beginning of a retrace time.

This approach slows the program down; if you don't mind a bit of temporary snow, you can leave it out. Or you can set it up as an option to be set up by a command line argument or by an environmental parameter.

A second area where we could improve the program is in additional handling for special characters. Control characters, for example, could be represented in the ^B form. The tab character could be used to insert spacing instead of printing out as a funny-looking character. Certain characters could be used to toggle reverse video or high-intensity properties by altering the attribute.

A third area of improvement would be to create further buffering. The standard file I/O buffer only holds about a quarter-screenful of data. Using a larger intermediate buffer would speed up the program further. Or by using a really good-sized buffer, say 32k, you could arrange for the program to move back and forth through text.

We leave such refinements to those of you who have the need for them or the curiosity to work them out. Our main point is that by using special features of the compiler, we can create programs that run much more quickly than generic ones. The negative side, of course, is that such programs are much less portable. This program, for example, depends on such specific items as the 8088's use of segmented memory, on specific BIOS calls, and on particular memory addresses and port addresses. You can see now why IBM compatibility comes in varying degrees.

Summary

The standard small-memory model confines code and data to 64K segments. In the medium-memory model, code can occupy more than one segment, and in the large-memory model, both code and data occupy more than 1 segment. The huge-memory model lets single data items exceed 64K segment in size. The extensions are accomplished by using 32-bit far pointers instead of 16-bit near pointers. The 16-bit pointer used in the small-memory model just holds the offset of the address. Data pointers measure the offset from the data segment, whose value is stored in the DS register. Code pointers measure the offset from the code segment, whose value is stored in the CS register. The far pointer holds the offset in the low-order 16 bits and the segment value in the high-order 16 bits.

With the keywords `near` and `far`, enabled by the `/Ze` compiler option, you can use a pointer that is not the default type for a particular model.

With some library functions you can work with segment values and offsets separately, rather than as parts of a single pointer.

With any of these approaches, you can implement programs that directly access the video memory. Such programs are hardware-specific, but perform much more quickly than those relying upon standard library or interrupt routines.

Answers to Questions in the Chapter

■ *10-1.* Yes. Bits 2 through 7 are evenly divisible by 4, so the remainder of a division by 4 would be the original 0 and 1 bits. Thus, if we mask all but bits 0 and 1 to 0, the result is the remainder. The proper mask is bits 0 and 1 set to 1, that is, the number 3:

```
shift = 2 * (3 - col & 03 );
```

■ *10-2.* The statement is

```
*(scrptr + offset ) ^= ( (color & CLMSK) << shift);
```

The expression

```
*(scrptr + offset )
```

tells the program to go to the address `scrptr + offset` and use the value found there. The `^=` operator causes the value there to be exclusively ORed with the following expression and the resulting value to be placed in the indicated location. The expression

```
(color & CLMSK)
```

leaves bits 0 and 1 unchanged and masks the rest to 0; this ensures that the resulting expression is a two-bit color code. The expression

```
(color & CLMSK) << shift
```

shifts the two-bit color pattern to the proper position within a byte. The combined effect of all these operations is to use EXCLUSIVE OR on the indicated color with the current settings of the two bits controlling the pel at the indicated row and column.

Exercise

Implement and test the improvements we suggested for the *fastshow.c* program.

11

Introducing Assembly Language

- Machine language
- Machine architecture
- Assembly language
- Instruction mnemonics
- Assembly directives
- Assembly modules
- C-assembly interface
- C compiler as tutor
- Improving compiler-generated code

Introducing Assembly Language

In Chapters 8 through 10 we saw how the IBM C Compiler allows you rather precise control over the IBM PC-DOS operating system, the BIOS, and the system hardware. The highest level of control, however, comes from using assembly language, which is very closely tied to the innate machine language of the processor. There is no "best" choice for programming. Assembly language fully exploits the capabilities of the processor, and it does so with compact, fast-running programs. But it is a very detailed language, one that easily leads to subtle and unsubtle errors. A high-level language like C, on the other hand, makes it much easier to structure a program into logical, functional modules. The readability of a high-level language makes it is easier to check for logical and syntactical errors. To some extent the strengths and weaknesses of assembly language and C complement each other. In this and the next chapter, we'll look at assembly in the context of using it with C programs.

What can you gain by studying assembly language? While the overall structure of most programs is best handled using a high-level language such as C, you occasionally may wish to incorporate an assembly language module to handle some specific task. Such modules can be incorporated easily into a C program as long as certain setup conventions are followed. The IBM C Compiler itself can be used to generate assembly code. By looking at that code, you can get an inside view of how C programs actually work and of how assembly programs are put together. Once you get that far, you may find that you can use assembly language to modify and improve code produced by the C compiler.

To learn assembly language, you'll have to study a whole book or its equivalent. But we can outline the philosophy and capabilities of assembly language so that you can gain a sense of what an assembly language program does. Then you can judge if it is a subject you wish to pursue further. This chapter provides that introduction.

Because our intent is to provide an overview of assembly language rather than detailed instruction, the beginning of the chapter surveys the general features of assembly language and includes a summary of many of the instructions. Once you have developed a good background, you are ready for the chapter's specific examples. In particular, we will use the IBM C Compiler to generate assembly code. Comparing the code to the C original will provide insight into how assembly code does its work. In addition, we'll see the features needed to make an assembly module compatible with a C program. If you already are familiar with assembly language, you may wish to scan the first part of this chapter.

Assembly Language, Machine Language, and Machine Design

The heart (or is it the brain?) of the IBM PC is the 8088 microprocessor. As we have learned, it contains several registers capable of holding binary values. It also has access to the system memory. The processor recognizes a large number of *machine language* instructions. These instructions are on the level of "put this number in the CX register" and "put this item in the stack." Each instruction is represented by a binary number. Ultimately a C program is converted to a sequence of such binary machine instructions stored in memory. The CS (code segment) register contains the segment value for the beginning of the code, and the IP (instruction pointer) register contains the offset of the next instruction to be executed. Once a program starts, it marches through the machine code instructions, using the IP register to tell it which instruction to do next. Figure 11–1 illustrates the concept.

Different processors have different built-in instructions, so each processor has its own machine language. In general, a program written in machine language will work only for one particular processor, or, perhaps, for a family of processors. The 8088 and 8086 processors compose one such family. The only difference between the two chips is that the 8088 accesses the memory a byte at a time, while the 8086 accesses it two bytes at a time. The 80286 processor used in the IBM AT is a close relative—the 8088 instructions are a subset of its own machine language. Thus, an 80286 will run 8088 programs, but the 8088 may not run 80286 programs.

Programming on the most primitive level would involve placing the required binary codes in the proper memory locations; it is a tedious, error-intensive process. Assembly language eases the task by providing mnemonics for the actual machine instructions and by providing directives, or "pseudo-ops" to handle particular aspects of assembling a program. For example, the mnemonic

```
mov ah,19
```

represents moving the value 19 into the AH register, and the DB data-byte directive

```
bigbyte DB 255
```

allocates a byte, initializes it to 255, and assigns it the name bigbyte. A

Figure 11–1
CS and IP Registers

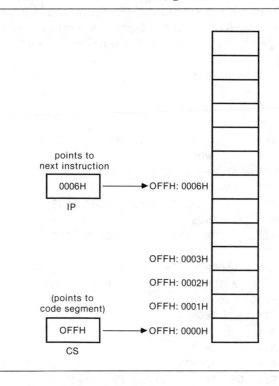

program called an *assembler* actually converts mnemonics and directives to machine code. Figure 11–2 summarizes the conversion. The mnemonics represent machine-language instructions to be executed during run time, while the directives represent instructions for the assembler to follow during assembly time. Like machine language, assembly language is specific to a particular processor. Several vendors provide assemblers for the 8088/8086. The various assemblers provide different facilities and different mnemonics.

Figure 11–2
Converting Assembly Language to Machine Language with an Assembler

assembly language ──► │ ASSEMBLER │ ──► machine language

MOV AX, 19	1011	1000
	0000	0000
	0001	0011
JMP GO	1110	1011
	1111	1011

We will use the Microsoft's MASM assembler. It provides 65 basic mnemonics (plus many usage variants) and 57 directives for the 8088 processor. You can see why learning assembly language is more involved than learning, say, BASIC or C! Here, for example, is a fairly simple assembly module produced by the IBM C Compiler from a C program:

```
;  Static Name Aliases
;
TITLE    forloop

_TEXT      SEGMENT  BYTE PUBLIC 'CODE'
_TEXT      ENDS
CONST    SEGMENT  WORD PUBLIC 'CONST'
CONST    ENDS
_BSS       SEGMENT  WORD PUBLIC 'BSS'
_BSS       ENDS
_DATA      SEGMENT  WORD PUBLIC 'DATA'
_DATA      ENDS
DGROUP  GROUP    CONST, _BSS,       _DATA
          ASSUME  CS: _TEXT, DS: DGROUP, SS: DGROUP, ES: DGROUP
PUBLIC  _forloop
_DATA      SEGMENT
EXTRN   _printf:NEAR
_DATA      ENDS
_DATA      SEGMENT
$SG29   DB  '%5d',  0aH,  00H
          EVEN
$SG30   DB  0aH,  00H
_DATA      ENDS
_TEXT      SEGMENT
;        n=4
; Line 3
          PUBLIC  _forloop
_forloop    PROC NEAR
      push     bp
      mov      bp,sp
      sub      sp,2
;      i=-2
; Line 7
      mov        WORD PTR [bp-2],0
      jmp        SHORT $L20000
$F24:
; Line 8
      push     WORD PTR [bp+4]
      mov      ax,OFFSET DGROUP:$SG29
      push     ax
      call      _printf
```

```
        add       sp,4
        inc       WORD PTR [bp-2]
$L20000:
        mov       ax,[bp+4]
        cmp       [bp-2],ax
        jl $F24
; Line 9
        mov       ax,OFFSET DGROUP:$SG30
        push      ax
        call      _printf
; Line 10
        mov       sp,bp
        pop       bp
        ret
_forloop   ENDP

_TEXT      ENDS
END
```

This may look intimidating if you haven't worked with assembly language before, but by the end of this chapter you should be able to analyze this program line by line.

Assembly instructions are closely tied to the architecture of the processor. We can gain insight into assembly language by reviewing the processor design and seeing how specific instructions relate to that design.

Registers

Let's review and extend what we have discussed about the 8088 chip. Of paramount importance are the registers. They form the workspace used by the microprocessor. Each register is capable of holding 16 bits. There are 4 general-purpose registers. Their main use is to hold values for logical and arithmetic operations. Then there are 4 pointer-and-index registers; these are used to hold the offset portion of addresses. The 4 segment registers serve to hold the segment values. There is 1 instruction pointer register. Finally, there are 9 single-bit "flags" that can be set and unset by various events.

The registers and flags are the chief tools used by the assembly language instructions. Let's take a closer look at them.

General-Purpose Registers—The general-purpose registers are named AX, BX, CX, and DX when they are used as 16-bit registers. Figure 11–3 diagrams them. Each register can also have its low and high bytes used independently. The high byte of AX is called AH, the low byte AL, and so on for the other registers.

Most arithmetic and logical operations can be applied equally well to all the general registers, but the registers are not entirely equivalent to one another. Each has particular tasks as its specialties; let's see what they are.

Figure 11-3
The General-Purpose Registers

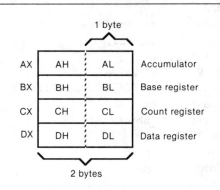

The AX register, or "accumulator," is used for division and multiplication. It also is used to hold values transmitted by the in and out instructions. These are the assembly language instructions for communicating with ports.

The BX, or "base," register often is used to store an offset address. For instance, it can serve as the assembly version of a pointer. That is, some instructions, instead of saying "use the value in BX," will say, "use the value found at the address given by BX." BX is the only general register that can be used in this "indirect address" mode.

The CX, or "count," register, is used as a counter by some instructions.

The DX, or "data," register is used to hold the port number used by the in and out instructions. It also takes part in division and multiplication when there are too many bits for the accumulator to handle alone.

Segment Registers—An assembly program can keep track of up to four memory segments at a time. The segment registers hold the segment values for these segments. The four registers are named CS, DS, SS, and ES. The CS register is used for the code segment, DS for the data segment, SS for the stack segment, and ES for the extra segment. Certain pointer registers, as we will soon see, are assumed to measure offsets from these values.

Pointer/Index Registers—These four registers are named SP, BP, SI, and DI. They are 16-bit registers, and they are used to hold address offsets. Assembly language for the 8088 is designed with stacks in mind, and the SP and BP pointers are used to describe the stack. The BP (base) pointer typically holds the offset of the stack base, while the SP pointer typically holds the offset of the top of the stack. With C programs, the base pointer is reset each time a function is called to provide a local stack base (called a *frame*) for the current function. The offsets are measured relative to the stack segment (SS) register. It is these registers, for example, that are used to locate the automatic variables generated by a C program. Remember that the stack grows towards smaller memory addresses, so the top of the stack has a lower address than the stack base; both, however, are higher than the stack segment address. Figure 11-4 shows their positions.

Figure 11-4
Pointers to the Stack

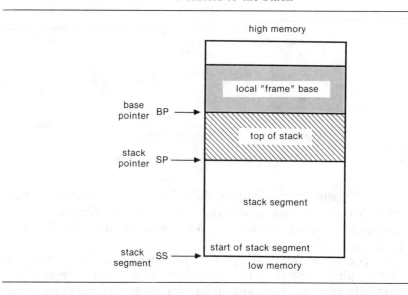

The SI and DI index registers usually measure offsets from the data segment (DS) register. They might be used, for example, to refer to external variables set up by a C program. Certain instructions, however, imply different interpretations. For instance, there is a string-copying command for copying data from one location to another. In that case, the SI index contains the starting offset of the source (measured from DS), and the DI index contains the starting address of the destination (measured from ES); for this reason, these registers sometimes are termed the *source index* and the *destination index*.

The Instruction Pointer—The instruction pointer (IP) register contains the offset of the next instruction to be executed. This offset is measured from the current CS value. Program flow can be altered by altering the value of this pointer.

You may have noticed how different pointer and index registers measure offsets relative to different segment registers. Figure 11-5 summarizes which registers are used with the various segment registers. Note that the default use may be overridden in some cases; we'll see how in Chapter 12.

The Flags—The 8088 has nine flags. Each is a one-bit switch. Some, called "status flags," are set by the processor in order to note the result of some

Figure 11–5
Segment and Offset Registers

segment registers	pointer and index registers					
	SP	BP	BX	SI	DI	IP
CS	no	yes with override	yes with override	yes with override	yes with override	yes
DS	no	yes with override	default	default	default (non-string)	no
SS	yes	default	yes with override	yes with override	yes with override	no
ES	no	yes with override	yes with override	yes with override	default (strings)	no

action. Others, called "control flags," are set by the user to control actions. Many of the machine-language instructions use flag values as a means of choosing a subsequent action. We'll describe the flags briefly in order to give you a feel for what they do.

The status flags are set after an operation. For example, an addition may result in a number requiring more bits than the register holds. In that case, it's said that the most significant bit has been "carried out," and the carry flag (CF) is set to one. If there is a carry out for the four least significant bits, the auxiliary carry flag (AF) is set to one. The overflow flag (OF) is set to one if the result is an out-of-bounds signed value. The zero flag (ZF) is set to one (not 0) if the result of an operation is 0. If the result is a negative number, the sign flag (SF) is set to one. Finally, if the parity is even (an even number of ones in a binary number), the parity flag (PF) is set to one.

☐ *Question 11–1* Is having both a carry flag and an overflow flag redundant?

There are three control flags. The trap flag (TF) enables the single-step processing mode used in debugging. The interrupt enable flag (IF) enables external interrupts. A 0 value for this flag causes the processor to ignore all external interrupts except for the nonmaskable interrupt (NMI) generated by severe problems. Finally, the direction flag (DF) controls the direction (beginning to end, or vice versa) for certain string-related instructions.

Memory and Ports

Although the CPU is a clever manipulator, it is not able to remember the sequence of instructions needed to run it nor the results of this work. Memory is needed for that. The instruction pointer and code segment give the processor access to its instructions, and various assembly language instructions give the program access to the system memory. As you probably have noticed by now, the CPU can address up to 1Mb of memory. Conceptually, the memory is divided into 64K segments, since up to 64K addresses can be specified by a 16-bit pointer register. A segment must start at a memory location that is evenly divisible by 16. These particular locations are called paragraph boundaries. Thus, we can say that all segments must start at paragraph boundaries. A segment register specifies a particular segment by storing its segment value, which is the actual address divided by 16. Typically, a location is specified by giving the segment and the offset:

$$\text{absolute address} = 16 \times (\text{segment value}) + \text{offset}$$

Nothing prohibits the overlapping of one segment with the other. The small memory model, for example, has the data segment and the stack segment set to the same value. Static variables get stored near the bottom of the segment, and stack variables get stored nearer to the top.

As you saw in Chapter 8, the CPU has 64K ports available for communicating with other devices, such as keyboards, timers, and printers. They are addressed by number; the 64K possible ports means that only a 16-bit address is required, so port addresses don't use the segment method.

Assembly Language Instructions

Now that we have seen the arena in which assembly language works, we can investigate the particular kinds of tasks assembly instructions must perform. The instructions fall into several categories. Some instructions move data around. Some perform arithmetic operations, and some perform bitwise operations. Others operate on strings of bytes. (A *string* in assembly is a series of related bytes; it corresponds more closely to a C array than to a C string, since no terminating character is involved.) Other instructions, such as the jump family, relate to program control, that is, determining the next instruction to be executed. (They reset the IP value.) A few instructions relate to the flags, and, finally, some instructions serve to coordinate the CPU with an 8087 floating-point coprocessor. This coprocessor, if present, steps in when floating-point calculations are needed.

We'll take a quick look at some of the more important or interesting (or perhaps both) instructions.

Transferring Data

Perhaps the most frequently used assembly instruction is MOV. This instruction moves data from a source to a destination. It can be used to move data from memory to register, from register to memory, from register to register, and to set register values. When moving data between a register and memory, it can do so by mentioning the memory address directly *(direct addressing)* or by telling where to find the address *(indirect addressing)*. This is the same distinction we find in C between using a regular variable (direct addressing) or using a pointer (indirect addressing).

Using assembly language you can also create a symbolic name for a memory location; that is, you can create a named variable. This is an assembly language convenience for you, because in machine language the name gets translated to a particular address. Thus, the assembly language label is just a more convenient form of direct addressing.

As an example of a MOV instruction, consider this:

```
mov ax,cx
```

This moves the contents of the CX register to AX. Note that MOV, like other assembly data transfer instructions, lists the destination first and the source second.

We'll see examples of different forms of MOV soon.

The PUSH and POP pair are stack-related operations. PUSH puts data into the stack, and POP removes it. Recall that the SP pointer points to the current top of the stack. Suppose you give this instruction:

```
push ax
```

First, this instruction decreases SP by two. It decreases the value because the stack (as described in Chapter 6) grows downward, to lower addresses. It decreases by two because the AX register holds two bytes. Then the two bytes in AX are placed in the two new bytes of the stack.

The operation

```
pop ax
```

reverses the process, copying the top two bytes of the stack into AX and incrementing the stack pointer SP by two. Incidentally, the memory in the stack is not erased, but it will be overwritten by the next PUSH. Figure 11–6 shows how four operations (a–d) are affected.

Assembly programs often use PUSH to save the current values of the registers so that the registers can be used for other purposes. When the task is finished, POP is used to restore the original values.

To access the ports, assembly language uses the IN and OUT instructions; they perform the same function as IBM C's inp() and outp() functions. The latter, of course, are implemented using the former.

For example, the following instruction reads port 61H into the AL register:

```
in      al,61h
```

Note that assembly uses the h suffix to indicate hex values.

Figure 11–6
PUSH and POP

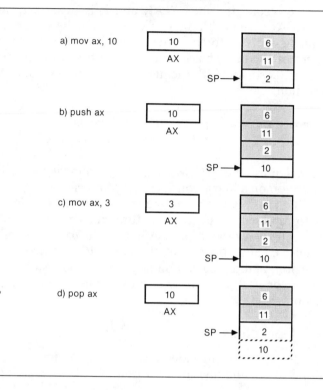

Similarly, the instruction

```
out     61h,al
```

sends the current AL value out the 61H port.

Both instructions must use either the AL or the AX register for the value to be read or written.

The data-moving instructions we've mentioned so far have close C analogs. The next two don't. First, XCHG exchanges the contents of two registers. This avoids the three-step procedure using temporary storage that we must use in C. For instance, to exchange the contents of AX and CX, just do this:

```
xchg ax,cx
```

This instruction also can be used with eight-bit registers. For example, to switch the high and low order bytes in AX, do this:

```
xchg al,ah
```

Since an exchange is involved, the order of listing the two registers is immaterial.

The second is called XLAT, and it is used to transfer a value from a table to AL. The table in this case would be an array of bytes, with the beginning address stored in the BX register. Suppose we want, say, the fifth element of the table placed into AL. Just as in a C array, table numbering starts at 0, so the fifth element has the index four. So we can give this instruction:

```
mov al,4      ;move index 4 into AL
xlat          ;place table item #5 into al
```

Here we've use the MASM assembler comment method: anything following a semicolon on a line is considered a comment.

One possible use would be in a program to convert the EBCDIC code uses to represent characters on IBM mainframes to ASCII representation. Table entry 0 would be the ASCII code for the character represented by EBCDIC 0, and so on. Put the EBCDIC character in AL, give the XLAT instruction, and the corresponding ASCII code is placed in AL. If your program needs fast byte-to-byte conversions, you may wish to try this instruction.

Arithmetic Operations

The instruction set includes instructions for integer addition, subtraction, multiplication, and division. For example, the instruction

```
add ax,cx    ; add contents of cx to ax
```

adds the contents of CX to AX, even if you omit the helpful comment. The result is placed in AX, and CX is left unchanged.

However, life is a bit more complicated in assembly than in C. For instance, a separate add instruction (ADC) is used if you need to keep track of the carry flag. This could happen, for example, in adding 32-bit integers, since the registers could handle just 16 bits at a time. Similarly, there is a regular subtraction instruction (SUB) and an instruction for subtraction with borrowing (SBB).

Division and multiplication each come in two forms, also. One set (MUL and DIV) is used with unsigned values, and a second set (IMUL and IDIV) is used with signed values.

Like C, assembly language provides incrementing (INC), decrementing (DEC), and sign-changing (NEG) operations. In addition, it has a comparison operation (CMP) that compares two values by subtracting one from another and tossing away the answer. This seemingly senseless waste actually is useful, for actual subtraction changes the value of one of the operand registers. The CMP operation changes no registers, but it does affect flags; for example, if the two values are equal, the subtraction yields 0, setting the zero flag

(ZF) to one. The flags, as we will soon see, are used to control program flow, so an instruction that just affects flags is a useful one, acting much like a test condition in a C program.

You may have noticed that we haven't mentioned any floating-point operations. That's because the 8088 processor doesn't have any. Floating-point calculations can be handled by programs that use integer arithmetic to construct the proper sequence of calculations to find floating-point values. The C library, for example, provides such functions. A faster way is to add a coprocessor, such as the 8087 or 80287 chip, specifically designed for floating-point operations. The IBM C library also includes functions designed to use a coprocessor.

Bitwise Operations

One distinction between C and most high-level languages is that it supports several bitwise operations. In that, it follows the lead of assembly language.

The AND, OR, XOR, and NOT operations in assembly are similar to C's bitwise &, |, ^, and ~ operations. With the assembler operations, the result is left in the leftmost operand. For example, the operation

```
and bx,cx
```

leaves the result of the ANDing in register BX.

Assembly language adds a TEST operator to the logical repertoire. It works like AND, except the result is discarded, leaving the original registers or memory locations unchanged. Like CMP, TEST is used for its effects upon the flags.

Assembly provides counterparts to the left-shift and right-shift operators. There are two varieties. The shift logical left (SHL) and shift logical right (SHR) operators use zero extension (for details, see Chapter 4). The shift arithmetic left (SAL) and shift arithmetic right (SAR) operators, however, use sign extension for right shifts; typically they would be used with signed quantities. (The SAL and SHL operations are identical, since both fill the vacated bits with 0's.)

The C shift operations use one or the other set of assembly shift operations, depending on whether signed or unsigned quantities are involved.

There are four assembly bitwise operations with no C counterpart. The rotate left (ROL) and rotate right (ROR) operations do what their names suggest; they rotate the bits in a register. For example, the instruction

```
rol ax,1
```

rotates the 0 bit to the 1-bit position, the 1-bit to 2, and so on, with the 14 bit going to the 15-bit position, and the 15 bit going around to the 0-bit position. The instruction can also be used to rotate half registers, such as AL. Figure 11–7 illustrates the rotation.

Don't conclude from this example that changing the one to a two will produce a two-bit rotation. It is possible to rotate more than one bit at a

Figure 11–7
Bit Rotation

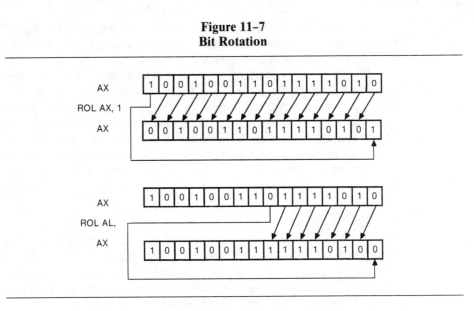

time, but for those cases you must put the desired number of bit positions to be rotated into CL, the count register. Thus, to produce a three-bit rotation to the left, you would use the following sequence:

```
mov   cl,3
rol   ax,cl
```

This is an example of how assembly language often is not as straightforward as are high-level languages.

Program-Control Instructions

C uses devices such as `while` loops, `for` loops, `switch` statements, `if` statements, function calls, and jump statements (`break`, `continue`, `goto`) to control program flow. Assembly language lacks the more structured of these forms, but it has a huge variety of jump statements. It also has ways of calling subroutines and interrupts.

Jumps—Assembler offers two classes of jumps: unconditional and conditional. An unconditional jump (`JMP`) says go to a certain address. A conditional jump tells the program to go to a certain address if a particular condition holds and otherwise to go on to the next instruction.

In addition, the assembler distinguishes between jumps to code in the same segment ("near jumps") and jumps to code in another segment ("far jumps"). Near jumps use a relative offset; that is, instructions like "jump ahead 10 bytes" or "jump back 20 bytes." Far jumps must specify a segment value and an offset. Near jumps are quicker and less cumbersome; they are used by IBM C's small-memory model.

Conditional jumps typically depend on particular flag values. For instance, the `JNZ` instruction means "jump if not 0"; it causes a jump if the preceding instruction resulted in the zero flag (ZF) being set to 0. The assembler recognizes over 30 mnemonics for conditional jumps. (Some of the names, however, are synonymous.)

The MASM assembler helps us to specify jump destinations by using address labels instead of numerical values. For instance, a code segment could look like this:

```
start:              ; a label
        dec ax      ; decrement AX
        jnz start   ; jump to start if result is not 0
```

Here, the `start` identifier is a label. Notice that it is followed with a colon when it is used to mark a location. The assembler will convert this code to machine language giving the size of the jump in bytes.

The `LOOP` instruction is a specialized form of jump which, in addition to jumping, decrements the CX register by 1. When the CX register reaches 0, the loop stops. Here, for example, is a waiting loop that counts CX down from 5000 to 0:

```
        mov cx,5000    ;put 5000 into CX
wait:
        loop wait      ;do-nothing loop
```

The basic mechanism for all these jump instructions is that they set the instruction pointer and, if necessary, the code segment to the values corresponding to the desired address.

Calls and Returns—The `CALL` instruction is slightly more elaborate than a jump. It is used to call subroutines. Just as for jumps, there are "near calls" for subroutines in the same segment, and "far calls" for subroutines in another segment. Let's see what is involved for a near call.

A subroutine should return to the calling routine when done, so it has to know which address to return to. The `CALL` instruction helps with this goal by saving the current value of IP by pushing it onto the stack. Remember that the IP value is the address of the next instruction. Next, it sets IP to the offset address of the desired subroutine. Thus, the next instruction executed is the one that begins the subroutine.

A `CALL` instruction looks like this:

```
call invert
```

Here, `invert` is the name of another procedure; this call transfers control to the beginning of that procedure.

A subroutine ends with a `RET` instruction. This tells the program to return to the calling program. It does so by popping the stored IP value off the stack and back into IP. Thus the next instruction executed after a RET is the instruction just after the original CALL.

Far calls and returns also push and pop the code segment (CS) register values.

Interrupts—An assembly program can process hardware-generated interrupts and generate software interrupts. The IF flag enables and disables external interrupt recognition. That is, if the IF is set to 1, interrupts from the outside are processed. If it is set to 0, they are ignored, except for the nonmaskable interrupt (NMI). For example, setting the IF flag to 0 will cause the program to ignore interrupts from the keyboard, such as CTRL-BREAK.

Generating a software interrupt is much like generating a subroutine call. For example, the various BIOS video routines of interrupt 10H are assembly language routines stored in the ROM. To access them from assembly, we use the INT instruction. (It, incidentally, is not disabled by the IF flag.) The INT instruction works like CALL, except that it also pushes the flag settings onto the stack. Interrupt routines themselves end with an IRET instruction instead of a RET instruction; IRET works like RET but also pops the flags back. This means that interrupt routines can use flags as they please without disturbing the calling routine flag settings.

Suppose, for instance, we wish to use interrupt 10H routine 15 to get the video display mode. This involves setting AH to 15, then invoking the interrupt:

```
mov ah,15       ;set AH to 15
int 10h         ;invoke 10h interrupt
```

This results in the current mode being set to AL, the number of character columns being placed in AH, and the current active page being placed in BH, just as for the int86() call we used in Chapter 8.

String Operations

In machine language, a string is a sequence of bytes in memory. It is not necessarily a string of characters, and it is not necessarily terminated by a null value. Assembly language offers several instructions designed to operate efficiently upon strings. In general, these instructions can operate on either a byte at a time or a word (two bytes) at a time. The MOVS instruction copies a string from one location to another. The CMPS instruction compares two strings to one another. The SCAS instruction scans a string for a particular byte or word. The LODS instruction loads a string element into the accumulator and moves a pointer to the next string element. The STOS instruction stores an accumulator value to a string and advances a pointer to the next string position.

We'll learn more details later, but there are three important features we wish to mention now.

First, these instructions can work either a word at a time or a byte at a time. One way to indicate which you want is to add a W suffix to the instruction if you wish to work with words, and a B suffix to work with bytes. Thus, `SCASB` will scan a string for a particular byte, and `SCASW` will scan for a particular word.

Second, it is very important to understand how these functions operate upon strings. In general there is a source string and a destination string, although some registers use just one or the other. The location of the source string is specified by two registers. The DS register holds the source segment value, and the SI register holds its offset. The ES register holds the destination segment value, and the DI register holds its offset. Suppose, for example, we initialize these registers to the desired values and then give this instruction:

```
movsb
```

The instruction uses the DS and SI registers to find the initial byte in the source, and it uses the ES and DI registers to find the initial destination byte. It copies the source to the destination, then increments both SI and DI by one. This sets up the next call to `MOVSB` to copy the next byte. If we were to use the `MOVSW` version instead, SI and DI would be incremented by two, setting up to copy the next word. Thus, SI and DI play the role of two pointing fingers, moving in sync from byte to byte or from word to word. Figure 11–8 illustrates the source and destination strings.

Figure 11–8
SI and DI in String Operations

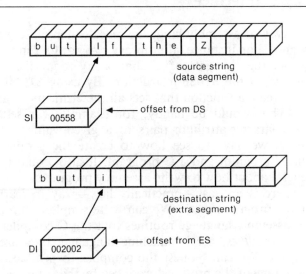

As described, the string operations affect only one byte or word of a string, but they do update the pointers. The third feature we want to mention is that there is a REP prefix designed to work with these string instructions. Prefacing the string instruction with REP causes the combined instruction to test if CX is 0 and to quit if it is. If it isn't, CX is decremented, the string instruction is executed, and the process is repeated. Thus, the REP instruction turns a string instruction into a counting loop. For example, to place 100 null bytes into a destination location specified by ES and DI, we can repeat the STOSB instruction, which copies bytes from AL to the destination string:

```
mov cx,100        ;set CX to 100
mov al,0          ;set al to 0
rep stosb         ;fill up destination with 100 zeros
```

To load words, we'd use STOSW and AX.

The REP prefix has two relatives. The REPE (repeat while equal) prefix is used to repeat a CMPS or SCAS instruction as long as the compared values are equal to each other. The REPNE (repeat while not equal) repeats those same instructions as long as the compared values are not equal. Note that the difference between CMPS and SCAS is that CMPS compares corresponding bytes (or words) of two strings, while SCAS compares a single byte (or word) to successive elements of a string.

As you can see, the string functions have the potential to create useful additions to the C library.

There are more assembly language instructions, but these examples should give you a good idea of what is possible.

The Assembly-C Interface

Our survey of assembly language reveals many interesting possibilities for C programs. For instance, the library memset() function offers a quick way to set all the elements of a char array to a given value. Presumably, it makes use of the STOSB instruction. By using STOBW instead, we should be able to create a function that sets all the elements of an int array to a given value. That would be handy, for example, for setting a block of video screen character-attribute pairs to a given value. Before getting that far, however, we have to see how to create the proper interface between an assembly program and a C program. It also would be useful to learn more in general about how to write assembly programs.

There is an easy—practically lazy—way to learn more about writing assembly program for C. We can write simple programs in C and then look at the assembly language routines that the C compiler produces. The object files, or *modules,* are in machine language; they are the files bearing the obj suffix. We can request the compiler to produce an assembly language version. One of the prompts produced by the compiler is this:

```
Object listing [NUL.COD]:
```

The NUL indicates that the default value is no file. Provide a name, however, and a listing for the object code is given. Let's try an example.

An Example That Adds Up

First, let's start with a C function that adds two to its argument and returns the new value. The function is simple to write:

```
/* incrs.c--increase argument by 2 */
increase ( n )
int n;
{
   return n = n + 2;
}
```

We could have written it more efficiently, but we wanted to include an assignment statement. Next we compile it. We used the /Gs option. Normally, the IBM C Compiler invokes a stack-checking function to prevent stack overflow. The /Gs option deletes this step and makes the code slightly easier to follow. Here is the object code listing produced by the compiler:

```
;         Static Name Aliases
;
          TITLE    incrs

_TEXT      SEGMENT  BYTE PUBLIC 'CODE'
_TEXT      ENDS
CONST    SEGMENT  WORD PUBLIC 'CONST'
CONST    ENDS
_BSS       SEGMENT  WORD PUBLIC 'BSS'
_BSS       ENDS
_DATA      SEGMENT  WORD PUBLIC 'DATA'
_DATA      ENDS
DGROUP   GROUP    CONST, _BSS,       _DATA
          ASSUME   CS: _TEXT, DS: DGROUP, SS: DGROUP, ES: DGROUP
PUBLIC   _increase
_DATA      SEGMENT
_DATA      ENDS
_TEXT      SEGMENT
;         n=4
; Line 2
          PUBLIC   _increase
_increase           PROC NEAR
          *** 000000  55              push bp
          *** 000001  8b ec           mov    bp,sp
```

379

```
; Line 4
        *** 000003  83 46 04 02    add   WORD PTR [bp+4],2
        *** 000007  8b 46 04       mov   ax,[bp+4]
        *** 00000a  5d             pop   bp
        *** 00000b  c3             ret
_increase   ENDP

_TEXT       ENDS
END
```

At first glance, this seems a lot messier than the C original, but it is not as bad as it may look.

The listing contains three main categories of text. There are assembler directives; these are in uppercase. There is the actual machine language coding. It consists of entries like this:

```
        *** 000001              8b ec
```

The *** 000001 represents the address. The final address is not determined until the function is linked to a program, and the program is loaded; hence the asterisks. The 8b ec represents the binary machine language instructions represented in hexadecimal notation.

Finally, text such as

```
mov     bp,sp
```

represents the assembly language equivalent to the machine language instructions.

Analyzing the Code

We don't have to worry about the machine-language instructions, but we should try to understand the rest. First, let's look at the assembly language code and see if we can follow what is happening. Here is just the code portion, along with a few added comments:

```
_TEXT       SEGMENT        ;the _TEXT segment is the code segment
;       n=4     this refers to the location of n, not its value
; Line 2        this identifies the C program line defining n
        PUBLIC  _increase  ;other modules can use this one
_increase PROC NEAR  ;it's a near procedure
        push    bp                      ;save old bp value
        mov     bp,sp                   ;make sp the new bp
        add     WORD PTR [bp+4],2        ;add 2 to n
        mov     ax,[bp+4]               ;place result in ax
        pop     bp                      ;restore old bp value
        ret                             ;return
```

```
_increase       ENDP                    ;end of procedure

_TEXT           ENDS                    ;end of code segment
END                                     ;end of module
```

Some of these statements are required by all C functions, and some are specific to this procedure. Let's go through this line by line. The assembly needs to know where to place its code and data. The `_TEXT SEGMENT` line indicates that the material between it and the `_TEXT ENDS` line should go into the code segment. All small-memory model C functions will have these statements.

Next, there is a comment stating n=4. A C function call places its arguments on the stack; this comment indicates that the variable n corresponds to the stack item with an offset of four from the stack base pointer, BP. Why four? We'll come back to that question. The following comment identifies the program line in which n was defined. Similar comments would be generated by any small-memory model program with a single integer argument.

Next there are two lines identifying the procedure name:

```
        PUBLIC  _increase   ;other modules can use this one
_increase       PROC NEAR   ;it's a near procedure
```

The assembler directive `PUBLIC` says that `_increase` is a public identifier; that is, it can be accessed by other modules. If we had used the C keyword `static` before the function name in the C program, the `PUBLIC` directive would have been omitted, indicating that only functions in the same module could call `increase()`. Of course, there are no other functions in this particular module, so that would be a poor choice. The following line says that `_increase` is the name of a near procedure; that is, it is a procedure that can be accessed by near calls. This is a consequence of using the small memory model, in which all code modules are assumed to go into the same segment. If we had used the medium or large memory model, the procedure would have been labeled `PROC FAR`. Note the name `_increase`; the IBM C convention is that a C function is represented in assembly by prefixing an underline character to its name. Many, but not all, C compilers follow this same convention.

Now we get to the assembly code:

```
push    bp                      ;save old bp value
mov     bp,sp                   ;make sp the new bp
```

First, recall the special meanings of the BP and SP registers. The BP register points to the base of the stack, and the SP register points to the current top of the stack. Also recall that the stack grows downward in memory, so SP is equal to or less than BP, and adding to the stack decreases SP.

The PUSH instruction saves the current value of the base pointer. As the procedure draws to an end, a POP instruction restores that original value, so the procedure leaves the larger order undisturbed.

The MOV instruction sets BP to SP; this makes the top of the stack into the new base. In effect, the procedure has its own stack within a stack to work with. These two stack-related commands are done for all C functions. Figure 11–9 illustrates how the stack is set.

Figure 11–9
Setting the Stack

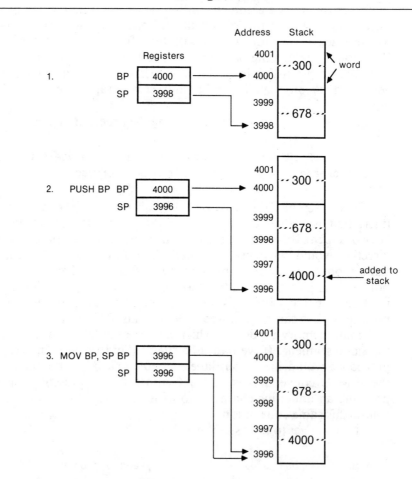

Next we have the most involved of the instructions:

```
add     WORD PTR [bp+4],2      ;add 2 to n
```

As indicated, it adds two to the current value of n, but the approach doesn't look very direct. The **ADD** instruction adds its two operands, placing the result in the place occupied by the left operand. The right operand is obvious enough; it's the two that gets added to n. Therefore, the left operand should be n. Let's untangle it.

BP, recall, is the base pointer, so the expression bp+4 is the address four bytes greater than BP. This represents a location "below" the current stack base, hence a location in the stack of the calling procedure. Earlier, we were told that n=4; this means that the _increase procedure expects to find a value for the n variable four bytes "below" the current stack base.

What about bp and bp+2? Recall that a function call pushes the instruction pointer (IP) value so that the called function will know what address to return to; that address is at bp+2. And the first thing this called program did was to push BP. That stored the current BP value at the top of the stack. Then the

```
mov bp,sp
```

made BP point to the current top of the stack, so BP points to an address containing its original value. Look again at Figure 11-9. In it, **BP+4** is 4000, the address of the passed argument; in this case the argument is 300. **BP+2** is 3998 and points to the address in the calling routine that _increase should return to; in this example, that address is 678. And BP itself points to the previous stack base value, 4000.

Anyway, bp+4 is an *address,* so we don't want to add two to it; instead we want to add two to the *contents* of that address. That is what the brackets represent; bp+4 is the address, and [bp+4] is the value at that address. In C terms, bp+4 is a pointer and the brackets are an indirect value operator, like C's *. The **WORD POINTER** part acts like a C typecast; it informs the assembler that bp+4 is the address of a word, not a byte. This means bytes bp+4 and bp+5 are used. After the addition, these two bytes hold the resulting value. In Figure 11-9, the 300 would become 302.

Not all registers can be used with the [] notation. In fact, just the base registers BP and BX and the index registers SI and DI can be used that way.

What this all amounts to is that the expression bp+4 represents the variable n, and the expression [bp+4] represents the value of n. So we can paraphrase the instruction as "add 2 to n and store the result at n." Or, in C terms, this line translates to the following:

```
n = n + 2;
```

Well, that's not surprising, since that's the C assignment expression we started with!

Next we have this statement:

```
mov     ax,[bp+4]              ;place result in ax
```

As before, [bp+4] represents the value stored at the address bp+4. The MOV instruction copies the value into the AX register. Because AX is a 16-bit register, 2 bytes are transferred automatically. In short, this line says to copy n to AX. There is an extremely important reason for including this instruction: C functions require that the return value be placed in the AX register. Actually, this is true just for 16-bit return values. Table 11-1 provides the complete picture.

Table 11-1
Register Use for C Return Values

Return Value Type	Register
8-bit and 16-bit integer types	AX
long, unsigned long	high order word in DX
	low order word in AX
struct, union, float, double	address in AX; value must be in a static memory area
near pointer	AX
far pointer	segment in DX, offset in AX

The code section ends with these statements:

```
pop     bp                  ;restore old bp value
ret                         ;return
```

The POP instruction restores the original stack base, and RET causes program flow to return to the instruction following the original CALL. In terms of Figure 11-9, BP is reset to 4000, and the instruction pointer (IP) is set to 678.

Finally, the following three assembler directives announce the end of the procedure, the end of the code segment, and the end of the module:

```
_increase   ENDP            ;end of procedure

_TEXT       ENDS            ;end of code segment
END                         ;end of module
```

To understand the distinctions between procedure, code, and module, we should look at assembly directives and at how assembly programs are put together.

Parts of an Assembly Program

As befits the 8088 architecture, an 8088 assembly program can contain a code segment, a data segment, a stack segment, and an extra segment. A small-memory model contains just one segment of each (although not all need be used), while larger models use additional segments.

Often an assembly program is put together from more than one file. The material in one particular file is assembled into a module, and the modules are linked together to form a program. The program as a whole, at least in the small-memory model, still will have just one code segment, one data segment, one stack segment, and one extra segment, if used. This means the code segments from the individual modules need to be merged together into a single code segment. The same holds true for the other segments. This is accomplished by using assembler directives to name the segments; the linker combines together material contained in segments of the same name. The larger-memory models then can use additional segment names, and particular names will guide code or data to particular segments.

Let's see how the directives in our sample accomplish this aim.

Assembler Directives

First, let's extract the directives from our sample function:

```
        TITLE   incrs

_TEXT       SEGMENT  BYTE PUBLIC 'CODE'
_TEXT       ENDS
CONST   SEGMENT  WORD PUBLIC 'CONST'
CONST   ENDS
_BSS        SEGMENT  WORD PUBLIC 'BSS'
_BSS        ENDS
_DATA       SEGMENT  WORD PUBLIC 'DATA'
_DATA       ENDS
DGROUP  GROUP   CONST, _BSS,        _DATA
        ASSUME  CS: _TEXT, DS: DGROUP, SS: DGROUP, ES: DGROUP
PUBLIC  _increase
_DATA       SEGMENT
_DATA       ENDS
_TEXT       SEGMENT
    PUBLIC  _increase
_increase   PROC NEAR
_increase   ENDP

_TEXT       ENDS
END
```

The TITLE directive provides a name for the module; it is just the filename stripped of its extension. If you produce a program listing, the title will get printed every 50 lines (the default value). This directive is not required.

Next, we have these lines:

```
_TEXT      SEGMENT  BYTE PUBLIC 'CODE'
_TEXT      ENDS
```

The **SEGMENT** directive marks the beginning of a segment, and the **ENDS** directive marks the end of a segment. So these lines represent an empty segment. Their purpose is to set up the code segment used by all small-memory model C programs. In these two directives, **_TEXT** identifies the name of the segment. Assembly programmers are free to choose a name, but modules to be used with the IBM PC Compiler must use this particular name for the code segment.

The **BYTE** is an alignment modifier; it indicates that the code must start on a byte boundary. Other alignment choices are **WORD**, **PARA**, and **PAGE**, indicating the code must start on a word, paragraph, or page boundary. (A *word boundary* is an address evenly divisible by 2, a *paragraph boundary* is evenly divisible by 16, and a *page boundary* is evenly divisible by 256.)

PUBLIC, in this context, is a "combine" modifier, indicating how segments having the same name will be combined. **PUBLIC** means that all segments having the same name are to be combined into a single, contiguous segment. This applies to segments within the module and, when linked, to segments in different modules.

The **'CODE'** modifier is a class name; it must be in single quotes. Its presence means that the segment name **_TEXT** belongs to the **'CODE'** class. The significance of belonging to a class is that different segment names belonging to the same class will be loaded in contiguous memory.

In short, these two lines define the code segment in a manner compatible with code produced by the IBM C Compiler.

Later in the file, the actual code is contained between **_TEXT SEGMENT** and **_TEXT ENDS** directives.

Next, several statements deal with data:

```
CONST     SEGMENT  WORD PUBLIC 'CONST'
CONST     ENDS
_BSS       SEGMENT  WORD PUBLIC 'BSS'
_BSS       ENDS
_DATA      SEGMENT  WORD PUBLIC 'DATA'
_DATA      ENDS
DGROUP    GROUP    CONST,  _BSS,       _DATA
```

The **CONST** segment is used to store read-only constants. IBM C, in anticipation of the forthcoming ANSII C standard, supports a keyword const that can be used to set up such constants. The **_BSS** segment is used for uninitialized static data, and **_DATA** is used for initialized static and global (defined outside of a function) data. This sounds like several data segments, but they are joined together into the **DGROUP** group. The net effect is that when modules are combined, all the **_DATA** segments are combined into one contiguous segment, all the _BSS segments are combined into another contiguous segment, and so on, with all the segments grouped together into a single group, with all offsets measured from the group segment value. Figure 11–10 shows how module segments are merged.

Figure 11–10
Merging Segments

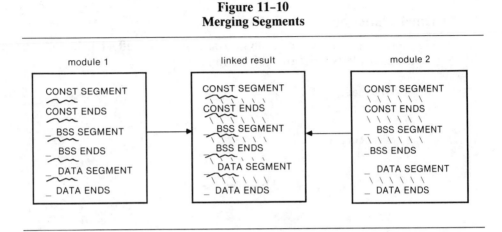

The ASSUME directive indicates which register is the default segment register for the various segments:

```
ASSUME  CS: _TEXT, DS: DGROUP, SS: DGROUP, ES: DGROUP
```

If, for instance, a variable is defined in the data group and its name is used in the code, the assembler will assume that the segment value for the variable is in the DS register.

The directives to this point can be considered to be a defining heading to be used with all small-memory model assembly modules intended to be used as C functions. The only variations would be in the title name and in the exact list of data segments to be used. We'll see other examples soon.

The subsequent directives pertain to our module in particular. First, _increase is proclaimed to be a public name. That _increase is declared twice to be PUBLIC is an artifact of the compiling process; one declaration will do. Next comes a data segment for this particular module; in this case, it is empty. Note that each SEGMENT directive has to be balanced by an ENDS directive. Then comes the code segment. This one contains one procedure, or routine; in general, there could be more. Each procedure would be marked off by directives marking its beginning and end:

```
          PUBLIC  _increase
_increase         PROC NEAR
_increase         ENDP
```

Note that each PROC is balanced by an ENDP.

Finally, END is used to mark the end of the entire module.

Even if we don't understand in full the reason for every line in the file, we still can use it as a framework for constructing assembly programs.

☐ *Question 11-2* How could you write a C function in assembly to add five to the function argument?

A Quick Variation

Let's change the C code slightly and see what effect it has on the code. In particular, let's write the C function this way:

```
increase ( n )
int n;
{
   return n + 2;
}
```

instead of the way we did before:

```
increase ( n )
int n;
{
   return n = n + 2;
}
```

The relevant assembly code becomes this:

```
;         n=4
          PUBLIC  _increase
_increase         PROC NEAR
      push      bp
      mov       bp,sp

      mov       ax,[bp+4]
      inc       ax
      inc       ax
      pop       bp
      ret
_increase         ENDP
```

Compare this to the previous code:

```
;         n=4
          PUBLIC  _increase
_increase         PROC NEAR
      push      bp
      mov       bp,sp
```

```
        add       WORD PTR [bp+4],2
        mov       ax,[bp+4]
        pop       bp
        ret
_increase         ENDP
```

Now that the procedure is freed from the necessity of resetting n to the final value, the compiler has taken a different approach. Register arithmetic is faster than memory arithmetic, so the addition has been moved to the registers. Second, the INC operation is faster than an ADD; indeed, the compiler seems to believe that two INC operations are faster than a single ADD.

Using an Assembly Language Function

Suppose we had written our sample assembly program ourselves. How would we incorporate it into a C program? First, we would need to assemble the module. The usual practice is that assembly source code files have an *.asm* extension, so we should place the assembly code in a file called, say, *incrs.asm*. Note that this file should not contain the machine-language code found in a COD file. (If you wish to modify a COD file, delete the machine code and change the filename extension to *.asm*.) Then we invoke the assembler:

```
A>masm incrs
```

The result is object code in a file called *incrs.obj*. This file then can be linked with object files produced by the IBM C Compiler. Suppose, for example, we have this source file:

```
/* useit.c--try the increase() function */
#include <stdio.h>
main()
{
   printf("increase(4) = %d\n", increase(4) );
}
```

Then we could compile *useit.c* with this command:

```
cc  useit.c
```

This will compile the *useit.c* file, producing a *useit.obj* file. Next, we use the linker to combine that file, the *incrs.obj* file, and modules from the library to produce the *useit.exe* file.

```
clink useit incrs
```

Because our *incrs.asm* file follows the same format used by the IBM C Compiler, the two object modules are compatible. Try it yourself.

Library Modules and the Start-Up Module

When the IBM C Compiler produces an object file, it encodes in the file the libraries to use. Thus, we normally need not specify libraries explicitly. The libraries contain more object modules conforming to the standard format used in C programs.

There is one library module that is incorporated into all C programs. (Actually, it comes in different versions for different memory modules.) It is called *crt0.obj*, and it is the start-up module. It executes before `main()`. Among other things, it sets up the stack segment. The stack needs to be set up just once, so our assembly functions don't include directives for setting up the stack. It also sets up a `NULL` segment at the very beginning of the data group. Since the offset of the `NULL` segment is 0, the `NULL` pointer points to that segment; if anything gets written there, it is a sign that a program is misbehaving.

Your Own Private Tutor

We can learn a lot more about assembly language, assembly directives, and about how C functions are put together by generating COD files for other simple C functions. In essence, we can use the C compiler as an assembly tutor. If we want to know how do something in assembly language, we can write an equivalent C program and see how the compiler does it. We'll devote the rest of this chapter to that kind of exploration.

Static and Stack Data

First, let's investigate how different storage classes are stored. Our first function didn't incorporate any built-in data. Let's modify it to include a static variable and an automatic (stack) variable:

```
/* incrs.c--stupid way to add 8 to a number */
increase ( n )
int n;
{
   int x = 3;
   static y = 5;

   return n + x + y;
}
```

According to what we have said, y, being an initialized static variable, should be placed in the _DATA segment, and stack space should be allocated for x. Let's look at the COD file generated by the compiler; we'll continue using the /Gs option to simplify the code:

```
;      Static Name Aliases
;
;      $S11_y      EQU      y
       TITLE   incrs


_TEXT     SEGMENT   BYTE PUBLIC 'CODE'
_TEXT     ENDS
CONST     SEGMENT   WORD PUBLIC 'CONST'
CONST     ENDS
_BSS      SEGMENT   WORD PUBLIC 'BSS'
_BSS      ENDS
_DATA     SEGMENT   WORD PUBLIC 'DATA'
_DATA     ENDS
DGROUP    GROUP     CONST,     _BSS,     _DATA
          ASSUME  CS: _TEXT, DS: DGROUP, SS: DGROUP, ES: DGROUP
PUBLIC  _increase
_DATA     SEGMENT
_DATA     ENDS
_DATA     SEGMENT
$S11_y    DW      05H
_DATA     ENDS
_TEXT     SEGMENT
;      n=4
; Line 2
          PUBLIC        _increase
_increase     PROC NEAR
          *** 000000     55          push     bp
          *** 000001     8b ec       mov      bp,sp
          *** 000003     83 ec 02    sub      sp,2
;      x=-2
; Line 4
          *** 000006     c7 46 fe 03 00      mov      WORD PTR
[bp-2],3
; Line 7
          *** 00000b     8b 46 04    mov      ax,[bp+4]
          *** 00000e     03 46 fe    add      ax,[bp-2]
          *** 000011     03 06 00 00 add      ax,$S11_y
          *** 000015     8b e5       mov      sp,bp
          *** 000017     5d          pop      bp
          *** 000018     c3          ret
_increase     ENDP


_TEXT     ENDS
END
```

Note that the file contains the same segment definitions as the first example. Since these definitions are common to all small-memory model C functions, we'll omit mentioning them in the future.

What's new? Near the beginning, there is a comment:

```
;$S11_y EQU y
```

The C compiler generates its own names for variables; this comment indicates that the module name for the C variable y will be $S11_y. Incidentally, the MASM assembler does offer an EQU directive that works much like a C preprocessor define. For instance, the line

```
VIDMEM EQU B8000H
```

establishes VIDMEM as a symbolic representation for the indicated address. The y example, however, is just a comment for our edification.

The next new point is that the _DATA segment no longer is empty:

```
_DATA       SEGMENT
$S11_y      DW      05H
_DATA       ENDS
```

The DW directive corresponds roughly to a C declaration. DW declares that the program needs a word of data memory. The 05H is the value placed in the word, and the $S11_y is a name assigned to the memory location. In other words, the line declares $S11_y to be a two-byte variable initialized to the value 05H. Remember, $S11_y corresponds to the static variable y, so that variable indeed was placed in the _DATA segment as promised.

Other assembly *data types* are DB (data byte), DD (data doubleword), DQ (data quadword), and DT (data 10-byte word).

□ *Question 11-3* How do you suppose you would declare a one-byte variable and initialize it to the ASCII code for A (0x41)?

The other new variable is the automatic variable x. Let's see how it was handled. Here is the relevant code:

```
sub     sp,2
;       x=-2
mov     WORD PTR [bp-2],3
```

The SUB instruction subtracts 2 from the current value of the stack pointer, SP. Initially, the stack pointer and base pointer have the same value, so this instruction adds 2 bytes to the top of the stack. This is the space allocated for the automatic x variable. The next line is a comment verifying this assignment; the x=-2 means that the address of x is 2 less than the base pointer value. Henceforth in this procedure, bp-2 will be used to represent the address of x and [bp-2] will be used to represent the value of x. The next instruction illustrates that point as it moves the value 3 into the x memory slot. The instruction itself is analogous to the

```
mov     WORD PTR [bp+4],2
```

instruction of our first example. The main difference is that the minus sign in the present instruction indicates we are using the procedure's stack (the current "frame"), while the plus sign in the first example indicates we are using the calling program's stack (the previous frame). See Figure 11–11 for an illustration of the stack frames. (Remember, the stack grows "up" toward low memory, so a plus sign indicates something "below" the current stack base.)

Figure 11–11
Current and Previous Stack Frames

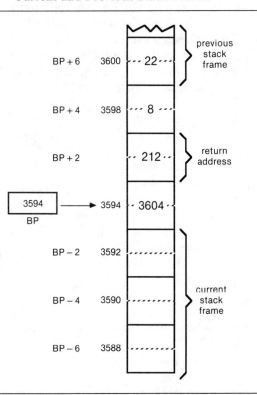

□ *Question 11–4* Wouldn't PUSH 3 have the same effect as the SUB, MOV sequence?

Note that creating and initializing the static variable y is a one-step operation, but creating and initializing the automatic variable x is a two-step operation. Note, too, that the initialization of x is in the code segment, so that it occurs each time the function is called. The initialization of y, however, takes place in the _DATA segment; that segment is put together when the modules are linked, so that initialization takes place just once, when the program is loaded. Also, if the function were to modify y, that modification will hold between function calls, while x, being on the stack, is lost. We can see now how C's rules for automatic and static variables reflect the architecture of an assembly program.

Now we come to the arithmetic; here is the relevant code with some added comments:

```
mov     ax,[bp+4]       ;move n to AX
add     ax,[bp-2]       ;add x to AX
add     ax,$S11_y       ;add y to AX
```

Once again, we see that automatic variables are represented by stack addresses in brackets, while a symbolic name is used to represent the static variable. At this point the desired value is in the AX register, ready to be returned to the calling program.

To test our analysis, we can alter the code, assemble it with MASM, link it to *useit.obj* with C LINK, and see if it works. For example, we can change the values of x and y. Here is the result of doing that:

```
_DATA       SEGMENT
$S11_y      DW      15H         ;change y to 15
_DATA       ENDS
_TEXT       SEGMENT
;       n=4
; Line 2
            PUBLIC      _increase
_increase       PROC NEAR
push    bp
mov     bp,sp
sub     sp,2
;       x=-2
; Line 4
mov     WORD PTR [bp-2],20   ;change x to 20
; Line 7
mov     ax,[bp+4]
add     ax,[bp-2]
add     ax,$S11_y
mov     sp,bp
pop     bp
ret
_increase       ENDP

_TEXT       ENDS
```

This should add 15H, or 21, and 20 to n, so that the result is n plus 41. Does it work? Try it and see. Don't forget to put back in the obligatory segment definitions.

Working with Addresses

We've seen how assembly programs deal with function arguments passed to them, local automatic variables, and static variables. Now let's try a pointer example and see what the compiler does with it. Here is a simple program that switches two values:

```
/* exchange.c--program to swap two values */
#include <stdio.h>
main()
{
   int x = 5;
   int y = 22;
   int swap();

   printf("x = %d; y = %d\n", x, y);
   swap(&x,&y);                        /* pass addresses */
   printf("x = %d; y = %d\n", x, y);
}

int swap( a, b)
int *a, *b;                      /* pointers */
{
   int temp;                    /* temporary storage */

   temp = *a;
   *a = *b;
   *b = temp;
}
```

This uses the standard C method for swapping values. Recall that simply passing x and y won't work, for then the called program will swap its copies of x and y, leaving the original values unaltered. Only by passing the addresses can we let the function know where to find x and y. The swapping algorithm is the same as used to switch the contents of two water glasses; a third glass has to be used for temporary storage.

Compiling the swap() function separately, we get this _TEXT segment from the COD file; for simplicity, we've removed the machine language portions:

```
_TEXT       SEGMENT
;       a=4
;       b=6
; Line 2
```

```
        PUBLIC      _swap
_swap       PROC NEAR
            push    bp
            mov     bp,sp
            sub     sp,2
            push    si
;       temp=-2
; Line 6
            mov     bx,[bp+4]
            mov     ax,[bx]
            mov     [bp-2],ax
; Line 7
            mov     si,[bp+6]
            mov     ax,[si]
            mov     [bx],ax
; Line 8
            mov     bx,[bp+6]
            mov     ax,[bp-2]
            mov     [bx],ax
; Line 9
            pop     si
            mov     sp,bp
            pop     bp
            ret
_swap       ENDP

_TEXT       ENDS
```

First, note the opening comments in the code segment:

```
;       a=4
;       b=6
```

This time two arguments are being passed to the function. The comment notes that the first formal argument is displaced four from BP, while the second is displaced six. This illustrates an important point about C functions in the IBM C environment: they place their arguments on the stack in reverse order. That is, the last argument is the first placed on the stack. Again, the downward growth of the stack means that the first argument, which is the last placed on the stack, has the lowest address.

Next, notice these instructions:

```
push    bp
mov     bp,sp
sub     sp,2
push    si
;       temp=-2
```

As before, the original BP value is saved on the stack, and BP is reset to the current stack top. Then two bytes are added to the stack to represent the variable `temp`; the comment documents that allocation. Finally, the SI value is saved on the stack. This is because the procedure turns out to use this register, and IBM C pledges itself to save its value. (The general registers aren't saved because they are considered to be workspace; the SI register, however, is reserved for the possible use of a type `register` variable.)

Now we start the actual work:

```
mov     bx,[bp+4]
mov     ax,[bx]
mov     [bp-2],ax
```

This looks strange, but it makes sense once we remember what's going on. Recall that `bp+4` is the address of the `a` variable, so the first MOV copies the *value* of a into the BX register. But a is a *pointer,* so its value is an *address.* In fact, when used with our sample calling program, it is the address of the x variable in the calling program. Suppose the second line in this segment had been this:

```
mov     ax,bx
```

That would copy the *address* of x into AX. But by using `[bx]` instead of `bx`, the actual line copies the *value* of x into AX. The procedure is using double indirection. The third line copies this value into `temp`. Figure 11–12 illustrates the possible contents of the stack at this stage.

What about the next set of three instructions? They look like this:

```
mov     si,[bp+6]       ;get b, the address of y
mov     ax,[si]         ;get value of y
mov     [bx],ax         ;put it in the address of x
```

They are similar to the last set. We should note three points. First, `bp+6` represents the second formal argument. That's b, which in our example is the address of y. Second, BX still holds the address of x in the calling program, so the final instruction in this set serves to assign to x the value found in the calling program's y. Finally, the reason SI was used instead of, say, CX, to obtain the y value is that the BX register and three of the index registers (BP, SI, and DI) are the only ones that can be used with the bracket notation.

The next set of three instructions completes the swap:

```
mov     bx,[bp+6]
mov     ax,[bp-2]
mov     [bx],ax
```

The first of these instructions resets the BX register so that it holds the

Figure 11-12
Stack Values after MOV AX,[BX]

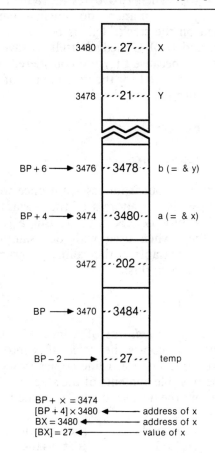

BP + x = 3474
[BP + 4] × 3480 ◄────── address of x
BX = 3480 ◄────── address of x
[BX] = 27 ◄────── value of x

value of b, which is the address of y. The second places the temp value into AX, and the final one copies this value to y. If bx is the address of y, then [bx] is the value of y.

The rest of the procedure restores SP, BP, and SI to their original values.

Looking at this program, we see that it rather faithfully reproduces the logic of the C version; each assignment statement in the C version is represented by three assembly instructions. A closer look, however, suggests we can do better. In C we needed to use a temporary variable so as not to lose one of the values. In assembly language, we already have temporary storage in the form of the registers, and temp really isn't needed. We can shorten the program significantly by using assembly language more efficiently. Here, for example, is one possible rewrite:

```
_TEXT       SEGMENT
```

```
;        a=4
;        b=6
; Line 2
         PUBLIC      _swap
_swap       PROC NEAR
push        bp
mov         bp,sp
push        si

mov         bx,[bp+4]       ;put value of a (an address) into BX
mov         ax,[bx]         ;put value a points to into AX

mov         si,[bp+6]       ;b value into SI
mov         cx,[si]         ;value b points to into cx

mov         [bx],cx         ;b value into location a points to
mov         [si],ax         ;a value into location b points to

pop         si
mov         sp,bp
pop         bp
ret
_swap       ENDP

_TEXT       ENDS
```

Here we've eliminated the need for a `temp` variable, and we've done away with four lines of code. We do use two registers (AX and CX) instead of one for temporary storage. Remember that only the BX, BP, SI, and DI registers can be used for indirect addressing. Since BX and BP were in use already, we could have used either SI or DI to transfer the value to CX.

☐   *Question 11-5*   Would we want to use XCHG in this procedure?

This example illustrates one of the benefits of using assembly language: the opportunity to improve the code produced by a compiler. Indeed, using the compiler as a first-draft resource may prove to be a faster way of developing assembly code than starting from scratch.

Trying a Loop

Let's see how the IBM C Compiler handles a simple `while` loop. Here is the C source code:

```
#include <stdio.h>
main()
{
```

```
    void countoff();

    printf("Here we go!\n");
    countoff(25);
    printf("Done!\n");
}
countoff ( n )
int n;
{
    while (n-- > T 0 )
        ;
}
```

Here, `countoff()` is a delay loop function. We compiled `countoff()` separately. Here is the relevant portion of the COD file, along with some added comments:

```
_TEXT      SEGMENT
;    n=4                       that is, [bp+4] is n
; Line 2
    PUBLIC    _countoff
_countoff      PROC NEAR
    push bp
    mov  bp,sp
; Line 4
$WC10:                         ;an address label
    mov  ax,[bp+4]             ;move n to AX
    dec  WORD PTR [bp+4]       ;decrement n
    or   ax,ax                 ;check if n was > 0
    jg   $WC10                 ;if n > 0, go to $WC10
; Line 6
    mov  sp,bp
    pop  bp
    ret
_countoff      ENDP
```

It's interesting to see how the compiler handles the `n--` notation, which means use the current `n` value, then decrement it. By copying `n` into AX before decrementing `n`, it saves the original value for use.

Next, let's look how the loop is set up. The basic structure is this:

```
$WC10:
    ...
    jg $WC10
```

The `$WC10` is a compiler-generated label identifying a particular address in the code. The JG instruction is the conditional "jump if greater" command. The question becomes, "if what is greater than what?" If the JG instruction follows a CMP (compare) instruction, the meaning is clear: is the left operand of the CMP greater than the right? But here it follows an OR instruction. Obviously, this bit of coding needs further discussion.

How JG Works—The JG instruction actually depends on the flag settings. More specifically, the jump takes place if the zero flag (ZF) is 0 *and* if the sign flag (SF) equals the overflow flag (OF). It turns out that if a CMP instruction results in these settings then the left operand was greater than the right operand.

To see how our code works, we have to analyze the flag setting produced by the OR instruction in the code:

```
or ax,ax
```

The result of ORing a value with itself is just the original value, so the only point to this operation is to produce flag settings. Let's check the various possiblities.

First, if AX is positive, the result is positive. This means that ZF is set to 0 (the result is not 0). It also means that SF is 0 (no sign). There can be no overflow, because the result is the same as the original value of AX; thus, OF is 0. The final outcome is ZF = 0 and SF = OF, so the jump occurs.

Next, suppose AX is 0. Then the result is 0, the zero flag is set to 1, and there is no jump. We don't have to check the second condition, for the failure of either condition to be met will prevent a jump.

Next, suppose AX is negative. The zero flag is set to 0, so that's okay. There is no overflow, so OF = 0. But the result is negative, so SF = 1. Now OF and SF are not equal to each other, and there is no jump.

The procedure would have been simpler to follow if the compiler had used

```
cmp ax,0
```

instead of the OR instruction. It turns out, however, that this instruction takes four clock cycles to execute, while the OR version only takes three clock cycles.

This seems a rather subtle approach for testing a loop condition. It points out how many tricks of the trade are built into the compiler.

Improving the Example—Subtle though the compiler may be, we still can improve the code by being straightforward. You may recall we mentioned a LOOP instruction. To use it, set CX to the desired number of loops, and LOOP will loop to a starting address, decrementing CX until it reaches 0. Here is a rewrite of the code using LOOP:

```
_TEXT        SEGMENT
;     n=4
; Line 2
     PUBLIC      _countoff
_countoff      PROC NEAR
     push bp
     mov  bp,sp

     mov  cx,[bp+4]   ; set cx to n
wait:                 ; an address label
     loop wait        ; loop until cx is 0

     mov  sp,bp
     pop  bp
     ret
_countoff      ENDP

_TEXT        ENDS
```

This code is shorter, faster, and easier to understand than the first version. Why didn't the compiler produce this? One reason is that the compiler was representing a while loop, and a while loop is more general in design than the simple counting loop we constructed. Secondly, in some circumstances, using LOOP can cause problems. We'll see an example soon.

Calling a C Function from Assembly

Let's find out how C functions are called from assembly language programs. Here is our investigative program:

```
main()
{
  void forloop();

  forloop(10);
}
#include <stdio.h>
void forloop (n )
int n;
{
  int i;

  for ( i = 0; i < n; i++)
     printf("%5d\n", n);
  printf("\n");
}
```

The forloop() function calls printf(). Let's see how that comes out in assembly; here is the relevent portion of the COD file, along with added comments:

```
_DATA     SEGMENT
EXTRN     _printf:NEAR          ;_printf is an external procedure
_DATA     ENDS
_DATA     SEGMENT
$SG29     DB      '%5d', 0aH, 00H  ; a C string
        EVEN                    ; alignment instruction
$SG30     DB      0aH,  00H
_DATA     ENDS
_TEXT     SEGMENT
;     n=4
; Line 3
        PUBLIC    _forloop
_forloop       PROC NEAR
     push bp
     mov  bp,sp
     sub  sp,2                   ;allocate space for i
;     i=-2
; Line 7
     mov  WORD PTR [bp-2],0      ;set i to 0
     jmp  SHORT $L20000
$F24:                           ;start for loop body
; Line 8
     push WORD PTR [bp+4]        ;put n on stack
     mov  ax,OFFSET DGROUP:$SG29 ;get string address
     push ax                     ;put it on stack
     call _printf                ;call printf()
     add  sp,4                   ;reset stack pointer
     inc  WORD PTR [bp-2]        ;increment i
$L20000:                        ;start for loop test
     mov  ax,[bp+4]             ;fetch n
     cmp  [bp-2],ax             ;compare i to n
     jl   $F24                  ;jump if i < n
; Line 9
     mov  ax,OFFSET DGROUP:$SG30 ;get string address
     push ax                     ;push it
     call _printf                ;call printf()
; Line 10
     mov  sp,bp                  ;reset SP
     pop  bp                     ;reset BP
     ret
_forloop  ENDP

_TEXT     ENDS
```

This module is more involved than the ones we have studied so far; we'll analyze the important sections now.

The Data Segment: External Functions and Strings—First, let's see what is new in the data section:

```
_DATA      SEGMENT
EXTRN      _printf:NEAR        ;_printf is an external procedure
_DATA      ENDS
_DATA      SEGMENT
$SG29      DB      '%5d',  0aH,  00H  ; a C string
      EVEN                            ; alignment instruction
$SG30      DB      0aH,  00H
_DATA      ENDS
```

The _DATA segment is used to announce procedures used—but not defined—in the module. The linker will interpret the EXTRN line as a request to search through other modules and indicated libraries for the _printf procedure. The NEAR directive indicates the code for that procedure will be placed in the same segment as the code in this module.

Next, the $SG29 identifies the beginning of a sequence of bytes stored in static memory. In general, the DB directive can be followed by a list of bytes to be stored consecutively. The bytes should be separated by commas, but printable ASCII characters can be represented by a sequence placed between single quotes, as shown. In this case, '%5d' results in the ASCII codes for these three characters being stored consecutively in memory. Then, 0aH is the hex value of '\n', and 00H is the null character used to terminate a C string.

Similarly, $S30 represents the newline argument for the second print statement.

The EVEN directive is an alignment instruction. The _DATA segment, you may recall, is aligned on word boundaries. The EVEN directive pads the data with an extra byte, if necessary, so that the next data item will start on an even address (a word boundary).

Because the compiler analyzes function declarations separately from data declarations, it places them in separate little compartments, each with its own _DATA SEGMENT and _DATA ENDS directives. Remember, however, that all _DATA segment instructions eventually are concatenated into a single segment in machine language. Later, when we write our own assembly programs from scratch, we'll lump the function declarations and data declarations together.

Function Calls—Now let's look at how the first call to printf() is handled. The C source code looked like this:

```
printf("%5d\n", n);
```

Here is the assembly version:

```
push WORD PTR [bp+4]            ;put n on stack
mov  ax,OFFSET DGROUP:$SG29     ;get string address
push ax                         ;put it on stack
call _printf                    ;call printf()
add  sp,4                       ;reset stack pointer
```

As we mentioned earlier, C functions have their arguments pushed onto the stack, beginning with the last argument. The last argument for this call is n. In the procedure, n is stored at address bp+4, so the contents of this location are pushed. Again, WORD PTR indicates to use a word, not a byte, for n.

The next argument, moving backwards, is the format string "%5d\n". The printf() function, you may recall, passes the addresses of strings, so the procedure needs to push the address of the format string. Earlier, $SG29 was established as an identifier for that string of bytes. The OFFSET DGROUP: directive says to use the offset address of $SG29 as measured from the data segment; thus, that instruction loads the string address into AX.

The next instruction pushes the address on to the stack. This completes the data setup for the function call. The CALL instruction is used to make the call.

Finally, the ADD instruction is used to reset the stack pointer. Loading n decreased SP by two (two bytes were pushed), and pushing the address decreased it by another two. Without this resetting, each call in the loop would result in four more bytes being added to the stack. This way, the same four bytes are used each loop cycle. Using ADD instead of popping the stack twice essentially discards the values once they have been used. Popping them would involve specifying a place to pop each value.

In this particular case, the same values of n and the format string are used each time, so it would make more sense to push these values once *before* the loop is started rather than push them each cycle, but the compiler is not sufficiently perceptive to notice such points.

Through the Loop—Now let's look at the looping scheme. The C code was this:

```
for( i = 0; i < n; i++)
    printf("%5d\n", n);
```

In terms of structure, this loop contains one expression that is done once, before the loop ever starts; that's the initialization of i. Then there is the comparison expression; it's done before each new loop cycle. The body of the loop, here the print statement, is executed each loop, and the incrementing of i is performed at the end of each loop.

The assembly language version uses jumps and address labels to implement this structure:

```
        ; here is the initializing--it's done just once
        mov  WORD PTR [bp-2],0      ;set i to 0
        jmp  SHORT $L20000          ;go to test

$F24:                              ;start of for loop body
        push WORD PTR [bp+4]        ;put n on stack
        mov  ax,OFFSET DGROUP:$SG29 ;get string address
        push ax                    ;put it on stack
        call _printf               ;call printf()
        add  sp,4                   ;reset stack pointer
        ; the body of the loop ends here

        ; now comes the incrementing at loop's end
        inc  WORD PTR [bp-2]        ;increment i

$L20000:                           ;start for loop test
        mov  ax,[bp+4]             ;fetch n
        cmp  [bp-2],ax             ;compare i to n
        jl   $F24                  ;jump if i < n
        ; if i>=n, procedure goes on to next instruction
```

The compiler sets up the code so that the test actually comes at the end of the loop. That way, if the jump condition fails, the procedure goes on to the next instruction. The JL instruction means "jump if less than." Like JG, its behavior depends on flag settings. However, in the context of following a CMP instruction, the effect is the jump takes place if the left operand of the CMP is less than the right operand. The CMP instruction can compare memory with a register or two registers, but not memory with memory; hence one memory value was shifted to a register first.

Although the test condition is at the end of this loop, it must be performed before the loop ever starts. Therefore a JMP (unconditional jump) instruction shifts program control to the test section immediately after initialization.

A Would-Be Improvement—The code can be simplified. As we mentioned before, the printf() argument stack need not be pushed each loop, since the contents do not change from cycle to cycle. That part of the code can be moved to the initialization section. Then the instruction that resets SP by adding four to it can be placed after the loop. Another plausible move is to replace the complicated loop structure with a LOOP loop. Here is coding that does that:

```
_DATA     SEGMENT
EXTRN     _printf:NEAR
```

```
_DATA      ENDS
_DATA      SEGMENT
$SG29      DB        '%5d', 0aH, 00H
           EVEN
$SG30      DB        0aH, 00H
_DATA      ENDS
_TEXT      SEGMENT
;     n=4
      PUBLIC      _forloop
_forloop  PROC NEAR
      push bp
      mov  bp,sp
      ;initialize i, stack, and CX
      push WORD PTR [bp+4]
      mov  ax,OFFSET DGROUP:$SG29
      push ax
      mov  cx, WORD PTR [bp+4]      ;set CX to n

ploop:                             ;here's the loop
      call _printf
      loop ploop

      add sp,4
      mov  ax,OFFSET DGROUP:$SG30
      push ax
      call _printf

      mov  sp,bp
      pop  bp
      ret
_forloop      ENDP

_TEXT      ENDS
```

Notice how much shorter this code is and how much easier it is to understand. Its chief drawback is that it doesn't work; the loop becomes endless. The problem is that the loop terminates when CX reaches 0. The LOOP instruction valiantly decrements CX each loop, but the knavish _printf function resets CX to some other value each time. The moral is that C functions treat the general registers as workspace. There is no guarantee that a C function will not meddle with general register values if called.

> ☐ *Question 11-6* How could you modify this program so that it would use putch() to print an * in the loop and a newline after the loop ends? Does putch() mess up the CX register?

What registers are safe? The only registers guaranteed to be saved by an IBM C function are the BP, SI, DI, DS, and CS registers. This has two implications for you as a programmer. First, if you write a C function in assembly that uses any of these registers, you must save their values and restore them at the end. Second, you cannot assume that a C function will leave any other register unaltered.

Compiler Optimization—The IBM PC attempts to optimize the code. In general, *optimization* means reducing the code size and increasing the speed. By default, the compiler favors code size in optimizing a module. The /Ot option causes the compiler to optimize for running time. The /Od option disables optimization. It's instructive to see what unoptimized code looks like. Here's the relevant code for the forloop() function, along with some added comments:

```
        PUBLIC   _forloop
_DATA       SEGMENT
EXTRN       _printf:NEAR
_DATA       ENDS
_DATA       SEGMENT
$SG29       DB      '%5d',  ØaH,   ØØH
        EVEN
$SG30       DB      ØaH,   ØØH
_DATA       ENDS
_TEXT       SEGMENT
;      n=4
; Line 3
        PUBLIC      _forloop
_forloop       PROC NEAR
push      bp
        mov      bp,sp
        sub      sp,2
        push     di                  ;saves DI,SI even though
        push     si                  ;they are not used
;      i=-2
; Line 4
; Line 7
        mov      WORD PTR [bp-2],0
$F24:
        mov      ax,[bp+4]
        cmp      [bp-2],ax
        jl       $+3                 ;means jump 3 instructions
        jmp      $FB26
        jmp      $F27
$FC25:
        inc      WORD PTR [bp-2]
        jmp      $F24
$F27:
```

```
; Line 8
        push    WORD PTR [bp+4]
        mov     ax,OFFSET DGROUP:$SG29
        push    ax
        call    _printf
        add     sp,4
        jmp     $FC25
$FB26:
; Line 9
        mov     ax,OFFSET DGROUP:$SG30
        push    ax
        call    _printf
        add     sp,2
; Line 10
$EX22:
        pop     si
        pop     di
        mov     sp,bp
        pop     bp
        ret
_forloop        ENDP
```

The jump logic for the loop is much more involved. What appears to be happening is that the compiler is following a general format for implementing a for loop. Notice, for example, that the test condition, the loop body, and the updating portion of the loop (the incrementing of i, in this case) each get separate sections of code. Clearly, the optimizer did some clever analysis to reduce the code to what we saw earlier. That version had two jumps and two address labels, while the unoptimized version has five jumps and five address labels, one unused.

Programmers, particularly C programmers, often use tricks that they think will speed up programs. A compiler with a good optimization scheme may use the same tricks or even better ones. For example, a popular C idiom, and one we've used in this book, is to say

```
while ( *pc )       /* pc is a pointer-to-char */
    {
    ...
    pc--;
    }
```

instead of

```
while ( *pc != '\0' )
    {
    ...
    pc--;
    }
```

The idea is that when *pc is not the null character, its value is non-0, hence "true"; and when it is 0, not only is the second test condition "false" (or 0), but so is *pc. Thus, the two test conditions are logically equivalent, but the first saves a comparison.

It turns out that the IBM C Compiler translates both forms into the same code! So one is no more efficient than the other, and the second form is clearer. Of course, this does not mean that all compilers render the two forms the same.

Summary

Assembly language for the 8088 processor is tied closely to the architecture of the 8088 processor. This processor uses registers, flags, ports, and memory in its work. Machine-language instructions work in that arena, manipulating registers, transferring bytes and words between register and register, register and port, and memory and register.

There are four general-purpose, 16-bit registers: AX, BX, CX, and DX. Each of these can be divided into two 8-bit registers called AH, AL, and so on. The H indicates the high byte, and the L the low byte. These registers form a work area. Values there can be manipulated arithmetically and by a flock of bitwise operators. They are not completely interchangeable, however. For example, the accumulator (AX) plays a special role in division and multiplication. The base register (BX) can be used to hold addresses, acting somewhat like a C pointer. The count register (CX) is used by several operators to provide a counting service. The data register (DX) has a special role in multiplication and division of 32-bit values.

The four segment registers reflect the segmented memory architecture of the 8088/8086. The code segment register (CS) holds the segment value of the current code segment. The data segment register (DS) holds the segment value of the current data segment. The stack segment register (SS) holds the current segment value for the stack. The extra segment register (ES) holds the current segment for an extra segment that a program can use.

Four pointer/index registers are used for offset addresses. The base pointer (BP) locates the current base of the stack, and the stack pointer (SP) locates the top of the stack. The source index (SI) and destination index (DI) are used to locate offsets for a set of string instructions; they also can be used to point to other data items.

The instruction pointer (IP) points to the next instruction to be executed. Certain instructions, such as JMP and CALL can alter the IP setting, thus controlling the program flow.

Various flags get set as the result of different operations. Flag values then may be used to determine the response of instructions like the conditional jumps.

Assembly language provides a wealth of mnemonic instructions that get translated directly into binary machine code. These instructions relate intimately to the hardware design of the processor. Assembly language also provides several directives. These are instructions to the assembler telling it how to put a program together.

Writing an assembly program designed to work with a C program involves knowing not only what machine instructions are needed, but also knowing which directives to use to set up the proper interface and which conventions to follow for compatibility. Learning all that from scratch is a tall order, but we can take advantage of the expertise built into the IBM C Compiler. One strategy is to write simple functions in C and then study the assembly code produced by the compiler.

Once you have the assembly code produced by a compiler, you can try to optimize it. That sounds like heavy-duty programming, but sometimes only a little knowledge of assembly is required to find ways of improving the code.

Answers to Questions in the Chapter

■ *11-1.* No. Recall that for signed numbers the high-order bit is zero for a positive number. Adding, say, 20000 to 20000 produces a value that sets the high-order bit to 1. In signed notation, this makes the result a negative number, and overflow has occurred. But the carry flag isn't set, for the result still is a 16-bit number.

■ *11-2.* Take the *.COD* file, delete the machine-language code, and replace the 2 with a 5. Then change the file extension from *.cod* to *.asm,* and use the assembler to assemble it.

■ *11-3.* Since only one byte of storage is needed, use DB instead of DW. For example, you can do this:

```
_DATA SEGMENT
      GRADE DB 41H
_DATA ENDS
```

Note that names don't have to begin with a $; that's just a convention used by the C compiler. Also, the assembler does recognize character values when enclosed in single quotes, so you can do this, too:

```
_DATA SEGMENT
      GRADE DB 'A'
_DATA ENDS
```

■ *11-4.* No. For one thing, PUSH works with memory locations and registers, not immediate numbers. Second, the procedure's approach distinguishes between two actions: creating the memory space, and placing a value in it. Often automatic variables are created and not initialized; in that case just the SUB SP,2 instruction would be used.

■ *11-5.* No. The XCHG instruction exchanges values in registers, whereas this procedure is supposed to exchange values in memory. You could move the memory values to registers and exchange them, but you still have to get the values back into memory.

■ *11-6.* We need to replace the references to _printf with references to _putch. And we need to refine the data suitably:

```
_DATA      SEGMENT
EXTRN      _putch:NEAR
_DATA      ENDS
_DATA      SEGMENT
STAR       DB      '*'
           EVEN
NL         DB      0aH      ; now a single character, no \0
_DATA      ENDS
_TEXT      SEGMENT
;      n=4
      PUBLIC      _forloop
_forloop      PROC NEAR
      push      bp
      mov       bp,sp
         ;initialize stack, and CX
      mov       ax,OFFSET DGROUP:STAR
      push      ax
      mov       cx, WORD PTR [bp+4]      ;set CX to n

ploop: call      _putch                  ;here's the loop
         loop ploop

         add sp,2                  ;just take 2 off instead of 4
         mov       ax,OFFSET DGROUP:NL
         push      ax
         call      _putch

         mov       sp,bp
         pop       bp
         ret
_forloop      ENDP

_TEXT      ENDS
```

This works fine, so putch() must leave CX unmolested.

Exercises

1. Use the compiler to see how if-else statements are translated into assembly language.

2. Use the compiler to see how a `switch` is translated into assembly language.

3. Investigate how arrays are handled. Try declaring both static and automatic arrays in a function.

4. Using the framework provided by the C compiler, write an assembly program to count the number of letters in a C string whose address is passed as an argument. Have one version that does the counting itself and a second version that calls the `strlen()` function.

12

Using Assembly Language

- Assembly language strengths and weaknesses
- High-level language strengths and weaknesses
- Integrating C and assembly modules
- The large-memory model interface

Using Assembly Language

Chapter 11 presented the rudiments of assembly language programming. In this chapter, we'll examine the blending of C and of assembly elements into a program. There are two important aspects to this task. The first is the decision-making aspect: when to use assembly language instead of C. The second is the technical one: ensuring that an assembly module interacts properly with the C portions of the program. Most of the chapter relates to the techniques for using assembly language, so let's take a little time now to look at when it is desirable to use assembly.

The Pros and Cons of Using Assembly Language Instead of C

The three most common justifications for using assembly language instead of a high-level language are these:

Assembly programs run faster than high-level language programs.

Assembly programs are more compact than high-level language programs.

Assembly programs allow you to do things that are difficult or impossible to do in high-level languages.

These arguments are weakened somewhat when the high-level language is C. C programs tend to run faster and be more compact than those of other high-level languages. C features such as pointers and bit-wise operators make it more versatile than many other high-level languages. Nonetheless, assembly still can have the edge in these matters.

The chief drawbacks to assembly language are two:

Assembly programs work only for a specific processor or, perhaps, a family of processors; thus, they are not particularly portable.

It is much simpler to make errors of remarkable subtlety and of devastating effect in assembly.

The enhanced error-making abilities of assembly stem, in part, from its power. You can overwrite code, destroy the interrupt table, disable input, and so on, with ease. Another source of error is that instructions have to be detailed. A related problem is that the main way of controlling program flow within a procedure is by using jumps; the structured forms of C have no direct analogs. For instance, we saw in the last chapter that a general `for` loop was translated using five jumps. Something like a multiple `if-else` or extensive `switch` can get quite hairy in assembly. The `for`-loop construction in C makes it fairly obvious if you have omitted one of the control conditions; it is much less obvious in assembly.

A reasonable approach is to use C to provide the overall framework for a program. It may well turn out that the speed and size of the C program are fine. And as far as capability goes, many compilers developed for the PC, including IBM C, have included facilities that give you access to the whole memory, to the ports, and to the BIOS and DOS interrupts. If, after writing a program in C, you find some specific part is too slow for your needs, then you can see if assembly can help.

If your compiler doesn't have some of these IBM adaptations, you may be able to create them in assembly. We'll give assembly-language examples for accessing ports, calling interrupts, and accessing other segments of memory.

In general, then, you most likely will be better off if you don't write vast segments of code in assembly. Instead, concentrate on small modules. If you then move on to another system, you can use the bulk of your code and only have to translate small, simple assembly procedures. We will provide some examples in this chapter, including procedures to set words in a block of memory to a given value and to find a given string in a second string.

General Rules for the Assembly-C Interface

The exact interface depends upon the C compiler and upon the memory model. We'll begin with the IBM PC small-memory model, and later we will look at the large-memory model. We'll use the Microsoft MASM assembler for our examples of assembly mnemonics and directives.

There are five main features to the interface that require your attention. First, in the assembly language program, you should prefix the C function name with an underscore character to obtain the procedure name. Second, you need to set up the segments properly, using the same segment names that the compiler does. Third, you need to preserve the values of the BP, SI, DI, CS, DS, and SS registers. Fourth, you need to access properly any values passed to the assembly procedure. Finally, you need to place any return value in the proper registers. We've mentioned these facts in the preceding chapters, but it won't hurt (we hope) to review them now.

Naming Conventions

A C program can access only those assembly routines whose names begin with an underscore. Thus, if you wish to call a function bango(), you should name the assembly procedure _bango, as illustrated in Figure 12-1. Do not, however, use double underscore beginnings, such as _ _fixit for a _fixit() function, for the C compiler uses the double underscore to identify certain routines it uses internally. Actually, the only problem is if you duplicate a name used by the compiler, but why take chances?

Figure 12-1
Assembly Program Names

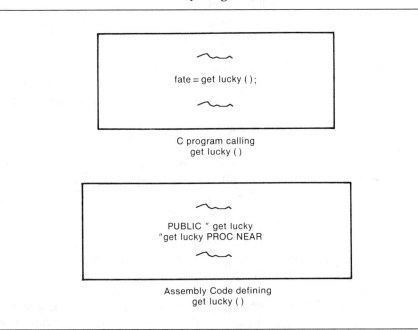

C program calling
get lucky ( )

Assembly Code defining
get lucky ( )

Some assemblers treat all names as if they were all one case, so they would consider the names _bebop, _Bebop, and _BEBOP to be the same, even though C considers them different. The MASM assembler, Versions 3.0 and later, lets you specify what kind of case interpretation you want.

Segment Names

Assembly programs, in general, define memory segments to be used by the program for the code, data, stack, and extra uses. When you write a module to be used with a C program, the safest thing to do is to start each assembly module with the same set of segment definitions produced by your C compiler. You've seen the definitions used by the IBM C Compiler; you should place them at the beginning of each assembly module. It would be nice if assembly had an include feature so that we could put that information into a header file. MASM does! To take advantage of that bounty, we'll create a file called *segdef.ah* that has this content:

```
;segdef.ah--segment definitions for the small-memory model
_TEXT       SEGMENT  BYTE PUBLIC 'CODE'
_TEXT       ENDS
CONST    SEGMENT  WORD PUBLIC 'CONST'
CONST    ENDS
_BSS        SEGMENT  WORD PUBLIC 'BSS'
_BSS        ENDS
_DATA       SEGMENT  WORD PUBLIC 'DATA'
_DATA       ENDS
DGROUP   GROUP   CONST, _BSS,        _DATA
            ASSUME  CS: _TEXT, DS: DGROUP, SS: DGROUP, ES: DGROUP
```

The file needn't have an extension, but we chose to use ah in order to mark it as a header file and to distinguish it from C header files. To use the include feature, insert this line near the beginning of the assembly file:

```
include segdef.ah
```

This assumes the file is in the same directory as the source file. You can, of course, create an *include* directory and use a complete pathname:

```
include c:\include\segdef.ah
```

This file sets up the names for the segments; it's up to you to provide the data and code to be placed in each segment. Let's look, in general, at what goes in each segment.

The __DATA Segment—If your procedure uses any initialized static data, use the _DATA segment for it. If it uses any routines from another module, identify the names in the _DATA segment; use the EXTRN and the NEAR or FAR directives:

```
EXTRN    _printf:NEAR
```

For small-memory model programs, use the NEAR type for C functions, since that is how the functions of the small-model library are set up.

Data can be set up as bytes, words, double-words, and quad-words, and 10-byte units; C programs generally use DB to create data bytes and DW to create data words. A directive such as DB can be used to create several bytes of data. Multiple data items are separated by commas, with each data item on a line being of the type given by the initial directive. Typically, a data name is given before the DB directive; it acts as a label. Here are some examples:

```
NORP      DB   89   ;allots 1 byte, initializes it to 89
          EVEN
PRON      DB   1,2,4 ;allots 3 bytes set to 1,2, and 4
          EVEN
NROP      DB   'Hoppy',0H ;allots the string Hoppy\0
          EVEN
RONP      DB   "HI!",0H   ;allots the string HI!\0
          EVEN
YEAR      DW   1986       ;allot word, set to 1986
          EVEN
```

Note that single quotes or double quotes can be used for a string of character bytes. The assembler does not add the null character required for C strings, so the terminating null character (0H) should be given explicitly.

The MASM assembly uses the EVEN directive to force each successive data item to start on a word boundary. This means, for example, that the PRON group will occupy three adjacent bytes and then will be padded with an extra byte so that NROP starts on a word boundary.

All data and external function names should be bracketed by the _DATA SEGMENT and _DATA ENDS directives. You can use separate sets of directives for data and function names, as does the compiler, or you can use a single set for both.

The __TEXT Segment—The _TEXT segment is used to hold the code for the program. This section opens with a _TEXT SEGMENT directive and ends with a _TEXT ENDS directive. Within this segment is the procedure. First, declare the procedure name to be public. Then identify the name to be a near procedure. Mark the end of the procedure with the name of the procedure followed by the ENDP directive.

A Format—We can combine these elements into a general format for a procedure designed to be used as a C function in an IBM C program:

```
        TITLE _name            ; optional
include segdef.ah
_DATA SEGMENT
        EXTRN  _cfunct NEAR ; declare other routines used
        datawd DW    values ; declare data
_DATA ENDS
_TEXT SEGMENT
        PUBLIC  _name
_name PROC NEAR                ; a near procedure
    ;place code here
```

```
     _name ENDP
     _TEXT ENDS
     END
```

Later, we will see that it is possible to have more than one procedure in the code segment.

Register Preservation

The third requirement for the C-Assembly interface is that the assembly module preserve the values of certain registers. IBM C functions preserve the values of the BP, SI, DI, CS, DS, and SS registers, so compatible assembly routines should do the same. The usual method is to note which registers your routine uses, push their values onto the stack at the start of the routine and pop the values off the stack into the correct registers at the end.

The IBM C Compiler uses a standard method of accessing arguments and of creating local variables that involves the stack, also. Thus, that method has to be coordinated with the pushing and popping. Here is the usual sequence:

```
     push    bp          ;save bp value
     mov     bp,sp       ;set up argument fetches
     sub     sp,n        ;n is bytes needed for local variables
     push    si          ;if necessary
     push    di          ;also push CS,DS,and SS as needed

;body of program goes here

     pop     di          ;pop in reverse order of pushing
     pop     si
     mov     sp,bp       ;discard local variables
     pop     bp
     ret
```

The reason for allocating local variables before pushing SI and DI is that it leaves these register values at the top of the stack so that they are available for popping at the end. The MOV SP,BP instruction skips the stack pointer over the local variables back to its starting value. At that point the top of the stack contains the BP value. After BP is popped, the top of the stack is the return address, which was placed there by the CALL that summoned this routine.

The key point here is the requirement to preserve certain register values; the strategy we've shown is just one of many workable ones.

Accessing Arguments

The next requirement for a successful assembly module is an ability to access the argument list provided by the calling function. To do that properly, we need to know how a C program transmits arguments.

The arguments to a C function are placed in the stack, with the final argument being pushed first, then the semifinal argument, and so on back to the initial argument. One-byte arguments are converted to two-bytes before being pushed; type `char` values are sign-extended, and `unsigned char` values are zero-extended. After all the arguments are placed on the stack, the return address is pushed.

Once the called routine is activated, it starts by pushing the BP value. Then the stack pointer is set to BP. At this point, then, the top of the stack is at address BP, and it contains the old BP value. The word beginning at `BP+2` contains the return address, and the `BP+4` marks the first argument of the calling function.

When a word is pushed onto the stack, the high-order byte is pushed first. When a two-word value is pushed onto the stack, the high-order word is pushed first. Figure 12–2 illustrates the stack sequence for a hypothetical function `use_em()` with three arguments: a `long`, an `int`, and a `char`. Hex notation is used, since each set of two hex integers corresponds to a byte; this makes it easy to see how a multibyte unit is decomposed into bytes.

The medium- and large-memory models use far procedure calls, so

Figure 12–2
A Function Call and the Stack

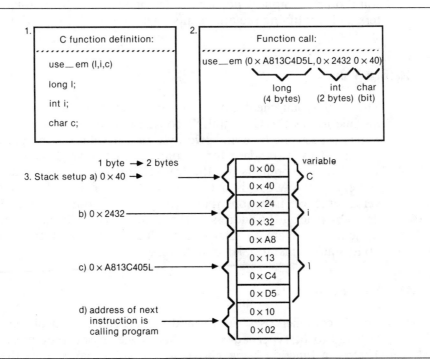

they require a segment value. In that case, the return segment value and the return offset value both are placed on the stack, meaning that the first argument winds up in BP+6.

The location of the second argument depends on the size of the first argument. If the first argument is a char, short, or int, signed or unsigned, or a near pointer, it takes two bytes, in which case the second argument is at BP+6 for the small model. Far pointers, double values, and float values (because they are expanded to double) take four bytes; if the first argument is one of these, then the second argument is at BP+8 for the small model. Similar calculations reveal the location of subsequent arguments. It is a good idea to include comments in the code to identify the locations in the stack of various arguments.

Suppose, then, that BP+4 is the location of the first argument. This means BP+4 is the address of the value, hence the equivalent of a pointer. The value itself is represented by [BP+4]. As we mentioned before, the brackets play the same role for an assembly pointer as the asterisk does for a C pointer.

One special case is that of passing an entire structure rather than the structure address as an argument. In that case, the entire contents of the structure are placed on the stack word by word, starting with the final word.

The system of pushing last arguments first is a standard practice with C compilers for the IBM PC. The particular method for accessing them described here, however, is just one possible method. You can use—and some other compilers do use—different methods for setting pointer registers and identifying the arguments. But we'll stick to the IBM C Compiler's strategy.

Return Values

The final requirement for the C-Assembly interface is that the assembly module follow the C compiler's conventions for return values. IBM C programs expect one-byte and two-byte return values to be placed in the AX register. This is standard for C compilers. Two-word return values, such as long and far pointers use the DX register for the high-order (or segment) value, and the AX register for low-order (or offset) value. This is not a universal practice. Functions that return float, double, structures, or unions do so by placing the address of the value in AX. The address must refer to a static area in memory so that the value remains after the procedure cleans up its stack. This, too, is not a universal practice.

Other Points to Note

The C compiler uses the SI and DI registers, if available, for variables declared to be type register. That is the reason they must be preserved. That is, a function using register variables may call another function. If that function modifies the SI and DI registers without restoring them, the original variables will get changed in an apparently mysterious fashion.

The second point we wish to discuss is allocating space in the stack for local variables. Up to now, we have reset SP to allocate space. That is, if we needed room for a two-byte automatic variable, we would do this:

```
sub sp,2    ; create space for int x
```

IBM C programs, however, normally use the _ _chkstk procedure to create stack space. This function checks to see if sufficient stack space is left before allocating it. If insufficient stack space is left, _ _chkstk halts your program and puts out a stack overflow error message.

To use this procedure, you first must declare it in the _DATA segment:

```
_DATA SEGMENT
      EXTRN _ _chkstk:NEAR
_DATA ENDS
```

Then, in the code section, set AX to the number of bytes needed and call _ _chkstk.

Suppose, for instance, that your procedure will use two one-word stack variables. The method we have used so far to allocate the space is this:

```
sub  sp,4       ;allocate 4 bytes in the stack
```

Here is _ _chkstk approach:

```
mov  ax,4       ;need 4 bytes
call _ _chkstk  ;find them or quit
```

This is the method used by the IBM C Compiler by default; the _ _chkstk procedure is part of the compiler library, not a feature of assembly language.

Some instructions depend on the value of the direction flag (DF). The C compiler assumes this flag has been cleared (set to 0). If you set the flag to 1, be sure to reset it to 0 by using the CLD (clear direction flag) instruction.

The small-memory model assumes that DS, SS, and ES are all set to the same value.

When calling a C function from assembly, you should first push the proper arguments onto the stack, then call the function. After the call, add to SP the number of bytes used in the pushes; this resets the stack pointer to where it was before the arguments were placed on the stack.

Let's move on to some examples.

Port Work

The IBM C Compiler provides nonportable functions for accessing the microprocessor ports of the 8088 chip. Let's see how we could write such functions ourselves.

The key, of course, is to use the assembly IN and OUT instructions. These instructions can identify the port number directly or indirectly. The direct calls look like this:

```
in    al,61h        ; read port 61h value into AL
out   61h,al        ; write AL into port 61h
```

Here 61H is the port number, and AL is used for the transferred byte. Some ports can handle a word; they would use AX. No other registers can be used for the port values to be read or written.

The indirect approach is this:

```
mov   dx,61h      ;place port number in DX
in    al,dx       ;read port value into AL
mov   dx,43h      ;place another port number in DX
out   dx,al       ;send AL value out to port
```

The second approach has two important advantages for our purposes. First, it can access all the ports, while the direct approach can only be used with the first 256 ports. Second, the indirect method makes it simple to represent the port number as a variable in a C function; just assign the argument value to the DX register.

Here is one implementation of a portin() function; it works like the inp() function. That is, its argument is the port number, and its return value is the value read from the port.

```
;   C function  portin()
;     int portin( port )
;     unsigned port;
;     Usage:  portvalue = portin(portnumber);

      TITLE    portin

include segdef.ah
_TEXT       SEGMENT
;   port is [bp+4]
      PUBLIC   _portin
_portin PROC NEAR
      push    bp                      ;set up bp and sp
      mov     bp,sp
```

```
        mov     dx,WORD PTR [bp+4] ;set dx to port
        in      al,dx             ;read port into al
        xor     ah,ah             ;clear ah

        mov     sp,bp             ;clean up
        pop     bp
        ret
_portin ENDP
_TEXT   ENDS
        END
```

This one is pretty elementary. There is just one argument, and it is at BP+4. We transfer it to DX, using the WORD PTR directive to indicate that BP+4 is the address of a two-byte value. The value is placed in the AL register, but C functions use the whole AX register, even for one-byte values. So we clear the high byte. The obvious way is to do this:

```
        mov ah,0
```

However,

```
        xor     ah,ah
```

is faster, and it produces the same end result, since any value XORed with itself is 0. (Remember, for the resulting bit to be one for an XOR operation, one or the other contributing bit must be one, but not both.)

□ *Question 12-1* How would you write an assembly portout() counterpart to the library outp() function?

A Word-Setting Function

The IBM C library offers a function (memset()) designed to assign the same value to each byte in an array. It would be useful to have a word counterpart that would set each word in an array to the same value. Note that we are using "word" here as it is used in assembly; that is, to indicate a two-byte unit of information.

It is simple enough to set array values using regular C:

```
int basis[500];
int i;

for ( i = 0; i < 500; i++)
    basis[i] = 1000;
```

The only justification for doing it in assembly is that we could then take advantage of assembly's string-related instructions. That might produce noticeably faster code. How much faster? Let's write a function in assembly and see.

The STOS Instruction

The key instruction we wish to use is STOS (store in a string). To store a word rather than a byte, we will use the STOSW variant. To use this instruction, we place the offset of the beginning of the string in the DI register. When used with string instructions, the DI register measures the offset relative to the extra segment. The word we wish to place in the string should be placed in the AX register. The STOSW instruction copies the word into the string and advances the DI pointer one word. If we use the REP prefix, this action will be repeated a number of times equal to the original setting of the CX register. Figure 12–3 shows how REP STOWS works.

Figure 12–3
REP STOWS

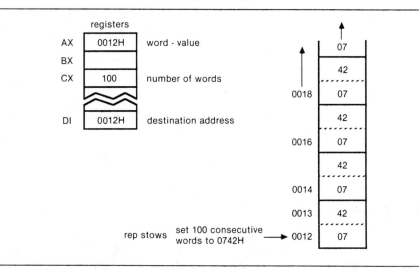

Using this instruction in a procedure, then, involves the following steps:

1. Pass the array address, the word value, and the number of words to be set to the procedure.
2. Since the array address is relative to the DS register, save the current ES value and set ES to the DS value.
3. Assign the address value to DI.

4. Assign the word value to AX.

5. Assign the word count to CX.

6. Invoke REP STOSW.

7. Clean up.

The Wordset Procedure

We've taken these steps in the following code. Note that at the beginning, we describe the routine in C terms.

```
                TITLE   wordset
; wordset()--sets words of an array to a given value
; function declaration:
; int *wordset(arradd, word, nwords)
; int *arradd;      /* address of array */
; int word;         /* assigned value */
; unsigned nwords;  /* number of words */
; this function returns the address of the last initialized word

include segdef.ah
_TEXT SEGMENT
    PUBLIC _wordset
_wordset          PROC NEAR
    ;bp+4 is address of array
    ;bp+6 is word
    ;bp+8 is nwords

    push    bp                      ;save register values
    mov     bp,sp
    push    di
    push    es

    mov     ax,ds                   ;set up
    mov     es,ax                   ;the registers
    mov     di, WORD PTR [bp+4]     ;for the
    mov     ax, WORD PTR [bp+6]     ;rep stosw
    mov     cx, WORD PTR [bp+8]     ;command
    rep     stosw
    sub     di,2                    ;get final address
    mov     ax,di                   ;place it in AX

    pop     es                      ;restore registers
    pop     di
    mov     sp,bp
    pop     bp
    ret
```

```
_wordset      ENDP
_TEXT         ENDS
END
```

Note that the setting of the ES register takes two steps; values cannot be moved directly from one segment register to another.

We decided to have this function return the last address set in order to provide a partial means of error checking. Suppose, for example, that the number of words we request to be set is greater than the remaining space in the data segment. DI is a 16-bit register, so an offset greater than 64K causes the register to pass through 0 and to start counting again with low values. If the returned address is lower than the starting address, something is wrong. The assembly program could check more carefully for errors of this kind, but we opted to keep the program short and fast. The C tradition is to favor compact code and to place the responsibility for using a routine correctly with the programmer.

How fast is it? We ran the following test on an IBM PC:

```
main()
{
    int ar[500];
    int i,j;
    long ts, te;
    long t_counts();
    int *wordset();
    int *last;

    ts = t_counts();
    for ( i = 0; i < 1000; i++)
        for ( j = 0; j < 500; j++)
                ar[j] = 2001;
    te = t_counts();
    printf("1000 setting loops take %ld counts\n", te — ts);

    ts = t_counts();
    for ( i = 0; i < 1000; i++)
            wordset(ar,2001,500);
    te = t_counts();
    printf("1000 wordsets take %ld counts\n", te — ts);
}
```

The program uses the t_counts() function we developed in Chapter 8; it should be linked in when the program is put together. Here is the output of this test program:

```
1000 setting loops take 322 counts
1000 wordsets take 29 counts
```

Well, it's over 10 times faster! Here is a case where using an assembly version seems justified, at least if your program has to set large arrays or many arrays.

Extending the Reach of Wordset()

As written, wordset() can be used for the data segment of the small-memory model. To set values elsewhere, such as in the video memory, we will have to modify the routine. One possibility is to follow the example set by the library movedata() function. As you may recall, this function can move data between segments because its argument list includes segment values. A second possibility is to write a version that works with the large-memory model. We can learn from each approach, so let's try both.

Using a Segment-Value Argument

Specifying a far memory location involves giving a segment value and giving an offset value. These values can be combined to form a single far pointer. But we also can transmit the two values separately, as does movedata(). One advantage to this approach is that it can be used with the small-memory model and without implementing the far keyword. Thus, this approach can be used with compilers that don't provide a large-memory model or far pointers.

We'll alter wordset by adding a segment value to the argument list, making it the first argument. First, let's visualize how the function will be called; we can do that by constructing a simple program to test the function. Here is one possibility:

```
/* testwsf.c--test wordsetf() function */
#include <conio.h>
#include color.h       /* defines colors, color macros */
#define CGSEG  0xB800   /* segment value for CGA video memory */
#define CL8025 3        /* color text mode */
#define ATTR  RED | (BCKGRND (BLUE) )  /* red on blue */
#define STOP ('\032')
main()
{
    int *wordsetf(); /* sets words far away */
    int ch;
    unsigned scrword; /* character-attribute pair */
    void setmode();   /* defined in Chapter 8 */

    setmode(CL8025);
    while ( (ch = getch() ) != STOP)
        {
```

```
                    scrword = ch | ((( unsigned ) ATTR) << 8);
                    wordsetf(CGSEG,0,scrword, 2000 );
                    }
            }
```

Once again we're using direct memory access to place information on the screen. Recall that in the text mode, each character position on the screen is represented by one word. The first byte (which is the low byte) contains the character code, and the second byte contains the attribute. Here we set the attribute to provide red on a blue background.

The word-setting routine, which we've called `wordsetf()`, has four arguments. In this case, the segment value corresponds to the beginning of video memory. The second argument is the offset; it is 0 because we wish to start at the beginning of screen memory. The third argument is character-attribute pair; in this case it consists of a character entered from the keyboard and the red-on-blue attribute. Finally, the last argument is 2000, the number of character positions on the screen.

To write `wordsetf()` in assembly, we can begin with `wordset()`, modifying it to recognize the additional argument and to set the ES register to it. These are rather minor changes, which we have marked with comments; here is the result:

```
                TITLE wordsetf   ; change name here and below
; rewrite function definition
; wordsetf()--sets words of a memory block to a given value
; function declaration:
; int *wordset(segval,offset, word, nw)
; unsigned segval; /* segment value */
; unsigned offset; /* memory offset */
; int word;        /* assigned value */
; unsigned nw;     /* number of words */
; this function returns the offset of the last initialized word

include segdef.ah
_TEXT SEGMENT
    PUBLIC _wordsetf
_wordsetf PROC NEAR
        ; new argument description
        ;bp+4 is segval
        ;bp+6 is offset
        ;bp+8 is word
        ;bp+10 is nw

        push bp
        mov  bp,sp
        push di
        push es
```

```
        mov   ax,WORD PTR [bp+4]
        mov   es,ax                ;place segval in ES
        mov   di,WORD PTR [bp+6]    ;place offset in DI
        mov   ax,WORD PTR [bp+8]    ;place word in AX
        mov   cx,WORD PTR [bp+10]   ;place count in CX
        rep   stosw
        sub   di,2
        mov   ax,di

        pop   es
        pop   di
        mov   sp,bp
        pop   bp
        ret
_wordsetf ENDP
_TEXT     ENDS
END
```

Trying out the test program, we found that each key, as struck, generated the corresponding character in all 2000 positions on the screen, so this method worked.

As a variant, we could have passed a single far pointer as an argument instead of the segment-offset pair, but the method we used is simpler to set up. In particular, we don't have to enable the far keyword with the /Ze compiler option to use our version.

A Large-Memory Approach

The wordsetf() function is suited for programs that don't require extra code segments. However, it is not compatible with the medium- or large-memory models, since those use far pointers by default for code and, in the second case, for data. Let's see how we could rework wordset() so that it could be used with the large-memory model.

An Exploratory Example—As a first step, let's see what the compiler docs when the large-memory model option (/AL) is specified. The wordset() function works with an address, so we'll investigate a very simple function that uses a pointer. In the large-memory model, a pointer is a far pointer (32 bits) by default, so we'll get to see how that kind of pointer is handled. Here is the simple function:

```
usefp(fp)
int *fp;
{
    *fp = 20;
    fp++;
}
```

This sets the pointed-to integer to 20, then increments the pointer. It is a most unuseful function, but, when compiled with the /AL option, it should show us what we need to know. Here is the COD file, with the machine code removed and with some comments added:

```
;          Static Name Aliases
;
          TITLE    usefp
; note new name for code segment
USEFP_TEXT      SEGMENT  BYTE PUBLIC 'CODE'
USEFP_TEXT      ENDS
CONST SEGMENT   WORD PUBLIC 'CONST'
CONST ENDS
_BSS   SEGMENT  WORD PUBLIC 'BSS'
_BSS   ENDS
_DATA SEGMENT   WORD PUBLIC 'DATA'
_DATA ENDS
DGROUP GROUP    CONST,_BSS,_DATA
        ASSUME CS: USEFP_TEXT, DS: DGROUP, SS: DGROUP, ES: DGROUP
PUBLIC _usefp
_DATA SEGMENT
EXTRN __chkstk:FAR              ;uses a FAR version of _ _chkstk
_DATA ENDS
USEFP_TEXT      SEGMENT
;fp=6
; Line 2
     PUBLIC _usefp
_usefp PROC FAR                ;a far procedure
     push bp
     mov  bp,sp
     xor  ax,ax                ;set AX to 0
     call FAR PTR _ _chkstk    ;request 0 stack space
; Line 4
     les  bx,[bp+6]            ;put seg in ES,offset in BX
     mov  WORD PTR es:[bx],20  ;segment override
; Line 5
     add  WORD PTR [bp+6],2    ;add 2 to offset
; Line 6
     mov  sp,bp               ;restore registers
     pop  bp
     ret
_usefp ENDP

USEFP_TEXT ENDS
END
```

So what's new? The large-memory model uses a code segment name consisting of the capitalized name of the routine with a _TEXT suffix. The procedure itself is declared a FAR procedure, meaning it can be called by procedures in different code segments. The _ _ckdstk function is evoked unnecessarily, since the procedure has no local variables. The only argument, fp, is located at BP+6 instead of at the BP+4 used for the small model. This, recall, is because the return address is now stored in segment and offset form, requiring two more bytes of stack.

The first really new feature is this line:

```
les  bx,[bp+6];     put seg in ES,offset in BX
```

The LES instruction assumes that BP+6 points to a 32-bit address in far pointer form. It places the segment portion of the address in the ES register, and the offset in the indicated register, here BX. The nice thing about this instruction is that it saves us the trouble of trying to remember which word of the address holds the segment and which holds the offset.

The second novel line is this:

```
mov  WORD PTR es:[bx],20 ;segment override
```

To understand it, first consider this instruction:

```
mov  WORD PTR [bx],20
```

This one means, "Place 20 in the location whose offset is stored in BX." By default, data offsets are measured from DS. But we want the offset to be measured from ES, since that is the segment value of the original pointer. The es: operation overrides the default interpretation; it tells the assembler to interpret the offset in BX as an offset from ES.

Finally, the fp++ expression is translated to this:

```
add  WORD PTR [bp+6],2  ;add 2 to offset
```

Note that 2, not 1, is added. That is because fp points to a two-byte integer, so the address must increase by two to point to the next integer. Second, the offset of the far pointer is at [BP+6], implying that the segment value is at [bp+8].

The Wordset() Function—Now let's apply what we have learned to create a large-memory model version of wordset() called lwordset(). We will have to change the name of the code segment to LWORDSET_TEXT and declare _lwordset to be a FAR procedure. The first argument will be found at BP+6 instead of at BP+4. Since the first argument will be a 32-bit far pointer, the second argument will be 4 bytes higher, at BP+10. To set up the ES register properly, we will use the LES instruction. Here are those changes implemented:

```
                    TITLE    lwordset
        ; lwordset() — sets a block of words, large-memory model
        ; function declaration
        ; int *lwordset(pb,word,nw)
        ; int *pb;    /* pointer to block of memory */
        ; int word;  /* value to be copied */
        ; unsigned nw;  /* number of words to be set */
        ; the function returns a far pointer to the last word set


        LWORDSET_TEXT    SEGMENT BYTE PUBLIC 'CODE'
        LWORDSET_TEXT    ENDS
        include lsegdef.ah          ;defines noncode segments
        ASSUME DS:LWORDSET_TEXT
        LWORDSET_TEXT   SEGMENT
            PUBLIC _lwordset
        _lwordset          PROC FAR
            ;bp+6 is pb
            ;bp+10 is word
            ;bp+12 is nw

                push     bp
                mov      bp,sp
                push     di
                push     es

                les      di,[bp+6]          ;set registers
                mov      ax,WORD PTR[bp+10]
                mov      cx,WORD PTR[bp+12]
                rep      stosw              ;set words
                sub      di,2
                mov      ax,di    ;return offset
                mov      dx,es    ;return segment value

                pop      es       ;restore registers
                pop      di
                mov      sp,bp
                pop      bp
                ret
        _lwordset          ENDP
        LWORDSET_TEXT   ENDS
        END
```

The only change in defining the segments was in the code name segment. Therefore we copied *segdef.ah* to *lsegdef.ah*, then deleted references to _TEXT from the latter file. As you can see, the changes are relatively minor. We can test this function with the following program:

```
/* testlws.c--test lwordset() */
#include <conio.h>
#include "color.h"
#define ATTR  RED ¦ (BCKGRND (BLUE) )
#define CLMEM ( 0xB800L << 16)  /* far pointer to video
memory */
#define STOP  ('\032')
main()
{
    int *wordsetf();
    int ch;
    unsigned scrword;
    void setmode();

    setmode(CL8025);
    while ( (ch = getch() ) != STOP)
        {
    scrword =  ch ¦ ((( unsigned ) ATTR) << 8);
    lwordset(CLMEM,scrword, 2000 );
        }
}
```

First, we used MASM to assemble lwordset(). Then we compiled the test program using the /AL option and linked with the lwordset object module. Note that lwordset() won't work if linked to code compiled using the small-memory model.

Again, the screen is filled with a character when the corresponding key is pressed.

Now that we've seen how to write simple assembly modules, let's look at a more complex example, one that involves a realistic integration of C programming with assembly programming.

A Word-Seeking Program

The assembly string-handling instructions seem to offer abilities that make it advantageous to use assembly. For another example using assembly string instructions, let's write a program that searches a file or files for a given word and prints out lines containing the word. We'll implement a low-budget grep. Grep is a UNIX/XENIX utility that searches files for a given word or phrase. It is more powerful than our version will be because it incorporates a pattern-recognition scheme. We'll settle for finding specific words, and we'll call the program *seek* to distinguish it from its more powerful relative.

There are two programming aspects to this project. The first is organizing the program so that it can inspect one or more files and recognize an option or so. The second is developing a method to search individual lines in a file for a particular word. The first task is best handled using C, while the assembly string instructions can be used for the second.

First, let's develop an overall plan. The main program will have the responsibility of scanning the command line arguments, identifying and affecting options, obtaining the search word, and cycling though files, opening and closing them. We'll have it call a second function; its responsibility will be to read a given file a line at a time, identifying and printing the lines containing the word. To identify the lines, it will use an assembly routine that scans a string for a given word.

The Main Program

We've already seen how to use the `ac--`, `av++` combination to process a series of command line arguments. The first argument after the filename is `av[1]`. We process it, decrement the argument count, increment the argument-list pointer, and now `av[1]` is the next command line argument. When the argument count reaches one, the list is exhausted.

We have to enhance that method, for this program will have three kinds of arguments: options, a search word, and filenames. To make things easy, we will require that the arguments come in that particular order.

The Option List—First, let's look at options. In DOS, command line arguments traditionally are identified by using a slash (/) as a prefix. Many commands now also recognize the hyphen (-) as an option prefix; this is in accordance with the UNIX/XENIX practice. We'll have our program recognize both. It will process arguments beginning with a slash or a hyphen as options; the first argument not beginning with one of these prefixes will be interpreted to be the search word.

Before expanding on the technique further, we should have some options in mind. We'll start with just one. The /n (or -n) option will indicate that the program should print line numbers as well as the matching lines. We'll set up the processing technique, however, so that the list can be added to easily.

To keep track of whether an option is set or not, we'll set bits in an `unsigned` variable called `flags`. Here is the portion of code needed to process the options:

```
#include "flags.h"
    ...
unsigned int flags = 0;
    ...
while ( ac > 1 && (av[1][0] == '-' || av[1][0] == '/') )
    {                              /* process options */
    switch ( av[1][1] )
        {
        case 'n' : flags |= NUMBER;
                   break;
```

```
        default  : fprintf(stderr,"%s: No such option\n",
                   av[1]);
            break;
        }
    ac--;
    av++;
    }
```

The `while` loop continues as long as there are arguments left beginning with a hyphen or slash. Since `av[1]` is a pointer to the first argument, `av[1][0]` is the first element of the argument, so we can inspect it to see if it is one of the valid prefixes. If so, we look at the second letter (`av[1][1]`) to see if it is an n. If it is, we set the `NUMBER` flag. The numerical value for this flag is stored in the *flags.h* file.

☐ *Question 12-2* What happens if we type something like `-night` or `/norbert` after the command name?

Note that this approach is simple to extend. Just add another case to the switch and another flag setting to the *flags.h* file.

☐ *Question 12-3* Modify the loop to include a `-c` option that causes the program to count the lines containing the search word and a `-s` option that suppresses the printing of matching lines. (Later questions will deal with implementing these options.)

The Search Word—After the option list is exhausted, there should be at least two more arguments, not counting the command name. There should be a search word and at least one filename. We can check the argument count to see if there are enough arguments left. If so, the next argument should be the search word. It also is `av[1]`, since the option loop increments `av` each cycle. Subsequently, `av` will be advanced to a filename, so we should save the address of the search word:

```
char *word;
...
word = av[1];          /* save pointer to search word */
ac--;
av++;                  /* go on to next argument */
```

The File List—At this point, the remaining arguments are interpreted to be filenames, and we can process them in the same fashion as we did with programs such as *show.c*. If a file cannot be opened, we'll print an error message and go on to the next one.

If more than one filename is provided, we'll have the program print out the filename to identify in which file a line is found. We'll use another bit in `flags` to turn on this option.

Code for the Main Program—Putting these points together, we can create the following main program:

```
/* seek.c--finds file lines containing a given word    */
/* Usage:  seek [-n] [/n] word file(s)                 */
/* -n or /n option numbers the lines                   */
/* filename is printed if more than one file is used   */
#include <stdio.h>
#include "flags.h"
main(ac,av)
int ac;
char *av[];
{
    FILE *fp;
    unsigned int flags = 0;     /* option settings */
    char *word;
    void seekw();

    while ( ac > 1 && (av[1][0] == '-' || av[1][0] == '/') )
        {                                /* process options */
        switch ( av[1][1] )
              {
        case 'n' : flags |= NUMBER;
            break;
              default  : fprintf(stderr,"%s: No such option\n",
                         av[1]);
            break;
                  }
        ac--;
        av++;
        }

    if (ac < 3)
        {
        fprintf(stderr,"Usage: seek [-n] ob/n] word file(s)\n");
        exit(0);
        }

    word = av[1];    /* save pointer to search word */
    ac--;
    av++;
    if (ac > 2)      /* set filename option if more than */
        flags |= NAMES;                          /* one file */

    while ( ac > 1 )
```

```
{
if ( (fp = fopen(av[1],"r") ) == NULL )
  perror(av[1]);        /* skip bad names */
else
   {
   seekw(word,fp,av[1],flags);
   fclose(fp);
   }
ac--;
av++;
}
}
```

Note the information that is being passed on to the next function, seekw(). It is told the search word, the file pointer, the filename (represented by av[1]), and the flag settings.

At this point, the *flags.h* file contains two flag values:

```
/* flags.h--flag settings for the seek.c program */
#define   NUMBER   1    /* number the lines */
#define   NAMES    2    /* print the filename */
```

Because each flag represents a particular bit, each should be a power of two. Thus, the next flag added to the list could use the value 4.

□　*Question 12–4*　Extend the *flags.h* file to include the options of Question 12–3.

The Seekw() Function

This function reads the opened file a line at a time. We'll use the standard fgets() function for that purpose. Then seekw() uses a function called strwrd() to determine whether or not the search word is in the line. This is the assembly routine we will have to write. If the word is found, the line is printed. Depending on the flag values, the filename and the line number may be printed, too. Here is the code for the function:

```
/*    seekw.c--reads file line by line, checks for word */
#include <stdio.h>
#include "flags.h"
#define SIZE 256                 /* maximum line length */
void seekw(wp, file, fname, flags)
char *wp;                        /* search word */
FILE *file;                      /* file pointer */
char *fname;                     /* filename */
int flags;                       /* flag settings */
{
    char line[SIZE];             /* holds input line */
```

```
        char *fgets(), *strwrd();
        long lc = 0;                    /* line count */

        while ( fgets(line,SIZE,file) != NULL )
          {
          lc++;
          if ( strwrd(line,wp) != NULL )
            {
            if (flags & NAMES)
               printf("%s:", fname);
            if (flags & NUMBER)
               printf("%4d: ", lc);
            fputs(line,stdout);
            }
          }
      }
```

Note that the `strwrd()` function returns a NULL pointer if it fails to find the word. We could have designed `strwrd()` as a Boolean function, returning a true or false value. That's all that is needed for this application. However, the function would be more useful in general if it were to return a pointer to the address within the string of the found word; that is what we chose to do.

☐ *Question 12-5* Can you alter `seekw()` to accommodate the options mentioned in Questions 12–3 and 12–4?

The Strwrd() Function

Now we come to the part of the program that will be coded in assembly language: searching a string for a specific word. The reason for choosing assembly for this task is that assembly has a `CMPS` (compare string) instruction that compares one string to another. Our hope is that by using assembly in general and by using this instruction in particular, we can speed up the search process. Later, we can investigate just how much using assembly helped.

Developing a Strategy—Before plunging into assembly programming, we need to develop a strategy for searching for a word in the string. One thing the routine should do is obtain the lengths of the string and of the word; if the word is longer than the string, the search is hopeless, and the function should report failure immediately. Otherwise, the function should compare the word with an equal number of characters at the beginning of the string. If there is a match, the function can report so by returning the address of the beginning of the string. If there is no match, and if there are more characters left in the string, the function must shift the comparison, this time comparing the word with the characters starting from the second character in the string. The process should continue until the word is found, or until the whole string has been searched. Figure 12–4 illustrates the matching process.

Figure 12–4
Matching Word to String

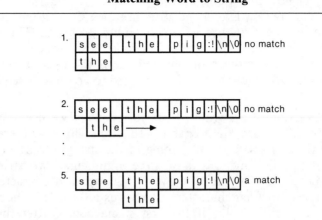

How can the function tell when to stop if there is no match? Well, if the string and the word are the same length, we need one comparison. If the string is one character longer than the word, we need at most two comparisons. In general, if the string is N characters longer than the word, we need at most N+1 comparisons. Figure 12–5 shows how the comparisons are made.

Figure 12–5
N+1 Comparisons

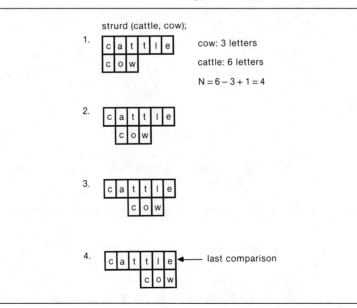

Now that we have a general idea of what is needed, we can begin to consider how to code it. At this point, it may be useful to try coding it in C first. One reason is that the structure of a C program usually is more obvious than the structure of an assembly program. This makes it easier to express the logic of the method in code. Also, we can link the resulting code with the rest of the program and see if the overall plan works. And if it works rapidly enough, we may not need to go on to assembly.

A C Version of Strwrd()—Let's review what we need. We need the lengths of the two strings; the `strlen()` function will serve there. We need to compare the word with the beginning of the string; the `strncmp()` function will do that. This function takes three arguments: two string addresses and a number n. It compares the two strings up to n characters or until the first difference between characters. It returns a 0 value if the substrings are identical, a positive value if the first string comes after the second in ASCII order, and a negative value otherwise.

If the comparison fails, the word should be compared with the next subsection of the screen. We can accomplish this by incrementing a pointer. If the word is found, we can return the pointer to where the word begins in the string. The maximum number of comparisons will be the string length minus the word length plus one.

Here is an implementation of these ideas:

```c
/* strwrd.c--C version */
#include <string.h>
char *strwrd(str,word)
char *str;                /* pointer to string to be searched */
char *word;               /* pointer to search word */
{
    int wl;               /* length of search word */
    int tries;            /* maximum number of comparisons */
    int cmp = 1;          /* set to 0 if match is found */

    wl = strlen(word);
    tries = 1 + strlen(str) - wl;
    if ( tries > 0 )
       while ( (cmp = strncmp(str,word,wl) ) && tries--)
            str++;
    if (cmp )             /* nonzero cmp means no match */
       return (char *) 0;    /* the NULL pointer */
    else
       return str;    /* value of str when match was made */
}
```

The heart of this fragment is the following loop:

```
while ( (cmp = strncmp(str,word,wl) ) && tries--)
        str++;
```

If a match is found, `cmp` is set to 0, and the loop ends. The pointer `str` points to the beginning of the word as it occurs in the string. If no match is found, the loop increments `str` so that the comparison will start with the next character in the string. This continues until a match is found or until `tries` reaches 0. If the last happens before a match is found, `cmp` is non-0, and we use that as a sign to return the null pointer.

☐ *Question 12-6* Can we condense this slightly by moving the incrementing of `str` to the `while` loop test condition as follows?

```
while ( (cmp = strncmp(str++,word,wl) ) && tries--)
        ;
```

We tried this function in the `seek` program, and everything seemed to work as intended. The next step, then, is to translate the function's logic to assembly language.

The Assembly Approach

Exactly what elements do we have to reproduce? The first important point is that we need the assembly equivalent of `strlen()`. Of course, we could call the `strlen()` library routine from the assembly program, but then we won't learn anything. Instead, we'll write our own assembly procedure to get the length of a string, and we'll include it in the code section.

Second, we need the assembly equivalent of the `strncmp()` instruction. Here the CMPS instruction, which compares elements of a string, will be useful.

Third, we need to build a loop to serve the same function the `while` loop in the C version did; that is, to compare the word to successive portions of the string.

The heart of the whole process is comparing two strings, so let's begin with that.

The REPE CMPSB Instruction—The CMPS instruction compares strings, and the CMPSB version does so byte by byte. It compares elements of two strings. One string is in the DS segment, and SI points to the element we wish to compare. The second string is in the ES segment and has DI pointing to the element that we wish to compare. Each time CMPS is executed, the SI and DI pointers are moved one unit. For CMPSB, the unit is one byte, and for CMPSW, the unit is one word. If the direction flag (DF) is cleared, the pointers move forward; otherwise, they move backward.

By itself, *CMPS* effects a single comparison, then advances the DI and SI pointers to the next elements. To compare whole strings, we'll use a variation of the *REP* prefix called *REPE* (repeat while equal). First, we set CX to the maximum number of repetitions. In our case, this will be the length of the search word. After each comparison, CX gets reduced by 1. The comparison of elements will continue until one of two conditions terminates it. The first terminating condition is that two elements don't match; as soon as there is a difference between the two strings, the comparison process ends. Otherwise, the comparisons continue until CX reaches 0. Thus, the combination REPE CMPSB acts in a way quite similar to strncmp().

How can we tell if there is a match? If there is no match, the comparison terminates before CX reaches 0. Therefore, a non-0 value for CX means the strings did not match, while a zero value means that all the tested elements did match. We can then use a *JZ* (jump if zero) instruction following the test to jump to a set of instructions to handle the case of a match being found:

```
repe    cmpsb   ; compare until no match or to end
jz      find    ; if all match, CX becomes 0
```

Here, find is the address label of the instructions to be executed if a match is found. These two lines form the heart of the procedure, but they require considerable support. For one thing, the module will have to determine the length of the search word so that it will know what to set CX to. For another, it will have to try matching the word to various parts of the string. It also needs to find the string length; if it is shorter than the word, it should bail out.

Anyway, we now have our strncmp() equivalent; now let's make a strlen() equivalent.

A String Length Procedure—Clearly, the strwrd module is more involved than our previous efforts in assembly. There is one simplification we can make. Note that we have to determine the length of two separate strings. In C, repeated tasks suggest using or devising a function for that purpose. In assembly, we can create a procedure to determine the length of the string, then call it twice. It can be in the same module as strwrd(). Since it is used just by this module, it can be a local (as opposed to PUBLIC) procedure. Also, because it won't be called directly by a C function, it need not follow the C conventions for arguments and return values.

The main tool we'll use to count characters in a string is the SCASB string instruction. It assumes that DI points to a byte in a string in the data segment. It compares the contents of the byte to the contents of the AL register, then advances DI by one. If the two bytes match, it sets the zero flag to one. Because C strings end with a null value, we can use SCASB to scan for 0. We need to place the instruction in a loop so that successive bytes are scanned, and we can use CX to maintain a count. When the zero flag is set, the loop should break, and CX will contain the number of characters before the null character. Let's look in more detail at the necessary steps. CX should be set to 0 before the counting starts; each time a new letter is found, CX will be incremented. AL should contain the character that

SCASB scans the string for. Since it scans to find the null character, AL should be set to 0.

After initializing these registers, we will use *SCASB* to see if the first character is a null character. If not, we increment CX and repeat the comparison. Note that the order is a comparison followed by paired increment-comparisons. In assembly, we can produce that sequence of events by setting up a loop that increments and then compares. The first time through the loop, however, we will jump immediately to the comparison. Here is code that does the trick:

```
        xor     cx,cx           ;set CX (the count) to 0
        xor     al,al           ;set al (the scan value) to 0
        jmp     SHORT inloop    ;go to first comparison
start:
        inc     cx              ;increment the count
inloop:
        scasb                   ;does byte match AL?
        jne     start           ;if test fails, go to start
```

The SHORT directive can used for absolute jumps of less than 256 bytes.

Next, we need to produce an interface between this fragment and the main procedure. Since the SCASB instruction expects DI to point to the string, we can require that the calling procedure place the starting address of the string in DI. Upon return, the calling procedure can then expect to find the count in CX. Since the SCASB function alters DI, the counting function should save the original DI value by pushing it at the beginning and popping it at the end. It also should restore any other registers (aside from CX) it uses. Note that we save time by using registers to communicate information between procedures. If we had set up the counting part as a C function, we would have had to go through the standard procedure of placing arguments on the stack in the calling procedure, having the called procedure read the stack, and placing the return value in AX. Here the DI and CX registers are the information channels. Here is the whole length-counting package:

```
cntlet      PROC NEAR
    push    ax
    push    di
    xor     cx,cx           ;set CX (the count) to 0
    xor     al,al           ;set al (the scan value) to 0
    jmp     SHORT inloop    ;go to first comparison
start:
    inc     cx              ;increment the count
inloop:
    scasb                   ;does byte match AL?
    jne     start           ;if test fails, go to start
```

```
        pop     di
        pop     ax
        ret
cntlet  ENDP
```

Note that we don't use an underbar prefix and that we don't declare the procedure name to be `PUBLIC`; that is because `cntlet` is used only in this module; it is not called directly by C programs or by other modules. We'll tuck the procedure in after the main procedure.

Designing the Loop—The loop, recall, should continue comparing the search word to successive portions of the string until a match is found or until a maximum number of searches have been made. Let's assume that the procedure has already calculated the maximum number of comparisons and has placed that value in the DX register. Then we can decrement that register each loop and stop the loop when DX reaches 0. (The CX register normally is used for such counting, but it already is being used by the `REPE CMPSB` instruction.) The overall loop design can look like this:

```
comloop:                    ;beginning of loop
    ;setup instructions go here
    repe    cmpsb           ;cmp until cx=0 or until no match
    jz      find            ;leave loop if match is found
    dec     dx              ;decrement DX
    jz      nofind          ;leave loop if DX reaches 0
    ;update here before starting next cycle
    jmp     comloop         ;loop end--go to beginning
```

Note the loop has two exits. First, there is a jump to `find` if a match is found. Second, there is a jump to `nofind` if no match is found after DX shifts the word along the string.

We need to fill in some details. Recall that the `REPE CMPSB` instruction wants SI to point to the initial character to be compared in the string, DI to point to the initial character in the word, and CX to contain the length of the word. As it makes its comparisons, `REPE CMPSB` changes the values of these three registers. That means they have to be reset at the beginning of the next loop cycle. DI and CX should be reset to the same values they had before, but SI should be increased by one so that the comparison starts one character later in the string. We need, then, to save the values of DI, SI, and CX. It is convenient to use registers. We'll use AX to store the CX value, and BX to store the SI value. That doesn't leave many registers free, so we'll use the stack to save DI. Storage will occur before the loop starts, and then the values can be reset in the loop from the stored values.

The update at the end of the loop consist of incrementing BX; this will cause SI to be reset to the next character in the string. Here is the loop with these additions:

```
comloop:                        ;beginning of loop
     mov     si,bx              ;set si to current start position
     mov     di,[bp-2]          ;set di to word start
     mov     cx,ax              ;initialize cx
     repe    cmpsb              ;cmp until cx=0 or until no match
     jz      find               ;a match was found
     dec     dx
     jz      nofind             ;nary a match
     inc     bx                 ;start from next character
     jmp     comloop            ;loop end--go to start
```

Creating a Procedure from the Elements—We have a procedure for finding the length of a string, we have a fragment for seeing if two strings match, and we have a loop for matching the word to successive portions of the string. Now we have to put these elements together. Here is one possible implementation:

```
        TITLE    strwrd
include segdef.ah
_DATA SEGMENT
EXTRN _ _chkstk:NEAR
_DATA ENDS
_TEXT SEGMENT
        PUBLIC _strwrd
_strwrd     PROC NEAR
; bp+4 is address of string
; bp+6 is address of word
     push    bp
     mov     bp,sp
     mov     ax,2                   ;set up stack for address
     call    _ _chkstk              ;of string beginning
     ;bp-2 will store initial string address
     push    di
     push    si
     push    es

     mov     ax,ds
     mov     es,ax             ;es same as ds
     mov     di,[bp+4]         ;di points to string
     call cntlet               ;str address in di, puts length in cx
     mov     dx,cx             ;stinglength in dx
     mov     si,di             ;si points to string
     mov     di,[bp+6]         ;di points to word
     call cntlet               ;wordlength in cx
     sub     dx,cx             ;difference in dx
     jl      nofind            ;word longer than string
     inc     dx                ;maximum number of searches
```

```
        mov     bx,si           ;si points to beginning of string
        mov     ax,cx           ;save word length
        mov     [bp-2],di       ;save beginning of word
        cld                     ;compare beginning to end

comloop:                        ;beginning of outer loop
        mov     si,bx           ;set si to current start position
        mov     di,[bp-2]       ;set di to word start
        mov     cx,ax           ;initialize cx
        repe    cmpsb           ;cmp until cx=0 or no match
        jz      find            ;yes, a match was found
        dec     dx
        jz      nofind          ;no match in whole string
        inc     bx              ;start from next character
        jmp     comloop         ;end of loop

find:                           ;go here if word is found
        mov     ax,bx           ;return its offset
        jmp     cleanup
nofind:                         ;go here if word is not found
        xor     ax,ax           ;return null value

cleanup:                        ;restore registers and return
        pop     es
        pop     si
        pop     di
        mov     sp,bp
        pop     bp
        ret
_strwrd ENDP
cntlet          PROC NEAR       ;counts chars in string
        push    ax              ;save registers
        push    di
        xor     cx,cx           ;initialize count to 0
        xor     al,al           ;set AL to null character
        jmp     SHORT inloop
start:
        inc     cx              ;increment count
inloop:
        scasb                   ;is current char a null char?
        jne     start           ;if not, repeat loop
        pop     di              ;restore registers
        pop     ax
        ret
cntlet  ENDP
_TEXT   ENDS
END
```

Note how both the _strwrd procedure and the cntlet procedure are placed in the same code segment. The names really act as labels. Because _strwrd is public, that label is recognized externally; for example, our seekw() function sees it. The underbar prefix lets C programs in particular recognize it. Cntlet, on the other hand, is hidden within the module.

☐ *Question 12-7*   Why is the string address first placed in DI, then moved to SI?

Trying the Procedure

Let's assemble this procedure and link it with the compiled object modules produced from the *seek.c* and the *seekw.c* files. To make the program more useful, we'll also link the *ssetargv.obj* file provided with the compiler. This module, recall, provides the code that allows the program to recognize wildcard symbols (* and ?) in the command line. We can use these commands:

```
masm strwrd;
clink seek seekw strwrd ssetargv
```

We can test the program on material for part of this chapter:

```
A>seek However ch12
However,
require extra code segments. However, it is not compatible with
what is needed for this application. However, the function would

A>
```

What Did We Gain?

Writing this program provided us with good experience in assembly programming. True, using jumps and subroutines isn't as elegant or as clear as using C's structured statements, but using the assembly string instructions increases the speed. Or does it? We saw it did for wordset(), but we won't know for sure with seek() until we compare it with the C equivalent.

We timed both versions through a search of a 50K text file relocated to a RAM disk. The assembler version took about 8 seconds, while the C version took about 19 seconds. The change is significant, but not close to the difference we saw for wordset().

Investigating Assembly-C Differences

Why was the assembly version faster? We were motivated by the success of the string instruction in wordset(), but there are several potential causes. First, the assembly version used string instructions, while the C version may not have; without having access to the library source code, we don't know. Second, the assembly version used registers to communicate information

451

between the string-length and string-comparison sections, while the C version used arguments, hence the stack. Third, the C strcmp() function does more than our assembly comparison. Not only does it see if the strings match or not, it reports on their relative ASCII ordering. Finally, the assembly version confined to one module what the C version did in three modules (strwrd(), strlen(), and strncmp()).

It is interesting to investigate the relative importance of some of these factors, and it also offers some programming practice. First, since we don't have access to library source code, we'll write our own versions of strlen() and strcmp() in standard C. Presumably, the compiled versions will not use the assembly string instructions; that can be checked. Then, to see the effect of using the string instructions, we can rewrite these two functions in assembly, using the string instructions. Third, we can modify our strncmp() so that it just returns 0 or one if the strings match or not, and not worry about the ASCII sequence. Finally, we can speed up strwrd.c by using register variables.

Our Very Own Strlen() and Strncmp()

We will write functions that behave as described in the library manual. For strlen(), that means it takes a string pointer as its argument and returns the length of the string. All the function has to do is count string characters until it reaches the terminal null character. Here is one implementation; to mark it as our version, we have changed the name:

```
/* st_len.c--returns the length of a string */
int st_len(s)
char *s;
{
    register ct = 0;  /* use a register for counting */

    while (*s++)       /* *s==0 marks end of string */
        ct++;
    return ct;
}
```

Each cycle the pointer s is incremented so it points to the next character. Before the incrementing takes place, the current character stored at s is checked to see if it is the null character. If it is, the loop quits; otherwise the count is incremented.

Using a register variable requests the compiler to use a register rather than a stack variable for ct. IBM C is one of the few compilers that support this storage class for the 8088 processor.

The strncmp() function is more involved. It must compare successive characters in two strings, quitting after N comparisons or after two characters don't match, whichever comes first. Then it must return a positive value if the first string is first in ASCII order, a negative value if the second string is first, and 0 if the strings match. Here is one approach to meeting these design goals:

```
/* s_ncmp.c--compare two strings up to a given number of bytes */
int s_ncmp (s1,s2,n)
char *s1, *s2;        /* pointers to the two strings */
int n;                /* maximum number of comparisons */
{
    while ( --in &&  *s1  &&  (*s1 == *s2) )
        {
        s1++;         /* advance first pointer */
        s2++;         /* advance the second pointer */
        }
    return ( *s1 — *s2);
}
```

The key section is the test condition for the `while` loop. The loop will quit when any one of the three expressions becomes zero, or "false."

The first expression, `--n`, provides the counting. Note that the prefix form causes n to be decremented before the test is made; thus, the loop quits when n is 1. This means the loop is transversed one less than n times. That's okay, however, for the `return` statement makes one more comparison after the loop. `return` is described later in the chapter.

The third expression, `*s1 == *s2`, becomes "false," or 0, when the character `*s1` differs from `*s2`, so it causes the loop to stop when nonmatching characters are met.

There is one other condition that should stop the loop, and that is if the end of either string is reached. We test for string 1 explicitly with the second test expression, `*s1`. If s1 points to the null character, `*s1` is 0, and the loop ends. Why don't we test whether `*s2` is the null character? Because we are slightly sly! Suppose `*s2` is 0. Then `*s1` either is 0 or it isn't. If it is, then the `*s1` condition halts the loop. If it isn't, then the `*s1 == *s2` condition halts the loop.

If the loop is not halted, s1 and s2 each are incremented. But halting the loop catches s1 and s2 at their current values. That is important for the `return` statement. The `return` statement returns `*s1 — *s2`, which is the ASCII difference between the last two characters tested. If, for instance, the loop quit because two characters didn't match, this step reports a positive number if `*s1` is greater than `*s2` and a negative number otherwise. If the loop quits because of the `--n` test, then the return value compares the nth characters, returning 0 if they are the same, and a positive or negative value otherwise. The sign of the return value lets us use s_ncmp, for example, to sort strings alphabetically.

We recompiled the `seek` program, using these functions instead of the library ones. The time for the 50K file was $16\frac{1}{2}$ seconds, $1\frac{1}{2}$ seconds faster than the library version, so we must have done something right.

Using Assembly Versions of the Library Routines

We can use elements of our original `strwrd` assembly program to provide assembly versions of `st_len()` and `st_ncmp()`. First, we can convert the `cntlet` procedure to the C function format:

```
        TITLE   st_len
; st_len()--returns length of a string
;   int st_len(s)
;   char *s;        /* pointer to string */

include segdef.ah
_DATA SEGMENT
_DATA ENDS
_TEXT SEGMENT
        PUBLIC _st_len
_st_len     PROC NEAR
; bp+4 is address of string
    push    bp
    mov     bp,sp
    push    di

    mov     di,WORD PTR[bp+4] ;move address to DI
    xor     cx,cx            ;set count to 0
    xor     al,al            ;set scan char to \0
    jmp     SHORT inloop
start:
    inc     cx
inloop:
    scasb
    jne     start
    xchg    ax,cx            ;put count in AX

    pop     di
    mov     sp,bp
    pop     bp
    ret
_st_len ENDP
_TEXT   ENDS
END
```

We've used the standard C format we learned from the compiler. The main changes from `cntlet` are that DI takes its value from the stack, and that the return value is placed in AX.

Next, we can use the core of `strwrd` to produce a `strncmp()` work-alike:

```
        TITLE    st_ncmp
;st_ncmp( s1, s2, n)  /* compares 2 strings, up to n chars */
;char *s1;    /* pointer to first string */
;char *s2;    /* pointer to second string */
;int n;        /* maximum number of comparisons */
include segdef.ah
_TEXT SEGMENT
        PUBLIC _st_ncmp
_st_ncmp      PROC NEAR
; bp+4 is address of string1
; bp+6 is address of string2
; bp+8 is maximum number of chars to be compared
    push    bp
    mov     bp,sp
    push    di
    push    si
    push    es

    mov     ax,ds
    mov     es,ax
    mov     si,WORD PTR[bp+4]     ;si points to string1
    mov     di,WORD PTR[bp+6]     ;di points to string2
    mov     cx,WORD PTR[bp+8]
    cld                           ;compare beginning to end
    repe    cmpsb                 ;cmp until cx=0 or no match
    jz      match                 ;cx=0 means a complete match
    dec     si                    ;back up to mismatch
    dec     di
    mov     ax,[si]               ;put string1 char into AX
    mov     dx,[di]               ;put string2 char into DX
    sub     ax,dx                 ;return ASCII difference
    jmp     cleanup
match:
    xor     ax,ax                 ;return 0
cleanup:
    pop     es
    pop     si
    pop     di
    mov     sp,bp
    pop     bp
    ret
_st_ncmp ENDP
_TEXT    ENDS
END
```

The comments explain the main points. The CMPSB advances the SI and DI pointers even if there is a mismatch, so we back them up to point to the mismatched characters. We then have to inspect the characters. Since SI points to a character, [SI] represents the character itself, and we load it into AX. Similarly, the other character is placed in DX. The characters are represented by their ASCII values, so the ASCII difference is returned.

We assembled these modules and relinked seek, using them instead of the C versions of the preceding section. This cut the running time of our test from 16½ seconds to 15½ seconds. Apparently, using the assembly string instructions instead of the regular CMP instructions used by the compiled C version makes only a small difference in this context.

A Simplified String-Comparison Routine—To make the comparison to our original assembly program more fair, we'll modify the st_ncmp() function so that it just reports on the success or failure of the matching problem. We'll replace the section that compares ASCII values with a statement that sets AX to 1:

```
        TITLE   st_ncmp1
;st_ncmp1( s1, s2, n)  /* compares 2 strings, up to n chars */
;char *s1;    /* pointer to first string */
;char *s2;    /* pointer to second string */
;int n;       /* maximum number of comparisons */
include segdef.ah
_TEXT SEGMENT
        PUBLIC _st_ncmp1
_st_ncmp1       PROC NEAR
; bp+4 is address of string1
; bp+6 is address of string2
; bp+8 is maximum number of chars to be compared
    push    bp
    mov     bp,sp
    push    di
    push    si
    push    es

    mov     ax,ds
    mov     es,ax
    mov     si,WORD PTR[bp+4]    ;si points to string
    mov     di,WORD PTR[bp+6]    ;di points to word
    mov     cx,WORD PTR[bp+8]
    cld                         ;compare beginning to end
    repe    cmpsb               ;cmp until cx=0 or no match
    jz      match
    mov     ax,1                ;return 1 if no match
    jmp     SHORT cleanup
match:
    xor     ax,ax               ;return 0
cleanup:
```

```
        pop     es
        pop     si
        pop     di
        mov     sp,bp
        pop     bp
        ret
_st_ncmp1 ENDP
_TEXT   ENDS
END
```

This change cuts the running time of the test from 15½ seconds to 15 seconds.

Register Variables

The two assembly programs for string length and string comparison use essentially the same code as the original *strwrd* assembly program did. However, the loop for matching the word to successive string positions is in the C function strwrd():

```
/* strwrd.c--C version */
#include <string.h>
char *strwrd(str,word)
char *str;              /* pointer to string to be searched */
char *word;             /* pointer to search word */
{
    int wl;             /* length of search word */
    int tries;          /* maximum number of comparisons */
    int cmp = 1;        /* set to 0 if match is found */

    wl = strlen(word);
    tries = 1 + strlen(str) - wl;
    if ( tries > 0 )
       while ( (cmp = strncmp(str,word,wl) ) && tries--)
            str++;
    if (cmp )                 /* non-zero cmp means no match */
       return (char *) 0; /* the NULL pointer */
    else
       return str;        /* value of str when match was made */
}
```

We can speed this up by using register variables. IBM C allows up to two register variables, so we should pick where they will do the most good. The variables altered most frequently in this program are tries and str. However, str is an argument, hence it must be a stack variable, not a register variable. But we can create a register variable within the program and assign it str's value:

```
/* strwrdr.c--strwrd.c modified to use register variables */
char *strwrd(str,word)
char *str, *word;
{
    int wl;
    register tries;
    register char *st;
    int cmp = 1;
    int s_len(), s_cmp();

    st = str;
    wl = s_len(word);
    tries = 1 + s_len(st) - wl;
    if ( tries > 0 )
        while ( (cmp = s_cmp(st,word,wl) ) && tries--)
            st++;
    if (cmp )
        return (char *) 0;
    else
        return st;
}
```

This change reduces the running time to 14 seconds. Table 12–1 summarizes the results. All times listed in the table are for seeking a nonexistent four-letter word in a 50K text file on a RAM disk on an IBM PC.

Table 12–1
Running Times for Various Seek( ) Versions

Version	Time
1. Library `strlen()` and `strncmp()`	19.0 sec
2. "Generic" C `st_len()` and `st_ncmp()`	16.5 sec
3. Assembly `st_len()` and `st_ncmp()`	15.5 sec
4. As above, but simplified `st_ncmp()`	15.0 sec
5. As above, but register variables in `strwrd.c`	14.0 sec
6. Assembly `strwrd.asm`	8.0 sec

The Moral

So much work should have some moral, so let's consider the implications of our findings. There are several reasons why an assembly program could run faster than a C equivalent. First, it can use assembly instructions not likely to be used by the compiler. With our `wordset()` function, that made a dramatic (if you consider tenfold dramatic) increase in speed. With the `seek` program, however, it made only a small difference, the one between versions 2 and 3 in Table 12-1.

When used in place of a general-purpose function, an assembly function (or C function, for that matter) offers advantages from having a simpler design objective. Again, for our case, the difference is small (version 3 versus version 4).

Another source of improvement is that assembly programs can make better use of registers. C programs use the stack to hold variables, and using the stack is slower than using registers. Using register variables in a C program can speed things up.

Comparing version 2 to version 5 shows that putting these factors together produces a modest increase in speed. What, then, accounts for the superiority of version 6 to version 2 or version 1? First, version 6 has few function calls; it just calls the `cntlet` procedure twice. The other versions have the main loop in a C program, so that the `strncmp()` procedure (or equivalent) may be called several times during the search of each file line; calling a procedure takes time. Second, when `_strwrd` does call `cntptr`, it uses registers, not the stack, for communicating values.

These results suggest the following techniques for speeding up a function by using assembly code:

1. If there is opportunity to use special assembly instructions such as the string instructions or the rotate instructions, use them.
2. If you use a loop, replace function calls within the loop with in-line code.
3. If you have more than one procedure, see if you can use registers to communicate between the two.

Accessing Interrupts through Assembly

In the *seek* program we had a choice between using standard C functions and assembly language modules. Sometimes we don't have that choice. For example, consider calling upon a BIOS or DOS interrupt. In IBM C, we can use `int86()` or one of its relatives, but they are not part of the standard C library. To produce those functions, or equivalents, compiler designers need to resort to assembly language. We can learn some interesting programming points by trying to follow that route ourselves.

We've used `int86()` frequently, so let's try designing a function along similar lines. We'll call our version `callint()`. The `int86()` function, recall, takes three arguments. The first is the interrupt number of the routine we wish to recall. The second is the address of a union holding values we wish to assign to the AX, BX, CX, DX, SI, and DI registers before making the interrupt call. The third argument is the address of a similar union meant to hold the values of these registers after the call. The union also has the carry flag (CL) flag value stored in it, since this flag is used to indicate errors for certain DOS interrupts. The union itself is defined in the *dos.h* file as type union `REGS`.

We will have to overcome several programming hurdles. One is that we will have to use the address of a union as a means of accessing union members; we'll have to do that for the input and the output unions. Second, we'll have to set several register values and use register values without misplacing information. Third, there is a problem with using the assembly INT instruction. With the port instructions, recall, we could use the DX register to hold the port number to be used; in essence, this allows the port number to be a variable. The `INT` instruction is not so cooperative; the interrupt number must be given explicitly. That is, we can say this:

```
int 10h    ;standard way to call the 10h interrupt
```

But this doesn't work:

```
mov dx,10h
int dx     ;not allowed, alas
```

There is no point attempting the other hurdles if we can't clear this one, so let's see what we can do.

Self-Modifying Code

The most direct way would be to set up a sequence of jumps. If, say, the argument indicates the program should use interrupt 10H, the program can jump to a line that says INT 10H. You just have to have the patience to type in all the possibilities. (Or you could write a `switch` in C, create a COD file, and modify it as needed.)

We will try a different method: self-modifying code. Our code will be written with an `INT` call for a specific interrupt. But when the function is called, it will modify, in the code, the interrupt value, making it the desired interrupt number. Self-modifying code has a slightly shady image as a programming technique, but it does illustrate just how flexible assembly programming can be.

Let's risk using self-modifying code. What do we have to do? First, we have to obtain the desired value for the interrupt number. Second, we have to ascertain the address of the explicit interrupt number used in the code. Third, we have to move the desired value to that location.

Obtaining the interrupt value is simple. Because it is the first argument of our call, it will be located in the stack at the location `BP+4`. The interrupt number is a single byte, so we can place it in AL:

```
;bp+4 is address of interrupt number
```

```
        ...
        mov al, BYTE PTR [bp+4]          ;get interrupt number
```

This is the same method we've used before for arguments.

Next, to get the address where the interrupt number should be placed, we can use a symbolic label:

```
int_addr:                ;symbolic label
     int 64              ;64 is place holder
```

Here, int_addr represents the address of the next instruction, which is INT 64. Machine language is set up so that the INT instruction occupies one byte of memory, while the interrupt number (here 64) occupies the next byte. Thus, the address of the 64 is 1 byte greater:

```
BYTE PTR int_addr + 1
```

We use the BYTE PTR type cast to indicate that int_addr is the address of a byte; this makes int_addr + 1 the address of the next byte, that is, of the number 64.

Next, we have to move the AL value to this location. To do this right, we need to use a segment override. That is, the MOV statement normally interprets addresses to be data segment offsets, but int_addr is an offset relative to the code segment. So we should explicitly indicate that the code segment should be used:

```
    mov cs:BYTE PTR int_addr + 1,al  ;place AL in code segment
```

Once this instruction is given, the memory location formerly occupied by the 64 will be overwritten by the AL value.

Referencing a Union

With the INT call problem out of the way, we can turn to accessing the members of a union through the union's address. The address of the input union is the second argument of the call; that means it is found in the stack position BP+6. The address itself is represented by [BP+6], but we want the values stored beginning at that address. In other words, BP+6 corresponds to a double pointer.

We faced a similar situation in Chapter 11, when we investigated how the IBM C Compiler handled pointers used in a swap function. There, we saw a sequence along these lines:

```
    mov  bx,[bp+6]  ; move address of variable to BX
    mov  ax,[bx]    ; move value at address to ax
```

Unlike the C asterisk, the assembly brackets can not be applied twice to one value; that is, we can't say [[BP+6]]. But we can apply the brackets in succession to two values, as shown above.

The only modification we need to handle an array, structure, or union is to allow for multiple values. The REGS union essentially is a series of unsigned integers. That means that BX, after being assigned the address at BP+6, points to the first member, which represents the AX register. Then BX+2 points to the BX register, BX+4 points to the CX register, and so on. This information can be used with MOV to assign values from the union to the registers. The BX value should be the last to be assigned; if we change BX earlier than that, then it will point to some other part of memory instead of to the union.

The Callint() Function

We've used these ideas to put together callint(). A few other points need to be made, but let's look at the code first:

```
        TITLE callint
; callint.asm  calls an interrupt, sets and reports registers
; function heading
; #include <dos.h>
; int callint( inum, a_uin, a_uout )
; int inum;              /* interrupt number */
; union REGS *a_uin;   /* address of input union */
; union REGS *a_uout;  /* address of output union */
; returns AX
include segdef.ah
_TEXT SEGMENT
    PUBLIC _callint
_callint    PROC NEAR
    push bp
    mov bp,sp
    push di          ;save registers
    push si
    ;bp+4 is address of interrupt number
    ;bp+6 is address of in SEGS union
    ;bp+8 is address of out SEGS union

    mov al, BYTE PTR [bp+4]        ;get interrupt number
    mov cs:BYTE PTR int_addr + 1,al  ;place it in code segment
    mov bx,[bp+6]         ;get structure address
                         ;bx points to input union
                         ;load values into registers
    mov ax,[bx]          ;bx points to ax value
    mov cx,[bx+4]        ;bx+4 points to cx value
    mov dx,[bx+6]
    mov si,[bx+8]
```

```
        mov di,[bx+10]
        mov bx,[bx+2]
        push bp             ;save bp value int_addr:
        int 64              ;64 is place holder
        pop bp              ;restore bp value
        mov bp,[bp+8]       ;get address of out union
        mov [bp],ax         ;store ax in union
        mov [bp+2],bx       ;store bx in next union member
        mov [bp+4],cx
        mov [bp+6],dx
        mov [bp+8],si
        mov [bp+10],di
        push ax             ;save ax value
        pushf               ;push flag values onto stack
        pop ax              ;pop flag values into ax
        mov [bp+12],ax      ;put flag values in union
        pop ax              ;restore ax
        cld                 ;clear direction flag

        pop si              ;restore registers
        pop di
        pop bp
        ret
_callint ENDP
_TEXT ENDS
        END
```

Note that we pushed the BP value before the interrupt call and restored it afterwards. Although IBM C functions are pledged to preserve BP's value, interrupts are not. The screen scrolling interrupt, for example, alters BP's value and does not restore it. If we don't save the value, then the program will use the wrong BP value when deciding where to store all the register values.

Similarly, IBM C assumes that all functions clear the direction flag. That may not be true for interrupts, so we do it explicitly. (The direction flag, recall, determines in which direction string comparisons are made.)

The PUSHF instruction places the current flag settings in the stack. We then use POP and MOV to transfer the settings to the output union. Figure 12-5 shows which bit each flag occupies in a word.

Summary

We have only skimmed the surface of assembly programming and of the capabilities of the MASM assembler. Yet only a modest knowledge is needed to do useful work in assembly, especially if you have the support of a compiler to offer you examples in assembly programming.

The advantages of assembly language programs are speed, compactness, and total access to all the resources of the computer. The disadvantages are that there are a great number of instructions to learn, that the resulting code is not portable, that it is harder to program in assembly, and that the potential for error is greater.

C, on the other hand, offers the advantages of portability and of useful programming structures. More than most high-level languages, it can reach deeply into the computer's resources, but at the cost of reduced portability.

A sensible approach to programming is to design and write the entire program in C, using functions freely. If you locate a particular trouble spot, you can try to reprogram a particular function in assembly. Programming it first in C offers a good way to develop the logic and algorithms needed for the function. Furthermore, by generating a COD file for the function, you can get pointers on how to do it in assembly.

Closing Words

This is a book about C and about the IBM PC. It has dealt with general C topics, such as pointers and linked structures, and with matters specific to the IBM PC, such as ports, interrupts, and the video display. And we've seen a little of assembly language and how to incorporate assembly modules with C programs. One of the most important resources in these studies has been the IBM C library. Much of the library is shared with other C implementations, including UNIX and XENIX, making it possible to write highly portable programs. But the library also provides functions that relate to the special properties of the IBM PC. In using them, we sacrifice portability but gain a better fit between program and equipment.

With C on the IBM PC, you can approach a programming problem on several different levels of detail. You can stick to the standard library, and even there you may have choices. For example, you can use low-level I/O or the standard I/O package. You can use DOS interrupts, or, on a lower level, BIOS interrupts. You can use ports. For some applications, you can bypass BIOS routines and access memory (and ports) directly. And you can write assembly language routines to be used by a C program.

Our goal has been to advance your understanding of C, of the C library, and of the IBM PC so that you have the tools you need to face your programming problems. Of course, there is always more to learn, but this book has attempted to provide the necessary knowledge base to start you off in whatever direction you choose to go next.

Answers to Questions in the Chapter

■ *12-1.*

```
;  C function  portout()
;     int portout( port, value )
;     unsigned port;
;     int value;
;     This function returns value of indicated port

      TITLE    portout

include segdef.ah
_TEXT      SEGMENT
;    port is [bp+4]
;    value is [bp+6]
      PUBLIC   _portout
_portout PROC NEAR
      push    bp                     ;set up bp and sp
      mov     bp,sp

      mov     dx,WORD PTR [bp+4] ;set dx to port
      mov     ax,WORD PTR [bp+6] ;put value in AX
      out     dx,ax                  ;send value out port

      mov     sp,bp                  ;clean up
      pop     bp
      ret
_portout       ENDP
_TEXT     ENDS
END
```

■ *12-2.* The test only looks at the second character of the string, so additional characters are ignored; –night and /norbert each have the same effect as –n or /n. If that bothers you, you can check to see if av[1][2] is the null character or not. Or you can use strcmp().

■ *12-3.* We need to add a case label and flag-setting for each option.

```
while ( ac > 1 && (av[1][0] == '-' || av[1][0] == '/') )
    {                          /* process options */
    switch ( av[1][1] )
        {
        case 'n' : flags |= NUMBER;
            break;
        case 'c' : flags |= COUNT;
                break;
        case 's' : flags |= NOPRINT;
                break;
```

```
            default  : fprintf(stderr,"%s: No such option\n",
                             av[1]);
                       break;
            }
        ac--;
        av++;
        }
```

■ *12-4.* To the list in *flags.h*, add the following:

```
#define   COUNT     4    /* count lines having the word */
#define   NOPRINT   8    /* don't print matching lines */
```

■ *12-5.* Use the flags settings to control if statements. Note we want printing if the NOPRINT flag is *not* set, so we use the binary NOT operator.

```
/*   seekw.c--reads file line by line, checks for word */
#include <stdio.h>
#include "flags.h"
#define SIZE 256               /* maximum line length */
void seekw(wp, file, fname, flags)
char *wp;                      /* search word */
FILE *file;                    /* file pointer */
char *fname;                   /* filename */
int flags;                     /* flag settings */
{
    char line[SIZE];           /* holds input line */
    char *fgets(), *strwrd();
    long lc = 0;               /* line count */
    long mlc = 0;              /* matching line count */

    while ( fgets(line,SIZE,file) != NULL )
       {
       lc++;
       if ( strwrd(line,wp) != NULL )
          {
          mlc++;
          if (~(flags & NOPRINT) )
             {
             if (flags & NAMES)
                printf("%s:", fname);
             if (flags & NUMBER)
                printf("%4d: ", lc);
             fputs(line,stdout);
             }
          }
       }              /* end while */
    if (flags & COUNT)
       printf("%s: %s found %ld times\n", fname, wp, mlc);
}
```

■ *12-6.* Placing `str++` in the test condition changes the effect of the loop. Originally, the loop increments `str` only when a comparison fails; placing in the test condition causes it to be implemented whether the test fails or not. You can fix that by adjusting the value of `str` after the loop, but it is simpler and clearer to leave it as it is.

■ *12-7.* Eventually, the `strwrd` procedure expects DI to point to the word and SI to point to the string. But the `cntlet` procedure expects DI to point to the beginning of the string it is to process. So we start with DI pointing to the string, then assign the value to SI. Next, DI is assigned the word address so it can get its length. Since that also is the assignment expected by the `strwrd` procedure, no further changes are needed.

Exercises

1. Rewrite the `t_counts()` and `wait()` functions of Chapter 8 in assembly language.

2. Write your own version of `intdos()`; modify it so that the function number is the first argument.

Appendixes

A

The C Preprocessor

The C preprocessor is a labor-saving text processor that alters the text of a source file before it is compiled. It uses *directives,* which are identifiable by beginning with the character #. The most commonly used directives, and the only ones we have used in this book, are #define and #include. We'll discuss them in this appendix, along with #undef and the conditional compilation directives #if, #elif, #else, and #endif.

The #define Directive

This directive can be used to create symbolic constants, often termed *manifest constants,* and function-like constructions called *macros.* The original definition for the preprocessor required that the initial # be the first character on the line. The IBM and Microsoft versions follow the anticipated ANSII standard and relax this requirement so that the # must be the first nonwhitespace character on a line. This enables nested directives to follow the same indentation rules used for structured C statements.

Manifest Constants

To create a manifest constant, use the following form:

#define *identifier text*

Subsequent appearances of the identifier in the source file are replaced by the corresponding text. For example, the directive

#define LENGTH 80

causes appearances of LENGTH to be replaced by 80.

There are limitations, of course. LENGTH has to appear as a "token," that is, in a form separated from other elements by whitespace or by other recognizable separators, such as operators. Thus, SLENGTH would remain SLENGTH and would not become S80. Also, in an expression such as

```
printf("What LENGTH, please?\n");
```

an identifier enclosed in quotes is left unaltered.

The identifier has to meet the same rules as a C identifier, that is, it can consist of uppercase and lowercase letters, digits, and the underscore symbol. The first character cannot be a digit. Usually, uppercase letters are used for manifest constants so that they can be spotted easily in program code.

The text can contain nearly any combination of symbols, but it should make sense in the context in which it will be used.

If the text is too long to fit on one line, you can precede the newline generated by the RETURN key with a backslash to extend the text:

```
#define MESSAGE     "You have attempted to open a nonexistent \
file; please be more careful."
```

It's important to know that these substitutions are made literally; no simplification takes place. That is, a directive such as

```
#define FIVE 2+3
```

causes the preprocessor to substitute 2+3 and not 5 for each occurrence of FIVE.

You can check the effect of the preprocessor by using the compiler's P option. This causes only the preprocessor to be invoked, and the resulting code is placed in a file with the same root name and a *.i* extension. Here, for instance, is a sample source file:

```
#define TRUE  1
#define FALSE 0
#define BOOLEAN int
#define SIZE 256
#define BASE (5 + 2)
#define REM  (BASE -3)
main()
{
    BOOLEAN boxes[SIZE];
    int i;

    for ( i = 0; i < SIZE; i++)
        if ( i % BASE == REM )
          boxes[i] = TRUE;
        else
          boxes[i] = FALSE;
}
```

Here is the preprocessor output:

```
main()
{
    int boxes[256];
    int i;

    for ( i = 0; i < 256; i++)
        if ( i % (5 + 2) == ((5 + 2) -3) )
          boxes[i] = 1;
        else
          boxes[i] = 0;
}
```

Note how `BASE` is replaced by `(5 + 2)`, not by 7. However, the compiler does evaluate constant expressions, so the final machine code will use 7. Also note how one manifest constant can be used to define another.

One advantage of manifest constants is that they help document the meaning of various numerical values. Second, they offer a shorthand representation of strings that are used more than once. (However, under standard C, each instance of a string constant is stored separately. Using a string constant twice, either directly or as a defined constant, uses twice the memory required for using the string once.) Third, they make it easy to modify a program. Just alter the defined value, and all the appearances of the constant throughout the program are altered.

Macros

You can include a parameter list with a `#define` directive; the text portion then indicates how the parameters are to be used. Such a construction is called a *macro*. For example,

```
#define SQR(X)   ( (X) * (X) )
```

defines a squaring macro. Suppose we have this text in the source file:

```
y = SQR(z);
j = SQR(a + b);
m = 50.2 / SQR(y + 2);
```

In each case actual argument for `SQR()` is substituted for `X` in the defining relationship:

```
y = ( (z) * (z) );
j = ( (a + b) * (a + b) );
m = 50.2 / ( (y + 2) * (y + 2) );
```

Because macros perform literal substitution and don't evaluate arguments, it's important to enclose each parameter as well as the whole defining expression in parentheses. Suppose, for example, we had defined `SQR()` this way:

```
#define SQR(X)   X * X
```

Then the original text will have been changed to the following:

```
y = z * z;
j = a + b * a + b;
m = 50.2 / y + 2 * y + 2;
```

The precedence rules make the second and third expressions mean something entirely different from what was intended.

Liberal use of parentheses will make a macro produce the proper precedence, but nothing will prevent some macros from producing odd results if increment or decrement operators are used. For instance,

```
y = SQR(z++);
```

produces the following code:

```
y = ( (z++) * (z++) );
```

If z starts out as 10, it gets incremented twice to 12. Also, since the multiplication occurs between incrementation, y is assigned 110 instead of the 100 one might expect. The moral is to avoid using the increment and decrement operators with macros.

To avoid confusing the preprocessor, do not use any whitespace when you set up the identifier and parameter list; however, it's okay to use whitespace in the text portion of the definition:

```
#define SQR(X)   ( (X) * (X) )     /* okay */ #define
SQR (X)    ( (X) * (X) )    /* no good */
```

Here's an example using two parameters, and another example that uses a quoted parameter in the text portion:

```
#define MAX(X,Y)   ( (X) > (Y) ? (X) : (Y) )
#define PR(X)   printf("X = %d\n", X)
#define MINN 10
#define MINM 15
main()
{
    int n,m;

    scanf("%d %d", &n, &m);
```

```
        n = MAX(n,MINN);
        PR(n);
        m = MAX(m,MINM);
        PR(n + m);
    }
```

And here is the preprocessor output:

```
main()
{
    int n,m;

    scanf("%d %d", &n, &m);
    n = ( (n) > (10) ? (n) : (10) );
    printf("n = %d\n", n);
    m = ( (m) > (15) ? (m) : (15) );
    printf("n + m = %d\n", n + m);
}
```

Note that the print statements will print the actual argument literally, then print the evaluated expression.

Often a short routine can be written either as a function or as a macro. Why choose one or the other? Both save you typing, at least if the function or macro is used a few times. Every use of a macro, however, is translated into code, so ten uses of a macro produce ten copies of its code. A function is translated to code just once; when a function is called, the program jumps to the function location, then returns.

What this implies is that macros, if used several times, use more machine code than a function. But because no jumps and returns are involved, macros run faster. Macros are somewhat more flexible, since they use no data types; the `MAX()` macro can be used just as easily with `double` values as with `char`. But functions offer greater insulation, since they use their own local variables; `sqr(x++)` will work correctly if `sqr()` is implemented as a function.

Scope, #define, and #undef

A `#define` directive holds from its first occurrence to the end of the file containing it. It is an error to try to redefine a defined identifier:

```
    #define BIG 256
    ...
    #define BIG 512        /* an error */
```

However, it is fine to use the same definition again. That might happen if you combine two files together that use the same defined constant.

The `#undef` directive removes the current definition of an identifier, causing the compiler to ignore subsequent references to it. With `#define` and #undef, you can set up definitions that are restricted to a specific region within a file.

The #undef directive will undefine macro definitions as well as constant definitions. For example, the toupper() routine exists both in macro form in the *ctype.h* file and as a function in the library. If you need to use the *ctype.h* file for some of the other macros but wish to use the library toupper(), you can do this:

```
#undef toupper
```

The #include Directive

The #include directive is used to include material from another file in a given file. In effect, the material is placed in the file at the location of the #include directive. The filename should be enclosed in double quotation marks or in angle braces:

```
#include <dos.h>
#include "color.h"
```

If double quotes are used, the preprocessor first searches the current directory for the file. If it doesn't find it there, it searches directories named in the command line. The I option is used to provide that list. Finally, it searches standard directories. With IBM or Microsoft C, the standard directories are specified by the INCLUDE environmental variable.

The angle brackets mean to search the command line directories first, then the standard directories.

One common use is to include files containing a set of related definitions. For instance, we defined several color-related values and macros in the *color.h* file. Not only does that free us from having to remember the exact codes for blue and red, it makes it simpler to combine different files. As long as each file includes the same *color.h* file, we know they can use the same set of references.

A second common use for an include file is to provide function declarations for sets of related functions. The system *string.h* file is one example. This helps ensure that all references to the same function are type-compatible.

Conditional Compilation

The preprocessor provides directives that can be used to control compilation of a program. The main tool is a form of if-else statement. The general preprocessor form looks like this:

```
#if constant-expression
        . . .
#elif constant-expression
        . . .
#elif constant-expression
        . . .
      #else
        . . .
     #endif
```

The #if and #endif are required. The #elif (for else if) directive can appear 0 times or as many times as needed. There can be at most one #else. Here, for instance are some of the possible constructions:

```
#if   ...
   ...
#endif

#if  ...
   ...
#else
   ...
#endif

#if ...
   ...
#elif ...
   ...
#endif
```

If the first *expression* is true, the text between the #if and the next directive is incorporated into the final code. Otherwise, the next expression is tested until a true one is found, or until an #else or #endif is reached. The first true #elif expression results in its text segment being used. If all the expressions are false, the #else text, if present, is used.

The expressions can use constants and most operators, but no variables. The sizeof operator, type casts, and enumerated types cannot be used. One special operator that can be used is the defined operator, which yields a "true" (non-0) value if you have used the #define function on the identifier that follows it.

For example, suppose you have a program that uses several variables that need to be 16-bit variables. You want to use the program on 3 different machines, one of which uses short for 16 bits, one that uses int for 16 bits, and one that uses long for 16 bits. (Remember, this is a hypothetical example.) Then you can do the following:

```
#if defined(VAX)
    #define BITS16   short
```

```
#elif defined(IBMPC)
    #define BITS16   int
#elif defined(MIDGE)
    #define BITS16   long
#endif
```

In your program, you would use `BITS16` to declare the appropriate variables. If you were going to compile the program on an IBM PC, you would initially define `IBMPC`:

```
#define IBMPC
```

This form of definition defines `IBMPC`, but assigns no value to it. It's enough, however, to satisfy the `defined` test, and `BITS16` will be interpreted as `int`.

The conditional compilation directives can appear anywhere in a program, and the text can be regular C code as well as preprocessor directives.

```
#if defined(IBMPC)
    ch = getch();
#elif defined(VAX)
    ioctl(0,TIOCSETP,&tty); /* set tty for no buffer, no echo */
    ch = getchar();
#else
    ch = getchar();
#endif
```

This allows you to circumvent portability problems in which one system uses different function calls from another.

Other constant expressions can be used as test conditions:

```
#if PLEVEL == 1
    printf("%d\n", gstat.num);
#elif PLEVEL == 2
    printf("%s: %d %d\n",gstat.dept, gstat.num, gstat.date);
#endif
```

The #ifdef and #ifndef Directives

These are older conditional compilation directives that are retained for compatibility. The `#ifdef` directive is "true" if the following identifier is defined, and the `#ifndef` directive is "true" if the following identifier is not true. Thus,

```
#ifdef FRODO
```

has the same effect as the following:

```
#if defined(FRODO)
```

The second form, however, can be used with `elif`, while the first cannot.

Become familiar with the preprocessor. It can lessen the typing you have to do, increase program reliability, facilitate program modification, and enhance program portability.

B

Binary, Octal, and Hexadecimal Numbers

Binary Numbers

The way we usually write numbers is based on the number 10. As you probably learned in grade school, a number like 4652 has a 4 in the thousands place, a 6 in the hundreds place, a 5 in the tens place, and a 2 in the ones place. This means we can think of 4652 as being

$$4 \times 1000 + 6 \times 100 + 5 \times 10 + 2 \times 1.$$

But 1000 is 10 cubed, 100 is 10 squared, 10 is 10 to the first power, and, by convention, 1 is 10 (or any positive number) to the 0 power. So we also can write 4652 as

$$4 \times 10^3 + 6 \times 10^2 + 5 \times 10^1 + 2 \times 10^0.$$

Because our system of writing numbers is based on powers of 10, we say that 4652 is written in *base 10*.

Presumably, we developed this system because we have 10 fingers. A computer bit, in a sense, only has 2 fingers, for it can be set only to 0 or 1, off or on. This makes a *base 2* system natural for a computer. How does it work? It uses powers of 2 instead of powers of 10. For instance, a binary number such as 1101 would mean

$$1 \times 2^3 + 1 \times 2^2 + 0 \times 2^1 + 1 \times 2^0.$$

In decimal numbers this becomes

$$1 \times 8 + 1 \times 4 + 0 \times 2 + 1 \times 1 = 13.$$

The base 2 (or *binary*) system expresses any number (if you have enough bits) as a combination of 1's and 0's. This is very pleasing to a computer, especially since that is its only option. Let's see how this works for a 1-byte integer.

A byte contains 8 bits. We can think of these 8 bits as being numbered from 7 to 0, left to right. This "bit number" corresponds to an exponent of 2. Imagine the byte looking as shown in Figure B-1.

Figure B-1
Bit Numbers and Bit Values

bit number	7	6	5	4	3	2	1	0

Here 128 is 2 to the seventh power, and so on. The largest number this byte can hold is one with all bits set to 1: 11111111. The value of this binary number is

$$128 + 64 + 32 + 16 + 8 + 4 + 2 + 1 = 255.$$

The smallest binary number would be 00000000, or a simple 0. A byte can store numbers from 0 to 255, for a total of 256 possible values. Or, if it is a signed byte, it can store the values −128 to 127.

Signed Integers

How does the computer represent a negative number? Perhaps the most obvious way would be to use the leftmost bit to represent the sign, with 0 indicating a positive number and 1 a negative number. This has been done, but the method is inconvenient in practice. For one thing, it produces two 0 values: plus 0 and minus 0. The IBM PC uses a different system, one called the *two's complement*.

To see how the scheme works, let's work with a single-byte example. With the two's complement approach, the numbers 0 through 127 represent themselves, while the numbers 128 through 255 represent the negative numbers −128 through −1. Note that in this scheme that a 1 in the leftmost bit does indicate a negative number, for the numbers 128 to 255 all have that bit set to 1. So, if we have a signed byte, and if the leftmost bit is a one, we subtract 256 from the stored number to get the actual value. Thus, if 255 is stored (all 1's), we subtract 256, getting a value of −1. Going the other direction, if you want to store a value of −30, the computer will subtract 30 from 256 and store 226. In general, the absolute value is subtracted from one plus the maximum unsigned number. Thus, if −30 were to be stored in a short integer, the actual value stored would be 65536 −30, or 65506.

One consequence of this approach is that the same bit pattern could mean −30 or 65506, depending on whether the computer thinks a location holds a signed or unsigned quantity. To check out the system, assign a negative number to a signed short integer, then print it out using both the %d and the %u modes.

Other Bases

Computer workers often use number systems based on 8 and on 16. Since 8 and 16 are powers of 2, these systems are more closely related to a computer's binary system than is the decimal system.

Octal

Octal refers to a base 8 system. In this system, the different places in a number represent powers of 8. We use the digits 0 to 7. For example, the octal number 451 (written 0451 in C) represents

$$4 \times 8^2 + 5 \times 8^1 + 1 \times 8^0 = 297 \text{ (base 10)}.$$

Hexadecimal

Hexadecimal (or *hex*) refers to a base 16 system. Here we use powers of 16 and the digits 0 to 15. But since we don't have single digits to represent the values 10 to 15, we use the letters A to F for that purpose. For instance, the hex number A3F (written 0xA3F or 0xa3f in C) represents

$$10 \times 16^2 + 3 \times 16^1 + 15 \times 16^0 = 2623 \text{ (base 10)}.$$

Conversions to and from Binary

Converting from binary to octal or hexadecimal and back is simple because the various bases are all powers of two. Because 8 is the third power of 2, each octal digit corresponds to 3 binary digits. Similarly, because 16 is the fourth power of 2, each octal digit corresponds to 4 binary digits. Let's see how this works.

For octal numbers, the rule is to convert each octal digit to the corresponding 3 binary numbers. Suppose we have the octal number 06. This is 6 in decimal and 110 in binary. Okay, now consider 066. Each 6 is represented by the same binary pattern, 110, so the binary equivalent is 110110. What about 061? We must remember to represent the octal 1 by a 3-digit binary number; that is, we must use 001, and not just 1. Thus the binary equivalent of 061 is 110001.

To go from binary, to octal, just reverse the process. Starting from the right, break up the binary number into groups of 3 digits and translate each group of 3 to the corresponding octal digit. Suppose a byte contains the pattern 01011101. Think of the number as looking like this:

$$001\ 011\ 101$$

We added an extra 0 to the left to make the final group three digits. Well, 001 is just 1 in octal, 011 is $2 + 1$, or 3, and 101 is $4 + 1$, or 5. This makes the octal equivalent 0135.

With hexadecimal, we use the same general method, except each digit corresponds to a 4-digit binary number. For example, 0x6 becomes 0110. This really is the same value as octal 06, but now consider 0x66. This becomes 01100110, which is quite different from octal 066 (00110110), for now one of the extra 0's occurs in the middle of the number.

Keep in mind that hexadecimal has the extra digits A, B, C, D, E, and F. Try converting 0xC4. C is 12 in decimal, or $8 + 4$, making it 1100 in binary. The 4 is 0100, so 0xC4 becomes 11000100 in binary.

Going from binary to hex, break up the number into groups of 4 digits. Let's go back to 01011101 and convert it this time to hex instead of octal. First, break it up into groups of 4:

$$1011\ 0011$$

The pattern 1011 is $8 + 2 + 1$, or 11 in decimal, and B in hex. Similarly, 0011 is 3, so 10110011 becomes 0xB3 in hex.

Numerical Conversion to ASCII

DEX X_{10}	HEX X_{16}	OCT X_8	Binary X_2	ASCII	Key
0	00	00	000 0000	NUL	CTRL/1
1	01	01	000 0001	SOH	CTRL/A
2	02	02	000 0010	STX	CTRL/B
3	03	03	000 0011	ETX	CTRL/C

4	04	04	000 0100	EOT	CTRL/D
5	05	05	000 0101	ENQ	CTRL/E
6	06	06	000 0110	ACK	CTRL/F
7	07	07	000 0111	BEL	CTRL/G
8	08	10	000 1000	BS	CTRL/H, BACKSPACE
9	09	11	000 1001	HT	CTRL/I, TAB
10	0A	12	000 1010	LF	CTRL/J, LINE FEED
11	0B	13	000 1011	VT	CTRL/K
12	0C	14	000 1100	FF	CTRL/L
13	0D	15	000 1101	CR	CTRL/M, RETURN
14	0E	16	000 1110	SO	CTRL/N
15	0F	17	000 1111	SI	CTRL/O
16	10	20	001 0000	DLE	CTRL/P
17	11	21	001 0001	DC1	CTRL/Q
18	12	22	001 0010	DC2	CTRL/R
19	13	23	001 0011	DC3	CTRL/S
20	14	24	001 0100	DC4	CTRL/T
21	15	25	001 0101	NAK	CTRL/U
22	16	26	001 0110	SYN	CTRL/V
23	17	27	001 0111	ETB	CTRL/W
24	18	30	001 1000	CAN	CTRL/X
25	19	31	001 1001	EM	CTRL/Y
26	1A	32	001 1010	SUB	CTRL/Z
27	1B	33	001 1011	ESC	ESC, ESCAPE
28	1C	34	001 1100	FS	CTRL<
29	1D	35	001 1101	GS	CTRL/
30	1E	36	001 1110	RS	CTRL/=
31	1F	37	001 1111	US	CTRL/-
32	20	40	010 0000	SP	SPACEBAR
33	21	41	010 0001	!	!
34	22	42	010 0010	,,	,,
35	23	43	010 0011	#	#
36	24	44	010 0100	$	$
37	25	45	010 0101	½	½
38	26	46	010 0110	&	&
39	27	47	010 0111	'	'
40	28	50	010 1000	(	(
41	29	51	010 1001	)	)
42	2A	52	010 1010	*	*
43	2B	53	010 1011	+	+

44	2C	54	010 1100	,	,
45	2D	55	010 1101	–	–
46	2E	56	010 1110	.	.
47	2F	57	010 1111	/	/
48	30	60	011 0000	0	0
49	31	61	011 0001	1	1
50	32	62	011 0010	2	2
51	33	63	011 0011	3	3
52	34	64	011 0100	4	4
53	35	65	011 0101	5	5
54	36	66	011 0110	6	6
55	37	67	011 0111	7	7
56	38	70	011 1000	8	8
57	39	71	011 1001	9	9
58	3A	72	011 1010	:	:
59	3B	73	011 1011	;	;
60	3C	74	011 1100	<	<
61	3D	75	011 1101	=	=
62	3E	76	011 1110	>	>
63	3F	77	011 1111	?	?
64	40	100	100 0000	@	@
65	41	101	100 0001	A	A
66	42	102	100 0010	B	B
67	43	103	100 0011	C	C
68	44	104	100 0100	D	D
69	45	105	100 0101	E	E
70	46	106	100 0110	F	F
71	47	107	100 0111	G	G
72	48	110	100 1000	H	H
73	49	111	100 1001	I	I
74	4A	112	100 1010	J	J
75	4B	113	100 1011	K	K
76	4C	114	100 1100	L	L
77	4D	115	100 1101	M	M
78	4E	116	100 1110	N	N
79	4F	117	100 1111	O	O
80	50	120	101 0000	P	P
81	51	121	101 0001	Q	Q
82	52	122	101 0010	R	R
83	53	123	101 0011	S	S

84	54	124	101 0100	T	T
85	55	125	101 0101	U	U
86	56	126	101 0110	V	V
87	57	127	101 0111	W	W
88	58	130	101 1000	X	X
89	59	131	101 1001	Y	Y
90	5A	132	101 1010	Z	Z
91	5B	133	101 1011	[	[
92	5C	134	101 1100	\	\
93	5D	135	101 1101	]	]
94	5E	136	101 1110	^	^
95	5F	137	101 1111	−	−
96	60	140	110 0000	`	`
97	61	141	110 0001	a	a
98	62	142	110 0010	b	b
99	63	143	110 0011	c	c
100	64	144	110 0100	d	d
101	65	145	110 0101	e	e
102	66	146	110 0110	f	f
103	67	147	110 0111	g	g
104	68	150	110 1000	h	h
105	69	151	110 1001	i	i
106	6A	152	110 1010	j	j
107	6B	153	110 1011	k	k
108	6C	154	110 1100	l	l
109	6D	155	110 1101	m	m
110	6E	156	110 1110	n	n
111	6F	157	110 1111	o	o
112	70	160	111 0000	p	p
113	71	161	111 0001	q	q
114	72	162	111 0010	r	r
115	73	163	111 0011	s	s
116	74	164	111 0100	t	t
117	75	165	111 0101	u	u
118	76	166	111 0110	v	v
119	77	167	111 0111	w	w
120	78	170	111 1000	x	x
121	79	171	111 1001	y	y
122	7A	172	111 1010	z	z
123	7B	173	111 1011	{	{

124	7C	174	111 1100	¦	¦
125	7D	175	111 1101	}	}
126	7E	176	111 1110	~	~
127	7F	177	111 1111	DEL	DEL,RUBOUT

C

Compiling and Linking

Before using the IBM or Microsoft C Compiler—or any other compiler—you should take the time to go through the manual. You don't need to absorb everything the first time through, but you should get an idea of what material is covered. The IBM and Microsoft manuals are good, but they also are quite large. One volume discusses the compiler and the C language, and a second volume documents the library.

The manual (or its updates) should be the final authority for using the compiler, but you might like to trace the steps that take you from a program as written in C (the *source code*) to the final product (the *executable code*). For now, we'll assume that the original code is confined to a single file. In the C tradition, the name of the file holding the C code should have a *.c* extension; that is, the filename should be something like *xta.c* or *falla.c*.

The Cc, Clink, Msc, and Link Commands

The next step is to run the compiler on the file. For the IBM C Compiler, use the `cc` command. The Microsoft near-equivalent is `msc`:

```
cc   xta;      ◄— Using the IBM version
msc xta;       ◄— Using the Microsoft version
```

Note that we can drop the *.c* extension; when given the name *xta,* the compiler automatically searches for a file called *xta.c*. You can, however, leave the extension on. The semicolon suppresses further queries from the compiler. If you omit it, you will be given the chance to override the default name for the output file, and you will have the opportunity to request an assembly code file. The same information also can be provided on the command line, but we will ignore these elaborations for the present.

Anyway, once you give this command, the C preprocessor performs the various macroprocessor directives (`#include`, `#define`, and so on).

When that is done, the compilation process begins. The compiler is a four-pass compiler, and the `cc` or the `msc` command executes all four passes. (The preprocessor is invoked by the first pass.) The program is optimized automatically. That means that after an initial code is produced, subsequent passes refine it to improve the running speed and to reduce the program size.

The final product is a file of *object code* that consists of a machine-language translation of the original C code. Machine language is the innate programming language of the computer's processor—an Intel 8088 chip for the IBM PC. The file is identified by an *.obj* extension. For our example, then, the resulting file would be called *xta.obj. Object module* is another term for such files.

Although the object file consists of machine-language code, it does not represent a complete program. For instance, the code for any functions used, such as `printf()`, has to be added. Also, some standard code setting up the interface between the program and the disk operating system is needed. The `clink` command (IBM) or the `link` command (Microsoft) takes care of these matters:

```
clink xta;      ◄─ IBM version of the linker
link xta;       ◄─ Microsoft version of the linker
```

The *.obj* extension can be omitted, for `clink` and `link` automatically interpret *xta* to mean *xta.obj*. Again, the semicolon suppresses questions the linker would pose otherwise. One of the questions is what libraries to search. Normally, we needn't provide that information, for either the IBM or Microsoft compiler encodes that information into the object file.

The result of this process is an executable file. It bears an *.exe* extension and represents a complete program. For our example, this file would be called *xta.exe*. It could be loaded into memory and run by typing the root name:

```
A>xta
```

The Cl Command

The Microsoft C Compiler offers a second approach. It initiates the same sequence of events with a single compile-and-link command:

```
cl xta.c
```

Note that this time we included the *.c* extension to the root name. The `cl` command accepts both source code files and object code files; if the extension is omitted, it assumes the name is of an object file.

You will need a hard disk or a 1.2Mb drive to use this command, since the compiler and linker will not fit on a single 360K disk.

Compiler Options

The compiler has a few dozen options, which you may read about in the manual. We will refer to options occasionally, so let's see how to use them. The options are identified by a slash (/) prefix, or, equivalently, a hyphen (-) prefix. With the `cc` and `msc` commands, the options can appear anywhere before the terminating semicolon on a command line:

```
cc /Od falla;
msc flop -Od;
```

For either example, the `Od` option (disable optimization) is evoked. (Using this option speeds up compilation.) Don't confuse the slash (/) with the backslash (\) used by DOS for identifying directory paths.

☐ *Question C-1*   If you were asked to use the `/Ze` option (and you will be) when compiling a program, what would you do?

With the `cl` command, the options must come between the command and the filename:

```
cl /Od ant.c
```

Multiple Files

One method to compile multiple files is to apply `cc` or `msc` to each file separately, producing a object module file for each source file. Then `clink` or `link` can be used to combine the object code modules together into a single program. This is the method outlined in Chapter 2.

If, however, you are using the `cl` command, you can use it with several filename arguments. For instance, the command

```
cl one.c two.c three.c
```

will create the three object modules `one.obj`, `two.obj`, and `three.obj`. Then it will link them into a file called *one.exe*. If you subsequently modify, say, `two.c`, you can give this command:

```
cl one two.c three
```

The `two.c` module will be recompiled, and its object module will be linked with the existing `one.obj` and `three.obj` modules.

Environmental Variables

The compiler uses environmental variables to tell it where to look for the compiler, the linker, the libraries, the include files, and for temporary work space. The values you assign to these variables depend on how you set up your directories. For example, suppose you place the compiler and the linker in *c:\bin*, the libraries in *c:\lib*, the include files in *c:\include*, and that you will use a RAM disk (drive D) for temporary files. Then you would set up these variables:

```
SET PATH=C:\BIN
SET LIB=C:\LIB
SET INCLUDE=C:\INCLUDE
SET TMP=D:
```

The PATH variable is a system variable used by DOS; it tells DOS where to look for executable programs. The other three environmental variables are used by the compiler and the linker.

Answer to the Question in the Appendix

■ *C-1.* We hope you would do something along these lines:

```
msc /Ze trinket;
```

You could use a hyphen instead of the slash:

```
cc -Ze trinket;
```

Index

HOWARD W. SAMS & COMPANY

The Waite Group

Advanced C Primer + +
Stephen Prata, The Waite Group

Programmers, students, managers, and hackers will learn to master the C programming language. Anyone who knows the basics of C will learn practical C tips never before published.
ISBN: 0-672-22486-0, $23.95

C Primer Plus, Revised Edition
Waite, Prata, and Martin, The Waite Group

The perfect tutorial for beginning C programmers and students, this book includes key additions about the C language and object-oriented programming using C + +.
ISBN: 0-672-22582-4, $23.95

Microsoft® C on the IBM® PC
Robert Lafore, The Waite Group

A tutorial for the beginning programmer with enough information to write useful and marketable programs for the IBM PC family, featuring hands-on interaction with the C compiler and the PC.
ISBN: 0-672-22515-8, $24.95

Inside XENIX®
Christopher L. Morgan, The Waite Group

Through easily-read-and-understood XENIX references and tutorials, this comprehensive text examines in detail its unique internal structure including its shells and utilities.
ISBN: 0-672-22445-3, $21.95

Advanced UNIX® — A Programmer's Guide
Stephen Prata, The Waite Group

An advanced guidebook beyond the basics of UNIX and with details of the system's key components and various programming mechanisms. It shows how to use simple and complex commands, including the Bourne Shell, shell scripts, loops, and system calls.
ISBN: 0-672-22403-8, $21.95

Tricks of the UNIX® Masters
Russell G. Sage, The Waite Group

This book contains the shortcuts, tips, tricks, and secrets programmers want, using a "cookbook" approach ranging from I/O functions and file operations to porting UNIX to a different computer.
ISBN: 0-672-22449-6, $22.95

UNIX® Primer Plus
Waite, Martin, and Prata, The Waite Group

Learn about the amazing UNIX operating system as this book presents UNIX in a clear, simple, and easy-to-understand style. It is fully illustrated and includes two summary cards for quick reference.
ISBN: 0-672-22028-8, $19.95

UNIX® System V Primer, Revised Edition
Waite, Martin, and Prata, The Waite Group

This edition provides a comprehensive overview and introduction to the UNIX System V operating system for the beginner, including a new chapter on the extended electronic mail program and the use of the new shell layer manager.
ISBN: 0-672-22570-0, $22.95

UNIX® Communications
Bryan Costales, The Waite Group

This book will clarify the complexities of the UNIX communication facilities. It gathers the knowledge and techniques needed to use, administer, and program UNIX-to-UNIX communication and UNIX mail.
ISBN: 0-672-22511-5, $26.95

UNIX® SystemV Bible
Prata and Martin, The Waite Group

This is a comprehensive reference for programmers working with the UNIX operating system documentation, covering intermediate to advanced level programming for professionals who have prior experience programming in C or using UNIX.
ISBN: 0-672-22562-X, $24.95

UNIX® Papers
Edited by The Waite Group

Collection of learning tutorials, issue papers, and case histories that provide insightful information on the UNIX operating system and UNIX business market, revealing the more hidden and obscure truths about UNIX.
ISBN: 0-672-22578-6, $26.95

Discovering MS-DOS®
Kate O'Day, The Waite Group

This comprehensive study of MS-DOS commands begins with information about operating systems then shows how to produce letters and documents; create, name, and manipulate files; use the keyboard and function keys to perform jobs faster; and direct, sort, and find data quickly.
ISBN: 0-672-22407-0, $15.95

MS-DOS® Bible
Steven Simrin, The Waite Group

This book helps intermediate users explore this operating system's capabilities from system start-up to creating, editing, and managing files, handling data, and customizing the keyboard. It includes detailed coverage of the tree-structured directories and DOS filters.
ISBN: 0-672-22408-9, $18.95

MS-DOS® Developer's Guide
Angermeyer and Jaeger, The Waite Group

This is a guide for programmers with a working knowledge of 8088 ALC, who want to learn tricks for getting their software running in the MS-DOS environment. Included are assembly coding tips, explanations, MS-DOS versions, and higher-level language debuggers and aids.
ISBN: 0-672-22409-7, $24.95

Understanding MS-DOS®
O'Day and Angermeyer, The Waite Group

This introduction to the use and operation of the MS-DOS operating system includes fundamentals and advanced features of the operating system.
ISBN: 0-672-27067-6, $16.95

HOWARD W. SAMS & COMPANY

The Waite Group

Product Number	Quantity	Price	Total
	Subtotal		
	All states please add sales tax		
	Standard shipping & handling		$2.50
	Total		

WC 339

Name _____

Title/Company _____

Address _____

City _____

State/Zip _____

Signature (required) _____

☐ Check   ☐ Money Order   ☐ MC   ☐ VISA   ☐ AE

Account # _____   Exp. Date _____

To order by phone call 800-428-SAMS.

Offer good in U.S.A. only. Prices and availability subject to change without notice. Full payment must accompany your order.

Tricks of the MS-DOS® Masters
Angermeyer, Jaeger, Fahringer, and Shafer, The Waite Group

This reference provides the personal user with advanced tips and tricks about the operating system, including advanced tips on using popular software packages such as dBASE III®, Lotus 1-2-3®, and WordStar®.
ISBN: 0-672-22525-5, $24.95

Soul of CP/M®: How to Use the Hidden Power of Your CP/M System
Waite and Lafore, The Waite Group

Recommended for those who have read the CP/M *Primer* or who are otherwise familiar with CP/M's outer layer utilities. It teaches how to use and modify CP/M's internal features, including how to modify BIOS and use CP/M system calls in your own programs.
ISBN: 0-672-22030-X, $19.95

CP/M® Bible: The Authoritative Reference Guide to CP/M
Waite and Angermeyer, The Waite Group

Already a classic, this highly detailed manual puts CP/M's at your fingertips. Instant one-stop access to all CP/M keywords, commands, utilities, and conventions are found in this easy-to-use format.
ISBN: 0-672-22015-6, $19.95

CP/M® Primer, Second Edition
Waite and Murtha, The Waite Group

This companion to the CP/M *Bible* is widely used by novices and advanced programmers. It includes the details of CP/M terminology, operation, capabilities, and internal structure, plus a convenient tear-out reference card with CP/M commands.
ISBN: 0-672-22170-5, $16.95

Desktop Publishing Bible
The Waite Group

A collection of essays by experts in their subject areas, these are the nuts and bolts of desktop publishing. Concentrating primarily on the technical aspects of the hardware and software, this book will be useful to anyone planning to buy a personal publishing system.
ISBN: 0-672-22524-7, $22.95

PC LAN Primer
Kleeman, Anderson, Angermeyer, Fisher, McCoy, The Waite Group

PC LAN *Primer* explores the Token Ring — IBM's grand strategy to tie together IBM micros, minis, and mainframes with Local Area Networks providing the communication feature.
ISBN: 0-672-22448-8, $22.95

68000, 68010, 68020 Primer
Kelly-Bootle and Fowler, The Waite Group

Beginning with an introduction to the 68000 chips, this book is written to introduce novice or experienced programmers to the instruction set and addressing modes common to the 68000 family.
ISBN: 0-672-22405-4, $21.95

Pascal Primer
Waite and Fox, The Waite Group

This primer will swiftly guide you through Pascal program structure, procedures, variables, decision-making statements, and numeric functions.
ISBN: 0-672-21793-7, $17.95

Printer Connections Bible
Marble and House, The Waite Group

This book contains all the information necessary to make the proper connections to get a printer printing. It focuses on the hardware side of connecting, particularly the main interface — the cable itself.
ISBN: 0-672-22406-2, $16.95

Modem Connections Bible
Curtis and Majhor, The Waite Group

This book describes modems, how they work, and how to hook ten well-known modems to nine name-brand microcomputers. It also features a "Jump Table" and an overview of communications software, the RS-232c interface, and a section on troubleshooting.
ISBN: 0-672-22446-1, $16.95

Inside the Amiga™ With C
John T. Berry, The Waite Group

This book is written for the experienced computer user who wants to put the powerful programming features of the Amiga to work using the C language.
ISBN: 0-672-22468-2, $22.95

Artificial Intelligence Programming on the Macintosh™
Dan Shafer, The Waite Group

Those with a basic understanding of computers and programming will be fascinated by the possibilities of music generation, robotics, and problem-solving available on microcomputers, and this book will show you how.
ISBN: 0-672-22447-X, $24.95

BASIC Programming Primer, Second Edition
Waite and Pardee, The Waite Group

A cornerstone of the Sams/Waite Primer series, this classic text contains a complete explanation of the fundamentals of the language, program control, and organization.
ISBN: 0-672-22014-8, $17.95

The Official Book for the Commodore 128® Personal Computer
Waite, Lafore, and Volpe, The Waite Group

This book examines Commodore's powerful computer with its three different operating modes, details how to create graphics and animation, and how to use the 64 mode to run thousands of existing Commodore 64 programs.
ISBN: 0-672-22456-9, $12.95

These and other Sams books are available from your local bookstore, computer store, or electronics distributor. If there are books you are interested in that are unavailable in your area, order directly from Sams by calling toll-free **800-428-SAMS** (in Alaska, Hawaii, or Indiana, call 317-298-5699).

PLACE
STAMP
HERE

Howard W. Sams & Company
Department DM
P.O. Box 7092
Indianapolis, IN 46206